AFTER DISCOURSE

T0403370

After Discourse is an interdisciplinary response to the recent trend away from linguistic and textual approaches and towards things and their affects.

The new millennium brought about serious changes to the intellectual landscape. Favoured approaches associated with the linguistic and the textual lost some of their currency, and were followed by a new curiosity and concern for things and their natures. Gathering contributions from archaeology, heritage studies, history, geography, literature, and philosophy, *After Discourse* offers a range of reflections on what things are, how we become affected by them, and the ethical concerns they give rise to. Through a varied constellation of case studies, it explores ways of dealing with matters which fall outside, become othered from, or simply cannot be grasped through perspectives derived solely from language and discourse.

After Discourse provides challenging new perspectives for scholars and students interested in other-than-textual encounters between people and the objects with which we share the world.

Bjørnar J. Olsen is Professor of Archaeology at UiT – The Arctic University of Norway.

Mats Burström is Professor of Archaeology at Stockholm University, Sweden.

Caitlin DeSilvey is Professor of Cultural Geography at the University of Exeter, where she is Associate Director for Transdisciplinary Research in the Environment and Sustainability Institute.

Þóra Pétursdóttir is Associate Professor of Archaeology in the Department of Archaeology, Conservation and History at the University of Oslo in Norway.

Routledge Archaeologies of the Contemporary World

John Schofield
University of York

A historian once described, 'all history as contemporary history'. All archaeology is contemporary for the same reason - in its persistence, its resilience, its place in the contemporary world, on or beneath its surface. But increasingly archaeologists are focusing attention on the contemporary world itself, its materiality, the behaviours that underlie it, and the heritage it creates. Archaeology provides a distinctive and meaningful contribution to understanding the contemporary world – a contribution grounded in materiality, and in seeking to understand the often complex relationships between people, their behaviours, and things. This series of books will generate new and deeper explorations of these relationships, creating and promoting archaeologies of the contemporary world through a range of formats (single-authored works, edited collections, Research Focus outputs) encouraging diversity of approach towards new interdisciplinary encounters with our supposedly 'familiar past'.

Archaeology of The Teufelsberg
Exploring Western Electronic Intelligence Gathering in Cold War Berlin
Wayne D Cocroft and John Schofield

After Discourse
Things, Affects, Ethics
Edited by Bjørnar J. Olsen, Mats Burström, Caitlin DeSilvey, and Þóra Pétursdóttir

For more information about this series, please visit: https://www.routledge.com/Routledge-Archaeologies-of-the-Contemporary-World/book-series/RACW

AFTER DISCOURSE

Things, Affects, Ethics

Edited by Bjørnar J. Olsen, Mats Burström, Caitlin DeSilvey, and Þóra Pétursdóttir

Routledge
Taylor & Francis Group

LONDON AND NEW YORK

First published 2021
by Routledge
2 Park Square, Milton Park, Abingdon, Oxon OX14 4RN

and by Routledge
52 Vanderbilt Avenue, New York, NY 10017

Routledge is an imprint of the Taylor & Francis Group, an informa business

© 2021 selection and editorial matter, Bjørnar J. Olsen, Mats Burström, Caitlin DeSilvey and Þóra Pétursdóttir; individual chapters, the contributors

The right of Bjørnar J. Olsen, Mats Burström, Caitlin DeSilvey and Þóra Pétursdóttir to be identified as the authors of the editorial material, and of the authors for their individual chapters, has been asserted in accordance with sections 77 and 78 of the Copyright, Designs and Patents Act 1988.

The publishers have made every effort to contact copyright holders to obtain permission to publish images. This has not been possible in every case, however, and we would welcome correspondence from those individuals/companies whom we have been unable to trace. Any omissions brought to our attention will be remedied in future editions.

Trademark notice: Product or corporate names may be trademarks or registered trademarks, and are used only for identification and explanation without intent to infringe.

British Library Cataloguing-in-Publication Data
A catalogue record for this book is available from the British Library

Library of Congress Cataloging-in-Publication Data
Names: Olsen, Bjørnar, editor. | Burström, Mats, editor. |
DeSilvey, Caitlin, editor. | Þóra Pétursdóttir, 1978– editor.
Title: After discourse : things, affects, ethics / edited by Bjørnar Olsen,
Mats Burström, Caitlin DeSilvey and Þóra Pétursdóttir
Description: Abingdon, Oxon ; New York, NY : Routledge, 2021. |
Includes bibliographical references and index.
Identifiers: LCCN 2020023568 (print) | LCCN 2020023569 (ebook) |
ISBN 9780367190460 (hardback) | ISBN 9780367190484 (paperback) |
ISBN 9780429200014 (ebook)
Subjects: LCSH: Material culture–Philosophy. | Archaeology–Philosophy. |
Object (Philosophy) | Affect (Psychology)
Classification: LCC GN406 .A34 2021 (print) |
LCC GN406 (ebook) | DDC 930.101–dc23
LC record available at https://lccn.loc.gov/2020023568
LC ebook record available at https://lccn.loc.gov/2020023569

ISBN: 978-0-367-19046-0 (hbk)
ISBN: 978-0-367-19048-4 (pbk)
ISBN: 978-0-429-20001-4 (ebk)

Typeset in Bembo
by Newgen Publishing UK

CONTENTS

FIGURES

CONTRIBUTORS

Doug Bailey, San Francisco State University, USA; email: dwbailey@sfsu.edu

Torgeir Rinke Bangstad, UiT – The Arctic University of Norway, Norway; email: torgeir.r.bangstad@uit.no

Hein B. Bjerck, NTNU: Norwegian University of Science and Technology, Norway; email: hein.bjerck@ntnu.no

Levi R. Bryant, Collin College, USA; email: lbryant@collin.edu

Mats Burström, Stockholm University, Sweden; email: mats.burstrom@ark.su.se

Denis Byrne, Western Sydney University, Australia; email: D.Byrne@westernsydney.edu.au

Caitlin DeSilvey, University of Exeter, UK; email: C.O.Desilvey@exeter.ac.uk

Curtis L. Francisco, Pueblo of Laguna, USA; email: curtislfrancisco@gmail.com

Alfredo González-Ruibal, Spanish National Research Council, Spain; email: alfredo.gonzalez-ruibal@incipit.csic.es

Lucas D. Introna, Lancaster University, UK; email: l.introna@lancaster.ac.uk

Timothy James LeCain, Montana State University, USA; email: tlecain@montana.edu

Robert Macfarlane, Cambridge University, UK; email: rgm20@cam.ac.uk

Jeff Malpas, University of Tasmania, Australia; email: jeff.malpas@utas.edu.au

Saphinaz-Amal Naguib, University of Oslo, Norway; email: s.a.naguib@ikos.uio.no

Bjørnar J. Olsen, UiT – The Arctic University of Norway; email: bjornar.olsen@uit.no

Þóra Pétursdóttir, University of Oslo, Norway; email: thora.petursdottir@iakh.uio.no

Christopher Witmore, Texas Tech University, USA; email: christopher.witmore@ttu.edu

ACKNOWLEDGEMENTS

This book is the outcome of two closely related research initiatives, *Object Matters and After Discourse*. The first was an international research project funded by the Norwegian Research Council (2015–19), focusing on things, heritage, and the archaeology of the recent past. The other, from which this book has borrowed its name, was a research group funded and hosted by the Centre for Advanced Study (CAS) in Oslo during the academic year 2016/17. Gathering scholars from a number of disciplines, both projects aimed to scrutinize the reception and consequences of the so-called "material turn" within disciplines already dedicated to the study of things and materiality. At the same time, these projects also explored how the knowledge and skill acquired in these disciplines may advance a critical and more empirically-grounded awareness of objects and matter in the humanities and social sciences more broadly.

We are indebted to the Norwegian Research Council and CAS for their respective funding of these two projects, and we especially thank CAS for generously providing additional funding for the preparation of this book. Our gratitude also goes to the CAS staff for making the year at the Centre so productive and memorable. A special thanks to Vigdis Broch-Due, at the time director of CAS, for her constant support and enthusiasm for our research.

The chapters in this book are written by scholars who, in one way or another, participated in the two projects. Some participated as members of the Object Matters team, some as After Discourse fellows at CAS, and others as contributors to the many workshops and lectures organized at the Centre and elsewhere. Additionally, a number of other scholars contributed to projects and events, and provided valuable comments and contributions. With regards to the themes covered in this book, we would especially like to thank Sylvia Benso, Vigdis Broch-Due, Matt Edgeworth, Stein Farstadvoll, Ingar Figenschau, Paul Wenzel Geissler, Graham Harman, Sven Ouzman, Kerstin Smeds, Marek Tamm, and Marzia Varutti.

Marek, who was a member of both projects, has recently edited a published volume with Laurent Olivier, *Rethinking Historical Time* (2019), which originates from one of our CAS After Discourse workshops. We are also indebted to series editor John Schofield, Matthew Gibbon and Katie Wakelin at Routledge, and Narmada Sugunan and the production team for making the processing of the book so smooth, and to Ingar Figenschau for compiling the index.

Bjørnar J. Olsen
Mats Burström
Caitlin DeSilvey
Þóra Pétursdóttir

1

AFTER DISCOURSE

An introduction

Bjørnar J. Olsen, Mats Burström, Caitlin DeSilvey, and Þóra Pétursdóttir

Over the last half century, notions of posteriority and subsequence (most often expressed as 'post' and 'after') have conspicuously made their way into the academic nomenclature. The prefix 'post' has become especially prominent as a conceptual game-changer, radically redefining the well-established meanings of intellectual and political projects such as structuralism, processualism, modernism, colonialism, and humanism. Not surprisingly, one may add, as it epitomizes well the *post*modern *Zeitgeist*, signifying ruptures, ends, and, more generally, a restless striving for difference and distance. The preposition 'after' cannot boast a similar popularity, and is mainly used more specifically for framing issues and debates (e.g. 'after history,' 'after culture,' 'after interpretation,' 'after nature,' etc.). This also relates to the subtle, but still effective, connotative difference between the two terms. Despite often considered semantically identical, a significant distinction emerges from the way these prepositions are used. The prefix 'post' often implies a state of opposition and, thus, inevitably, definition through negation. The notion of 'after,' on the other hand, is used in a less binary sense, and retains more of its purely chronological signification – as being subsequent to, representing an aftermath and, perhaps, a pause.

This distinction should be kept in mind when considering the title of this book. The label *After Discourse* originally named a research group at the Centre of Advanced Studies in Oslo (2016/17),[1] which gathered scholars from history, heritage studies, cultural geography, anthropology, and archaeology. It was itself an offspring of a larger research project, *Object Matters*, and this book is a combined outcome of these two closely affiliated research initiatives, focusing on things, heritage, and the archaeology of the recent past. Titles are crucial for scholarly branding and it is easy to read into these project names an opposition between language and things, and to assume that we are presenting 'things' as a kind of theoretical 'post' to text and language. This, however, is not the case, nor is the related assumption that we can claim to be entering a post-discursive phase. What *After Discourse* does refer to, and what it was intended to designate, is a concern with what happens *after* and in the wake of the heyday of linguistic and textual approaches, which came to significantly alter the ways things, heritage, and archaeology are understood.

During the last three decades of the 20th century, the works of poststructuralists such as Roland Barthes, Julia Kristeva, Michel Foucault, and Jacques Derrida laid the foundation for what became known as the linguistic or textual turn.[2] The immense impact of this turn was based on the idea of the 'limitless text,' by which the meaning-constitutive qualities of the text (e.g. its multivocality, inter-textuality, and 'play of difference') was considered equally relevant for understanding non-discursive phenomena, including actions, space, landscapes, and things (e.g. Ricoeur 1973; Derrida 1978; Sturrock 1979; Tilley 1990; Olsen 2006). Nevertheless, when this turn faded and lost impact during the 1990s and early 2000s, it was probably due to precisely the realization of the *limits* of the text, especially as scholars started to redirect their attention to reality as tangibly experienced and manifested. However, rather than seeing this as a dismissal of the insights created by the textual turn, it is better understood as a new concern for that which fell outside, became othered, or simply could not be grasped through perspectives derived from language and writing alone (Figure 1.1).

After Discourse, thus, refers to the new intellectual landscape that opened up in the aftermath of the textual turn and which involved a new curiosity and concern for things and natures, including what these beings are in their own constituency.

FIGURE 1.1 After discourse: collapsed hospital archive, Teriberka, Murmansk Oblast, Russia. Photo: Bjørnar J. Olsen

In his 2009 paper on the future of history, Frank Trentmann captures well what was flourishing in this aftermath:

> Things are back. After the turn to discourse and signs in the late twentieth century, there is a new fascination with the material stuff of life. Things have recaptured our imagination, from Jane Campion's film *The Piano* (1993), biographies of objects, and exhibitions in the Fifth Berlin Biennial for Contemporary Art, 'When Things Cast No Shadow' (2008), all the way to public debates about the transformation of human flesh and mind in an age of nanotechnology, cloning, and cyborgs.
>
> *(Trentmann 2009, p. 283)*

He proceeds by claiming the already radical outcome of this return: 'Like words in the postmodern 1980s, things today are shaking our fundamental understandings of subjectivity, agency, emotions, and the relations between humans and nonhumans' (ibid, p. 284).

Hence, for the last couple of decades, archaeology and heritage studies, and the humanities and social sciences at large, have been increasingly affected by what variously has been labelled the 'material turn' the 'turn to things,' or the 'ontological turn.' What initially seemed to be a fringe movement, confined primarily to science and technology studies, has taken the form of what might be characterized as an extensive paradigm shift, involving a radical rethinking of what things and natures are, and how we are affected by and relate to the non-human world. Prominent representatives of this turn include Bruno Latour and his actor-network theory, Jane Bennett's 'vital materialism,' Timothy Morton's 'new ecology,' Karen Barad's 'agential realism' and the object-oriented ontology/philosophy proposed by Ian Bogost, Levy Bryant, and Graham Harman. Though indeed a varied congregation of ideas, these approaches share a preoccupation with critiquing the anthropocentric constraints of modern thinking and, consequently, promote perspectives that reintroduce things and natures as co-producers and compatriots of the world. Crucial to this, moreover, has been the growing recognition of non-human agency and the calls for less hierarchical ontologies, tellingly labelled as 'flat,' 'object-oriented,' or 'multiple.' What furthermore characterizes this shift is not only the new significance assigned to things, natures, and human–non-human relations, but also that relations of interest are extended beyond those involving humans, to include interaction between other actors, such as plastic and sea currents, ruins and kittiwakes, snow geese, and toxic water.

A new scholarly engagement with the material world has also raised issues regarding how this involvement is experienced and brought to knowledge. This draws attention to the difference between emphasizing the world as primarily intellectually mediated – that is as something consciously "read" or interpreted – versus acknowledging the world as also bodily experienced and known through our tactile and lived engagement with it. The increased attention to the existential and aesthetic dimension of experience also brought a new concern for the ineffable impacts of things – the way they involuntarily affect us, and inflect the way we comprehend and engage with reality. The empowerment of the material world has also questioned the common modern understanding of things and natures as beings at our disposal, valued primarily for their use-value: that is, for what they have to offer us and our well-being. Consequently, yet another outcome has been a concern for ethics, and reflection on how an extension of agency to the non-human world may challenge and extend conventional ethical frameworks.

In tandem with *Object Matters, After Discourse* may be described as a research initiative aimed at scrutinizing the consequences of the material turn for traditionally thing-oriented disciplines – and, vice versa, an exploration of how the knowledge and skill acquired in these disciplines may advance a critical and more empirically-grounded awareness of things in the humanities and social sciences. While acknowledging and drawing on the profound contributions to thing theory made in philosophy, science, and technology studies and other fields, a grounding assertion of our shared work was a renewed trust in the material itself. We argue that a successful turn to things cannot be accomplished through theoretical and discursive reconfigurations alone, but must also be grounded in the tactile experiences that emerge from direct engagements with things – including broken and stranded things (Figure 1.2).

This book presents some outcomes of these research efforts. It offers a range of reflections on things, what they are, how we become affected by them, and the ethical concerns they give rise to. Combining theoretical mediations and concrete field studies, it focuses on three main themes:

- what things *are*; i.e., the ontology of things, and how their being impinges on what can be known and said about them
- what things *do*; i.e., how their presence involuntarily and ineffably affects us, and influences the way we comprehend and sense the world
- what things ask of *us*; i.e., how things draw us into relations of care, and challenge conventional ethical frameworks with their unintended afterlives

In this introduction we shall briefly provide a background to the book and research themes covered. However, rather than introducing and summarizing the chapters that follow, which is catered for in the thematic introductions, the current introduction should be read more as an independent contribution to the book. It contains the editors' reflections on the themes as these have developed through research and numerous discussions in our projects, and thus also covers perspectives that extend beyond and hopefully bridge the scope of the individual chapters. However, it is not an attempt to bring them together in any overall whole – the contributions are, fortunately, all too unruly for such handling.

Turning to things

As mentioned, an initial focus of the *After Discourse* project was investigation of how theories and ideas associated with the material turn were affecting scholarship

FIGURE 1.2 Turning to things tactilely: moving through an abandoned research station in Dalnyie Zelentsy, Murmansk Oblast, Russia. Photo: Bjørnar J. Olsen

in disciplines traditionally devoted to things, especially archaeology and heritage studies. While their reception indeed is varied, there is no doubt that the ideas generated by the material turn have triggered theoretical and metaphysical reassessment, stirring new debates about thing agency, human–non-human relations, representation, interpretation, and affects. Still, talking about a material turn, or a turn to things, in this context may raise some reasonable concerns and suspicions. While identifying such a turn makes perfect sense in most social sciences, where things (with some notable exceptions) were largely ignored in much 20th century research, such a turn would appear to be utterly redundant for the disciplines of concern here. Why, for example, should archaeology, the discipline of things par excellence, be in any need of orienting itself towards what for nearly two centuries has consistently constituted its disciplinary foundation?

This seeming paradox, however, highlights what may be diagnosed as an unresolved tension within archaeology and the fields of material culture studies more generally. Despite the fact that archaeology has consistently and faithfully devoted itself to things, its engagement with the material record has been somewhat Janus-faced, leaving a genuine material orientation somewhat overshadowed by an anthropocentric metaphysics and a pretext of the social/ human a priori. As tellingly heralded in popular disciplinary slogans, such as that archaeology is about 'digging up people, not things' (Wheeler 1954), or about reaching the 'Indian behind the artefact' (Braidwood 1958), this metaphysics did not welcome any sincere understanding of things as *part of* the human past, or of the subjects urged for. It rather assigned them an epiphenomenal and derivative status as more or less reliable *sources* through which humanity might be accessed. The same pretext applied to culture and societies, which were largely conceived of as assemblages of people held together by social and cultural relations that were equally non-materially understood. Yet another outcome was that meaning was seen as primarily humanly derived, leaving things, monuments, and landscape mostly drained of significance prior to their cultural construction or social embodiment.

Given this predominant metaphysics, the new materialist approaches in many ways came to represent a welcome theoretical emancipation. Archaeologists and others took notice of Latour's message that people do not occupy positions *behind* things (through which they may be accessed), but actually become human by living with and mixing with things. Things and natures are not extra to society, but are part of the very fabric of intimate relations that link and associate people and non-humans in heterogenous collectives. Humans and things, in short, should no longer be defined by oppositions, dualities or negativities, but by their relations, collaboration, and coexistence (Latour 1993, 2005).

One perhaps less anticipated and acknowledged outcome of this exchange with the new materialism, however, was that it also helped reveal the difference grounding the archaeological project, herein archaeology's other and uncompromised material side, the *doing* of archaeology. In its low-key empirical version, archaeology is a practice driven by a consistent devotion to things in their material mundanity and unruliness. No object is too small, too inconspicuous, too fragmented or too soiled to become a matter of archaeological concern. This dedicated material engagement with sites and things, which archaeologists share with museum workers, curators, heritage scholars, and other field practitioners, also brings forth a mode of familiarity and understanding that is hard to achieve through an intellectual involvement alone. Working directly with the messy spoils of the past creates a crucial and distinctive thing knowledge, an intimate expertise and care for things big and small in their various, and often quite derelict, modes of being.

Such care and skill constitute a scholarly affordance of great significance, and which we find crucial also for developing – and *materializing* – the material turn, which so far has been realized mostly as a theoretical turn. Thus, while our thing-oriented disciplines have gained from creatively engaging with the important theoretical discourses emerging out of this turn, our reciprocal intellectual offering may be an articulation of the insights embedded in this affordance, and an extended theoretical perspective informed by material encounters. Even though the positive impacts of this remarkably influential turn are immense, one should also address the biases or shortcomings present, which the disciplinary skills of the object-oriented disciplines may help to balance.

Firstly, it is worth considering which kind of things actually are turned to and, thus granted agency, vitality, and personality. Though the selection admittedly seems to have become less exclusive, it still holds true that it is mostly significant and successful objects, and indeed often rather special objects, that are attended to – or which now are 'back,' to use Trentmann's phrase. Accidently, perhaps, but the list he provides to substantiate the return of things may actually be quite telling: film, biographies, art exhibitions, human flesh (and mind), nanotechnology, cloning. Monsters, air pumps, and prostheses are also quite popular, and somewhat overrepresented compared to, say, paving stones, pigeons, broken pots, fishing nets, post holes, doorknobs, bunk beds, sheds, and sewer pipes. Thus, Latour's old call for the 'missing masses' seems to still have some validity (Latour 1992).

Secondly, and closely related to this material elitism, is the tendency to keep concrete engagements with things conveniently at arms' length. Even in approaches that claim to be post-discursive, textual or otherwise mediated encounters are commonly preferred to direct engagements with things themselves in their concrete and messy manifestations. Similarly, despite the assertion that they represent the prime object of interest, scholars often seem far less eager to approach and apprehend things qua things than, for example, Kant or Heidegger's philosophical reasonings about them. In other words, theories and concepts still seem to perform a function far more central and accessible than the multifarious material entities we actually live with. Thus, while things may be back, the old pedagogy of learning by hand, from direct encounters with things, clearly hasn't enjoyed the same welcome, reinforcing the modern mantra that all knowledge is theory-dependent. Accordingly, when establishing what counts as knowledge or is accountable for knowing, things and our immediate experiences of them seem less likely companions and contributors. As acknowledged by Karen Barad, 'we would rather put our faith in representations instead of matter, believing that we have a kind of direct access to the content of our representations that we lack towards that which is represented' (Barad 2007, pp. 380–1).

Finally, when assessing how these things are addressed and credited significance in their new social embrace, another notable feature is the repertoire of positive and largely desirable human qualities and virtues consistently ascribed to them. Indeed, articulating the status of things as equally vibrant and playful actors may well have helped facilitate their much-celebrated social repatriation; in fact, the effect is not very different from early functionalist anthropology's rationalization of the human others by showing them to be basically like us (i.e. rational and calculative actors) (Sahlins 1976, pp. 74–5). Nevertheless, what is little addressed is how this 'humanizing' attitude may have deprived things of their difference and glossed over their unruly capacity to act. Moreover, and no less importantly, things also do bad things: they can harm us and other animate and inanimate beings. This, however, should not be taken to imply that they necessarily are monstrous per se,

FIGURE 1.3 Atmosphere in a northern town: the sculpture park and playground in Nikel, Murmansk Oblast, Russia. Photo: Þóra Pétursdóttir

or suggest that scholarship should be limited to objects especially prone to such monstrosity (González-Ruibal 2019, pp. 171–8). In their afterlife, released from our intentions and programs for them, even ordinary and intentionally innocent things and practices, including synthetic cloths, plastic toys, rubber granules (for artificial football-pitch turf), solar panels, internet gaming, and livestock farming, may become radically transformed into monstrous beings such as marine debris, greenhouse gasses, and toxic pollutants. Thus, turning to things and taking things seriously necessitates a far more profound exploration also of their otherness, including their various less pleasing affordances (Figure 1.3).

Sensing things

Since the pioneering works of German 19th-century philosophers Droysen and Dilthey, interpretation (*verstehen*) has been considered a defining feature of the methods and rationale of the historical sciences and humanities at large (Mueller-Vollmer 1985; Johnsen and Olsen 1992). This also applies to archaeology and heritage studies, where things consistently have been approached within a framework of meaning and representation, which has also shaped theoretical and methodological concerns. Things, monuments, and landscapes are basically approached from an observer's point of view as study objects to be scrutinized and interpreted; that is, as objects to be made sense of, rather than sensed. During the last two decades, however, and partly in tandem with the material turn, there has also been what may be called an 'affective turn' driven by scholars exploring aspects of experience, knowledge, and sensibility that cannot be grasped by the dominant hermeneutics of meaning and representation (Thrift 2007). One of our claims in this volume is that our inclinations to understand and find meaning have overshadowed, and even suppressed, involuntary and non-conscious experiences that may be prior to, and perhaps independent of, our interpretations. The second section of this volume explores possible ways to come to grips with and account for our immediate and affective responses to material encounters.

As originally proposed by Spinoza, the concept of 'affect' refers generally to the capacity to affect and be affected. Seen as aroused most easily by factors over which we have little control, affect may be defined as non-conscious experiences of intensity (Shouse 2005), experiences that equally apply to encounters with humans, things, and natures. These experiences often defy meaning in the conventional sense and thus cannot be easily decoded into meaningful analytical or interpretative statements. Acknowledging this affective experience of presence, however, does not imply any downgrading or ignorance of scholarly skills and knowledge-making. What it involves, however, is an effort to take seriously also the values and insights that may be derived from encounters and experiences that are not theoretically mediated – acknowledging the significance of what Terry Eagleton once described as 'the body's long inarticulate rebellion against the tyranny of the theoretical' (Eagleton 1990, p. 14).

The affective turn can be seen as a reaction to the assumption that the elucidation of reason and meaning is the only legitimate and adequate way to deal with the world academically. This perspective was forcefully expressed more than fifty years ago by Susan Sontag in her famous paper 'Against Interpretation' (1966), where she accused the art-field of being obsessed by an 'aggressive hermeneutic.' What characterized this hermeneutic, she claimed, was an 'overt contempt for appearances,' where the world as it appears is rendered shallow and suspicious, and thus something to be unveiled in order to reach what she called a 'shadow world of meaning' (Sontag 1966, pp. 6–7). Her critique may very well also apply to a wider tendency in 20th-century social and cultural research, characterized by suspicion of reality and a prevailing critical urge to search beneath appearances and beyond surfaces. It is hardly a too far-fetched suggestion that the obsession with meaning and interpretative depth, and the closely associated inclination to theorize, intellectualize, and abstract this meaning, made us lose sight of both the wondrous *and* the ordinary aspects of the world. And, accordingly, it may be argued that this sustained focus on critique created a void – and perhaps a longing for something more.

Nevertheless, when there has been, and still is, reluctance to include this 'more,' it is probably due to a common inclination to think of wonder and affection as extra to, or even incompatible with, appropriate scholarly conduct. These elements of experience are taken to represent a kind of insignificant excess, ornamental sentiments without any real acknowledged value. On a personal level one may of course appreciate and value the excitement and affection of an archaeological find or an impressive monument, but it is assumed that this response does not make a significant contribution to understanding either the past or the present. And maybe it doesn't in a narrow interpretative sense, if by 'understanding' one assumes reaching conclusive answers to predefined questions. Still, the affective aspects of our own encounters may prove extremely valuable in nearing the past, not least when considering the role affect, wonder, joy, fear, and other experiential qualities may have played for those people whose lives we strive to understand. In other words, that they themselves may have been affected by those very things and places that also affect us (Hamilakis 2013). Moreover, these moments of affective encounters may also provide clues to aspects of things' being that are otherwise difficult to grasp in our intellectual and habitual interaction with them. Precisely in such moments, when objects, as Nicholas Thomas (2010, p. 7) nicely phrases it, are 'happened upon,' we might get glimpses of unforeseen qualities or affordances that carry the potential to disrupt and destabilize existing accounts and understandings, thus enabling new insights. As moments of revelation, they expose aspects of things' being that are not exhausted by use or signification, revealing fragments of the surplus or excess that is otherwise hidden or held in reserve (Harman 2016).

Another common assumption in scholarly endeavour is that susceptibility to wonder is a trap for the novice or the unprepared – and thus something we are presumed to filter out as we become cleverer, more knowledgeable and more skilled, and shed our immature or even ignorant sentimental attachments. The more we know, the less we wonder (Daston 2014). Nevertheless, though experience may render us less prone to be affected, having knowledge about things, even of how to explain their presence, does not necessarily preclude an affective and wondrous response. As Jeff Malpas convincingly argues (2012, pp. 253–8), there is a distinction between a phenomenon as such, which we may have good knowledge about (e.g. the rainbow), and its sudden presencing, which is the very source of wonder and affect. Every child may know what causes a rainbow to appear, but to hold this knowledge does not erase the wonder triggered by its appearance. Upon encounter wonder emerges – and is neither explained away by nor reduced to what we already know to be true (Figure 1.4).

We might further add that appearance and encounter are often closely associated with anticipation and waiting; with a state of non-presence or a not-yet realized presence (Malpas, ibid.). For example, much fieldwork, archaeological or otherwise, is motivated by presentiment of something which is yet to be recovered, which might never appear, and which itself is an affective aspect. Some might even claim this is the very thrill of our trade. Though archaeological fieldwork in many ways is an encounter with otherness, with 'strange strangers,' to use Timothy Morton's (2012) term, the strange in an archaeological context is not necessarily represented only by the things themselves in their individuality. It is often rather the odd conditions, the new modes of being and hybrid mingling that things, in-themselves familiar, have established. Especially in a contemporary archaeological setting, it is not least this othering of the familiar and ready-to-hand that generates affective and often uncanny experiences. These experiences are also enhanced by the fact that such encounters usually take place far outside the comfort of our habitual everyday settings, in places where our own being is rendered strange and insecure, and thus perhaps more vulnerable to what Descartes called 'animal passions.' Those

FIGURE 1.4 Wonderstruck? Summer night in Finnkongkeila, Finnmark County, Norway. Photo: Þóra Pétursdóttir

moments when we become lost among things – moments we find both fascinating and alluring, but at the same time, and upon second thought, almost inappropriate or at least irrational – are where wonder lies.

Ethics and caring for things

In an influential paper from 1973, 'The Shallow and the Deep,' Norwegian philosopher Arne Næss introduced the term 'deep ecology' (Næss 1973; Keller 2008). He coined the term to oppose what he saw as the 'shallow' ecological concern of the western environmental movement, which he claimed was rooted only in human interests. Its rationale for fighting pollution, conserving wilderness, and preserving biodiversity was consistently anthropocentric, Næss claimed, where everything was tied to concerns for *our* well-being. Nature was prized mainly for its use-value and seemed to have no right to existence save to serve man (Keller 2008, p. 206). Deep ecology, in contrast, was based on the idea that humans held no superior position in the world and that all organisms were equal in intrinsic worth. Thus, one of Næss' main tenets was the principle of biocentric egalitarianism, which denied any differential valuation of organisms and which even assigned them equal rights. In the words of Næss, 'the equal right to live and blossom is an intuitively clear and obvious value axiom' (Næss 1973, p. 96).

Much may be said about Næss' vision of 'deep ecology,' including that things do not really feature as part of it. Nevertheless, his distinctive and alternative view offers a challenging entrance to a reflection on ethics and things. Ethics has long been a recurring theme in the thing-oriented disciplines of archaeology and heritage studies, as conspicuously flagged in discourses on dispossession, repatriation, and the right to an acknowledged and protected past. While these discourses clearly are concerned with matter, with very tangible sites and monuments, the importance, and hence ethical significance, of these things has been primarily related to their value as things-for-us. Especially as part of heritage discourses, things tend to become tools employed to reach contemporary social or moral ends – in much the same way as with nature in Næss' depiction of 'shallow environmentalism.' Despite the commonly voiced concerns with the material past, things themselves, qua things, have not been the object of much attention in debates on ethics in archaeology and heritage studies.

This is hardly surprising, one may claim, since ethics, for sure, traditionally denotes concern for fellow humans. In other words, though animals may be embraced, ethics is normally not extended to inanimate things. In fact, much modern ethical and philosophical concern has been preoccupied precisely with *saving* the subject from being reduced to 'a thing.' Nevertheless, the current fading of ontological polarities and the growing recognition of non-human agency, has arguably rendered an ethics of things both a conceivable and somewhat anticipated step (e.g. Benso 2000; Verbeek 2009; Introna 2014; Dalton 2018) – a development which can be understood, in part, as a response to the ecological and societal challenges associated with the Anthropocene. The final section of this volume explores some of the obvious provocations, and perhaps paradoxes, involved in such an undertaking. That is, since ethics is so closely related to human relations, to the *humane* and to our thinking about human others, a certain anthropocentrism seems unavoidable.

This pertains to another obstacle for an ethics of things, namely that this cannot simply be a question of extending the normative ethical domain. That is, subjecting things to an anthropocentric discourse on 'rights,' as also exemplified in Næss' manifesto, may in fact work against the intention of caring for their otherness. As with the extension of agency, the outcome of such well-meaning acts of inclusivity is likely to simply mold things in our own image. The alternative we propose, therefore, is to explore how ethics may be shifted through a sincerer attentiveness to things' being and the very diverse ways in which they exist, participate, and act in the world (Benso 2000, p. 131). Importantly, this shift also entails attentiveness to less attractive aspects of their being. In other words, we propose that a possible first step towards a humbler ethics must be grounded in a serious concern with how things manifest themselves, including how they may persist and outlive us. This implies taking seriously the worrying and monstrous aspects of things, both in terms of what they are and what they may become. Moreover, considering their recently enhanced status as beings endowed with agency and social capacities, one may even ask – polemically and likely also anthropocentrically – why moral implications and shared responsibilities should not follow suit?

Extending ethics beyond human fraternity also enables a rethinking of care as something more than an exclusively human virtue (cf. Puig de la Bellacasa 2011). From the Latin root *cura*, care and caring implies devotion, nurturing, and thoughtfulness directed toward something or someone. Conceived as a conscious, rational, and altruistic action, care has in modern understanding become a virtue generally assigned only to humans – and though a form of care is acknowledged to exist among at least some animal species, it is still considered one of the criteria that define humans' exceptional place in the world. Without reducing the distinctiveness of human care, we ask whether it would be possible to understand care also as a 'capacity' that becomes realized within actual material ecologies – 'when species meet' (cf. Haraway 2007), join forces and form alliances. Such an extended notion of care can be seen as ontologically impartial, and constitutes a possible way to articulate the numerous connections between objects, environments, people, and animals inhabiting a shared world (Figure 1.5).

From this point of departure, it also seems possible to discuss and analyze how things themselves extend a kind of care, both for us and for other non-human entities. For example, consider how bogs and wetlands offer conditions of preservation superior to any humanly implemented conservation, or how abandoned and ruinous buildings provide home and shelter for animals, birds, and plants, enabling new ruin ecologies to emerge. Extending care beyond its conventional association with humane acts of salvation and healing, also, however, opens up the possibility for explorations of how care, for example in the field of heritage practices, may occasionally be extended through acts of 'release' or 'letting go' (Heidegger 1966; Introna 2009; DeSilvey 2017); that is, through an attitude of non-involvement.

FIGURE 1.5 Unforeseen care: Renault F17 tank used by Wehrmacht occupation forces preserved by Arctic nature. Photo: Bjørnar J. Olsen

While leaving something to itself normally would be associated with *carelessness* and disrespect, and thus challenging the very foundation on which heritage practices rest, it can also be seen as a recognition and appreciation of things' material integrity and autonomy. Such impulses towards *release*, allowing things and sites to decay and wither, are made manifest in some indigenous conceptions of heritage. While release can be seen as part of a natural course of evanescence, and thus an element of things' constantly evolving stories, care through preservation and restoration may be regarded rather as interruptive, and even, in certain contexts, destructive (Ouzman 2006; DeSilvey 2017). Although such thinking presents a challenge to the traditional tropes of protection and rescue, it offers a potentially productive avenue for addressing questions of legacy and acknowledging the ties that bind people and things in relation.

Conclusion

After Discourse is the outcome of an extended dialogue, a long interdisciplinary and inter-ontological conversation between a group of affiliated scholars and the array of things that have been brought to our attention in the aftermath of the linguistic and textual turn. For logistical and somewhat arbitrary reasons, the book splits the conversation into three thematic sections. However, observant readers soon will realize that the actual contributions transverse these sections, in their attempts to grapple with the crooked paths of things as they manifest themselves through numerous and varied cases, from Elisabeth Bay, Australia, to Olderfjord, Arctic Norway. Things, in one way or another, are thus intimately interwoven with the authors' diverse concerns with wildness and writing, exceptionalism and evolution, touching and destruction, memory and nostalgia, Anthropocene thinking and intentional indifference. And things are made present in the book in a variety of forms, represented variously by ballast, ruins, cave paintings, paths, uranium mines, slides, longhorns or bowerbirds.

Notions of what things *are*, what they *do*, and what they ask of us, are not unaffected by these conceptual and material encounters. While the volume engages in thematic segregation and aligns with dominant strands of thinking and their effective histories, it also attends to how things become articulated and enrolled in academic projects, and highlights how specific examples and cases are employed in that endeavor. In other words, discourses on ontology, affects, and ethics are influenced not only by philosophical homilies and traditions, but also by the things and cases they become expressed through and entangled with. This material impact, or cross-contamination, is alive to the experiences and knowledge gained from attending to things and the way they articulate themselves upon encounter.

The awareness and knowledge produced in response to these material articulations should therefore be seen as making a decisive contribution to the rethinking of things 'after discourse.' For example, how did the fading of ontological polarities and the growing recognition of non-human agency actually come about? Does this rethinking stem solely, or even primarily, from pure reasoning and philosophical speculations? Or is it rather triggered by the way things have increasingly, and not least so in the Anthropocene, asserted themselves, as always-already blending with other objects, humans, and natures, and thus refusing to 'add up' in an orderly way? What such thing-oriented perspectives suggest is that the weakening and fragmentation of the prevailing Cartesian ontological framework may be seen as the outcome of confrontations with such messy assemblages, which in turn have provoked the emergence of current alternatives (Latour 1993; Pétursdóttir and Olsen 2018, pp. 107–8).

The situatedness of these theoretical strands and their immediate and intimate connection to the world equally explains, perhaps, the renewed attention given to affects and ethics. The enmeshment with a becoming world, which is perceived to be increasingly fragmented and fragile, both requires and facilitates a new awareness and responsiveness. As stated by Kathleen Stewart,

> matter in an unfinished world is itself indefinite – a not yet that fringes every determinate context or normativity with a margin of something deferred or something that failed to arrive, or has been lost, or is waiting in the wings, nascent, perhaps pressing
>
> *(Stewart 2008, p. 80).*

Attending to this unfinished world may seem futile and unpromising, especially since things give rise to much more than new 'problems of *thought*' (Stewart 2008, p. 72, emphasis added). In their novel expressions, things also generate real material problems, create fear and uncertainty, and force us to question established truths about right and wrong. In this world of new becomings it is indeed difficult to distinguish things' being from their affects and ethics. This remind us yet again that although our discourses on these matters commonly adopt a stance of rational debate and conform to theoretical constructs of coherency and logic, these discourses are also, inevitably, the outcome of direct material engagements, and thus demand of us responses that are attuned to, and loyal to, the trouble (cf. Haraway 2016).

Notes

1 After Discourse: Things, Archaeology and Heritage in the 21th Century, led by Bjørnar J. Olsen with co-authors among ten research fellows.
2 This turn, of course, also included the originating structuralist and semiotic insight of Ferdinand de Saussure, and the way this was later developed by e.g. Jakobson, Hjelmslev, and Propp, and notably expanded outside its traditional linguistic home-ground thanks largely to the anthropological structuralism of Claude Lévi-Strauss.

References

Barad, K., 2007. *Meeting the Universe Halfway: Quantum Physics and the Entanglement of Matter and Meaning*. Durham: Duke University Press.
Benso, S., 2000. *The Face of Things: A Different Side of Ethics*. Albany: State University of New York Press.

Braidwood, R., 1958. J. Vere Gordon Childe 1892–1957. *American Anthropologist* 60, 733–6.

Dalton, D. M., 2018. Towards an object-oriented ethics: Schopenhauer, Spinoza, and the physics of objective evil. *Open Philosophy* 1(1), 59–78.

Daston, L., 2014. Wonder and the ends of inquiry. *The Point Magazine*, Issue 8, summer 2014.

Derrida, J., 1978. *Writing and Difference*. London: Routledge.

DeSilvey, C., 2017. *Curated Decay: Heritage Beyond Saving*. Minneapolis: University of Minnesota Press.

Eagleton, T., 1990. *The Ideology of the Aesthetic*. Oxford: Basil Blackwell.

González-Ruibal, A., 2019. *An Archaeology of the Contemporary Era*. London: Routledge.

Hamilakis, Y., 2013. *Archaeology and the Senses: Human Experience, Memory, and Affect*. Cambridge: Cambridge University Press.

Haraway, D., 2007. *When Species Meet*. Minneapolis: University of Minnesota Press.

Haraway, D., 2016. *Staying with the Trouble: Making Kin in the Chthulucene*. Durham: Duke University Press.

Harman, G., 2016. *Immaterialism: Objects and Social Theory*. Cambridge: Polity Press.

Heidegger, M., 1966. *Discourse on Thinking*. New York: Harper and Row.

Introna, L.D., 2009. Ethics and the speaking of things. *Theory, Culture & Society* 26(4), 398–419.

Introna, L.D., 2014. Ethics and flesh: Being touched by the otherness of things. In: B. Olsen and Þ. Pétursdóttir, eds., *Ruin Memories: Materiality, Aesthetics and the Archaeology of the Recent Past*. London: Routledge, 41–61.

Johnsen, H., and B. Olsen. 1992. Hermeneutics and archaeology: On the philosophy of contextual archaeology. *American Antiquity* 57(3), 419–36.

Keller, D.R., 2008. Deep ecology. In: J. Baird Callicott, ed., *Encyclopaedia of Environmental Ethics and Philosophy*. Belmont, CA: Cengage Learning, 206–11.

Latour, B., 1992. Where are the missing masses? The sociology of a few mundane artifacts. In: W.E. Bijker and J. Law, eds., *Shaping Technology/Holding Society*. Cambridge, MA: MIT Press, 151–80.

Latour, B., 1993. *We Have Never Been Modern*. Cambridge, MA: Harvard University Press.

Latour, B., 2005. *Reassembling the Social*. Oxford: Oxford University Press.

Malpas, J., 2012. *Heidegger and the Thinking of Place: Explorations in the Topology of Being*. Cambridge, MA: MIT Press.

Morton, T., 2012. Thinking ecology: The mesh, the strange stranger and the beautiful soul. *Collapse* VI, 195–223.

Mueller-Vollmer, K. ed., 1985. *The Hermeneutics Reader: Texts of the German Tradition from the Enlightenment to the Present*. New York: Continuum.

Næss, A., 1973. The shallow and the deep, long-range ecology movement: A summary. *Inquiry: An Interdisciplinary Journal of Philosophy and the Social Sciences* 16, 95–100.

Olsen, B., 2006. Scenes from a troubled engagement. Post-structuralism and material culture studies, In: C. Tilley, W. Keane, S. Kuechler, M. Rowlands, and P. Spyer, eds., *Handbook of Material Culture*. London: Sage, 85–103.

Ouzman, S., 2006. The beauty of letting go: Fragmentary museums and archaeologies of archive. In: C. Gosden, W. Edwards, and R. Phillips, eds., *Sensible Objects: Museums, Colonialism and the Senses*. Oxford: Berg, 269–301.

Pétursdóttir, Þ. and Olsen, B.J. 2018. Theory adrift: The matter of archaeological theorizing. *Journal of Social Archaeology* 18 (1), 97–117.

Puig de la Bellacasa, M., 2011. Matters of care in technoscience: Assembling neglected things. *Social Studies of Science*, 41(1), 85–106.

Ricoeur, P., 1973. The model of the text: Meaningful action considered as a text. *New Literary History* 5 (1), 91–117.

Sahlins, M., 1976. *Culture and Practical Reasons*. Chicago: University of Chicago Press.

Shouse, E., 2005. Feeling, emotion, affect. *M/C Journal* 8.6 (http://journal.media-culture.org.au/0512/03-shouse.php).

Sontag, S., 1966. *Against Interpretations and Other Essays*. New York: Farrar, Straus and Giroux.

Stewart K., 2008. Weak theory in an unfinished world. *Journal of Folklore Research* 45(1), 71–82.

Sturrock, J., ed., 1979. *Structuralism and Since: From Lévi-Strauss to Derrida*. Oxford: Oxford University Press.

Thomas, N., 2010. The museum as method. *Museum Anthropology* 33(1), 6–10.

Thrift, N., 2007. *Non-Representational Theory: Space, Politics, Affect*. London: Routledge.

Tilley, C., ed., 1990. *Reading Material Culture: Structuralism, Hermeneutics and Poststructuralism*. Oxford: Blackwell.

Trentmann, F., 2009. Materiality in the future of history: Things, practices, and politics. *Journal of British Studies* 48(2), 283–307.

Verbeek, P.P., 2009. Cultivating humanity: Toward a non-humanist ethics of technology. In: J. K. Berg, E. Selinger, and S. Riis, eds., *New Waves in Philosophy of Technology*. New York: Palgrave Macmillian, 254–60.

Wheeler, M., 1954. *Archaeology from the Earth*. Oxford: Clarendon Press.

PART I

Things: Writing, nearing, knowing

Þóra Pétursdóttir

'To take the side of things is to take the side of *existence*', Joshua Corey (2016, ix) notes in his acclaim to Francis Ponge, the poet with the boundless passion for everyday objects, small and humble. And there is truth in this. While the turn to things has oftentimes been accused of turning concern away from the human and humane, the contributions to this volume share between them a very different view. 'Ponge's work …', Corey continues, '… does not de-humanize so much as it redistributes subjectivity' (ibid., iii). A turn to things, in other words, is as much a concern for the question of what it means to be human as it is an acknowledgement of how the non-human cannot be reduced to such subjective concerns. 'Man is a curious body whose centre of gravity is not in himself', Ponge claimed in one of his works (1979, p. 47). In many ways the contributions to this section reverberate around the search for this outer centre of gravity, in the in-between amid things and us. The aim, thus. is not to bring things close in order to render them fully explicable and knowable, but rather to ask in what way their integrity, difference and reluctance to surrender to our grasp, may affect our means of writing, nearing and knowing them?

As mentioned in the introduction to this volume, one conspicuous feature of the recent turn to things is the repertory of positive *human* qualities and virtues often ascribed to them in the process – qualities such as agency, vitality and personality. While this has proved vital for things' social inclusion, it is questionable to what extent this well-intended cultivation actually allows for an embracing of their difference. One aim of this section, therefore, is to address the question of what it actually implies to turn to things' alterity and otherness, and to explore how doing so can be motivated by the way things themselves already refuse to align with the Cartesian legacy? Moreover, how does the altered ontological position of things and natures affect the relationship between theory and data, the production of knowledge, and the notion of epistemology more generally? And what language will allow us to articulate the significance of things at present – in the aftermath of discourse and at the dawn of the Anthropocene?

This last question is the focus of two of the contributions in particular, 'Writing things after discourse' by Bjørnar J. Olsen and myself and 'Thick speech and deep time in the Anthropocene' by Robert Macfarlane. Drawing on archaeology and the nature of archaeological materials – which often display as muddy, fragmented, indistinct and muddled – Olsen and I address the divergence between 'the language of things' and the way they have been accounted for in academic writing. Suggesting that the turn to things may need a linguistic turn of its own we further ask, whether the language dominating social sciences and humanities today – a genre inherited from 20th-century critical thinking where the object was largely scorned and demonized – will be able to attune to such ambitions? For, how do we articulate not only the disclosure of things' otherness in the Anthropocene, but also their non-verbal expression more generally? Following this, and even more concerned with the challenges of this novel geological epoch, Robert Macfarlane recalls his encounter with the Greenland ice and his revelation that, as a writer, he utterly lacked the language to describe this phenomenon – ice in the Anthropocene. Faced with the contemporaneity of, on the one hand, the momentary and subjective and on the other the vast, entangled 'chrono-mashups' of this mutable body of ice, words would not adhere to what he saw and written notes only slide off their icy subject. How, indeed does the Anthropocene affect our speech?

Also concerned with the articulation of things, Levi Bryant starts out by probing the implications of the volume's title, after discourse, in his *Wild Things*. Traversing 20th-century thinking, touching upon the ideas of Barthes, Lacan, Derrida Luhmann, Kant and many more, Bryant scrutinizes the effective legacy of the linguistic turn and the intricate relations between signs and signifiers, discourse and being, before exploring the possibility of cultivating an attentiveness to the wildness in things. 'Is it possible', he asks, 'that there is something dangerous, something wild, about the non-discursive thing behind (after), beyond, and outside of discourse?', and in what way can we promote an aesthetics that is open to this 'danger' rather than immediately prone to pacify it?

On a related note Jeff Maplas asks in his essay 'In the presence of things', to what degree the claimed material turn feels at home in a world where social, cultural and economic structures rather tend towards an understanding of things as spatial, distributed and networked. Where does that leave the essential characteristics of the tangible, concrete thing – its place and bound? Drawing on what he refers to as a form of romantic materialism, Malpas explores the role of things in materialist thinking, and the intricacies of what it actually means to be in their presence.

The final contribution to this section is Torgeir Rinke Bangstad's 'On the face of things: Surficial encounters with the memory of architecture.' Picking up from Malpas' discussion of things as bound and/or dispersed, Bangstad focuses on the poignant surfaces of things and thus neatly bridges over to the following section on affects. Exploring surfaces as anything but superficial, the chapter approaches the exterior planes of buildings and structures not as physical boundaries but as permeable membranes that blur distinctions between buildings and their environment.

References

Corey, J. 2016. Introduction: The challenge of Francis Ponge. In: F. Ponge *The Partisan of Things*, pp. i–xi. Translated by J. Corey and J.L. Garneau. Chicago: Kenning Editions.

Ponge, F. 1979. *The Power of Language*. Translated by S. Gavronsky. Berkeley: University of California Press.

2

WRITING THINGS AFTER DISCOURSE

Bjørnar J. Olsen and Þóra Pétursdóttir

Academic writing has recently become subject to new criticism and attention. Setting the scene for much of this is the rising current of scholarship performing under legends such as post-humanism, environmental humanism, new materialism, and object-oriented ontology. One specific concern has been the question of how matters of Anthropocene and climate change are approached and articulated within these new discourses. To some critics, the language applied has increasingly been dominated by airy deliberations filled with poetic and ambiguous expressions that prevent a clear analytical grasp of the situation and, in the end, therefore serve reactionary and anti-humanist interests. Anthropologist Alf Hornborg, for example, comments that the 'styles of thinking and writing recently encouraged in the environmental humanities are not conducive to *analytical clarity, theoretical rigor*, or *effective critique* of the practices and discourses that generate global inequalities and unsustainability,' and what is even worse, 'that the *haziness, inconsistency*, and *inaccessibility* of so-called post-human deliberations on the Anthropocene ultimately serve to promote the destructive economic forces that are responsible for such change' (Hornborg 2017, p. 61, emphasis added).

There seem to be at least two assumptions in this criticism that call for attention. Firstly, that there are certain ways of writing that are considered (in themselves) analytical, rigorous, and effective. And secondly, that there is currently a trend in some academic fields to exchange this presumably analytical, rigorous, and effective language for alternative and less transparent genres. In this chapter we will address both these assumptions. The chapter is, however, not aimed at the Anthropocene particularly. It is rather concerned with the modes of thinking and writing that are stimulated in its wake and which more generally may be seen as concerning the articulation of matter and material compounds. Despite the human connotations of its naming, the Anthropocene has announced itself through the proliferation of new things, substances, and more-than-human relations. These changes considered, it is probably no coincidence that we in the last decades also have seen a 'material turn,' which pertinently has sought to substitute preceding linguistic or textual models of the world with more tangible references such as things, material agency, and assemblages, and spurred concerns with alternative and object-oriented ontologies.

Moving from discourse to things, however, does not mean that language matters less than before. It matters and it matters differently. Language is still the inevitable medium of scholarly exchange. There is little escape from language and writing when we want to articulate our knowledge, theories, arguments, and concerns. The material turn, of course, makes no exception to this – and it should be a matter of concern how this turn is brought to expression, and what sort of language it may require. Perhaps because of being campaigned, initially at least, as a riot against the linguistic paradigm, such concerns have remained surprisingly unaddressed. Despite voiced critique of scholars experimenting with alternative styles of writing (e.g. Ribeiro 2019, p. 43;[1] Hornborg 2017; Ion 2018), we contend that the actual *articulation* of the material turn has not really received any serious notice. And notwithstanding important examples of alternative narration and storytelling in the wake of Anthropocene (e.g. Rose 2011; Kohn 2013; Tsing 2015; Haraway 2016), the material turn has in general *not* augmented any greater change neither in how we write *nor* in how we conceive of language and writing as such. Perhaps it may even be claimed that the turn to things is in need of a linguistic turn of its own? For, how do we articulate not only the disclosure of things' otherness in the Anthropocene, but also their non-verbal expression more generally? Is the language and genre we rely on in the social sciences and humanities – a language largely inherited from 20th-century critical thinking where things were either demonized or ignored as sources of significance – attuned to such ambitions (Figure 2.1)?

With footing in our own thing-oriented discipline of archaeology, we will address some of these concerns in this chapter. We think engaging with *archaeological* things provides a significant experience helpful for discussing these questions. For one, revealing themselves often as muddy, fragmented, indistinct or muddled, archaeological assemblages conspicuously bring to attention the discrepancy between 'the language of things' and the ways they have been accounted for in academic narratives. Moreover, the difference brought to expression by the idiosyncrasy of the archaeological record may not only accentuate the need of different modes of articulation but even suggest alternative ways of writing the past. Keeping this is mind, we underline that our aim is not to disprove claims of ambiguity, poetic deliberations or lyrical metaphors, and we even see a potential value and affordance in such formulations. That is, embracing and accounting for archaeological things in their fragmented and muddled being may in fact welcome such alternative genres. At the same time, it is important to maintain that academic writing is scholarly and that it has to base its mediations in features such as logic, analysis, and empirically grounded arguments. For this reason, it cannot be judged by the same standards as those pertaining to novels or poetry. Academic writing has other and committing

FIGURE 2.1 The ineffable matters of concern in the Anthropocene? Beach debris, Ringvassøya, Arctic Norway. Photo: Þóra Pétursdóttir

attachments to truth and knowledge, and should indeed differ. This, however, does not render language and writing any less significant as methodological or theoretical concerns.

Academic language and literature

Thinking about the theoretical and methodological repertoire of archaeology, writing is not what first comes to mind. It is certainly something we do – all the time even – but, with few exceptions, writing, as such, is rarely considered a key activity of archaeological work (Lucas 2019). It is mostly treated as a helping device, in form of fieldnotes, reports, catalogues, and, of course, as an indispensable means for outreach – translating analysis, results, and thoughts into a communicative and durable format. The writing process is generally supposed to move hierarchically and irreversibly from signified to signifier, from content to form, and from idea to text. Our attitude to academic language and writing thus continues to be characterized by what Roland Barthes once called the 'illusory privilege … of a slave language' (1986, p. 7). In this conception, illusory as it may be, language should be pliant and 'invisible,' allowing the scientific content, the argument, to shine through without much disturbances and 'noise':

> For science, language is merely an instrument, which it chooses to make as transparent, as neutral as possible, subjugated to scientific matters (operations, hypotheses, results), which are said to exist outside it and to precede it: on one side and *first of all*, the contents of the scientific message which are everything, and on the other and *afterwards*, the verbal form entrusted with expressing these contents, which is nothing.
>
> *(Barthes 1986, p. 4, emphasis original)*

While both science and literature are discourses, science, unlike literature, rarely assumes or acknowledges language as constitutive for its practices and existence. Scientific language is appreciated primarily for its representative and communicative services, and the only widely recognized 'style' or genre guiding such authorship is 'clarity.' One telling manifestation of this utilitarian appropriation of language, is how academic journals have increasingly formalized standard narrative structures for their articles, most eloquently represented by the widely used IMRAD format (introduction, methods, results, and discussion). The claimed advantage of this model is that it makes communication more direct and effective, helps prevent repetitions and digressions, and thus to emphasize main points and 'highlights.' As Isabelle Stengers has argued in her 'plea for slow science,' one result may be that academic and scientific communication increasingly takes the form of a PowerPoint presentation, where ones' points are made 'in a striking, authoritative and schematized manner. In "bullets" (just listen to this word …)' (Stengers 2016, p. 64). They are, quite literally, as Walter Benjamin (1968, p. 89) puts it in the *Storyteller*, 'shot through with explanation.'

Understood in this way, academic writing is not really about language or writing as such. Actually, as Adorno once claimed, to be named a 'writer' is not necessarily a scholarly compliment (Adorno 1984, p. 151). While rhetoric for long was a recognized part of academic activity, the modern urge for value-free and neutral knowledge has discredited or veiled its acknowledged significance. Nevertheless, findings and arguments must be presented in ways that create trust and assurance, and in order to convince an audience and readership various rhetorical means are explicitly and implicitly applied. Erasing signs of vulnerability and uncertainty from the text, including the subjective presence of authors themselves, is probably among the most common. Actually, the very aspired-to ideal of textual transparency and mimesis may itself be seen as an effective rhetoric, advocating academic writing as an innocent tool of representation (e.g. Derrida 1978, p. 22; Barthes 1986). It may be telling for the ontologization of this ideal that the International Committee of Medical Journal Editors gave the thumb up to the IMRAD format precisely because it allegedly represents a 'direct reflection of the process of scientific discovery.'[2]

Considerable critique has of course been raised against this neutral and utilitarian conception of scholarly language. An important feature of the linguistic and textual turn of the 1970s and 80s, was exactly to problematize the ignorance of language and literary formation processes in academic discourses. The argument was that by belonging to the same discursive medium as the epic, the novel, and the drama, also scholarly texts were affected by the underlying codes and structures of textual production. Narrative formation processes and literary techniques and conventions (rhetoric, metaphors, tropes, plots, aesthetics) will therefore, to various extents, always intervene in the writing of our subject matter – sometimes even in ways that are at odds with our intentions (e.g. Barthes 1976; 1977; Derrida 1973; 1978; White 1973; 1978).

This recognition of the formative power of the text was made particularly relevant in late 20th-century anthropological writing, where the 'crisis of representation' led to a new focus on both ethnographic autobiography and writing 'the other' (e.g. Clifford and Marcus 1986; Clifford 1988; Hastrup 1992). Similar concerns also found their way into archaeology, where they triggered debates and reflections on how things and the past were written and experimentations with alternative styles of writing and narration (e.g. Baker and Thomas 1990; Shanks 1992; Solli 1996; Hodder et al. 1995; Pluciennik 1999; Campbell and Hansson 2000; Rudebeck 2000; Joyce et al. 2002; Ballard 2003; Bender, Hamilton, and Tilley 2007; van Dyke and Bernbeck 2015). An important outcome of the textual turn, thus, was that the strict delineation between scientific and fictional writing was questioned. Since both are conditioned by language, it becomes hard to exclude that elements of fictionality intrude in what is otherwise conceived of as results, facts, and knowledge.

Writing and the archaeological record

Despite that segments of the humanities and social sciences have become far more aware of themselves as communities of writing (e.g. Haraway 1976; Latour 1987; Gross and Keith 1997; Lucas 2019), it is for the large majority of scholars still business as usual that applies. Writing continues to be thought of solely as a means of communication and is rarely scrutinized for its meaning-*producing* services. Indeed, there is little doubt that our common academic plots often work well to frame an analysis or an argument, as evident in many of the works discussed here and also in this very chapter. In their familiarity, such plots are effective and productive, especially because they relate to discourses, modes of thoughts, and logics that might be said to exhibit similar features. Things, the non-human world, or the past, however, do not necessarily comply with the format of such discursive or cognitive constructions. And from the perspective discussed here, serious problems arise when a particular mode of writing is self-evidently applied as if it is isomorphic with its (or any given) subject matter. The persistently strong position culture-historical narratives hold in archaeological writing of the past provides a particularly intriguing case in this respect.

In archaeology, cultural history, and to write such history, has often been stated as an ultimate disciplinary goal. Ian Morris, for example, states that 'Archaeology is cultural history or it is nothing' (Morris 2000, p. 3). Similarly, in his recent book, aptly entitled The Times of Their Lives: Hunting History in the Archaeology of Neolithic Europe, Alasdair Whittle claims that archaeology can and must write history by offering narratives of individuals, groups, and sites (Whittle 2018). There

FIGURE 2.2 Ready to be narrated? Floor assemblage in a WW2 barrack, Sværholt prisoner of war camp, Arctic Norway. Photo: Þóra Pétursdóttir

is little doubt that archaeology can write such history, or that hunting history has been a major preoccupation for archaeology since the first half of the 20th century (e.g. Childe 1925). What is remarkable, however, is the taken for granted-ness of this trope, since the stories we write hardly can be claimed inherent to the archaeological record or in any other way afforded by the way the archaeological past unfolds and exposes itself (Figure 2.2).

This discrepancy has of course been repeatedly addressed (e.g. Shanks 1992, 2003; Pluciennik 1999, 2010; Burström 2013; Tringham 2015; Olsen 2012; Olsen and Pétursdóttir 2014, 2017), and equally so in the presumed model discipline of history. Most prominently by Hayden White who questioned the presumed realism of the traditional historical account, if for no other reasons than that 'real events do not offer themselves as stories' (White 1980, p. 8). Or, as he elaborates in his more comprehensive critique:

> Since the second half of the nineteenth century, history has become increasingly the refuge of all those "sane" men who excel at finding the simple in the complex, the familiar in the strange. ... The historian serves no one well by constructing a specious continuity between the present world and that which preceded it. On the contrary, we require a history that will educate us to discontinuity, more than ever before; for discontinuity, disruption and chaos are our lot.
>
> *(White 1978, p. 50)*

While White's harsh comments were grounded in his concerns for an increasingly more fragmented present, the archaeological discrepancy (or paradox) appears as a negation or denial of our always-already fragmented record. As archaeologists we work with the messy spoils of the past, however distant or recent. In fact, it can be claimed that the fragmented, the discontinuous, and accidental have always been *our* lot. This constitutes a disciplinary difference of great, even emblematic, significance, as Michel Foucault correctly realized in his philosophical branding of the name (Foucault 1970, 1972).

Traditionally, however, this has mostly been viewed as a main problem, a disciplinary Achilles heel representing loss, failure, and defect, and which therefore must be corrected in order to heal the material past as history. Because history, as a means of bringing reason, consistency, and flow to the past, has always been an implicit ideal of archaeological thinking; a pre-configured past which the archaeological material consistently has been seen as a distorted representation of. Writing coherent narratives has in many ways become the prescribed cure to our wounded record; accounts that smoothen, fill in the gaps, and provide the logic, clarity, and consistency that the record itself is lacking. Being more than sequentially ordered stories, narratives provide coherence through their inherent textual plots, whereby events and circumstances dealt with appear as a logical consequence of previously described conditions (Pluciennik 1999, p. 653). The narrative offers events, fragmented things, and instances with a connecting and consequential significance; that is, 'a meaning produced by discourse' (White 1987, p. 43). As such, these narratives unwittingly make manifest a rarely addressed feature: the crucial role writing plays in the construction of the archaeological past as history.

Sometimes this lack of attention to how literary formation processes operate in and through our writing is rather revealing. In his criticism of those archaeologists that in the 1980s found inspiration in a textual analogy in their *reading* of material culture, Colin Renfrew pertinently pointed out that 'it is a feature of written text that they are in essence linear: the words need to be in the right order.' He concluded, accordingly, that, '(w)hen we turn to an archaeological site consisting of a palimpsest of structures and rubbish pits, constructed and deposited at different periods, the analogy breaks down altogether' (1989, pp. 35–6). Strangely, however, he and other archaeologists seem little concerned with the opposite and no less cardinal move: how this fragmented and palimpsestal record is unproblematically *written* into linear and coherent texts and narratives (Figure 2.3). In other words, there is a lack of concern for the performative nature of texts – how they work beyond representation, and thus what they do and accomplish (Lucas 2019, pp. 11–12).

The heritage of language

Structuralists and post-structuralists often saw language as an autonomous structure, and thus seemed less concerned with how things spoken about *in* language had a locus and significance outside of it (van Beek 1991, p. 359). An

FIGURE 2.3 Joined in decay: fragments of papers and other things in an abandoned office, Eyri herring-oil factory, NW Iceland. Photo: Þóra Pétursdóttir

object-oriented approach, however, requires a different and possibly more 'leveled' conception. While acknowledging the internal dynamics and properties of language, it is also necessary to incorporate an understanding of language as embedded in the world and that it thereby becomes affected by the attitudes, dreams, and struggles of the speaking community. Such commitments are evident for example in nationalist language, revolutionary language, feminist language, etc., and in the ways of expression, vocabulary, and metaphors mobilized by these discursive communities.

To a larger or lesser extent this commitment also applies to scholarly language, which exemplifies an additional feature of its connectivity. New modes of thinking, or new subject matters, require or foster new articulations and though often born out of a context of novelty and critique, such critical language may subsequently take on a different role. Through repeated use and canonic texts it becomes sedimented into the discursive repertoire of developing academic traditions, constituting effective and, subsequently, often constraining historical legacies – a 'heritage of a common spirit' (Gadamer 1975 [1960], p. 72). Martin Heidegger's philosophical works represent a remarkable case both with respect to the power of language and as a rebellion against the constraints of such discursive heritage. More radically than Husserl, Heidegger molded phenomenology as a profound break with the idealist tradition, including its conceptual framework (Heidegger 1927). This, however, also urged a whole new vocabulary of neologisms free of – or in opposition to – the idealist linguistic deposits (see Inwood 2000). At first glance Heidegger's concepts may seem philosophically (and linguistically) odd by their strange mix of detachment and almost trivial familiarity, but this oddness also affords both a reflexive distancing and immediate glimpses of crucial aspects of his phenomenology. This is emblematically exemplified by terms such as *Dasein, thrownness,* and *being-in-the-world* (with the hyphens). In a vivid and straight-forward way these terms articulate our being as inevitably situated and entangled – while simultaneously signifying the central role this *grounded* terminology plays in molding the *difference* of Heidegger's philosophical universe.

Similarly, it can be claimed that current attempts to include things more sincerely through new and object-oriented approaches, must also involve a consideration of our own troubling language legacies. Here, an obvious object of attention should be the critical discourses that characterized much social and cultural research throughout the 20th century, where anthropocentric concerns and a pervasive hostility and suspicion towards things, technology, and nature were normative. Moreover, a grounding tenet of this research was an ingrained distrust in appearances, in the world as it appears to us, and which thus required digging into the deeper strata where more true meanings supposedly were to be exposed (Sontag 1966). The conceptual legacy of this critical attitude – and material resentment – is still very present in the common conceptual repertoire of social science and humanist writing. Just consider how crucial terms such as *objectification, reification, naturalizing,* and *instrumental reason* evoke a very specific mode of negativity and distrust, and which today is neatly paired with the persistently negative connotation associated with the notions 'materialist' and 'materialism' as characteristics of modern living.

Actually, when Roland Barthes in the quote above argues that language is for science 'merely an instrument' (1986, p. 4), he draws precisely on this legacy of negative thing allegories. Its meaning goes without saying precisely because it is shaped and sustained by the specific and suspicious conception of things and technology in 20th-century thought, where objects largely were deprived of significance beyond their use-value as things-for-us (Heidegger 1993). This discursive legacy is equally made effective through more general 'terms of suspicion,' or abstractions, commonly applied in the humanities and social sciences. Just consider the habit of articulating phenomena as *regimes* (of display, writing, historicity, etc.), *disciplinary* (societies, technologies, institutions), *invented* (the invention of tradition, authenticity, culture) or *imagined* (communities, ethnicities, cultures), as particularly witnessed in those fields which find it imperative to add the prefix 'critical' to their conducts.

For sure, this critical attitude and language have played a productive and emancipatory role in analyses of power and ideology, and also helped to bring attention to the marginalized and suppressed. But perhaps less so when it comes to articulating the marginalized themselves and their modes of expression, everyday experiences, worries, and affections? Moreover, how can new and attentive attitudes to things and natures be accommodated and articulated in a language that exhibits so many conspicuous traces of their demonizing? In other and more ontological words, how can a turn to things be realized without seriously considering the legacy

FIGURE 2.4 Articulating the marginalized themselves: flat assemblage in an abandoned apartment block in Nikel, Murmansk Oblast, Russia. Photo: Bjørnar J. Olsen

of a normative academic language, casted in the divided world currently averted (Figure 2.4)?

Writing as nearing

Debates about academic language and writing have, as noted above, often boiled down to whether or not it fulfils the ambition of clear and convincing transmission of knowledge. How language is ontologically situated, and also contributes to shape and generate meanings and objects of science, has been a matter of less concern. Given the assumption of a smooth transition from idea and content to textual form, we may for a moment consider the process of writing this very text. It is true that here, in its published form, it does appear as a relatively coherent whole, where the language employed may indeed seem to constitute a smooth and logical mediation of arguments that precede and exist outside it. Thinking back on the process of writing, however, it is evident that many also take form, or become tuned, altered, and scrapped, in the struggle with words and expression, and hence that the product presented cannot really be said to truly predate its articulation. In this sense, there is a certain semblance between the practice of writing and the practice of excavating – for example to follow and expose an archaeological feature like a cut (cf. Edgeworth 2012). While the latter requires employing various tools and methods in 'a constant adaptation to the unfolding and changing reality of the cut itself' (Edgeworth 2012, 78), writing similarly involves a struggle with words and the constant interaction between the account and the accounted for. The silhouette of the idea, the content, and the archaeological feature, is there to begin with, but the result equally takes form through the engagement with words and writing.

Acknowledging this is not to announce any fallacious return to the textual precedence. It is rather to attest to an ontological balance between words and things and how both are reciprocally constituted. Words do things to your thoughts. They act on how you conceive the world and your subject matter, and though they may, as addressed above, contribute to a distancing from things and the everyday, they may also assist a *nearing*. Language brings things to mind, helps us recognize their properties, as exemplary shown by Heidegger's conceptual artistry as well as those legacies of language born out of close proximity with things and nature (Macfarlane 2015). Such experience-near legacies – including our everyday language – help articulate things, imaginably making possible the seeming paradox of letting 'the world without words speak without me' (Serres 2015, p. 118).

Based on such understanding, it is perhaps even possible to reclaim text and writing as *instruments;* not in the sense of obediently transporting meaning but as phenomena that work on and affect the world and which, moreover, by fulfilling their tasks of expressing and naming things also help us *knowing* and nearing them. If nothing else, this understanding would allow for a reconsideration of the negativity and subjugation associated with the 'instrumental' being of language, as if this is merely a being at our disposal. That is, to acknowledge that much like things language has instrumental capacities and affordances, including unforeseen and hidden ones, that ought to be embraced and taken seriously as productive and enabling in the endeavour to bring things close. Rather than born out of purely cognitive relations, language and writing evolve in close proximity with things and chores (Benjamin 1999, pp. 72–3). Thus, and following Laura Micciche, we may say that language and writing are characterized as much by *with*ness as witness: 'Writing is contaminated, made possible by a mingling of forces and energies in diverse, often distributed environments. Writing is defined, ultimately, by its radical *withness'* (Micciche 2014, p. 502) (Figure 2.5).

The discursive environments of science and academia make no exception to this. Though undoubtedly also characterized by abstraction and distancing, academic languages, especially those of the empirically grounded disciplines, have evolved in close proximity with their objects and practices. This is manifested by their rich and detailed vocabularies. Archaeologists, for example, have a rich portfolio of words for what they do, the features and things they excavate, and for how they expose, document, and categorize them. This may include typological and designating concepts such as *pit-house, three-aisled longhouse, posthole, shell midden, passage grave, water-logged site, hearth-row site, bell beaker, pit-comb pottery, thick-butted axe, boat axe, end scraper, microlith,* and *bipolar core.* We also have a range of fieldwork terms such as *fieldwalking, test pitting, trial trenching,* and *single-context recording,* and other methodological

FIGURE 2.5 Attending to buried things: excavating a WW2 barrack floor in the Sværholt prisoner of war camp, Arctic Norway. Photo: Chris Witmore

concepts such as *closed find*, *horizon marker*, *seriation*, *ecofact*, and *site formation processes*. These names and 'technical words' may perhaps, to outsiders, appear alienating and confining, and accusations of disenchantment and scientific anesthetization may easily follow suit. However, for a large part this is an experience-near and associative vocabulary that has emerged through a profound interest in and concern for the objects engaged with and is thus very different from the critical and abstract 'social' vocabulary addressed above.

The way language, both ordinary and scholarly, attunes to its objects and practices may be said to be an example of what Heidegger, calls 'de-severance' (*Ent-fernung*[3]) or bringing close (1962, p. 139). To him, being-alongside and bringing close is essentially an empathic attitude that implies 'a kind of concernful being towards what is brought close and deseved' (Heidegger 1962, p. 140). Thinking of science this way is evidently at odds with Heidegger's own conception, where science (and technology) by large was seen as exemplifying a more calculative attitude to the world. To him, poetry would be a far more appropriate expression of such concernful and contemplative being. However, and against presumptions about scientific sterility and calculative motifs, science and poetry may not be that different after all. Both share a concern with perceiving and naming things and in this sense, as argued by Lily Huang, there may be a similitude and complementarity between science and poetry:

> Poetry and science aid each other in the work of perceiving, in setting things in motion. Both are in attendance at the stirring of objects into sacredness – into communion with the imagination – and they do not, I think, simply attend the same phenomenon in contrary spirits. The words by which science comes to know things have manners and movements intrinsic to them as poetic names do. Even a scientific understanding of constitutive processes or parts – the dreaded woof and texture of things – can lend an object a more pronounced identity, more ways to "deal out being." Is it disenchanting to discover what the summit of Mount Everest is made of? ... With a name a thing comes to life – a premise so basic to poetry that it cannot be from poets that the charge of intellectual anesthetization comes.
>
> *(Huang 2014)*

Karen Barad (2007, 2012) has made a somewhat related claim about the scientific undertaking of measurements. They are performative and 'world-making,' and matter and meaning, therefore, become co-constituted through the act (or intra-acting) of measure, observation, engagement (Barad 2012, p. 6). The performative aspect of science is likewise emphasized by Andrew Pickering (2011), who suggests this as an alternative to a representational understanding of scientific practice. While the latter furthers an ontological separation between the things scientists work with and their representations thereof, a performative understanding conceives of this as an outcome of a mutual translation, a dialectic of resistance and accommodation.

Writing and speaking things is, indeed, a very specific mode of translation. We may normally think of translation as transference from an original language to another, a transition that, hence, poses a potential threat to the original's authenticity, accuracy, and clarity (cf. Derrida 1977). Following the line of thought outlined above, however, translating things into words can also be seen as a mutual process and, thus, as a movement towards the thing expressed In this sense, language becomes less a means for representing things than one for *actualizing* them, and may in this mode of presencing, perhaps, even help articulate some of their 'essence,' if only in an allusive or indirect way (Harman 2016). The conception of language as born in opposition to mute objects, thereby shifts towards an understanding where it is seen as an instrument which *can* offer closeness. Much like an archaeological excavation, the act of putting things into words is not simply about mediating what is *already* revealed, but equally about carving something out through literally *engaging* with it.

Writing an archaeological past

We shall end this chapter by adding a few comments on archaeology and archaeological writing. As noted, archaeology has a rich and idiosyncratic vocabulary for its things and practices. Far from being arbitrary or unmotivated signifiers, these names are born out of attentiveness to artefacts and features, and out of concern and loyalty to the way they show themselves to us; *cup mark, funnel beaker, slab-lined pit*. Naming things helps articulate their particular features, and thus to bring them to knowledge in a concrete and associative way.

The same, however, cannot be said for many of the stories we write about them, exemplified by the culture historical narratives still found imperative to archaeological mediations. As argued above, these stories often seem more motivated by adhering to a historical ideal of the past than by the actual material articulations of the archaeological record itself. There are several reasons for this bias. For one, our expectations to the past have long been dictated by historical narratives, even to the degree that the past itself is consistently confused with history. This, moreover, has led to an inherited distrust in alternative accounts that abolish the narrative logic of connection and consequential significance. And, the methodological habit of conceiving the fragmented nature of the archaeological record as a distortion corrupting a previous lived order, has provided further legitimacy for constructing coherent and continuous accounts.

Nevertheless, what we would emphasize here is precisely the archaeological material's incongruence with history as traditionally conceived. This dissonance is not only rooted in the material's fragmented and scattered mode of being, but also in another and more profound sense – in its durability. Archaeological things are things that last. Through aging and transforming they stubbornly linger on, making the archaeological past slow, a past that stretches and postpones, and which thereby quite literally objects to the pace and passing of history. This material persistency, moreover, is actually what constitutes the condition of possibility for the archaeological project, and what implicitly grounds it as a project born out of resistance to the historical (Foucault 1972, p. 369; Heidegger 1962, pp. 388–9). A project perhaps better captured, thus, by Walter Benjamin's ideas about the past as topological and accumulative, rather than linear and biographical; in short, a past configurated by the ruins 'blasted out' of the historical continuum (Benjamin 1999; pp. 473–6) (Figure 2.6).

In his own meticulous attempt to go against the grain, Benjamin's solution was quite literally to *show* the past as scattered and ruined (Benjamin 1999, 2012; cf. Buck-Morss 1999). In a similar vein, staying faithful to the archaeological record will imply to relinquish the urge to hunt for historical coherence among its wounded survivors and rather try out options attentive to their own way of expressing themselves. By interrupting the historical expectations of the have been and the becoming, and by refusing to comply with wilful and conscious recollection, archaeological assemblages suggest modes of writing that care for and exhibit

FIGURE 2.6 Blasted out of the historical continuum: table assemblage, Eyri herring-oil factory, NW Iceland. Photo: Þóra Pétursdóttir

these qualities (e.g. Shanks 1992, 2003; Witmore 2020). And if we need a trope or model to further conceptualize the archaeological, one that takes the fragmented record seriously for what it is, we are perhaps better off with memory than history (cf. Olivier 2011). Just like things, memories don't come to us as coherent and plotted stories. Prior to any biographical retro-fitting, they reach us without any clear order, bending and braiding in a disorderly manner. Memories are fragmented and often accidental in their recalling of events big or small, much in the same way as what is materially recalled and encountered in an excavation trench: finds decaying and surviving without being subjugated – a priori – to any hierarchy of significance.

Its similitude with memory notwithstanding, archaeology has at its disposal the sufficient tools to undertake its own rewriting. It has an experience-near and thing-oriented language and, in the archaeological record, also a model for how to conceive of and articulate the past. What remains a challenging obstacle for such rewriting, however, is the constraint of a deeply sedimented historicist legacy – possibly most conspicuously manifested by the almost ontologized conflation of history with the past. In countering these discursive legacies, archaeology may find allies among those scholars who in the face of the bulging and frightening materiality of the Anthropocene have started to experiment with other and alternative styles of writing. Importantly, and contrary to the existing and expected accusations of irrationality, poetic deliberations, or obscure metaphors, this is not about making archaeological accounts that are more playful, abstract, ambiguous or poetic. Quite the contrary, such texts should rather be seen as born out of a serious, academic effort to make them more empirically grounded and archaeological; that is, attuned to the record we do rely on. Thus, when returning to the question initially posed about how to articulate the disclosure of things' otherness and their non-verbal expressions more generally, a simple advice may be to follow the still largely unfulfilled ambition of turning to things themselves.

Notes

1 "Instead of logical clarity, much of the writing surrounding object agency is hidden behind nonsensical allusions and poetic metaphors, or, as Alf Hornborg (2017, 2) has described it, it is something more akin to 'dinner conversations after some glasses of wine'. It seems obvious that archaeology requires much more theoretical engagement than it currently manifests, but I also believe that this engagement needs to be less cryptic and considerably more sober."

2 https://web.archive.org/web/20100706184319/http://www.icmje.org/urm_full.pdf

3 Literally abolishing distance.

References

Adorno, T. W. 1984. The essay as form. *New German Critique* 32: 151–71.

Baker, F. and Thomas, J. (eds.) 1990. *Writing the Past in the Present*. Lampeter: Saint David's University College.

Ballard, C. 2003. Writing (pre)history: Narrative and archaeological explanation in the New Guinea Highlands. *Archaeology in Oceania* 38 (3): 135–48.

Barad, K. 2007. *Meeting the Universe Halfway: Quantum Physics and the Entanglement of Matter and Meaning*. Durham: Duke University Press.

Barad, K. 2012. What is the measure of nothingness? Infinity, virtuality, justice. *Documenta* 13: 4–17.

Barthes, R. 1976. *The Pleasure of the Text*. London: Cape.

Barthes, R. 1977. *Image-Music-Text*. London: Fontana.

Barthes, R. 1986. *The Rustle of Language*. Oxford: Blackwell.

Beek, G. van. 1991. Words and things: A comment on Bouquet's "Images of artefacts." *Critique of Anthropology* 11(4): 357–60.

Bender, B., Hamilton, S. and Tilley, C. 2007. *Stone Worlds: Narrative and Reflexivity in Landscape Archaeology*. Walnut Creek, CA: Left Coast Press.

Benjamin, W. 1968. The storyteller: Reflections on the works of Nikolai Leskov. In: W. Benjamin *Illuminations* (ed. H. Arendt), pp. 83–109. New York: Schocken Books.

Benjamin, W. 1999. *The Arcades Project*. Cambridge, MA: Belknap Press of Harvard University Press.

Benjamin, W. 2012. *100 Notes, 100 Thoughts: Documenta Series 045*. Berlin: Hatje Cantz Verlag.

Buck-Morss, S. 1999. *The Dialectics of Seeing: Walter Benjamin and the Arcades Project*. Cambridge, MA: MIT Press.

Burström, M. 2013. Fragments as something more. Archaeological experience and reflection. In A. Gonzales-Ruibal (ed.), *Reclaiming Archaeology: Beyond the Tropes of Modernity*. London: Routledge

Campbell, F. and Hansson, J. (eds.) 2000. *Archaeological Sensibilities*. Gothenburg: Department of Archaeology, Gothenburg University.

Childe, V. G. 1925. *The Dawn of European Civilization*. London: Kegan Paul, Trench, Trubner & Co.

Clifford, J. 1988. *The Predicament of Culture: Twentieth-Century Ethnography, Literature, and Art.* Harvard: Harvard University Press.

Clifford, J. and Marcus, G.E. 1986. *Writing Culture: The Poetics and Politics of Ethnography.* Berkeley: University of California Press.

Derrida, J. 1973. *Speech and Phenomena, and Other Essays on Husserl's Theory of Signs.* Chicago: Northwestern University Press.

Derrida, J. 1977. *Of Grammatology.* Baltimore: Johns Hopkins University Press.

Derrida, J. 1978. *Writing and Difference.* Chicago: University of Chicago Press.

Edgeworth, M. 2012. Follow the cut, follow the rhythm, follow the material. *Norwegian Archaeological Review* 45 (1): 76–92.

Foucault, M. 1970. *The Order of Things: An Archaeology of the Human Sciences.* London: Tavistock.

Foucault, M. 1972. *The Archaeology of Knowledge.* London: Tavistock.

Gadamer, H.G. 1975. *Truth and Method.* London: Bloomsbury.

Gross, A.G. and. Keith, W.M. (eds.) 1997. *Rhetorical Hermeneutics: Invention and Interpretation in the Age of Science.* Albany: State University of New York Press

Haraway, D.J. 1976. *Crystals, Fabrics, and Fields: Metaphors of Organicism in Twentieth-Century Developmental Biology.* Yale: Yale University Press.

Haraway, D.J. 2016. *Staying with the Trouble: Making Kin in the Chthulucene.* Durham: Duke University Press.

Harman, G. 2016. *Immaterialism.* Cambridge: Polity Press.

Hastrup, K. 1992. Writing ethnography: State of the art. In: J. Okely and H. Callaway (eds.), *Anthropology and Autobiography.* London: Routledge.

Heidegger, M. 1927. *Sein und Zeit.* Tübingen: Max Niemeyer Verlag.

Heidegger, M. 1962. *Being and Time.* Malden: Blackwell Publishing.

Heidegger, M. 1993. *Basic Writings.* D.F. Krell (eds.) London: Routledge.

Hodder, I., Shanks, M., Alessandri, A., Buchli, V., Carman, J., Last, J., and Lucas, G. (eds.) 1995. *Interpreting Archaeology: Finding Meaning in the Past.* London: Routledge.

Hornborg, A. 2017. Artifacts have consequences, not agency: toward a critical theory of global environmental history. *European Journal of Social Theory* 20 (1): 95–110.

Huang, L. 2014. In praise of things. *The Point Magazine* 8 (June 11, 2014). Available online: https://thepointmag.com/examined-life/praise-things/

Inwood, M. 2000. *A Heidegger Dictionary.* Oxford: Blackwell.

Ion, A. 2018. A taphonomy of a dark Anthropocene: A response to Þóra Pétursdóttir's OOO- inspired 'Archaeology and Anthropocene'. *Archaeological Dialogues* 25 (2): 191–203.

Joyce, R.A. et al. 2002. *The Languages of Archaeology: Dialogue, Narrative, and Writing.* Oxford: Blackwell.

Kohn, E. 2013. *How Forests Think: Toward an Anthropology Beyond the Human.* Berkeley: University of California Press.

Latour, B. 1987. *Science in Action: How to Follow Scientists and Engineers through Society.* Cambridge, Mass.: Harvard University Press

Lucas, G. 2019. *Writing the Past: Knowledge and Literary Production in Archaeology.* Routledge: London.

Macfarlane, R. 2015. The word-hoard: On rewilding our language of landscape. *The Guardian* (February 27, 2015). Available online: www.theguardian.com/books/2015/feb/27/robert-macfarlane-word-hoard-rewilding-landscape.

Micciche, L.R. 2014. Writing material. *College English* 76 (6): 488–505.

Morris, I. 2000. *Archaeology as Cultural History: Words and Things in Iron Age Greece.* Oxford: Blackwell Publishing.

Olivier, L. 2011. *The Dark Abyss of Time: Archaeology and Memory*. Lanham, MD: Alta Mira Press.

Olsen, B. 2012. After interpretation: Remembering archaeology. *Current Swedish Archaeology* 20: 11 – 34.

Olsen, B. and Pétursdóttir, Þ. 2017. Sværholt: Poetics of memory. In: J. Kaila and J. Knuutila eds. *Inside and Beside the Camp*. Helsinki: The Academy of Fine Arts, University of Helsinki, pp. 88–95.

Pétursdóttir, Þ. and Olsen, B. 2014. An archaeology of ruins. In: B. Olsen and Þ. Pétursdóttir (eds.) *Ruin Memories: Materiality, Aesthetics and the Archaeology of the Recent Past*. London: Routledge, pp. 3–29.

Pickering, A. 2011. Ontological politics: Realism and agency in science, technology and art. *Insights* 4 (9): 2–11.

Pluciennik, M. 1999. Archaeological narratives and other ways of telling. *Current Anthropology* 40 (5): 653–78.

Pluciennik, M. 2010. Is narrative necessary? *EAZ – Ethnographisch-Archäologische Zeitschrift* 51 (1/2): 48–63.

Renfrew, C. 1989. *Archaeology and Language: The Puzzle of Indo-European Origins*. London: Penguin Books.

Ribeiro, A. 2019. Against object agency 2: Continuing the discussion with Sørensen. *Archaeological Dialogues* 26 (1): 39–44.

Rose, D.B. 2011. *Wild Dog Dreaming: Love and Extinction*. Charlottesville: University of Virginia Press.

Rudebeck, E. 2000. *Tilling Nature Harvesting Culture. ACTA Archaeologica Lundensia*. Series in 8°, No.32. Lund: Almqvist & Wiksell Intl.

Serres, M. 2015. *The Five Senses: A Philosophy of Mingled Bodies*. London: Bloomsbury

Shanks, M. 1992. *Experiencing the Past: On the Character of Archaeology*. London: Routledge.

Shanks, M. 2003. *Classical Archaeology of Greece: Experiences of the Discipline*. London: Routledge.

Solli, B. 1996. Narratives of Veøy. On the poetics and scientifics of archaeology. In P. Graves-Brown, S. Jones, and C. Gamble (eds.), *Cultural Identity and Archaeology*. London: Routledge.

Sontag, S. 1966. Against interpretation. In S. Sontag (ed.), *Against Interpretation and Other Essays*. London: Penguin, pp. 3–14.

Stengers, I. 2016 "Another science is possible!" A plea for slow science. In H. Letiche, G. Lightfoot, and J.-L. Moriceau (eds.), *Demo(s). Philosophy – Pedagogy – Politics*. Rotterdam: Sense Publishers.

Tringham, R. 2015. Creating narratives of the past as recombinant histories. In R.M. Van Dyke and R, Bernbeck (eds.), *Subjects and Narratives in Archaeology*. Colorado: University Press of Colorado, pp. 27–54.

Tsing, A. 2015. *The Mushroom at the End of the World: On the Possibility of Life in Capitalist Ruins*. Princeton: Princeton University Press.

Van Dyke, R.M. and Bernbeck, R. (eds.) 2015. *Subjects and Narratives in Archaeology*. Colorado: University Press of Colorado.

White, H. 1973. *Metahistory: The Historical Imagination in Nineteenth-Century Europe*. Baltimore: The Johns Hopkins University Press.

White, H. 1978. *Tropics of Discourse: Essays in Cultural Criticism*. Baltimore: The Johns Hopkins University Press.

White, H. 1980. The value of narrativity in the representation of reality. *Critical Inquiry* 7 (1): 5–27.

White, H. 1987. *The Content of the Form: Narrative Discourse and Historical Representation*. Baltimore: The Johns Hopkins University Press.

Whittle, A. 2018. *The Times of Their Lives: Hunting History in the Archaeology of Neolithic Europe*. Oxford: Oxbow Books.

Witmore, C. 2020. *Old Lands: A Chorography of the Eastern Peloponnese*. London: Routledge.

3

WILD THINGS

Levi R. Bryant

I would like to begin this chapter by reflecting on the title of this collection: After Discourse. In English, the preposition 'after' can signify one of two things. 'After' can refer to one event following another in the order of time. 'After' can also signify 'behind,' as in the sentence 'they stood in line one after the other.' Setting the second sense of 'after' to the side for the moment, the title 'After Discourse' could plausibly be taken to signal a sort of apocalypse or catastrophe where discourse has ceased and now, in its aftermath, we find ourselves in the midst of something else, something that is not discourse. The skeptical or willfully obtuse reader cannot fail to sense an air of paradox here. On the one hand, the articles collected in this book claim to aim at something after discourse. Yet on the other hand, *all of this transpires in discourse*.

The skeptical, perhaps hostile, reader exclaims 'your project is absurd from the outset, for it can only unfold within discourse and you are therefore powerless to escape discourse!' I am, of course, taking the title of this collection far more literally than it is intended. Or rather, I am misconstruing the referent of the term 'discourse' in the title. I am treating 'discourse' in a very general and extended sense to refer to any form of speech, writing, talk, or communication. However, the title 'After Discourse,' no doubt, refers to something far more narrow: it refers to a moment across a variety of disciplines in the humanities and social sciences where a variety of different theories of discourse were the dominant mode of analysis. Perhaps we are unable to escape discourse in the first sense, yet maybe we can produce something 'after discourse' in the second sense. However, perhaps through an intentional, literal misreading we might get at something fundamental about this moment where discourse in the second sense intended by the title reigned supreme, getting at what is at stake in aiming at something after discourse.

The second half of the twentieth century witnessed an extraordinary attentiveness to the nature of language, signs, and discourse as they function in our cognition, conception of reality, politics, and society. In certain respects, this comes as no sur-prise given transformations that then took place in our technologies and how per-vasive and ubiquitous these technologies became in our lives. As Barthes noted,

> [t]here is no doubt that the development of mass communications confers a particular relevance today upon the vast field of signifying media, just when the success of disciplines such as linguistics, information theory, formal logic and structural anthropology provide semantic analysis with new instruments. There is at present a kind of demand for semiology, stemming not from the fads of a few scholars, but from the very history of the modern world.
>
> *(Barthes 1967, p. 9)*

In a world where radio, television, cheaply available print of all kinds, and later the internet came to invade every aspect of our life, there could not fail to be a deep interest in how images act upon us and how language, signs, and discourse affect us. We thus got a series of 'turns.' There was the linguistic turn, the hermeneutic turn, the semiotic turn, the semiological turn, deconstruction, the rhetorical turn, and the discursive turn. There was hardly a discipline in the humanities and the social science where these 'turns' were not deeply felt. All of these orientations were deeply varied and therefore defy generalization beyond their focus on how lan-guage, signs, and discourse contribute to how we conceptualize reality, the nature of society, and politics.

These positions differed in their degree of radicality, but there was an unmistak-able *tendency* towards linguistic or semiotic idealism. In 1973, the great French psy-choanalyst Jacques Lacan would declare that, '[t]here's no such thing as a prediscursive reality. Every reality is founded and defined by discourse' (Lacan 1998b, 32). Later in the same seminar he would sum this thesis up in the beautiful aphorism '[t]he universe is the flower of rhetoric' (ibid., 56). Lacan is, of course, famous for his claim that 'the unconscious is structured like a language,' showing how symptoms are rhetorical formations that can, in part, be dissolved by tracing the logic of those signifiers in the speech of the analysand or patient. However, we get a sense of how this thesis might function elsewhere in a 1957 article where he presents two doors with the signifiers 'Gentlemen' and 'Ladies' over top of them. There he remarks that '[t]he point is not merely to silence the nominalist debate with a low blow, but to show how the signifier in fact enters the signified– namely, in a form which, since it is not immaterial, raises the question of its place in reality' (Lacan 2006, p. 417). The point here is that there is nothing about the physical doors that makes one a mens room and the other a ladies room, but rather that their being as such is constituted by the signifier. It is not difficult to extrapolate from this example to all systems of categorization for ethnicities, sexual orientations, plants, even elements. Indeed, we can imagine the Lacanian response to the question of whether or not Pluto is a planet: 'There are no planets, for being-a-planet is merely a rhetorical effect of a differential system of signifiers!' The claim, I think, is not that there is not something other than language – though Lacan does refer to this idea as 'mythological' (Lacan

1998b, p. 32) – but that we never can have any *access* to what that being might be. We are, according to Lacan, trapped in a play of the signifier without any outside. I confess that I am here being unfair to Lacan, for he has the category of the real that cannot be represented within language, but that nonetheless produces all sorts of effects within language. We will return to this later.

A similar point is made by Derrida in *Of Grammatology*. There Derrida will remark that '[t]here is nothing outside of the text.' Just before he will say that,

> if reading must not be content with doubling the text, it cannot legitimately transgress the text toward something other than it, toward a referent (a reality that is metaphysical, historical, psychobiographical, etc.) or toward a signified outside the text whose content could take place, could have taken place outside of language, that is to say, in the sense that we give here to that word, outside of writing in general
>
> *(Derrida 1997, p. 158)*

Derrideans are quick to argue that by 'text,' Derrida does not literally mean books, articles, etc. Rather, he is referring to the play of *différance* or differing-deferral by which anything is made present regardless of whether it is a novel or a tree.[1] I have, in fact, attempted to outline precisely what a Derridean framework would have to look like when applied to beings that are not texts in the more conventional sense (Bryant 2014). However, notice that despite the defense that textuality or *différance* is the condition for any and all presencing and givenness, in both Derrida and his defenders, there is almost an *exclusive* focus on the deconstructive analysis of *texts* in the more literal – always a dangerous term in Derrida! – and commonplace sense. In other words, we seem to get something of the sort of linguistic idealism defended by Lacan.

Elsewhere, in the discipline of Sociology, there is Niklas Luhmann and his claim that all of society is composed of communications (Luhmann 1995). I cannot here give a detailed outline of Luhmann's intricate meta-sociological theory, but perhaps it would not be an over-generalization to suggest that it is composed of four central claims: 1) Society is composed of communications, not people (he claims that people belong to the environment of social system or are outside of society). 2) Social systems are autopoietic systems that must perpetually reproduce themselves through communication. 3) social systems are 'operationally closed' in such a way that they can only 'observe' the world through distinctions they have drawn for the sake of determining what is to be observed and what is to be ignored. And finally 4) these distinctions are inherently paradoxical because they only exist *for* the system that draws the distinction. In other words, the distinction between system (what is inside) and environment (what is outside) – for Luhmann the first and most fundamental distinction organizing every system (ibid., 16) – is not a distinction that exists out there in the world, but only exists for the system drawing the distinction.

As a consequence, every system is self-referential and paradoxical. An environment is *only* an environment *for* a system. Now note how Luhmann's sociological *meta-theory* plays out when he engages in concrete sociological analyses. In works like *Ecological Communication*, Luhmann makes the case that we cannot analyze the environment because the environment is always a distinction drawn by the social system itself between itself and that which is outside it (Luhmann 1989). In other words, we cannot, for Luhmann, investigate environment, but can only investigate *talk* or *discourse* about environment, investigating those system-specific distinctions that determine what belongs to system and environment, what a social system is open to in the environment, and how that system of *communication* evolves. Suppose we take a commonplace discussion with a Luhmannian friend. You begin by discussing some sort of environmental issue such as the disappearance of Lake Chad in Africa since the 1960s. You refer to how the lake has shrunk dramatically, the impact on local agriculture and fishing, the refugee crises that have arisen from this in Chad, Niger, Cameroon, and Nigeria and how that might be related to violence in the region. Your Luhmannian friend contemplatively strokes his beard and says, 'but have you explored the *discourse* that constitutes this as a crisis and how the social system has been able to register or be open to these things at all?' You began by referring Lake Chad, the people surrounding it, and the wildlife and plants *themselves*, but now you are no longer talking about *Lake Chad*, but are instead talking about talk about Lake Chad. It is not that there is no value in talk-about-talk-about Lake Chad, but that there is a way in which the *being* of Lake Chad – what Lacan referred to as a mythological pre-discursive reality of Lake Chad – is erased in this move. We don't talk about Lake Chad. We end up talking about what people say about Lake Chad. That is the discursive turn.

Perhaps we were not wrong to begin with an obtuse and literal interpretation of the title 'After Discourse.' The title is clearly about a certain moment in theory where language, signs, and discourse reigned supreme as a frame for analyzing the world. Ironically I am now talking-about-talk-about language and signs. Yet it would appear that there is a very basic argument based on the generalized sense of discourse that the moment of the 'empire of discourse' in the world of theory is based on. Years ago I had a phone conversation with my future partner who lived in New Mexico at that time. She was telling me about New Mexican green chiles; magical and divine chiles that can only be found in this region of the world and perhaps the entire universe. She says, 'well, they are green, and come in varying degrees of heat, and have this very particular flavor, and …' What tumbles out of her mouth is not the *color* green, nor the *heat*, nor the *texture*, nor the 'very particular flavor' *that differs from farm to farm*. No. What comes out of her mouth are *signifiers*, discourse. 'Are they like jalapenos' I asked? 'No.' 'What about poblanos?' 'No.' 'Serranos?' 'No.' New Mexican green chiles are like New Mexican Green chiles. Yet, this very simple truth cannot be put into *discourse*. And as a consequence, Hegel, anticipating the discursive turn will say,

It is as a universal too that we *utter* what the sensuous [content] is. What we say is:

> 'This', i.e. the *universal* This; or, 'it is', i.e. *Being in general.* Of course, we do not *envisage* the universal This or Being in general, but we *utter* the universal; in other words, we do not strictly say what in this sense-certainty we *mean* to say. But language, as we see, is the more truthful; in it, we ourselves directly refute what we *mean* to say, and since the universal is the true [content] of sense-certainty and language expresses this true [content] alone, it is just not possible for us ever to say, or express in words, a sensuous being that we *mean*.
> *(Hegel 1977, p. 60)*

We cannot *say* or *utter* what we *mean*. And from here it is but a short leap from the claim that we cannot say the thing or materiality to the claim that the thing or materiality *is* language. If A = B and B = C, then A = C. If New Mexican green chiles can only be expressed as signifiers and signifiers are language, then New Mexican green chiles are creations or constructions of language. There is no pre-discursive reality of the green chile, regardless of what it might do to your delicate digestion later.

It is not difficult to discern that the discursive turn is a variant of correlationism. As articulated by Meillassoux, correlationism is 'the idea according to which we only ever have access to the correlation between thinking and being, and never either term considered apart form one another' (Meillassoux 2008, p. 5). In this instance, the correlation is not between thought and being, but rather language and being. We are unable to ever know being as it might be, the defender of the discursive turn argues, apart from language. Or, to put it in a slightly different key, we can only ever speak of what being is *for* and *in* language. To be clear, the point here is not that we must use language to *discuss* being and objects. This point is obvious, and both the realist and idealist are here agreed. Rather, the point is that for the discursive correlationist, the object *is* a being of language. Hjelmslev presents a striking example of this with respect to how the Danish, German, and French languages divide up the world (Hjelmslev 1969, p. 54) (see Figure 3.1).

The point here is that the three languages 'cut' up distinctions between trees, woods, and forests differently. In Danish we do not find the intermediary category

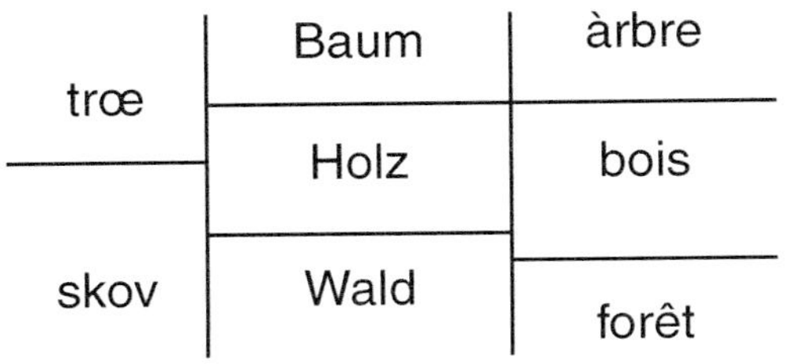

FIGURE 3.1 Hjelmslev's example of linguistic divisions

of woods at all, instead only having a distinction between tree and forest. In French the category of woods is broader than it is in German. In Danish the category of 'tree' is broader than it is in French and German. Similarly, in American English, rivers and streams are distinguished by their size, such that streams are smaller than rivers. By contrast, in French, *un fleuve* is a body that flows into the sea, whereas *une rivière* is a river that flows into a *fleuve* or *rivière*.

Countless examples such as this can be given and it is for this reason that translation is such a difficult, if not impossible, task. Faced with such observations, it is difficult not to reach the conclusion that reality is discursively constructed and that the Danish, French, Germans, and Americans live in different universes. What we encounter here is a linguistic version of the Kantian thesis that objects conform to our mind, rather than our mind to objects (Kant 1998, p. Bxvi). The claim that objects conform to our mind rather than our mind to objects is the claim that the mind is not merely a passive mirror of beings, but rather that it actively produces them through various cognitive operations. In Kant, these features of mind – the pure forms of intuition or time and space and the categories of the understanding – are universal, which is to say that they are shared by all rational beings. In the linguistic variants of correlationism, it is not mind that is doing this work, but language. And insofar as there is no one language, there is also no *one* being or reality. Where for Kant there is a single reality insofar as all rational beings share the same structure of thought, in discursive correlationism, there will be many realities defined by the different structures of language. Insofar as it is mind or language that structures reality, it follows that we cannot say what reality might be *apart* from mind or language. In the most extreme forms of discursive correlationism we can ask whether there are, in fact, rivers and streams in France.

Confronted with the claim that there are no rivers and streams for the French, one responds 'but regardless of what we call these things, surely there is something!' Hegel returns. "You say there is something, so *say* [utter] what it is." In frustration I find that as I strive to *say* what I *mean* only words tumble out of my mouth. And, to make matters worse, try as I might the words that flow from my mouth will be governed by the differential logic of the language I speak, again raising the question of whether there are rivers and streams in France. Later, Wittgenstein will intervene and say that '[w]hereof one cannot speak, thereof one must be silent' (Wittgenstein 1990, p. 189). Not only are we told that it is impossible to utter the real, but we are told that we must not attempt to utter the real. We here encounter a strange sort of prohibition, an imperative that prohibits us from doing something we are incapable of doing anyway.

I pause here with this prohibition. With Hegel, Lacan, Derrida, and Luhmann, it is a question of representing the limit of language within language. No matter how hard I attempt to refer to something other than language, I find that I am still within language. As a sort of retort, it is difficult not to think of Magritte's famous 1929 painting *La Trahison des images*. We are presented with an image of a pipe with the sentence '*Ceci n'est pas une pipe*' below it. The message is simple, it seems: the image is not the thing. In other words, through the juxtaposition of the image and the

FIGURE 3.2 The stony beach outside Sværholt fishing hamlet, Finnmark, Norway. Photo: Levi R. Bryant

sentence, Magritte at least marks existence of an outside to the order of words and images. Similarly, we can imagine a lost painting by Magritte entitled *La Trahison des mots*. This painting would be as follows:

> *Une pipe.*
> *Ceci n'est pas une pipe.*

Through the simple juxtaposition of two sentences we would, at least, have marked the limit of representation, of the discursive, pointing out the obvious: that the word or sentence is not the thing. While we have not *uttered* the thing – we readily agree that this is impossible – we have nonetheless marked or hallowed a space within language that indicates its own limit. And in doing so, we have introduced a fissure or crack into the transitive law – if A = B and B = C, then A = C – where, through Hegel's gesture we sought to collapse thing into language. This is such an obvious move that I am almost embarrassed to mention it.[2] Given the obviousness of such a gesture, might Wittgenstein's prohibition and the rush to collapse the thing in discourse resonate differently? Is it possible that there is something

FIGURE 3.3 The remains of a gun turret at Sværeholtsklubben, Finnmark, Norway. Photo: Levi R. Bryant

dangerous, something wild, about the non-discursive thing *behind* (after), beyond, and outside of discourse? Might we wish to prohibit speaking of what can never be said because that which cannot be said nonetheless endlessly disturbs and upsets discourse in all sorts of incalculable ways?

To excavate what this wildness of the thing might be, let us begin by looking at the conceptual effects of the discursive turn. In *Difference and Repetition*, Deleuze carefully draws a surprising distinction between generality and repetition. Where we might think that generality and repetition are synonymous, Deleuze claims that they differ in kind. The order of generality, Deleuze observes,

> presents two major orders: the qualitative order of resemblances and the quantitative order of equivalences. Cycles and equalities are their respective symbols. But in any case, generality expresses a point of view according to which one term may be exchanged or substituted for another. The exchange or substitution of particulars defines our conduct in relation to generality.
>
> *(Deleuze 1994, p. 1)*

What Deleuze here says of generality can equally be said of language and discourse. When Hegel points out that we cannot *utter* what we *mean*, he is making the claim that in uttering what we mean, the thing falls into the order of exchange, equality, and substitution. Speech retains only what can be substituted or exchanged for the thing. I wish to say *that* amazing curry that my friend made in a tent in the uninhabited region of Svaerholt in Norway, but as Hegel points out, all that comes out of my mouth is the universal 'this' that can be exchanged with all other thises (Hegel 1977, p. 60). The same would be true of the signifier 'curry.' Thus Lacan will say that '... the symbol first manifests itself as the killing of the thing' (Lacan 1998a, p. 206, 262). In the name of very different aims directed at a defense of realism, Harman will remark in another context that

> direct knowledge of anything is impossible because to be truly direct, knowledge of a thing would have to be that thing itself. As long as my knowledge of a tree does not actually become a tree, taking root in the soil and bearing fruit, then knowledge about it is obviously not a direct translation ..., because there remains a difference between the tree and knowledge of it.
>
> *(Harman 2013, p. 33)*

The treeness of the tree is lost in knowledge and signification. The being of the tree falls away and is replaced by a generality or universal, whereas the tree is this singular tree. With the signifier, the thing as *that* thing falls into the order of universality and is therefore erased in its singularity. The signifier freezes the thing, transforming it into a statue in a museum. However, where Hegel deploys this argument to erase the tree, Harman uses it to defend the reality of the tree.

By contrast to the order of generality, Deleuze will claim that

> repetition is a necessary and justified conduct only in relation to that which cannot be replaced. Repetition as a conduct and as a point of view concerns non-exchangeable and non-substitutable singularities. Reflections, echoes, doubles and souls do not belong to the domain of resemblance or equivalence; and it is no more possible to exchange one's soul than it is to substitute real twins for one another. If exchange is the criterion of generality, theft and gift are those of repetition.
>
> *(Deleuze 1994, p. 1)*

A reflection *repeats* what it reflects, but cannot *replace* what it reflects. Indeed, insofar as it inverts what it reflects, they are enantiomorphs that map on to their doubles without it being possible to substitute the one for the other.

Indeed, Kant notes precisely this in the *Prolegomena* remarking that,

> [w]hat indeed can be more similar to, and in all parts more equal to, my hand or my ear than its image in the mirror? And yet I cannot put such a hand as is seen in the mirror in the place of its original; for if the one was a right hand, then the other in the mirror is a left, and the image of the right ear

is a left one, which can never take the place of the former. Now there is no inner differences here that any understanding could merely think; and yet the differences are inner as far as the senses teach …

(Kant 1997, p. 38)

Kant's point is that *conceptually* (from the standpoint of generality or what can be uttered) there is no difference between the two gloves, yet nonetheless there *is* a difference … A non-conceptual, non-linguistic difference that can only be sensed or intuited. Kant's example is all the more powerful in that it is a *universal* feature of *all* enantiomorphs. All enantiomorphs evade exchange and substitution in this way; yet, nonetheless this difference between the two symmetrical objects is something that cannot be put into words but can only be sensed. We can refer to it, gesture to it, allude to it, without being able to *say* it. What we encounter in enantiomorphs and repetition are differences that can only be alluded to, that can only be intuited, without it being possible to utter them. One must sense them to know them.

Within the framework of the discursive turn, the thing, object, 'this,' or materiality is erased and replaced by the symbol. This is an instance of what Graham Harman calls 'overmining.' We overmine objects when 'one treats them as needlessly deep or spooky hypotheses by comparison with their tangible properties or effects' (Harman 2016, p. 10). In this instance, the thing is reduced to our concept of the thing, its form, or the sign or signifier. As Stacy Alaimo remarks, '[m]atter, the vast stuff of the world and of ourselves, has been subdivided into manageable "bits" or flattened into a "blank slate" for human inscription' (Alaimo 2010, p. 1). In short, the thing, the this, or matter itself will contribute nothing, but will instead be reduced to a mere vehicle, a screen, for the inscription of human meanings. The thing will become a *symbol* or *text* to be deciphered. Thus, when we open the pages of Baudrillard's *The System of Objects*, we expect to encounter a discussion of the thingliness of things, but are instead treated to a discussion of the *meaning* of furniture, interior design, and the domestic layout of the home (Baudrillard 2005). There is a sense in which, for Baudrillard, the furniture is not really there at all, as if it contributes nothing. Like a game of chess where you have lost a knight and replace it with a quarter, the furniture only matters insofar as it is a screen for a differential system of meaning that could just as easily be dispensed with or replaced by other entities. Speaking in a similar vein with regard to this phenomenon in archaeology and ethnography, Bjørnar J. Olsen remarks that,

What strikes me after reading many recent books and papers on rock art is the never-ending urge to intellectualize the past: a constant search for a deeper meaning, something beyond what can be sensed. According to this unveiling mode a boat, an elk, or a reindeer can be claimed to represent almost everything – ancestors, rites of transitions, borders, supernatural powers, and so on – apart, it seems, only from themselves. A boat is never a boat; a reindeer is never a reindeer; a river is always a 'cosmic' river.

(Olsen 2010, p. 86)

The thing itself comes to be replaced by the meaning, text, or the narrative of the thing. Presumably this is not merely a matter of how rock art is approached, but extends to how the ethnographer might approach living, breathing reindeer themselves. Perhaps the role that the *reindeer* play in the lives of the Sami comes to be replaced by the 'deeper meanings' Olsen here refers to. In short, the thing itself has been *erased*.

Adorno refers to this phenomenon as the 'idealist misconception,' that arises from thinking that 'because we cannot speak about anything … which is not mediated by form, form must therefore be the only thing which *is*' (Adorno 2001, p. 67). The peculiarity of the *concept* of matter, Adorno observes, is that it is the concept of something that is not a concept. It refers to something that is not conceptual (ibid.). Insofar as we can only speak of form, the discursive, we therefore conclude that matter does not exist at all. We reduce the thing to what can be exchanged: the signifier, the sign, the text.

We have seen that the thing gets erased because the thing is precisely that which cannot be exchanged. The thing, in its essence, is a non-substitutable,

FIGURE 3.4 Abandoned fishing boat in Sværholt, Finnmark, Norway. Photo: Levi R. Bryant

non-exchangeable singularity. It is the this which cannot be uttered, but which can only be *meant*. At this point, it will be objected that we exchange things all the time. I exchange some homemade cookies with my neighbor in return for some tulips. Yet as counter-intuitive as it might seem, never in the entire history of history has a single thing be exchanged, and this for the very simple reason that only that which is subject to substitution and replaceability can be exchanged. What is exchanged is a symbol, an equivalence, never a thing. The thing, like Baudrillard's furniture, is treated as being merely a vehicle for the symbol. The thing is overmined in exchange and replaced by the symbol. Insofar as, following Hegel, the thing is that which can only be meant and never said, it cannot, by definition, be exchanged. As Derrida remarks, '[t]he *without-goal*, the *without-why* of the tulip is not significant, is not a signifier, not even a signifier of lack. At least insofar as the tulip is beautiful, *this* tulip' (Derrida 1987, p. 95). It is a strange paradox. Insofar as only a symbol or sign can be exchanged, it follows that it is impossible to exchange a thing. As Lacan remarks, 'the real is the impossible' (Lacan 1998b, p. 165), which is to say, the impossible to *represent*. It is precisely that which falls outside the system of exchange, whether it be linguistic or otherwise.

Why, then, is there this perpetual erasure of the thing? The reasons are legion. There is, first of all, the real as the impossible which favors the erasure of the real and reduction of it to the conceptual. Yet there is also something, no matter how minimally, *traumatic* about the real. Drawing on Aristotle's concept of *tuché* or chance, Lacan defines the *tuché* as an encounter with the real (ibid., 53). In particular, Lacan defines the *tuché* – which he equates with trauma –with the *missed* encounter (ibid., 55). What must be true in order for it to be possible for there to be a missed encounter? And why is the encounter with the real or trauma a *missed* encounter? Ordinarily when we think of trauma we think of it as an encounter. The train hits my car. Such an experience is traumatic. There does not seem to be anything missed here. Indeed, it seems as if the problem is precisely that the train did not miss.

To unpack this mystery, let us recall Heidegger's analysis of equipment in *Being and Time* (Heidegger 1962). In his discussion of equipment, Heidegger is careful to note that there is never *an* equipment. Rather, equipment always belongs to a referential totality that he refers to as 'worldhood.' The hammer refers to the nails and the boards to be fastened and the home to be built so as to shelter us from the elements and create a place of gathering and living. In short, the hammer belongs to an entire system of meaning or significance. In my use of the hammer the hammer disappears and almost becoming an extension of my body, because I project myself towards the future embodied in my task of building. In other words, the thingness of the hammer disappears or gets erased. When, then, does the hammer appear *qua* thing? The hammer appears as a thing when, for instance, it breaks and becomes unusable (ibid., 102–7). When the hammer is broken it falls outside of the system of meaning or significance, becoming a 'mere' thing in its obtrusiveness.

Heidegger's analysis of equipment sheds light on Lacan's claim that the encounter with the real is a missed encounter. Our ordinary concernful dealings with the world are characterized by a system of meaning in which we are able to *anticipate* how it is with things, how things will go. There is a system of meaning that carries a sense of being-at-home in the world or that the world has been mastered. When the tool breaks, this being-at-homeness is shattered. If trauma, the encounter with the real, is a *missed* encounter, then this is because it is the eruption of something, an event, for which there was no signifier, meaning, or anticipation. The signifier or concept was not there. This is precisely what the *tuché*, chance, is. Chance is that for which there are no signifiers or systems of meaning and anticipation, erupting into the world of our everyday experience. It is for this reason that in response to trauma we never cease to speak of it, dream about it, and repeat it in action as in the case of the childhood victim of abuse who later in life seems to encounter new instances of abuse in all sorts of ways. As Lacan will elsewhere say, the real 'is that which doesn't stop … being written' (Lacan 1998b, p. 59). In the aftermath of an encounter with the real or the missed encounter, we endlessly circle about the hole produced in the system of signification seeking to name it, while endlessly missing it.

While I do not wish to suggest that an encounter with the thingliness of things is equivalent to severe traumas such as those suffered by soldiers in the wake of having something horrific happen to them, I do wish to suggest that there is something minimally traumatic about the thing in its sheer materiality. In this connection, it is difficult not to recall Roquentin's encounter with the chestnut tree in Sartre's *Nausea*.

> The roots of the chestnut tree were sunk in the ground just under my bench. I couldn't remember it was a root any more. The words had vanished and with them the significance of things, their methods of use, and the feeble points of reference which men have traced on their surface. I was sitting, stooping forward, head bowed, alone in front of this black, knotty mass, entirely beastly, which frightened me.
>
> *(Sartre 2007, pp. 126–7)*

Roquentin continues,

> If anyone had asked me what existence was, I would have answered, in good faith, that it was nothing, simply an empty form which was added to the external things without changing anything in their nature. And then all of the sudden, there it was, clear as day: existence had suddenly unveiled itself … The veneer had melted, leaving soft, monstrous masses, all in disorder— naked, in a frightful, obscene nakedness.
>
> *(Ibid., 127)*

Denuded of the concept, we are presented with the wild thing, the monstrous thing, that eludes our ability to utter it or master it. It is the real, the missed encounter which is missed not because it is not there, but precisely because there are no words that are adequate to it.

Perhaps, then, the erasure of things arises not because we are unable to utter them as Hegel contended, but because there is something traumatic about the thing due to how it evades our ability to master and domesticate it. If this is true, then suddenly an entire series of binary oppositions governing Western thought would take on a new sense: form/matter, mind/body, culture/nature, theoretical sciences/applied sciences, theory/practice, anthropology/archaeology, literary studies/media studies, etc. In each case, the term associated with form, signification, exchange, meaning, and therefore mastery is treated as being higher in dignity than the term associated with materiality. If this is the case, then the reason that the term associated with things and materiality is treated as lower in dignity is because they confront us with the unruliness of existence, the wildness of being. Thingliness, materiality, confronts us with that which evades our mastery. And what is it that we are truly confronted with when confronted with that which evades our mastery? We are confronted with our own finitude, with the possibility of our death. When, in uninhabited region of Svaerholt, I stand in the shadows of 10,000 year old pre-historic home foundations (Figure 3.2), the World War II Russian POW camp there, portions of the Nazi Atlantic Wall (Figure 3.3), and the abandoned fishing village dating back centuries (Figure 3.4), I encounter my own finitude. I encounter my own finitude *not* because people once lived here and are now gone and I realize that that is my fate as well – though that too – but because, like Roquentin, I encounter a foreignness, an alien being of things that have taken on a life of their own beyond humans. Following the reflections of Þóra Pétursdóttir in her haunting and disquieting article 'Things out-of-hand,' those of us who seek to theorize things often restrict ourselves to the 'domesticated thing,' the good thing, or the thing that assists us in our living and tasks like the hammer (Pétursdóttir 2014). We theorize the meaningful thing, the symbolic thing, and the useful thing. In her encounter with the office at the Eyri herring station in Iceland, Pétursdóttir, like Sartre's Roquentin, encounters the wild, emancipated thing that is behind and before discourse, that has taken on a disquieting life of its own beyond human meanings and uses. Like the uncanny and disquieting experience of the doll's head that has become the home of a hermit crab, thereby becoming something utterly foreign to its original being as a child's toy, in these instances we encounter a thingliness and materiality that is not ours and that is not merely the uses that we put things to and the meanings that we drape over them like lines of latitude and longitude that we lay over the earth on a map. It is in this sense that an encounter with things is an encounter with our finitude: it is the disquieting recognition that the things are not simply mirrors or reflections of us. They are not our screens.

Our initial reaction might be 'so what?' We have conceded that the thing itself cannot be uttered, yet have also seen that as something behind discourse they can be encountered and they spur us to all sorts of talk. Nonetheless, if wild things are as Sartre's Roquentin describes them, what is to be gained from speaking of them at all?

Husserl famously declared that 'we must go back to the "things themselves"' (Husserl 2000, p. 252). Yet oddly despite all that the phenomenologists teach us about how we experience objects, there is a strange way in which the things themselves evaporate and are once again placed under erasure. In an article reflecting on the contributions of the symmetrical archaeologists, Jeff Love and Michael Meng reflect on how our historical narratives can cultivate a gaze that prevents us from seeing what is there before us (Love and Meng 2016). As a result of our historical narratives, the things dug in a midden pit, for example, become ventriloquized things that speak what we expect them to speak, rather than speaking what they might have to speak. In their archeological work at the Russian POW camp at Svaerholt, the archaeologists find curious things such as cologne bottles, alcohol bottles, and game pieces. Our historical narratives tell us that conditions in the Nazi prison camps were brutal, yet in this instance we encounter things suggestive of modest acts of kindness, hinting at a more sympathetic relationship between the guards and the prisoners (Olsen and Witmore 2014). We encounter a mystery. Why, when conditions were so horrific in other prison camps, do we find very modest suggestions of kindness in this place? The point is not that the Nazi's were good people after all, but that in this instance we encounter something that does not fit with our narratives. So long as our vision is guided by these narratives, we might overlook these things out of place altogether. However, if we cultivate an aesthetics of the wildness of things, of their unruliness – and here 'aesthetics' should be understood in the Kantian sense of sensibility or receptivity – we might be more open to seeing what is there before us, rather than erasing them beneath the signifier or meaning.

However, there is another reason we should cultivate an attentiveness to things out of place, to the wildness of things, to the unruliness of things. As we find ourselves at the height of the Anthropocene where humankind has fundamentally transformed the nature of the earth and where we are everywhere threatened by the effects of climate change, we should recall that part of how we got here was through the erasure or repression of things and our belief that we have mastered them and that they are simply reflections of our own meaning and uses. A posthuman conception of things as wild things in excess of human meanings and uses might very well be precisely the sensibility we need to cultivate to begin addressing the ravages of climate change.

Notes

1 Since the rise of Actor-Network Theory, New Materialism, and Object-Oriented Ontology this has been a very common response to the critique of these respective positions and their criticism of the dominance of variants of the linguistic or discursive turn in the humanities and social sciences. Most recently Jack Caputo made this argument in response to a talk I gave at Texas A&M in February 2019.
2 This is not, of course, intended as a refutation of the correlationist argument, but instead to allude to how we can point beyond language. For a more detailed discussion of how we might escape the correlationist circle cf. (Bryant 2011, Chapter 1).

References

Adorno, T.W. 2001. *Metaphysics: Concepts and Problems*. Translated by Edmund Jephcott. Stanford: Stanford University Press.

Alaimo, S. 2010. *Bodily Natures: Science, Environment, and the Material Self*. Bloomington: Indiana University Press.

Barthes, R. 1967. *Elements of Semiology*. Translated by Annette Lavers and Collin Smith. New York: Hill and Wang, 1967.

Baudrillard, J. 2005. *The System of Objects*. Translated by James Benedict. London: Verso Books.

Bryant, L.R. 2014. "The Time of the Object: Derrida, Luhmann, and the Processual Nature of Substances." In *The Allure of Things: Process and Object in Contemporary Philosophy*. Edited by Roland Faber and Andrew Goffey. London: Bloomsbury Press.

Deleuze, G. 1994. *Difference and Repetition*. Translated by Paul Patton. New York: Columbia University Press.

Derrida, J. 1987. *The Truth in Painting*. Translated by Geoff Bennington and Ian McLeod. Chicago: Chicago University Press.

Derrida, J. 1997. *Of Grammatology*. Translated by Gayatri Chakrovorty Spivak. Baltimore: John Hopkins University Press.

Harman, G. 2013. *Bells and Whistles: More Speculative Realism*. Winchester, UK: Zero Books.

Harman, G. 2016. *Immaterialism*. Cambridge: Polity Press.

Hegel, G.W.F. 1977. *Phenomenology of Spirit*. Translated by A.V. Miller. Oxford: Oxford University Press.

Heidegger, M. 1962. *Being and Time*. Translated by John Macquarrie and Edward Robinson. San Francisco: Harper Collins.

Hjelmslev, L. 1969. *Prolegomena to a Theory of Language*. Translated by Francis J. Whitfield. Madison: The University of Wisconsin Press.

Husserl, E. 2000. *Logical Investigations: Volume I*. Translated by John N. Findley. Amherst, NY: Humanity Books.

Kant, I. 1997. *Prolegomena to Any Future Metaphysics*. Translated by Gary Hatfield. Cambridge: Cambridge University Press.

Kant, I. 1998. *The Critique of Pure Reason*. Translated by Paul Guyer and Allen W. Wood. Cambridge: Cambridge University Press.

Lacan, J. 1998a. *The Four Fundamental Concepts of Psycho-Analysis*. Translated by Alan Sheridan. New York: W.W. Norton & Co.

Lacan, J. 1998b. *The Seminar of Jacques Lacan, Book XX, On Feminine Sexuality, The Limits of Love and Knowledge 1972–1973*. Translated by Bruce Fink. New York: W.W. Norton & Co.

Lacan, J. 2006. *Écrits: The First Complete Edition in English*. Translated by Bruce Fink. New York: W.W. Norton & Co.

Love, J. and M. Meng. 2016. Histories of the dead? *Time & Mind*. 9(3): 223–44.

Luhmann, N. 1989. *Ecological Communication*. Translated by John Bednarz, Jr. Chicago: University of Chicago Press.

Luhmann, N. 1995. *Social Systems*. Translated by John Bednarz, Jr. with Dirk Baecker. Stanford: Stanford University Press.

Meillassoux, Q. 2008. *After Finitude: An Essay on the Necessity of Contingency*. Translated by Ray Brassier. London: Continuum International Publishing Group.

Olsen, B. 2010. *In Defense of Things: Archaeology and the Ontology of Objects*. Lanham: AltaMira Press.

Olsen, B. and C. Witmore. 2014. "Svaerholt: Recovered Memories from a POW Camp in the Far North." In *Ruin Memories: Materialities, Aesthetics and the Archaeology of the Recent Past*. Edited by Bjørnar Olsen and Þóra Pétursdóttir. New York: Routledge.

Pétursdóttir, Þ. 2014. "Things Out-of-hand: The Aesthetics of Abandonment." In *Ruin Memories: Materialities, Aesthetics and the Archaeology of the Recent Past*. Edited by Bjørnar Olsen and Þóra Pétursdóttir. New York: Routledge.

Sartre, J-P. 2007. *Nausea*. Translated by Lloyd Alexander. New York: New Directions Books.

Wittgenstein, L. 1990. *Tractatus Logico-Philosophicus*. Translated by C.K. Ogden. New York: Routledge.

4

IN THE PRESENCE OF THINGS

Jeff Malpas

Modernity and materialism

Despite the contemporary talk of a 'material turn' or the many references to 'object oriented' ontologies in the contemporary literature (see for instance, Bennett 2009; Harman 2018; also Coole and Frost 2010), the social, cultural, and economic structures that are most salient in the contemporary world are precisely such as to lead *away* from things. Perhaps one of the simplest examples of this is to be seen in the character of photographs as cultural artefacts. 'People take pictures of each other', sang The Kinks in the 1960s, 'Just to prove that they really existed' (The Kinks 1968). People do still take pictures – of others, of themselves, and of their meals and much else besides. But whereas the pictures that were taken used to be things that one kept in picture books or boxes, or carried in a wallet or purse, and for many were the things they would least want to lose (see Slater 1995, p. 138), they now appear most often as digital images. Such images are no longer constrained in their proliferation or replication by the physical limits associated with film. They have their primary existence, not in the private space of the personal or familial nor in the form of physical prints kept in box, book, or pocket, but in the public realm of the social media site and in the form of the digital image or electronic file.

The photographic example is not an unusual one: modernity and its technologies tend inevitably towards the submersion of the thing into a spatialized network of connectivity in which what is essential to the thing – its place and bounds – are effaced. This effacement extends well beyond the photograph alone. It is characteristic of modernity and, as such, is evident across almost every aspect of contemporary life and activity. As a result, things tend no longer to appear primarily *as things*, but rather as elements within networks of production, commodification, and consumption. They appear as commodities, representations, resources, quantities – ultimately as mere nodes in systems of convergent connectivity (see Heidegger 1977; Malpas

2018a, 2018b). In this respect, the so-called 'internet of things' captures a key feature of modernity – the drawing of everything into a single connected system – even though the idea that what is at issue is indeed an internet *of things* also misrepresents the tendency towards the disappearance of things as they are submerged into such connectivity.

The effacement of things is not to be construed as merely the effacement of a certain *kind* of thing or of a certain mode of being of things – as if in modernity things simply take on a different character, appear in 'different materialities'. Indeed, I would argue that there is no other materiality than the materiality *of things* – which is also to say, of embodied being in the world – and modernity does not cease to be material, just as it does not cease to materialize itself in and through things. In this respect, the effacement of things in modernity is not their obliteration, but the wiping out of their appearance – it is a form of obscuring that hides its own character as an obscuring.

It is this phenomenon – the effacement of that which nonetheless persists – that makes modernity problematic. What is effaced in the effacement of things is not only the genuine appearance of things as things, but also the character of human being and of the world as given shape and form in and around things, and in and around the places to which things are inevitably bound (see Malpas 2018a). If modernity effaces things, so too does it efface the genuine character of the world and of human being in the world. The concern with things, then, is also a concern with the human and the worldly. Since I take the human and the thingly to be bound together, my own interest in things is not an interest that stands apart from the human (although what this means is something about which I have more to say below) – and so my own interest in things in not an interest in the 'post-human'. Indeed, that which is 'post-human', I would argue, is also 'post-thing'.

It is because the human is bound up with things, and so also with materiality, that I refer to my own position as a form of romantic materialism. This is not quite the same as the 'romantic materialism' that is used by Gillian Beer to refer to the combination of romanticism and materialism in Darwin's early thought (Beer 1983, p. 37), though it is not entirely disconnected from the romanticized conception of nature evident in some of the thinkers of the late eighteenth and early nineteenth centuries. Romantic materialism as it applies in my work refers to the idea that memory and affect are given only in and through the materiality of things at the same time as the materiality of things is given only in and through memory and affect – things (and the larger material/environmental structures in which they are located) are thus the proper focus for the externalization of self, society, and culture.

At issue here is a larger argument about the formation of the self, and of the collectivities in which the self participates, as always materialized. This is an argument that applies to the self, and its own materiality in the body, so that, as Wittgenstein puts it (in a way that seems almost to invoke Aristotle – see Aristotle 1957a, esp. pp. 412aff), 'the human body is the best picture of the human soul' (Wittgenstein 1953, II, §178). But it also applies to the self in its relation to the concrete singularity of things. It is in the materiality of the world that we find ourselves, *as bodies* but also as oriented *to things*, and only thus. The thinking to this conclusion is driven by diverse sources: not only such as Wittgenstein and Heidegger, but also Blake and Coleridge, Proust and Camus. Here too, the focus on things, and on the externality of self as given in and through things, is tied to a focus on place – it is only in place that things themselves come to appearance. The effacement of things in modernity is thus also an effacement of place.

Although 'romantic materialism' might be said to be convergent with the so-called 'material turn' in contemporary theory, it nevertheless stands apart from that turn. One reason it does so is that the material turn, much like the other turns that have arisen over the last twenty years or so – the spatial, the linguistic, the discursive – tends largely to assume that *to which* it supposedly turns: in this case, to assume (at the same time as it also expands and even occludes) the notion of the 'material' and the 'thingly'. And it does so at the same time as it frequently also assumes that what it turns *away from* – the linguistic, the discursive, the ideal, the human – treating them as if they are already known, have already been understood, have already been dealt with.[1] Moreover, the 'material turn' often, though not always, appears as simply another turn 'in theory', rather than offering any deeper engagement with the issues at stake, and is frequently driven by what is largely a prior political agenda, rather than by the matter itself. It is thus that in many of the 'new materialisms' in which the material turn is instantiated, the tendency is not to engage in any direct or genuine fashion with the larger critical or philosophical tradition on which those materialisms nevertheless also and inevitably draw.

Instead those materialisms frequently seem to set themselves in opposition to that tradition in its entirety – a tendency perhaps most exemplified by some forms of speculative realism. Even the emphasis on supposed non-anthropocentrism that is such a central feature of many forms of such materialisms seems often to consist in a simple refusal to engage with the question of the human as such, a consequent failure to think through the potential differences between the human and the non-human (alongside a tendency towards the anthropomorphization of things and the world), and a refusal to engage with the question of the inevitably human standpoint to which such materialisms remain attached.

It is thus that Slavoj Žižek treats such materialisms (he takes Jane Bennett, 2009, to be an especially salient example) as failing to escape the anthropocentrism that they also criticize, and as also failing to constitute any genuine turn back to the material as such, writing that 'if New Materialism can still be considered a variant of materialism, it is materialism in the sense in which Tolkien's Middle Earth is materialist: as an enchanted world full of magical forces, good and evil spirits etc. …' (Žižek 2014, p. 12). In the material turn, the materialism of the material is typically assumed, not only conceptually, but also argumentatively, and consequently it frequently remains unclear to what extent the espousal of the 'material' moves beyond the metaphorical or the merely rhetorical, and so, indeed, to what extent materiality is indeed brought to the fore. What is genuinely material about materiality is seldom a question that is ever put, let alone answered, and so the idea of the material is not itself directly interrogated.[2]

A key idea that lies behind my own 'romantic materialism' is not only an attempt to rethink the idea of the material, and so also of things (in a way somewhat different from Žižek's attempt to re-found materialism dialectically, even though it is also sympathetic to some of Žižek's motivations and concerns), but also to take more seriously what a genuine turn to the material might mean, and so to take issue with the 'metaphorization' of thought, and specifically with the metaphorization of the language of thing, materiality, and place (something argued further in Malpas, in press). This does not derive from any suspicion of language – such suspicion being one of the problematic features of much that goes under the heading of the material turn – but, on the contrary, requires a genuine attentiveness to language and the linguistic. Language and things do not stand apart from one another, but instead each is infused within the other in a closeness that goes beyond any mere 'correlation'.[3]

The task is to think the ideas at issue here – the ideas that cluster around the notion of the material – in ways that neither reduces them to what they are not nor treats them as referring to something else. This is not only a problem that concerns the failure to address notions like 'material' and 'materiality, but appears also in the way terms now proliferate in their usage in ways that have often severed any connection with their original contexts (something like this occurs in relation to the anthropomorphizing tendencies of many new materialisms, and especially in the tendency to apply notions of agency, seemingly univocally, to non-intentional things and processes). What I aim to do here is to explore the role of things in this romantic materialist thinking, and so to spend some time thinking through just what it is genuinely to be in the presence of things. Moreover, to be clear: my interest is not in another move within contemporary theory – it is not a matter of taking a polemical stance against some previously dominant theoretical position as it may have been at work in a certain field. Instead, my intention is to engage, in preliminary fashion, in thinking through what it is to be in the world, what it is to be among things, what it is to be 'here'.

Things and the primacy of touch

As soon as we find ourselves in a world, as soon as we find ourselves alongside others, then we also find ourselves in the presence of things. It is in and through things that our sense of self, of others and of world is articulated. Of course, things themselves do not appear other than amidst this three-way entanglement, but it is also things that provide the focal points for action and affect – without which no entanglement or encounter would be possible. It is precisely because of the role of things in this regard that a philosopher such as Martin Heidegger focuses on the relation to the thing over the relation to the other or to the self (see Ott 1972, p. 190).

Our first encounter with things, and so with the world, is through *touch*. This is perhaps why, when we see something (for those of us who are sighted), our first impulse is often to reach out for it, to hold it, to feel its surface. To be in the presence of things is thus first and foremost to be engaged with them *by touch* – even when we cannot or do not touch. Touch is first not only because it is first chronologically or genetically, but because, in an important sense, it underlies the other senses, and so one might say that it is first 'ontologically'. According to Aristotle, touch is the primary sense (Aristotle 1957a, pp. 434b9–17), and he takes all the senses as essentially to be understood on the model of touch. Indeed, for Aristotle, the senses are themselves understood 'materially', in that the very character of a sense is its *receptivity* (perhaps the primary characteristic of matter), that is, its capacity to take on the forms of things or almost, one might say, to become one with things. The eye thus takes on the colour of that which it sees, and the skin the heat of that which it touches. This basic idea is one repeated, though in a slightly different form, by Hans Jonas (Jonas 1954, pp. 507–19, also Jonas 1966), and more recently by Mathew Ratcliffe among others (see Ratcliffe 2013).[4]

Touch is the touch of the hand, but touch is also at issue in the sense of bodily engagement in the world – the feel of the ground beneath one's feet, the freedom of space into which one can move, the very feel of a place (including its 'atmosphere', in all the sense of that term), and one's active's orientation within it. Touch thus belongs to the hand, but not only to the hand, nor even to the skin – touch encompasses the body and is that sense to which our active embodiment is most directly connected. Because touch is so fundamental, so the touch of things is the primary means by which things announce themselves as things. In touching, and this is obviously so in the touching of the hand, there is a sense of the thing touched as both apart and as affecting that is not so evident in the case of other senses. When we hear or when we see, there is not the same communion with the thing heard or seen, and this is partly because we cannot, merely in seeing or hearing, interact in any sort of reciprocal fashion with the thing.

It is true that to participate in any sensory modality is to give oneself over to the medium of that modality – so to touch is to be given over to the domain of the tangible, to be seen is to be given over to the visible, to hear is to be given over to the audible. But this does not mean that in any every act of perceiving one is also, by that very fact, opened up to being oneself perceived in the same way and at the same time (and this is true despite the sorts of analyses one finds in Sartre and elsewhere concerning the doubling that supposedly occurs in perception – including visual perception[5]). Consequently, seeing does not itself mean that we are seen, nor hearing that we are heard (even though there may be cases in which this is so), but to touch is always to be touched.

Touching and being touched are one and the same event in a way that is not matched by seeing and being seen or hearing and being heard. Indeed, we may say more generally that, in touch, we encounter things as things in a way that is not possible in any other sensory modality. In this respect, the old adage that 'seeing is believing' is not entirely correct – *touching* is believing and seeing is believing only inasmuch as seeing presupposes the possibility of touch. Thus, the apostle Thomas – the 'Doubting Thomas' of the New Testament – was not satisfied with a mere *vision* of Christ to convince him of the resurrection, but instead needed to touch Christ's wounds. Only in the *touch* was the doubt properly resolved (Figure 4.1).

FIGURE 4.1 Carravagio, The Incredulity of Saint Thomas, 1601–1602, Sanssouci, Potsdam. https://commons.wikimedia.org/wiki/File:The_Incredulity_of_Saint_Thomas-Caravaggio_(1601–2).jpg

To be in the presence of things is, therefore, to be 'in touch' with things – even if the touch itself is potential rather than actual (if the touch is a touch imagined or anticipated, rather than realized). Moreover, in this sense of the potentiality of touch, so touch can itself be given through the visual image even when what is presented in the image is itself removed from touch: we look at the image of the derelict room and we already have a sense of the touch of the room and the things in it – the sense of touch and of surface is given in the image itself. This does not mean, it should be noted, that the sense of touch is always accessible in the image – being able to connect seen shapes and felt shapes, for instance, is not something that one has immediately – it is rather something learned.[6] But this should not be surprising. Being able to engage perceptually with the world, and in a way integrated with thought and action, is itself learned. That it is so does not, however, diminish it as a genuine engagement with the world or with things.

Consequently, even though the ability to discriminate and to identify through touch is a capacity that must be developed, still it remains true that through touch one has a sense of surface and texture, as well as of density and weight, of resistance, of shape and configuration. It is through touch that one gains a definitive sense of the extent of a thing, of its own bounding surface as this is revealed in the contact between surfaces. Moreover, in touch one is also drawn to awareness of the bounding surface of one's own body. Touch is primarily the experience of that which itself touches the body, and through which both the body and the thing are brought to a reciprocal affectivity. Touch is above all else the experience of being here, in this place – of one's active, embodied, placing *in the world*.

Here the relation between touch and activity – both in action and reaction – is especially significant. And this is all the more so when we treat touch as connected with more than just the touch of the skin, but with the feel of the world as that occurs through the extended bodily sense of touch that we might think of as associated with proprioceptive awareness and bodily orientation. Activity itself draws the senses together – perceptual integration is indeed a precondition of the bodily integration necessary for integrated behaviour, that is, for action – and that drawing together of the senses, and so of the body too, is directly connected to the integration that occurs in the thing. The latter is not some sort of idea 'in the mind', it is not primarily an integration of perceptions, as if the thing were nothing other than a collection of sense-data nor indeed is it reducible merely to a bundle of properties. Rather, the thing is irreducible in character, and stands in an essential relation to the world.

This is a point made evident in an especially salient way in Martin Heidegger's analysis of the thing in terms of what he calls 'the fourfold' (*das Geviert*) – the differentiated unity of earth, sky, gods, and mortals are (see Heidegger 1971, pp. 163–86). Here the thing works as that in which the elements of world – including even that element which is the being of the human – are gathered inwards and reflected outwards as part of a single, unitary, but also complex and differentiated structure. And once again, the way the thing works in this regard is not merely as a passive 'object', and certainly not as an object standing over against a perceiving 'subject'. Rather it is the thing as itself active as well as the focus of action – thus as integrated and integrating – that underpins the role of the thing in the happening of the world.

Some hint of the character of the thing in this regard is suggested by the Greek term for things: πράγματα (*prágmata*). The term has connotations of the thingly as well as the real (see Liddell and Scott 1940, p. 1457), and it comes down to us in talk of the 'pragmatic' and of 'pragmatism'. Such talk of the 'pragmatic', at least in this context, should not be taken to imply any refusal to attend to the realities of things (as if all that mattered were some form of pure instrumentalism), but rather to indicate a commitment to the 'real' that is oriented to activity and to thing, and so also, one might add, to that which can be felt and touched, to that which is concretely *here*.

Place and materiality

The primacy of touch in the encounter with things is what underpins the idea of the materiality of things: the material is that which is given first to touch, that which can be touched, that which is receptive to touch. The material is, one might say, identical with the palpable, the tangible, the touchable, but also, I would say, with the placed, and so with the encounterable. From this also follows the emphasis on the material as that which can be acted upon as well as that which itself has an active effect. In the writings of Albert Camus, touch becomes the primary way in which Camus expresses his own materialism – a materialism that consists in a commitment to the world and that is bound to the experience of place. In Camus' case, the place that is most at issue is his native Algeria, and his materialism is in his commitment to his embodied existence in that place, to his singular 'being-there', over any set of ideas or abstractions: 'Between this sky and the faces turned toward it there is nothing on which to hang a mythology, a literature, an ethic, or a religion – only stones, flesh, stars, and those truths the hand can touch' (Camus 1968, p. 90) (Figure 4.2).

FIGURE 4.2 Albert Camus, by Jean-Paul Follacci. http://esmma.free.fr/mde4/camus_jb2.htm

Touch is itself inseparable from place. Only that which is in some place (and in virtue of being there also stands in relation to other things – to be placed is always *to be in relation*, and to be in relation is *to be placed*) can touch or be touched, and it is through touch that we first find ourselves in place. One might say that touch is *proximal*, whereas sight and sound are *distal*, but the very possibility even of distance is first given in touch and in the contact between surfaces that allows us to first make sense of their distinctness and separation. Only on the basis of touch can distance itself open up. In touch is the possibility of nearness, but nearness also brings distance with it. Distance is, one might say, a modification of nearness – something implicit in Heidegger's questioning of what has become of both the near and the far, and so also of the thing, under the impact of modern technology (see Heidegger 1971, pp. 165–82). For Heidegger, the effacement of the thing is directly tied to the transformation in the character of the near and the far – directly tied to a form of pure spatialization. In this way, the effacement of the thing, as Heidegger sees it, is tied to the effacement of place – which also suggests, though much more would have to be said here, a certain effacement of touch.

The Greek word, ὕλη (*hyle*), which our words 'matter' and 'material' can be taken to translate, originally seems to have referred to wood – that from which things can readily *be made* (see Liddell and Scott 1940, pp. 1847–8). 'Matter' and 'material' both come from the Latin, *materia*, and so relate to *matrix* (womb) and to *mater* (mother), and the idea of matter or material also connects with one of the central Greek terms for place: χώρα – *chōra*. Plato calls this the 'receptacle [ὑποδοχή – *hypodochê*] of becoming', as well as the 'nurse' of becoming (Plato 1960, p. 49a), and some translators and commentators treat it as 'womb' or 'matrix' (the *chōra* is that which holds things in such a way as to allow them to come to appearance or to emerge into being). The emphasis on its receptivity (present in Plato's use of *hypodochê* or 'receptacle') leads Aristotle famously to claim that Plato identifies *chōra* with matter (Aristotle 1957b, o, 209b18) – a claim that arises in Aristotle's own discussion of the nature of place (where the term used is τόπος – *tópos*). *Chōra* is itself translated sometimes as 'place' as well as 'space'. However, its bounded character makes it closer to place than to space *simpliciter* (see Malpas 2017, pp. 69–81).

The connection between *chōra* and matter or material is significant, although not because *chōra* is simply identical with matter as it might ordinarily be understood (or as Aristotle seems to view it in the *Physics*). Rather, it indicates a way of understanding matter itself in terms of place – of materiality as given only in terms of being-placed or being-here (so that matter is no longer some sort of fundamental 'stuff' out of which things are 'made') – and at the same time it also indicates how place, understood in terms of *chōra*, is precisely that which first allows materiality, and so also, that which first allows for the possibility of touch. *Chōra* gives *room* to things (which is why it does indeed have a connection to space). Moreover, *chōra* in giving room to things, *chōra* also gives room to the possibility of encounter *between* things. Such encounter is given in the very materiality of things, since the between of encounter is always a between that opens up amidst bodies (indeed, the between is always the between of bodies), and on the basis of their being placed. One might say that the very first materiality is the materiality of place – not in the sense that place is given in some material form, but rather because place is that which allows the materiality of things to appear, is that which allows for touch, that opens up to the possibility of touch, and it is in touch that the first possibility of being in place emerges.

The primacy of the body as a mode of placing is itself highlighted by this connection between materiality and place. To be in the presence of things is to be placed – and to be placed is also to find oneself amidst things, as a body amidst other bodies (and as an active body amidst other active bodies). The very character of presence is to be found in the presencing of things, and of bodies, and so in the presencing of place. This presencing and placing, since it is indeed a *placing*, is always *bounded*. Put crudely, to be present is to be somewhere, and to be somewhere is not to be everywhere or anywhere, but to be *here* – to be present within these bounds, in terms of this body, within this horizon. The boundedness of place does not imply, however, the limitation of things or of the possibilities of presence. The boundedness of place is what allows the opening into the singularity of presence, of place itself, and of things, and this singularity is itself an opening into the unbounded as it arises within bounds – as transcendence arises *within* immanence. There is thus a genuine infinity, an inexhaustible depth, that opens up within the bounds of any and every place.

The finitude of things

The singularity of place and thing, the singularity of presence, does not imply any absence of *relationality*. Indeed, it is characteristic of place that it is essentially relational – as relationality is itself topological in character – and the thing too is embedded within and constituted in terms of its own dense relationality. But precisely because of the way this relationality is bounded, as is all genuine relationality, so the relationality of things is indeed tied to their singularity, which is to say, it is tied to their being just that which they are, to their being this very thing, *here*. Relationality and singularity go together, rather than being in any way opposed. It is this relationality of the singular that is reflected in the way the same thing can be taken up from multiple perspectives and in multiple ways. In its singularity, the thing is a nexus of relations, even as it also stands out within the place in which those relations articulate themselves.

Here, in the connection between singularity and relationality, a key contrast emerges between the genuine topology in which things are embedded – and which is especially evident in the phenomenon of touch – and the structure of spatialized *connectivity*, to which I referred at the start of this discussion as characterizing contemporary technological modernity, in which things are effaced. Connectivity and relationality must here be distinguished, since the connectivity that characterizes technological modernity is a connectivity in which everything dissolves, not so much into 'air' as in Marx and Engel's famous phrase (see Marx and Engels 1975–2004, 6: 487), but into number and quantity, transmissible and transformable, part of an enormous and ever-expanding network of spatialized flow. Thus the photograph, to go back to my original example, ceases to be a singular material *locus* for memory and narrative, and is instead replaced by the digitized image that can itself be manipulated and transformed, reproduced and transmitted, and that is easily lost within the proliferating network of images and sites that constitutes the contemporary domain of digital and social media. Memory, like 'truth', 'history', even knowledge itself, becomes fragmented and dissociated.

Under the purely spatialized, and so also, *quantitized* mode of ordering that is at issue here (the spatial and the quantitative being closely tied together), nothing appears as standing in any genuine relation, since relation presupposes that which is related also retaining a singularity that belongs to it within the relational structure. The connectivity of the spatial reveals no more relationality than does the array of elements in a purely linear sequence. Genuine relationality, like any form of genuine integration or unity, presupposes difference (and vice versa), which is to say that relationality presupposes *boundedness* – precisely what technological modernity, and the progressivism so much associated with it, refuses (on this general issue see Malpas 2018b). It is boundedness that is at the heart of place and being-placed. The effacement of the thing is thus an effacement of place, but also an effacement of singularity, of boundedness, and of genuine relation.

It is ironic that the rhetoric of connectivity and flow is not only to be found as a central element in the mode of self-presentation as well the organizational impulse of contemporary technologized modernity – which is to say, of contemporary technologized capital – but it is also present as a key element in much contemporary theory, and especially in those modes of theory that give emphasis to the *global* and the *digital*, and thereby also to the purely *spatial*. To some extent, moreover, it even manifests itself in some of the new 'materialisms' inasmuch as they too often lose sight of the bounded and the finite, and thereby (once again there is a clear irony here) lose sight of the genuine materiality and thingliness of things – which also means of their singularity and their boundedness. Finitude does not belong only to the human – it belongs essentially *to things* just in virtue of their own essential being-placed. One might add that the finitude of the human is itself a function of the finitude of things and of place. It is because of the necessary dependence of human being on the thingly and the placed (which is to say that human being only emerges, to repeat a phrase from Marcia Cavell, 'here, in the midst of things' – Cavell 1993, p. 41), that human being is an essentially finite being (see Malpas 2018a, pp. 194–5). The inexhaustibility of the world is founded in such being-placed. Here is another aspect of the 'romantic materialism' whose elaboration has been one of the aims of this essay: its commitment both to the inexhaustibility of things and the world and to the idea that such inexhaustibility arises only in and through the concrete things and places that surround us and in relation to which our lives are shaped – only in and through, as Camus has it, 'stones, flesh, stars, and those truths the hand can touch.' The opening of the world to that which is unbounded – to that which is inexhaustible and infinite, even to the possibility of transcendence – occurs only in and through the finitude of place and thing. It arises in the play of nearness and distance, of sameness and difference, of multiplicity and unity. And to all of these we come first through touch and through the being-placed that belongs essentially with it.

Notes

1 This is not to say that recent and contemporary critiques of the representational or discursive are essentially mistaken, but only that the truth that underlies those critiques is often misunderstood or misappropriated.

2 One might make the same charge against Žižek as well as Bennett, except that Žižek is able to draw on a much richer philosophical background – deriving from Hegel and Marx – that does indeed provide some additional elucidation of what the commitment to materialism might mean. And even if that were not so, the critical point at issue here would remain valid. Does Žižek's criticism of the 'enchantment' at work in Bennett's account also apply to my own 'romantic' materialism? I would argue not in as much as the problematic character of such 'enchantment' is tied to its problematic retention of a form of anthropocentrism. Although there is a sense of enchantment or 're-enchantment' at work in my own account, it is rather different from Bennett's.

3 The closeness of the belonging of word and thing is not something that there is the space to pursue adequately here but see, e.g. Heidegger 1971b, esp. 57–110; see also Malpas 2019, pp. 14–15.

4 Radcliffe's work is part of a much larger exploration of touch in contemporary philosophy of perception – see De Vignemont and Massin 2015.

5 It is true that all perception involves a degree of self-referentiality, but this does not itself imply reciprocity of perceptual presentation of the sort that appears in the case of touch across any or every sensory modality.

6 As the final resolution of Moyneaux's question demonstrates, see Held et al. 2011; on Molyneaux' question in general, see Morgan 1977.

References

Aristotle, 1957a. On the soul. In *On the Soul/Parva Naturalia/On Breath*, trans. W.S. Hett. rev. edn., Cambridge: Loeb Classical Library.

Aristotle, 1957b. *Physics I–IV*, trans. P.H. Wicksteed and F. M. Cornford. rev. edn., Cambridge: Loeb Classical Library.

Beer, G., 1983. *Darwin's Plots: Evolutionary Narrative in Darwin, George Eliot and Nineteenth-Century Fiction*. Cambridge: Cambridge University Press.

Bennett, J., 2009. *Vibrant Matter: A Political Ecology of Things*. Durham, NC: Duke University Press.

Camus, A., 1968. Summer in Algiers. In *Lyrical and Critical Essays*, ed. Philip Thody, trans. Ellen Conroy Kennedy. New York: Alfred A. Knopf, pp. 80–92.

Cavell, M., 1993. *The Psychoanalytic Mind: From Freud to Philosophy*. Cambridge: Harvard University Press.

Coole, D. and S. Frost (eds.), 2010. *New Materialisms: Ontology, Agency, and Politics*. Durham, NC: Duke University Press.

De Vignemont, F. and O. Massin, 2015. Touch. In M. Matthen, (ed.), *The Oxford Handbook of the Philosophy of Perception*. New York: Oxford University Press.

Harman, G., 2018. *Object-Oriented Ontology: A New Theory of Everything*. London: Pelican.

Heidegger, M., 1971. *Poetry, Language, Thought*, trans. Albert Hofstadter. New York: Harper and Row.

Heidegger, M., 1977. *The Question Concerning Technology and Other Essays*, trans. William Lovitt. New York: Garland.

Held, R., and Y. Ostrovsky, B. Degelder, T. Gandhi, S. Ganesh, U. Mathur, and P. Sinha, 2011. The newly sighted fail to match seen with felt, *Nature Neuroscience*, 14: 551–3.

Jonas, H., 1954. The nobility of sight: A study in the phenomenology of the senses, *Philosophy and Phenomenological Research*, 14: 507–19 (also in Jonas 1966, pp. 135–56).

Jonas, H., 1966. *The Phenomenon of Life: Towards a Philosophical Biology*. New York: Harper and Row.

Kinks, The, 1968. *The Kinks Are tne Village Green Preservation Society*. London: PRT Records.

Liddell, H. G. and R. Scott, 1940. *A Greek–English Lexicon*. Oxford: Clarendon Press.

Malpas, J., 2017. Five theses on place (and some associated remarks): a reply to Peter Gratton, *Il Cannocchiale: rivista di studi filosofici* 42: 69–81.

Malpas, J., 2018a. *Place and Experience: A Philosophical Topography*. Abingdon, Oxon.: Routledge.

Malpas, J., 2018b. The spatialization of the world. Technology, modernity, and the effacement of the human, *Phainomena*, 27: 91–108.

Malpas, J., 2019. Topologies of history, *History and Theory* 58: 3–22.

Malpas, J., in press. "The House of Being": Poetry, language, place, In Günter Figal et al. (eds.), *Heidegger's Later Thought*. Bloomington: Indiana University Press.

Marx, K. and F. Engels, 1975–2004. *Collected Works*. New York: International Publishers.

Morgan, M.J., 1977. *Molyneux's Question: Vision, Touch and the Philosophy of Perception*. Cambridge: Cambridge University Press.

Ott, H., 1972. Hermeneutic and personal structure of language. In J. J. Kockelmans (ed.), *On Heidegger and Language*. Evanston, IL: Northwestern University Press, pp. 169–94.

Plato, 1960. *Timaeus*. In *Timaeus/Critias/Cleitophon/Menexenus/Epistles,* trans. R.G. Bury. Cambridge: Loeb Classical Library.

Ratcliffe, M., 2013. Touch and the sense of reality, In Zdravko Radman (ed.), *The Hand an Organ of Mind; What the Manual tells the Mental,* Cambridge: MIT Press, pp. 131–57.

Slater, D., 1995. Domestic photography and digital culture. In *The Photographic Image in Digital Culture* ed. by Martin Lister. London: Routledge, pp. 129–46.

Wittgenstein, L., 1953. *Philosophical Investigations*, trans. G.E.M. Anscombe. Oxford: Blackwell.

Žižek, S., 2014. *Absolute Recoil: Towards a New Foundation of Dialectical Materialism*. London and New York: Verso.

5

THICK SPEECH AND DEEP TIME IN THE ANTHROPOCENE

Robert Macfarlane

I spent August and September 2016 in south-east Greenland, making ascents of several peaks in the coastal ranges north of Kulusuk, and also researching a long piece of writing about ice, time and memory in the Anthropocene. 2016 was a year of anomalously intense melt in the Arctic. For the previous decade, Greenland's ice cap had been losing mass at twice the mean rate of the preceding century; that year the mass-loss accelerated. Surface melt began in early April, a month earlier than usual, and flow rates in the meltwater rivers monitored by climatologists went on to reach unprecedented speeds. The increased area of meltwater on the surface of the ice cap led to an albedo feedback loop; more sunshine was absorbed by the darker water, resulting in more melt and therefore more absorption.

Yes, ice that year was spectacularly on the move. Up on the cap, the moulins roared. Down at sea-level, the calving faces of tidal glaciers boomed. Temperatures hit a historic high of 24C in Nuuk, Greenland's capital. The same month, polar scientists predicted a total absence of Arctic sea-ice by September; this did not occur, though sea-ice reached the second-lowest extent in the satellite data record. Across northern Canada and Eurasia, the Arctic was melting – and as it melted what was locked beneath its surface rose towards the light. On the Yamal peninsula between the Kara Sea and the Gulf of Ob, 12000 km^2 of permafrost thawed. Cemeteries and animal burial grounds turned to slush. Reindeer corpses that had died of anthrax seventy years earlier were exposed to the air, causing an outbreak of the disease: twenty-three people were infected by the spores, and a child died. In northern Greenland, a Cold War US missile base cut deep into the ice cap, abandoned in 1967 and still containing hundreds of thousands of litres of fuel and other contaminants, began to be revealed.

'Climate change is felt in our lives here strongly,' a Kulusukian called Frederick told me one afternoon in his village. 'New species have come here, old ones have gone. There is thunder and lightning sometimes in autumn. The sea ice used to be so deep always' – he gestured from the floor to the ceiling of the house we were in, a distance of eight or nine feet – 'but each year it is thinner and this spring it was *this* thin' – he placed his hands a forearm's length apart – 'It is harder to hunt. We can travel less far.' He shrugged. 'It is a change to our spirit, as well as our lives.' One day, camped a mile from the tidal snout of the Knud Rasmussen Glacier, my climbing team and I watched a huge calving event occur (Figure 5.1): the collapse of a section of the mile-wide face, to which we found ourselves only able to respond in the moment with cries of alarm and elation, and in the immediate aftermath with stuttered, rhetorically dead-ended re-tellings. *Did you see that …? What just happened?*

During my weeks in Greenland, I found myself – as a writer – unusually lost for words. I was at once frightened, exhilarated and confused by my encounter with ice in the Anthropocene. The thinning of the cryosphere thickened my speech and thought. I found it hard to think clearly or to write fluently. Note-taking felt futile, tending towards impertinent. In retrospect, I see that this inarticulacy had in part to do with what Cymene Howe (2016) has called the 'chrono-mashups' of ice – the multiple, disorderly temporalities it carries – which were beyond my powers to sort or historicize while still in the field. I also struggled in my note-taking to reconcile the need to register the presence-effects of being a socially situated, structurally privileged human with a body in that place, at that moment – while

FIGURE 5.1 Calving event, Knud Rasmussen Glacier, East Greenland. Photo: Helen Spenceley

also acknowledging the problems of taking myself as the focus of self-presence, given the countless more-than-human histories and deeper-time agencies that were operating simultaneously – and with planetary-scale aetiologies and consequences – around and within me. At times I felt entangled in hermeneutic questions of how to interpret the volatile matter of ice in this year of extreme melt, into which my own actions as consumer and citizen were inscribed. At other times I experienced the old representational difficulty of making language adhere to what I was seeing. Sign–signifier relations felt fragile, fissile: my written notes slid off their icy subject (Figure 5.2), to the degree that this sliding became its own displaced subject of scrutiny.

Ice has, of course, long disobeyed our categories. It thickens, thins, slips, slides, will not stay still. In the 1860s, when glaciology was emerging as a science, the discourse of glaciers was riven by the dispute over whether ice should be classified as liquid, solid, or some other kind of colloid-like matter altogether. It is unsurprising that ice should have proved so ungraspable to human habits of designation, for it is a shape-shifter and a state-shifter. It flies, it swims and it flows. It can be blue, green white and silver. Ice crystals at 30,000 feet set halos and parhelia shining around the sun and the moon. Ice falls as snow, as hail, as sleet; it crystallizes as feather and it gleams as mirror. Ice erases mountain ranges, but also preserves air bubbles for millennia and can be tender enough to bear a human body almost unriven for centuries. It is silent, and it creaks and thunders. It sharpens eyesight, and it breeds mirages.

FIGURE 5.2. Melting iceberg, Ammassilak Fjord, East Greenland. Photo: Helen Spenceley

In the Anthropocene, ice has gained a new and threatening liveliness. The 'frozen' poles are melting and the consequences of their melting are both locally experienced and globally felt. The Russian term for 'permafrost', вечная мерзлота, translates as 'the eternally frozen ground' – the name looks increasingly inappropriate. Greenland, Antarctica and the Arctic are now front-line territories, in which the fate of ice will shape planetary futures. As Rob Nixon (2018) observes, 'Glaciers in the twenty-first century constitute an *unfrozen* hazard [...] Language bends and buckles under pressure of climate change.' A 'glacial pace' used to mean movement so slow as to be almost static. Today's glaciers, however, surge, retreat, vanish. The recession of Himalayan glaciers threatens the livelihoods and lives of more than a billion people in Asia, who depend on the water that is seasonally stored and released by these ice rivers. The West Antarctic Ice Sheet is breaking up into bergs and sheets that drift unbiddably. Cartography cannot keep up with the shrinkage of Arctic sea ice. Globe-makers can no longer confidently cap their globes with white. Ice has become *dirty*, in the sense of Mary Douglas's (1966, p. 36) famous definition of dirt as 'matter out of place', and requires new means of reckoning as a result. 'In the event of the Anthropocene; or even in the case of ice,' writes Hester Blum,

> perhaps we lack the language to describe, or the vision to perceive, or the corpus to absorb information in its own terms. Maybe torqued, perceptual category shifts are more representationally apt – or have more explanatory power – in our Anthropocenic age [...] Our present planetary moment demands new modes of knowledge.
>
> *(Blum 2016)*

In indigenous cultures that have long lived adaptably and in close contact with ice, it has always been an ambiguous entity – and the stories told about glaciers have often blurred boundaries between human and non-human activity. Glaciers appear in these stories as actors – aware and intentful, sometimes benign and sometimes malevolent. In Athapaskan and Tlingit oral traditions from south-western Alaska, for instance, as the anthropologist Julie Cruikshank (2005, p. 3) documents, glaciers are both 'animate (endowed with life) and animating (giving life to) landscapes they inhabit'. In languages from this region, special verbs indicate the living power of what in English might be classified as passive landscape presences. These verbs recognize in ice both its actions and, vitally, its powers to act. Linguistic anthropologists refer to the enlivening influence of such verbs: their deep-level acknowledgement of a sentient environment which both listens and speaks recalls Robin Wall Kimmerer's (2017) wish for a 'grammar of animacy' that might acknowledge the autonomy of plant life.

While in Greenland, I found myself desiring a 'grammar of animacy' in my own language that might register the complex weaves of reciprocity at work in the lively ice that surrounded me, and over which I moved. Certainly, older aesthetic categories such as the 'sublime' seemed too fixed – too culturally *tethered* – for the alien display of matter on the move which we encountered. The pale blue ice we saw calving in such quantity from the above-water face of the Knud Rasmussen glacier, or the pyramid of ancient blue-black ice that we once saw rising from deep in the fjord following a below-water-level calving event, exhibited what was to me a new order of withdrawnness – one so extreme as at times to induce nausea.

Albert Camus (1942, p. 19) called this property of matter the 'absurd'. Confronted by matter in its raw forms, he wrote, 'strangeness creeps in':

> perceiving that the world is "dense", sensing to what degree a stone is foreign and irreducible to us, with what intensity nature or a landscape can negate us. At the heart of all beauty lies something inhuman [...] the primitive hostility of the world rises up to face us across millennia [...] that denseness and that strangeness of the world is the absurd.

I recognized a version of that 'density' – that 'absurdity' – in Greenland to an unprecedented degree. This was a landscape where dense matter drove language aside, and the object consistently refused its lexical profile. There was something not just uncanny but actively horrific in what I saw; an obscenity to the ice and its meltings, and specifically to its combination of vastness and vulnerability. The visceral affects of the ice brought to mind Jean-Paul Sartre's (1943, passim) descriptions of his existential nausea in *Being and Time* as produced by encounter with what he called *le visqueux*: matter that we encounter not as object or substance but as relation, in which we are always-already implicated (en-folded). For Sartre, to exist is to get stuck.

Viscosity can be a linguistic as well as an affective property. In her influential study of minor affects, *Ugly Feelings*, Sianne Ngai (2005) argues that Western aesthetic tradition has historically over-invested in major affects such as the sublime, fear and wonder, at the expense of unpretentious 'negative affects' (p. 3) including irritation, envy, paranoia and anxiety. In Ngai's account, these insufficiently acknowledged ugly feelings have proliferated within and been inflected by what she calls 'late modernity' (p. 1), and she investigates their ubiquitous but inconspicuous presence across recent culture, connecting them especially to the 'suspended agency' (p. 1) and dysphoria induced by capitalism. Recognizing that the extreme administrations of capitalism have brought new affects into being as well as re-configuring old ones, she also coins the term 'stuplimity' (p. 3) – a neologized portmanteau of 'stupor' and 'sublimity' – to refer to the contemporary dysphoric experience of paralyzed awe that can arise when a subject is confronted by the multiply-scaled, 'enormous, agglutinative' (p. 270) cultural and political constructs of late modernity. In such an encounter the subject experiences at once 'shock and exhaustion' (p. 271).

For Ngai, the fatigued urgencies of stuplimity are indexed linguistically by what she calls 'thick language'; a 'back-flowing discourse' (p. 249) that is characterized by jumbledness, and by the agglutination of language units (syllables, words, sentences, paragraphs). When writing thickly, language declines to flow, and instead pools and gums syntactically. It refuses conventional modes of reference in favour of internecine recoils and self-referential eddies. Such thick speech often exists as stuttered utterances which connote both stupefaction and over-awedness, and which distinctively combine hyperactivity with a lack of causal grip. When speaking thickly, Ngai notes, subjects are challenged in their usual ability to interpret or respond; this is true of reading, too. Instead of the lucid correspondences of fluid language, a congealed voice is produced, which assimilates other linguistic entities and fragments into itself to produce a new kind of lexiglomerate.

Ngai examines stuplimity and thick language at work only in literary texts such as Stein's *Americans* and Richter's *Atlas*, but – not least given the legacy of the Burkeian 'natural' sublime within her discussion – it is reasonable to extend her account of this affective relationship beyond cultural artefacts and towards those 'enormous, stupefying objects' (p. 270) of the post-natural Anthropocene which may also produce shock and exhaustion within the subject. Though Ngai was not explicitly addressing the Anthropocene context, her 'enormous, stupefying objects' stand in clear family resemblance with Timothy Morton's (2013a, p. 42) hyperobjects: those 'massive non-human, non-sentient entities' – including climate change and Styrofoam – which 'make decisive contact with humans, ending various human concepts such as "world," "horizon," "Nature" and even "environment" '. Morton (2013b, p. 27), like Ngai, reaches for metaphors of stickiness and thickness to figure the representational and experiential challenge of hyper-objects; one of their distinctive traits is 'viscosity'. We can no longer easily hold Anthropocene materials away from us, argues Morton; an out-there Nature is unavailable either as concept or praxis. The hyperobject, in Andy Weir's (2016) account, 'cannot be exhausted by perception, and the more we struggle to distance ourselves from it, the more "stuck" we become.' Morton's language here echoes Michel Serres's discussion, at the start of *The Natural Contract*, of Goya's painting of two men fighting while enmired in mud. With each blow the two fighters sink deeper into the marsh, seemingly unaware that they are sinking. For Serres the painting resonates as emblem of the contemporary predicament; humanity's unconscious worsening of its own footing upon the Earth, fighting one another for primacy while failing to perceive the catastrophic consequences of what Serres (1990, p. 2) calls 'the world of things themselves' reasserting their force: 'River, fire and mud are reminding us of their presence.'

Not only river, fire and mud; the thickening of synthetic matter has become a key feature of the Great Acceleration decades. 'A very present past', write Bjørnar J. Olsen and Þóra Pétursdóttir (2017, p. 2),

> is relentlessly and ever more rapidly accumulating around us; archipelagos of sea-born debris, industrial wastelands, sunken nuclear submarines, withering metropolises and regions of ghost towns: the acceleration over past two centuries of mass production, consumerism, disposal and replacement has created 'an empire of things' with its own unruly material afterlife,

generating 'a swelling topography of scrapped modernity which, despite ever more effective regimes of disposal, is increasingly confronting us with its pestering presence'. Nuclear waste accumulates in vitrified casks on the back of flat-bed trucks in parking lots, waiting for the underground tombs to be prepared into which it can be buried. The seas, rivers and oceans clot with plastic trash. $CO2$ accumulates in the atmosphere, leading in its turn to a thinning of the cryosphere.

While in Greenland that late summer and early autumn, one of the books I read was John Wyndham's postwar SF novel *The Chrysalids*. The book portrays a post-nuclear community of fundamentalists set on eliminating all those with inherited 'mutations' (1955, passim) from their society. Anyone born with a deviation from the prescribed physical or mental norm is prevented from reproducing, exiled or executed. The novel describes first the detection and then the escape of a small group of such 'mutants', whose 'deviance' is that they are able to communicate tele-pathically. Surrounded by fundamentalists in the novel's final scene, the telepathists are saved from death by the appearance overhead of airships that have been sent from New Zealand, where a technologically and morally progressive society of mutants – including telepathists – has survived and flourished.

At the novel's climax, a shower of thin, ultra-sticky plastic strands rains from the airships onto both the mutants and their pursuers. The strands adhere to any surface or object they touch. If that object – a struggling human body, say – moves, then the strands contract, thickening and tightening their grip until, if the feedback process of movement-leading-to-tightening persists, the victim dies of asphyxiation. Telepathically, the mutants are instructed to lie still and not move; they are rescued safely. Their pursuers, unwarned, struggle on; they are killed precisely by means of their attempts to free themselves. It was only after returning from Greenland that I realized how tellingly Wyndham's scene – itself one of the earliest significant uses of plastic as an active substance in fiction, pre-dating Roland Barthes's famous essay on the same subject by two years – anticipated the Anthropocene Catch-22 described by Weir: 'the more we struggle to distance ourselves from it, the more "stuck" we become'.

Stickiness has of course long been a quality implicit in traditional ecological dis-course: 'When we try to pick out anything by itself, we find it hitched to everything else in the Universe', wrote John Muir (1911, p. 110), recognizing the webby nature of biomes, and how hard it is to detach any one 'thing' from all else that adheres to it. Anthropocene viscosity is of a different order to the ecological stickiness perceived by Muir, however. Where Muir's journals and published works narrate a relational ontology with things that nevertheless leaves the human a largely intact and autonomous actor, contemporary interpretive subjects instead find themselves absorbed by the unforeseen entanglements which characterize Anthropocene activity. Thick speech, viscosity, mud and actively densening meshes of entangle-ment: across geology, geography, affect theory, cultural theory and literature, sticki-ness and thickness now recur as both textural and textual 'horizon markers' of the Anthropocene. Even the origin myth of the naming of the Anthropocene is associated with stickiness and what might be called 'st-utterance'. In 1999 at a con-ference in Mexico City on the Holocene, the Nobel prize-winning atmospheric chemist Paul Crutzen was struck by the inaccuracy of the Holocene designation. 'I suddenly thought this was wrong,' he later recalled to Howard Falcon-Lang (2011). 'The world has changed too much. So I said, "No, we are in the … in the … in the … Anthropocene." I just made the word up on the spur of the moment. But it seems to have stuck.' 'The Anthropocene': a stuttered neologism that has stuck.

So intransigent is the Anthropocene to representation, indeed, that numerous projects have been started around the world to gain the most basic of linguistic purchases upon it: a glossary of phrases and single words with which to denote its objects and affects. The Bureau of Linguistical Reality was founded by Heidi Quante and Alicia Escott (Quante and Escott 2014) 'for the purpose of collecting, translating and creating a new vocabulary for the Anthropocene.' Among the Bureau's terms were 'stieg', 'apex-guilt', and 'shadow-time', the last of these meaning 'the sense of living in two or more orders of temporal scale simultaneously' – an acknowledgement of the out-of-jointness provoked by Anthropocene awareness. Cymene Howe and Anand Pandian (2016) began constructing a 'Lexicon for an Anthropocene Yet Unseen' as part of their work with the journal *Cultural Anthropology*. In 2018 Linda Russo and Marthe Reed edited *Counter-Desecration: A Glossary for Writing Within the Anthropocene*, 'a book of ecopoetics that compiles terms – borrowed, invented, recast – that help […] focus and configure the emerging relations and effects of the Anthropocene' (2018, jacket description) and in 2019 the environmental philosopher Glenn Albrecht (2019) published *Earth Emotions: New Words For A New World*.

Among Albrecht's (2005, p. 43) 'new words' is 'solastalgia', coined by him to mean the 'form of psychic or existential distress caused by environmental change'. At the time of coinage, Albrecht was studying the effects of long-term drought and large-scale mining activity on communities in New South Wales when he realized that no word existed to describe the unhappiness of people whose landscapes were being transformed about them by forces beyond their control. 'A worldwide increase in ecosystem distress syndromes', wrote Albrecht (2005, p. 43), is 'matched by a corresponding increase in human distress syndromes'. He proposed his new term to describe this distinctive kind of homesickness. Where nostalgia refers to a longing for home brought about by displacement in space, solastalgia is produced in subjects who do not move anywhere. Solastalgia speaks of a modern uncanny, in which a familiar place is rendered unrecognizable by climate breakdown or corporate action: the home become suddenly unhomely around its inhabitants. *Solastalgia, stieg, geotraumatics, planetary dysphoria, hyper-objects*: all of these are ugly coinages for an ugly epoch, often produced by means of lexiglomeration and usually resistant to easy utterance. They enact both a 'thickness' of speech and what Ngai (2013) has elsewhere described as 'zaniness': a performatively hyperactive kind of pointing and naming. We cannot yet, as it were, call out the Anthropocene.

Specific genres and forms, as well as more basic units of lexis, have been either 'thickened' or scrapped by the representational obduracy of the Anthropocene and its associated crises. The 'academic essay' – as this collection, or Anna Tsing et al.'s (2017) *Arts of Living on a Damaged Planet*, show – is responding with historically typical agility, re-thinking how to write shorter-form Anthropocene-aware pieces that are often recursive and always reflexive. Magazines such as *Emergence* or the

New York Times climate and environment sections are re-imagining what an on-line multi-media essay might look like and how, ergodically, it might be read. In *The Great Derangement: Climate Change and the Unthinkable*, Amitav Ghosh (2016, p. 84) identifies three main representational challenges posed by the 'intransigent' nature of the Anthropocene to literature and culture: how to recognize the more-than-human world in all its liveliness; the 'other, fully aware eyes looking over our shoulders' (p. 66), how to represent unfoldings of agency and consequence within deep time, especially those which might be attributed to objects and matter that have hitherto fallen outside the category of 'life'; and how by extension to come to terms with the drastic decentring of human presence.

Despite his criticisms of the Western realist novel's adequacies in these respects, Ghosh remains hopeful that cultural response to the crisis epoch will be found. 'New, hybrid forms will emerge,' he writes, 'and the act of reading itself will change once again, as it has many times before' (p. 84). Those 'new, hybrid forms' are most visible in the field of non-fiction. Tonally adventurous climate-change reportage such as Elizabeth Rush's recent *Rising* (Rush 2018), major environmental histories like Bathsheba Demuth's 2019 study of the Bering Strait, *Floating Coast* (Demouth 2019), innovative long on-line essays such as Emily Raboteau's 'Climate Signs' (Raboteau 2019) – all are recognizing and registering the poly-temporal weaves of culpability, vulnerability, elementality and urgency that characterize the present situation. They are fulfilling literature's ability to offer regimes of perceptibility: making visible that which could not be seen in or through a different form. 'When readers turn to the art and literature of our time,' asks Ghosh – imagining a future reader looking back at the culture of the Anthropocene – 'will they not look first and most urgently for traces and portents of the altered world of their inheritance?' (p. 11).

Between 2012 and 2019 I grappled with a work of creative non-fiction called *Underland* (Macfarlane 2019), which sought in part to meet the challenges Ghosh identifies as posed by the intransigence of the Anthropocene, and to answer his call for writing that might actively unconceal the traces of our materially fast-altering world. In particular, I sought to find a means of writing about geological deep times, past and future, which could register something of the temporal complexities of the Anthropocene; its accelerations and minglings of epochs, its disrupting of any easy notions of Earth history as orderly in its sequence (with the deepest down being the furthest back). Epochs are currently entangling with distinctive consequences; burning the liquefied remains of Carboniferous forests melts glacial ice that fell as snow in the Pleistocene, leading to the raising of sea-levels in a future Anthropocene. Both time and place are undergoing a 'great derangement', wrought into new forms by the scales and speeds of anthropogenic change at a planetary level. 'The problem [of deep time],' writes Þóra Pétursdóttir (2018, p. 98), 'is not that things become buried far down in strata – but that they endure, outlive us, and come back at us with a force we didn't realise they had'.

As I worked on *Underland* I began to consider kinds of formal and stylistic means of representing the variable 'thicknesses' of deep time: how we might or should imagine ourselves inhabitants not just of a human lifetime or generation, but also as long-legacy-leaving individuals and communities; and therefore how we might politically register the complex and uneven cross-weaves of vulnerability and culpability that exist between us and other species, as well as between humans now and humans to come. *Underland* moved over its course from the dark matter formed at the universe's birth (studied in a subterranean laboratory cut into a halite seam three-quarters of a mile below ground) to the nuclear-waste futures of an Anthropocene-to-come (stored in an eternity chamber sunk half a kilometre beneath the Bothnian Sea). The attempt, at least, was to find a hybrid non-fiction form that might – by speaking both of the bright time of the present instant (a child, held lovingly by its parent) and the more-than-human resonances of deeper times (soil time, tree time, species time, the giant life of rock, stirring and shifting) – be at once ancient and urgent.

The time I spent in East Greenland formed part of the research for *Underland*. When, on returning from those inarticulate weeks in and on the ice, I turned my attention to how to write about that place at that time, I found that I was thickening and densening my own language in an attempt to generate an appropriate 'regime of perceptibility'. Instead of writing fluently, I broke paragraphs up into staccato series of single sentences; removed verbs and adverbs often entirely; left gaps and lacunae of sense that often worked to produce a 'back-flowing syntax', or a stuttered rhythm of record. I mixed registers of discourse, and allowed spiky thought-fragments or quotations to adhere to the main tone, present as italicized and unattributed phrases. Instead of the sometimes exclusory or unself-aware eye/I of 'nature writing' or 'travel writing', I sought means of enfolding evidence of my own culpability and entanglement. I worked with different tenses and with semi-fictional interludes which moved about within human and more-than-human spans of time. The effort over all was to seek utterance that might respond to what Morton (2013a, p. 39) describes as our

> disturbing uncanny co-existence with other entities, from radionuclides to melting ice to fungal spores we inhale, the microbiome of our gut flora, the eerie intermeshing to which we are all subject, the 'strange strangers' (ice, dust, gamma particles) with which we largely unwittingly co-exist.

In this way, I came slowly to understand, 'thick language' might indicate not a failure of utterance but rather an approach to an adequacy of utterance; the movement towards what Hester Blum calls a 'torqued, perceptual category shift'. (Blum 2016).

In *Slow Violence and the Environmentalism of the Poor*, his foundational examination of environmental politics and its relation to culture and capital, Rob Nixon (2011, p. 10) observes that writer-activists engaging with the slow violence of industrial toxicity – including climate breakdown – must:

> plot and give figurative shape to formless threats whose fatal repercussions are dispersed across space and time. The representational challenges are acute,

requiring creative ways of drawing public attention to catastrophic acts that are low in instant spectacle but high in long-term effects. To intervene representationally entails devising iconic symbols that embody amorphous calamities as well as narrative forms that infuse those symbols with dramatic urgency.

At its best, the thickening of language which I detect widely at work in contemporary writing about and within the Anthropocene is not a regression politically into inertia, but rather a version of Nixon's 'intervention', 'infusion' and 'embodiment' of the 'amorphous calamities' and 'formless threats' of the Anthropocene crisis. The shock of the Anthropocene demands a new time-literacy, already apparent in recent political movements: deep-time awareness is implicitly the catalysing context of inter-generational justice broadly understood; more specifically it is what frames and informs the activism of Greta Thunberg and the school climate-strikers, and the Sunrise campaigners in the US and their counterparts in Europe and the global south pushing for equitable Green New Deals.

A deep-time perspective requires us to consider not only how we will imagine the future, but also how the future will imagine us. To think well in deep time is not a means of evading our troubled present, but rather of re-imagining it; countermanding its short-term greeds and furies with older stories of making and unmaking – and far wider views of obligation. At its best, deep-time thinking contests both the world-numbed eschatologies of fundamentalism, and the chaotic short-termism of so much present politics, bringing us instead to contemplate what we are leaving behind for what Rebecca Solnit (2019) – writing of the school climate-strikers – calls the 'ghostly billions not yet born'. In this current crisis-epoch, it recognizes that the continued survival of the species depends upon just such a stretched perspective, rather than the crash-ended narrative arcs of disaster capitalism, or aestheticized apocalypse-dreams that foreclose action in preference for spectacle.

Astrida Neimanis and Rachel Loewen Walker (2013) have re-worked the notion of 'deep time', re-christening it 'thick time'. 'Thick time' is, they write persuasively, a 'temporal frame' that recognizes our 'transcorporeal stretching between present, future, and past', and that allows us 'to reimagine our bodies as archives of climate *and* as making future climates possible.' The task now, it seems to me as both a writer and a scholar, is to find a 'thick language' for 'thick time' and in this way to keep asking, urgently, a version of Jonas Salk's (1992, p.16) searching question: 'Are we being good ancestors?'

References

Albrecht, G., 2005. Solastalgia, a new concept in human health and identity. *Philosophy Activism Nature*, 3: 41–4.

Albrecht, G., 2019. *Earth Emotions: New Words for a New World*. Ithaca, NY: Cornell University Press.

Blum, H., 2016. Speaking substances: Ice. *Los Angeles Review of Books*, March 21. Available from: https://lareviewofbooks.org/article/speaking-substances-ice/#! [Accessed July 17, 2019].

Camus, A., 1942. *The Myth of Sisyphus*. Trans. Justin O'Brien. London: Hamish Hamilton, 1973.

Cruikshank, J., 2005. *Do Glaciers Listen? Local Knowledge, Colonial Encounters and Social Imagination*. Vancouver: University of British Columbia Press.

Demuth, B., 2019. *Floating Coast*. New York: W.W. Norton.

Douglas, M., 1966. *Purity and Danger: An Analysis of the Concepts of Pollution and Taboo*. London: Routledge.

Falcon-Lang, H., 2011. Anthropocene: Have humans created a new geological age? BBC, May 11. Available online: www.bbc.co.uk/mobile/science-environment-13335683 [Accessed July 17, 2019].

Ghosh, A., 2016. *The Great Derangement: Climate Change and the Unthinkable*. Chicago: University of Chicago Press.

Howe, C., 2016. Timely. Available from: https://culanth.org/fieldsights/timely [Accessed July 17, 2019].

Howe, C. and Pandian, A., 2016. Lexicon for an Anthropocene yet unseen. *Fieldsights*. January 21. Available online: https://culanth.org/fieldsights/series/lexicon-for-an-anthropocene-yet-unseen [Accessed July 17, 2019].

Kimmerer, R.W., 2017. Speaking of nature. *Orion Magazine*, March/April 2017. Available from: https://orionmagazine.org/article/speaking-of-nature/ [Accessed July 17, 2019].

Macfarlane, R., 2019. *Underland: A Deep Time Journey*. London: Penguin.

Morton, T., 2013a. Poisoned ground: Art and philosophy in the time of hyperobjects. *Symploke*, 21 (1–2): 37–50.

Morton, T., 2013b. *Hyperobjects: Philosophy and Ecology after the End of the World*. Minneapolis, University of Minnesota Press.

Muir, J., 1911. *My First Summer in the Sierra*. San Francisco: Sierra Club Books, 1988.

Neimanis, A. and Walker, R.L., 2013. Weathering: Climate change and the "thick time" of transcorporeality. *Hypatia* 29 (3). Available online: https://doi.org/10.1111/hypa.12064 [Accessed July 17, 2019].

Nixon, R., 2011. *Slow Violence and the Environmentalism of the Poor*. Cambridge, MA: Harvard University Press.

Nixon, R., 2018. The swiftness of glaciers: Language in a time of climate change. *Aeon*, March 19. Available from: https://aeon.co/ideas/the-swiftness-of-glaciers-language-in-a-time-of-climate-change [Accessed July 17, 2019].

Ngai, S., 2005. *Ugly Feelings*. Cambridge, MA: Harvard University Press.

Ngai, S., 2013. *Our Aesthetic Categories: Zany, Cute, Interesting*. Cambridge, MA: Harvard University Press.

Olsen, B., and Pétursdóttir, Þ., 2017. Unruly heritage: An archaeology of the Anthropocene. Tromsø: UiT The Arctic University of Norway. Available online: www.sv.uio.no/sai/forskning/grupper/Temporalitet%20-%20materialitet/lesegruppe/olsen-unruly-heritage.pdf [Accessed July 17, 2019].

Pétursdóttir, Þ. 2018. Drift. *Multispecies Archaeology*, ed. Pilaar Birch, S.E. London: Routledge. 85–102.

Quante, H., and Escott, A., 2014. The bureau of linguistical reality. Available online: https://bureauoflinguisticalreality.com [Accessed July 17, 2019].

Raboteau, E., 2019. Climate signs. *New York Review of Books*, February 1, 2019.

Rush, E., 2018. *Rising: Dispatches from the New American Shore*. Minneapolis: Milkweed.

Russo, L., and Reed, M., 2018. *Counter-Desecration: A Glossary for Writing Within the Anthropocene*. Middletown: Wesleyan University Press.

Salk, J., 1992. Are we being good ancestors. *World Affairs* 1 (2), 16–18.

Sartre, J.P., 1943. *Being and Nothingness*. Trans. H.E. Barnes. London: Routledge, 1969.

Serres, M., 1990. *The Natural Contract*. Trans. E. MacArthur and W. Paulson. Ann Arbor, University of Michigan Press, 1995.

Solnit, R., 2019. Thank you, climate strikers. Your actions matter and your power will be felt March 15, 2019. Available from: www.theguardian.com/commentisfree/2019/mar/15/climate-strikers-letter-thank-you [Accessed July 17, 2019].

Tsing, A. et al., 2017. *Arts of Living on a Damaged Planet*. Minneapolis: University of Minnesota Press.

Weir, A., 2016. Deep Decay. *Parse* (4). Available online: http://parsejournal.com/article/deep-decay-into-diachronic-polychromatic-material-fictions/#return-note-2793-18 [Accessed July 17, 2019].

Wyndham, J., 1955. *The Chrysalids*. London: Michael Joseph.

6

ON THE FACE OF THINGS

Surficial encounters with the memory of architecture

Torgeir Rinke Bangstad

In late May 2016 I was given permission to explore an abandoned house in the municipality of Porsanger in Finnmark, the northernmost county in Norway. The house from Olderfjord on the west shore of Porsangerfjorden would, three years later, reopen as a permanent museum exhibition in the open-air museum of Norsk Folkemuseum at the Bygdøy peninsula in Oslo, more than 1800 kilometers southwest of Olderfjord. The preparations for its relocation and ex situ conservation were already well under way, and the building had been boarded up the previous winter to keep it safe through the long Arctic winter. The southern and eastern façades were adorned by a scaffold, and a green tarpaulin canvas shielded the leaky tar paper roof (see Figure 6.1). The red front door and the windows were all covered by sheets of plywood. The dense foliage made it difficult to see the house from the road. Large birch trees had already sprung into leaf on the overgrown property, and in the driveway patches of grass and small bushes were gradually effacing the wheel tracks of the cars that used to park there. A pillar of lightweight concrete blocks supporting the front porch entrance had collapsed and the concrete foundation was fractured by large cracks next to the window in the basement.

On the inside it was dark, and it was evident that the building had been vacant for a long time (Figure 6.2). A marooned DIY felt and burlap Christmas decoration hung from a hook on the living room wall next to the lace-curtained windows. In the kitchen a local newspaper from 1982 lay on the counter next to a blue pencil, a wash bowl and a coffee tin. A pair of well-worn woollen slippers on the floor seemed to have been left in their regular place by the stove in the kitchen corner. In this tranquil scene of suspended domesticity, every single thing seemed to await the next move. The building was prepped for the next stage of the disassembling which would commence in the summer of 2016. A gravel road had been prepared for the lorry trucks that would unload and reload large containers holding building materials, furniture and household appliances that had accumulated over the years

FIGURE 6.1 The Olderfjord house. May, 2016. Photo: Torgeir Rinke Bangstad

FIGURE 6.2 Kitchen interior. Olderfjord, May, 2016. Photo: Torgeir Rinke Bangstad

from the house was built in 1951 until its permanent abandonment six decades later. The scaffolding, the plywood on the windows and the tarpaulin on the rooftop, had already detached the house from its familiar environment and dampened the effect of the wind, the sun and the rain. As the house turned in on itself, the interior space was couched in a dull, dark grey which dimmed the outlines of the things inside. In one of the upstairs bedrooms, the pink paint film on the wall was becoming brittle and tiny pieces of paint was found on the floor amidst mouse droppings.

These impressions from a field work some years ago when I set out to document and explore the house in Olderfjord before it was taken apart and moved to the museum, recount the initial encounter with a specific research object coated in a fairly recent material addendum that seemed to yield restriction, detachment and introversion. The outside environment was rendered hostile and a threat to the building's physical fabric and future existence as a museum object. The roof could no longer keep the rain out, the windows were broken and the fragile wooden walls were damaged by rot. In an abandoned building one encounters many different surfaces that bear the traces of interactions between materials and the world. Surfaces absorb past events in the physical fabric and over time, as they start to disintegrate, also co-determine the scope of conservation by facilitating the potential recovery of a building's hidden, historical layers. In the process of exfoliation, the building invites a glimpse of its former self and potentiates a recovery of past states when the architectural object seemed more at home with its own time.

Different notions of the composition, recovery of and conservation of historical knowledge in architecture are brought to bear on the Olderfjord house as a museum object *in spe*. In a conservation context, the surface brings together different practices, epistemologies, technologies and different notions of the historical. This is not simply a question of different perspectives on the same surface. The surface is enacted differently depending on professional training and disciplinary background, to the extent that we might suggest that in a conservation process different approaches will 'literalize different kinds of material object' (Jones and Yarrow 2013, p. 7). In piercing through the surface in a preservation context like this, several technologies and specific competencies come into play to shape new insights and specific temporalities. The surface is in this sense 'multiple' (Mol 2003), enacted and materialized differently by a home owner, a building's conservator, a house painter, an archaeologist or an artist.

This chapter will focus on three different ways of enacting and understanding the surface. The first one, which treats the architectural as surface as derivative of function, always already an after-effect, is often associated with architectural modernism. The modernist call for transparency stressed the correspondence between the outer appearance and the structural logic as a virtue of a constructional honesty and aesthetic clarity. Secondly, in culture historical studies of vernacular architecture, the surfaces of buildings were often seen as the recent, often entropic layers that rendered illegible the basic forms of the architectural grammar. This enabled an ethnological optic of piercing through the arbitrariness of the surface. The third mode of grasping the surface is my own attempt to reflect on the restrictions imposed on my field work in Olderfjord at a site that was, regardless of its battered appearance, the property of a museum, and hence calling for distance and caution. This compelled me to explore surfaces not as an opaque physical boundary restricting insight, but as a vibrant interface where the friction between the physical transformation and a conservation object is brought to the fore.

Surfaces are often seen as a threshold separating the accessible outward appearance from a deeper, interior realm. This is perhaps why they are often overlooked, or looked straight through. Tim Ingold (2017) has claimed that either our vision pierces the surface like a transparent window, or it bounces off the opaque exterior restricting access to their insides, it rarely stays there, to dwell in the surface. The chapter is an attempt to stay with the surface and try to recover some of its analytic vigor, in the sense that any surface has a cultural validity and material vibrancy that extends beyond acts of concealing or revealing. This chapter draws on the revaluation of surfaces in anthropology (Ingold 2017), archaeology (Harrison 2011; Sørensen 2020, forthcoming; Farstadvoll 2019) and architecture (Chatterjee 2009, 2017; Spuybroek 2011; Benjamin 2006) to explore the spontaneous 'creaturely' surface materializations, as a contrast – or also potentially an overlap – with epistemic practices and technologies in culture historical museum work that seem to require that conservators pierce through the surface to recover lost stories and chronological sequences.

Disintegrating buildings actualize latent material potentials that are normally mute in a functioning architectural ensemble. In the process of taking down the Olderfjord house, a heightened sense of the potentials and constraints of the materials in the long term develops from conservator's engagements with surfaces, the stories they cue and the events they infold. In abandonment contexts where ordinary functions are suspended and other processes become more apparent, materials assert themselves in a different way. As the 'creaturely' material transformation outpaces the stylistic evolution, surfaces engage us in ways that might prevent our gaze from bouncing off immediately in sheer disinterest.

Drapery and deceit

A binary of skeleton and mask has, according to the architectural theorist Lars Spuybroek (2011), defined the flimsy metaphysics of architectural history, and this makes it difficult to envision surfaces in terms of a substantial, constructive contribution to the ontology of buildings. Adornment is always already 'after', an 'after-effect' (Benjamin 2006, p. 16). The depthlessness of the late modern condition diagnosed by Fredric Jameson (1984), brought this metaphysics of skeleton and mask to its historical conclusion. It was claimed that the representational capacity of architecture in the postmodern age had imploded in the asignifying and structurally autonomous free-floating façade which pointed to nothing but itself and the sovereignty of flatness. In its postmodern guise, the exhilaration of surfaces echoed a deeper rupture in the historical fabric of art and architecture. The mode of representation in the commoditized, postmodern artwork was literal and flat, a symptom of the inadequacy of art to express something profound about the wider historical and political realities at the time. By contrasting Andy Warhol's *Diamond Dust Shoes* (1980) with Vincent Van Gogh's *A Pair of Shoes* (1886), the key point for Jameson was to draw attention to the emergence of a new depthlessness signaled by Warhol's series of pumps, high-heels, stilettos – a 'random collection of dead objects' – that refused a completion of the hermeneutic gesture that would 'restore to these oddments that whole larger lived context of the dance hall or the ball, the world of jetset fashion or of glamour magazines' (Jameson 1984, p. 60)

The apparent problem of appreciating surfaces is that the formation of knowledge and meaning has long presupposed a human subject penetrating the surface of the world (Gumbrecht 2004, p. 27). A more profound insight, tangential with the emotional, existential or historical depths of art in the hermeneutic mode, seems to require that a connection is forged between the present and literal and its always already 'vaster reality' (Jameson 1984, p. 59). Similarly the modern preoccupation with 'authenticity' which comprises all three of these different depths 'implies the downward movement through all cultural superstructures to some place where movement ends, and begins' (Trilling 1973, p. 12). When objects are detached from their vaster life-worlds and placed in museums, it is the hermeneutic gesture that attempts to restore life to what Jameson calls 'dead objects,' by expounding their cultural, historical contexts and by relating them to a reality outside of themselves. The claim that I will make in this chapter is, however, that much like the shell of invertebrates or the skin of human beings, surfaces of buildings articulate architecture's continuously changing, extensive relations with the wider world. As a membrane through which water, air and heat can circulate and that may also act as a shield for humans or accommodate small plants, mold, bacteria and fungi, surfaces are capable of articulating historical, cultural, material and biological life-worlds in and of themselves.

Historically, vernacular buildings and the material culture of the peasantry, were often expected to touch base with the deeper layer of cultural evolution, by retaining forms of folk culture that were untainted by aristocratic excess and artifice (Bendix 1997). In earlier articulations of the fear of depthlessness, collectors and conservators of the burgeoning folk museum movement in the late 19th century, derided the 'cocooned' domestic interiors of the 19th century that were so intricate materially that they threatened to engulf the residents. As Norsk Folkemuseum and other Scandinavian open-air museums evolved from dense and chaotic interior displays into more disciplined, scientific and systematic collections, one of the central concerns was, quite simply, to avoid cluttering. In the modern museum display of ethnographic artefacts and folk art, the surface, the fourth wall between the visitor and the exhibit, had to yield to a clear sense of order and curatorial self-discipline. It was claimed that whereas the romantic exhibitions of the early 1900s were overburdened with furniture, fabrics, art works and luscious palms, a disciplined, modern display required a consistent simplification (Shetelig 1944, pp. 208–9). The overriding curatorial priority at Norsk Folkemuseum in the age of order, was to give people a clear sense of characteristic cultural traits of different rural regions (Aall 1925, p. 40). For the key objects to stand out and convey a distinct sense of a specific regional tradition, the displays should avoid the excessive accumulation of things in small rooms (Aall 1925, p. 42).

The problem of romantic decorations and overcrowded displays in open-air museums, was compared to the lack of self-control in excessive bourgeois 19th-century interiors (Shetelig 1944). The exuberant display of collected exotica, trinkets, heavy furniture and drapery was regarded as the construction of a private, miniature world, a domestic encapsulation which detached the bourgeois home from the reality of the world and from any sense of continuity with homegrown traditions. The drapery would also be seen as a hallmark of the interior space of the *noveau riche*, and added to the sense of secluded, private realm. By virtue of its elaborate, multi-layered wall covers made from velvet, damask and satin, the domestic space increasingly lost contact with the real world physical environment, and detached the interior decoration from the architectural core that would traditionally act as structuring device determining the order of things in the domestic realm (Maleuvre 1999, p. 147).

The draped and cushioned space was built from the inside out, and not from the outside in. This was the problem of opaque surfaces that are still to this day often treated as an impenetrable boundary which distorts the relation between the individual home and a wider architectural grammar forged by tradition and the material, climatic and cultural conditions of a given period and place. Lavishly ornamented surfaces were criticized in the context of modernist's call for transparency and constructional honesty because they no longer bore any organic connection to contemporary culture, and were likely to degenerate into imitation and excess. In order for a museum display, an exhibited house or a domestic interior to connect to the historical fabric and carry the signature of an age, virtues such as honesty, simplicity and self-discipline were emphasized. Without this kind of restraint, the surface would become increasingly unmoored from the continuity of tradition and the structuring logic of the core construction.

Reconstruction architecture and the timeliness of form

The reconstruction architecture of the postwar years (1945–1960) to which the Olderfjord house belongs, can also be framed in terms of an attempt to transcend the momentary and excessive. The modesty and diligence that was required to rebuild the war-torn counties of Troms and Finnmark after the brutal scorched earth retreat of the occupying German Wehrmacht in 1944, required a reliable, simple and robust form of architecture. Einar Gerhardsen, who was Prime Minister for the Labor Party from 1945 to 1951 and from 1955 to 1963, claimed that the designers and architects involved in the reconstruction should resist 'unsightly' momentary ideals and whims of fashion: 'Such excesses may spice up life in more abundant societies. What we will build in the years to come, should be built to last. We cannot afford otherwise' (Gerhardsen 1946, p. 1). Excessive and redundant material adornments were discredited at an early stage of the reconstruction, and the form of building was required to resonate with the social reform policies of the post-war welfare state and yet transcend the momentary and the fashionable. Reconstruction houses were expected to fuse the timely and the timeless in a form of which rejected the superfluous and redundant (Bangstad 2019c).

A simple and rational design would not only minimize building costs, but also ease the daily chores and make cleaning simpler. The uniform style of reconstruction architecture also reduced the socio-economic differences which had been readily apparent in the built environment prior to the war. Already in 1940 the Committee for War Reparations (Krigsskadetrygdens gjenreisningsnemd) established a set of principles for the post-war rebuilding of domestic housing in Norway: 'The houses will have to satisfy the requirements of good architecture and, in a timely form, reflect regional building traditions' (Krigsskadetrygdens gjenreisningsnemd 1940, p. 18). Due to material scarcity and the plea for a modest architecture that would enhance social equality by providing sound and affordable housing, planners argued for an aesthetic sobriety that responded to the requirements of the post-war welfare state while also relying on the stylistic precedent of the pre-war buildings and older vernacular buildings (Figure 6.3). A typical reconstruction house would have a rectangular floor plan with a chimney in the middle to heat the adjacent rooms

FIGURE 6.3 The town of Berlevåg in Finnmark was completely destroyed in the scorched earth retreat. In 1962 the reconstruction was more or less complete, with parallel rows of houses extending in straight axes from the harbor area. Photo: Torgeir Rinke Bangstad

spread over two, or one and a half floors. The floor plans were often modelled after the cross plan, or the two-room house that was widespread in the Finnmark region before the war (Hage 1999, p. 143). Notably, the voguish flat roof modernist buildings of the interwar years with their rounded corners were considered too outlandish to function properly in the harsh, northern climate. The gable roof covered with slate or tar paper was considered far more reliable and also had a clear precedent in the vernacular regional building tradition.

In preparing for the ex situ conservation of the building and its interiors, the project management of the Finnmark project at Norsk Folkemuseum decided that the Olderfjord house would be restored at Bygdøy to a state resembling its 1956 appearance when electric power for lighting was first installed in the house. At that time, three generations lived under the same roof and the current museum exhibition is partly based on the home of this particular family. In contrast to many reconstruction houses in the region, and with the exception of a porch leading up to the front door entrance, the Olderfjord house had not been significantly altered since it was first built. In the mid-1950s the reconstruction was becoming increasingly manifest in the built environment of Troms and Finnmark. To convey to contemporary museum visitors the full scope of the social and political project of rebuilding large parts of Northern Norway more or less from scratch, the most effective strategy is to restore the building to its prime, to a time when its clear lines and bright surfaces pointed, as it were, straight into the future. Post-war progress was facilitated by the egalitarian and social democratic architecture of reconstruction that aimed to improve living conditions in the region from the poverty-ridden interwar years. The many reconstruction houses that have persisted in Finnmark and Troms, speak less clearly of this ambitious, social democratic housing project. They have often been amended or extended to such an extent that their distinctive and 'timely' signature has faded. This is perhaps also why the urge to go beyond the apparent is part of the backbone of culture historical building research. Recent additions and extraneous surface layers may obscure the particular lineage that a building belongs to, and undermine the legibility of constructional principles that aimed to transcend individual whims of fashion and personal preferences.

From the depths of tradition to surficial attunements

The surface was not only a recent addition articulating the more arbitrary and contingent choices of generations guided by individual choice rather than the rule of tradition, it was also a layer which potentially concealed the beauty and legibility of the architectural grammar. Researchers who studied profane, vernacular architecture in the 19th and early 20th century would frequently encounter properties that had been abandoned for a while and were deteriorating. They would also come across buildings that were facing demolition or buildings whose materials were sold to be reused in new buildings. Field work in rural contexts during the comprehensive economic restructuring of rural regions in the second half of the 19th century would have entailed frequent encounters with idle buildings, neglected farming areas, and a material culture that changed profoundly due to mechanization and rationalization of production. The transition from an autarkic subsidence farming to a market-based, mechanized production resulted in what historian Inge Krokann (1982) called 'the Great Exuviation' of rural, agrarian Norway in the second half of the 19th century. The residues of this exuviation, the relinquished skins of the old ways of life, resemble the rural contexts that contemporary archaeologists deal with in our time (e.g. Sørensen 2016; González-Ruibal 2005; see also DeSilvey 2006).

The sight of abandoned rural dwellings with their cluttered farm yards and contorted exteriors filled the early building collectors and researchers with a combination of awe and melancholia. Anders Sandvig (1862–1950), whose collection of buildings and antiquities, De Sandvigske Samlinger, became part of the open-air museum at Maihaugen in 1904, later recounted his first encounter with the 18th century house, Løkrestua in Skjåk in 1894 as meeting with an old, exhausted mother who had been forgotten and abandoned even by her next of kin. Its foundation walls were sliding, its roof perforated, the chimney had collapsed and the windows were broken, and Sandvig could not open the front door because the walls were sinking. The original interiors, however, were still intact and they yielded a sense of epiphany in the young collector:

> It was as if the home as a whole suddenly opened its doors for me. It was not an assemblage of random purchases from south and north. It was built for generations, and everything was rounded off in one form from its core to its edges, and with a harmony and culture about it that made me completely dizzy.
>
> *(Sandvig 1943, p. 97)*

A highly influential study of rural building traditions in Norway, was carried out half a century earlier by theologian and social scientist Eilert Sundt (1817–1875) who undertook comprehensive field work to study the living conditions and traditions of the peasantry during a time of profound cultural change in rural regions. In describing his research endeavours, Sundt conveyed the epiphanies engendered by the scientific gaze which enabled him to comprehend the deeper regularity obscured by the apparent irregularity of the built environment at the time:

> As I ventured out and entered more and more farms, it seemed as if the irregularity yielded for the vague impression of an originary rule and uniformity in the core. And it struck me that the unique beauty of the irregularity became more beautiful, the more I was trained in catching a glimpse of the rule and order half-concealed underneath.
>
> *(Sundt 1862, p. 1)*

By acting as a threshold between present-day appearance and past form, the surface conditioned the scientific method and the revelatory gaze looking past the exteriors and into the past. The ruins that Sundt encountered on some of his travels, such as the medieval 13th-century Jutul house, were eerie, 'doors since long of its hinges, windows and window sills gone, the exteriors all decayed and disturbed' (Sundt 1862, p. 24). Still, the ruinous structure also contained the faint traces of deeper origins:

> My vision endeavoured to look through the eeriness and up into the distant past, when the house was in its proper condition as the new-built home of the freeholder – I mean: half a thousand years ago, before the time of the Black Death.
>
> *(Ibid.)*

Sundt envisioned that a modern scientific gaze and the wealth of empirical data gathered, enabled him to look beyond the eerie appearances and into the historical fabric of a particular building. His comprehensive knowledge of traditional house plans would enable him to determine the location of pieces of furniture in individual rooms without ever stepping over the door sill. In a sense the surface, the apparent and the recent architectural layer, was always serving a greater epistemological purpose, an end beyond itself as a condition for, and boundary towards deeper historical insight. The scientific aim of identifying basic forms in the built environment, despite the apparent chaos on the ground, was premised on the ability to pierce through mere appearances and the masses of arbitrary forms introduced in the built environment by individual choice, fashion and mass produced furniture available in the modern market place. It is against this backdrop I wonder what encounters with abandoned buildings in similar contexts and in various states of disrepair actually amount to today. In how far does the attempt to dwell in the surface imply a disregard of history, tradition and memory? What I want to suggest in the following is that a form of 'reparative reading' (Sedgwick 1997) may recognize the literal and apparent as possessing a quality and reality of its own, allowing one to recognize the effect of the past in widely accessible forms such as the surfaces we encounter in domestic buildings or in our everyday environments.

Restoration work: Joining forces with past builders or arresting time?

In his important contribution to a rethinking of the relation between structure and ornament, depth and surface, architectural theorist Lars Spuybroek claims that the beauty of things is persistently explained by categories beyond themselves like utility, order, truth and imagination rather than 'between things, and between us and things' (Spuybroek 2011, p. 223). Rather than speaking of withdrawn essences, Spuybroek draws attention to the 'fringe' as the region that enables the outgoing and generous side of things (2011, p. 257). Spuybroek prefers the word 'sympathy' over the more mechanistic and commonly used 'affect' because in the latter things accidentally connect back to back, whereas in sympathy, they connect face to face (2011, p. 277).

Admittedly, the surficial relation to a specific field or a specific object of research may be considered a deficiency, a failed attempt of closer acquaintance and of getting to know something inside out. It may, nonetheless, compel the recognition that the material memory of things is not consigned to an obscure realm, always elsewhere and beyond reach. A common assumption of historical research, is that the past is always other, detached from the present and fundamentally unattainable through encounters in a present-day experiential realm. Materials of the past are enrolled as knowledge objects to different ends and through different means, but there is no clear-cut threshold which sets the historical apart from its current materialization through research, through different material conditions for preservation and

FIGURE 6.4 Removing wooden wall panel from the pink room. Each board is labeled with a number indicating room, wall and the order of assembly. Photo: Torgeir Rinke Bangstad

technologies of recovering traces of past lives. This is more an issue of where, and through what means, present-day building conservators join their efforts with an ever-emergent historical fabric.

Two distinct and fundamentally irreconcilable notions of the act or moment of preservation applies in this case. One view of the physical interventions that invariably occurs through conservation work, is that these activities take place as if 'outside of history' (Jones and Yarrow 2013), from a position where time is arrested and present-day activities are distinct from and should be distinguished physically and aesthetically from the organic, historical transformation of a building. The other, and qualitatively different view, is that skilled craftspeople's labour during conservation merges with the flow of time, locates material crossings where it may reconnect with the fabric of tradition by continuing the building operation, the caretaking, where previous builders left off (ibid.) (Figure 6.4). According to the first view, history stops with heritage conservation, and this contrasts with the idea that dutiful material care can be considered part of a building's ongoing, living history. Again we are confronted with the possibility of a fundamental disconnect between, on the one hand, the present articulation of and relation to an ongoing, continuing past and, on the other hand, a past that has already emerged, is complete and unattainable.

Interior walls with thick skins of consecutive layers of paint or wallpaper, begs the question of how deep the cut should go in specific restoration projects. What kind of historic figuration will prevail in the interiors on display and at what point should damaged building materials be replaced? In some cases, preservation welcomes the effect of a building's physical relation with the environment, with acidic rain, with weathering, its colonization by fungal and bacterial communities, or the sun's slow bleaching of a painted surface. In other preservation projects, attempts to arrest time in order to represent a distinct historical period detached from its spontaneous material, organic afterlife remains the overriding priority. The Olderfjord house would be restored to a time when it would still have had the faint scent of fresh wooden materials, shiny surfaces and oil paint, mixed with ephemeral smell of food cooking on kitchen stove.

Despite the decision to restore the house to its former self when it was only a few years old, the original materials carry a tremendous weight in efforts to forge a link between the present day, *ex situ* museum object and its past form *in situ* in the municipality of Porsanger in Finnmark (Bangstad 2019b). A house painter from the museum told me that the sense of authenticity conveyed through the original materials, was so important that it justified the extra work and long hours of mechanically scraping off the pink layer of paint that was non-contemporaneous with the temporal focal point of the exhibition. In paint conservation, different layers of paint are often exposed to gain knowledge about the cultural and material biographies of buildings (Figure 6.5). Different layers are revealed in small patches in what is called paint stratigraphy or paint exposure, showing the specific pigments and binders used in the course of time.

In the Olderfjord house, such samples showed that the bright pink, possibly alkyd paint had been applied sometime after 1956 over a layer of semi-transparent,

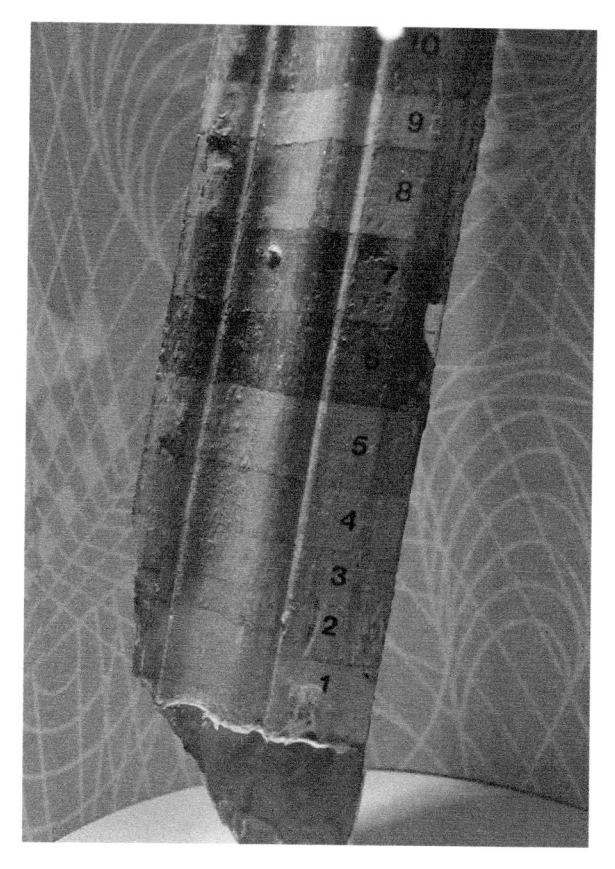

FIGURE 6.5 An exhibit at Norsk Folkemuseum showing the paint stratigraphy on a wooden trim from a 19th-century apartment building. Photo: Torgeir Rinke Bangstad

linoleic oil paint. It was established that the most recent layer of paint could be removed mechanically (Figure 6.6), which enabled the museum to reuse the original wooden panels instead of producing more affordable and less labor-demanding panel reproductions for the exhibition house. The pink layer of the original panels from Olderfjord was later removed *ex situ* in the workshop at Norsk Folkemuseum. Cheaper reproductions would compromise the notion of a continuous building operation, where the original building materials serve as a bridge between past traditions and present restoration (Jones and Yarrow 2013).

Abstract principles and guidelines of conservation can never be exhaustive and cover every conceivable scenario encountered during field work, and they need to be translated to the material context at hand and negotiated locally (Roede 2010). In this process, materials and practices are involved in a complex interaction between skilled experts and the restrictions and potentials of the 'historical fabric' which may or may not comprise the most recent, visible surface layer. As

FIGURE 6.6 Scrape or anti-scrape? Paint is removed from a pink board using a sheath knife. Photo: Torgeir Rinke Bangstad

an epistemic practice, the restoration of the Olderfjord house relies on enacting or materializing a specific notion historical insight by working its way through the surface in a form of 'learning-by-undoing' (Bangstad 2019a). During my second round of field work in Olderfjord in August 2016, I talked to one of the carpenters from the building preservation section at Norsk Folkemuseum, who told me that in the process of the disassembling of a building, he would acquaint himself with the house from the outside in. By working his way through and in taking apart all layers of paneling, he would be increasingly capable of understanding the mindset of the builder. This sense of going deep and reading the chronology of building, plays an important part in reconciling present-day conservation practices with the historical fabric of a building (Figure 6.7). It aims for the current museal manifestation to provide a legible connection to the mindsets, priorities and practices of another time. The potential for a carpenter to locate a joint, a line, a layer, a crack where present conservation work may meaningfully relate to the fabric of tradition, requires a close understanding of materials, an ability to follow the particular bent of materials to elicit their latent material and aesthetic potentials (Jones and Yarrow 2013, p. 20; Ingold 2012).

Other surfaces – material memory and 'what becomes of what was'

The cracks in the pink painted wall in the upstairs bedroom of the Olderfjord house contains many clues of the forces at work as materials cease to cohere and the surface coating and substrate detach. The specific form of craquelure at work here, is known as 'alligatoring' because it resembles the texture of alligator skin as the paint transforms from a continuous surface film to individual flakes. As it fractures a distinctive 'alligatoring' pattern emerges. Similar to other forms of paint failure, the pattern is formed when the mechanical stress exceeds the flexibility of the paint film, at which point it starts to disintegrate. When the cracks widen and bifurcate, the volatile material life intersects with the more coherent architectural edifice. Other material accretions may also present on exterior and interior surfaces, such as algae films, dust or efflorescence on concrete walls. The important point to note is that these are not extraneous or somehow discontinuous with a building's proper historical memory, rather they condition the surficial articulations of how material memory extend in time, in ways that no conservation agency has sanctioned. These processes are not necessarily parasitic, or unambiguously harmful. As bacteria, lichen and algae colonize surfaces of buildings they may form bioprotective films, helping to preserve the object they grow on (Farstadvoll 2020, forthcoming).

If crumbling paint is ordinarily conceived of as a form of gradual disclosure or unveiling, it is because some surfaces are considered extraneous, or somehow, less real from the outset. But cracking paint also presents textures of memory that enfold the unperceivably slow movement of materials and the interaction between different paint layers over time (Figure 6.8). The lively craquelure in the pink bedroom does not disclose a more profound layer, but manifests the interaction between several interlaced and mutually afflicting surfaces. The alligatoring pattern is formed through the co-involvement of surface and substrate, as well as the volatile relation between the indoor environment, the wooden panels, the fatty linoleic oil medium and the less flexible alkyd paint. The warping movement of shrinking wooden panels determines where the cracks will first appear, and later, it extends along the line where the strain of the paint film exceeds its ability to cohere. The source of this unintended ornamentation derives not from one isolated layer, instead every layer seems to form part of a complex, emergent surface.

This surface dynamism encourages a view of things as a compound of their present manifestation as well as of their past movements and emergent relations. The

FIGURE 6.7 A conservator from Norsk Folkemuseum revealing the original wooden wall panel in the living room. Photo: Torgeir Rinke Bangstad

seemingly incommensurable distance between separate temporal planes of what things have been, what they are and what they might become, sometimes enfold in one articulation of surficial becoming. Material processes are wild and exceed the well-defined memory objects with clear contours and a distinct, historical signature. The spontaneous or 'creaturely' memory suggests that things that perform their own past in and through their transformation articulate not the past as such, but its material memory in the form of 'what becomes of what was' (Witmore 2014, p. 213). The house from Olderfjord is since long enrolled in an oscillation between the sanctioned cultural archive and spontaneous memory deposited elsewhere, in things and in landscapes which may turn out to be unexpected repositories of memory and 'accidental archives' (Rigney 2017, 2015). This is the perhaps most intuitive sense in which surfaces reach out to us in generosity, and do so in ways that exceed the transcendent idea of a historical object or a building representing

FIGURE 6.8 Paint cracks in one of the upstairs rooms of the Olderfjord house. Original layer of oil paint underneath the absent electrical wiring. Photo: Torgeir Rinke Bangstad

a historical 'Zeitgeist' which predetermines its form. While the spontaneous, 'creaturely,' material memory unfolds more or less on its own accord, a culture historical memory is premised on the restoring the legible relation between present form and historical function in the tenor of 'what it was' or even sometimes, 'how it was meant to be.'

The 'wall veil' and the value of watching paint dry

The pink 'alligatoring' surfaces are adorned with faint traces of slow movements in the clayey ground in Olderfjord, ashes from the stove, dust and frequent exposure to sun light through the bedroom windows. These surfaces continuously enter into relations that extend or suspend certain capacities and innate material tendencies. The color of wall surfaces play a role here as well. Although we tend to think about the color of surfaces in terms of aesthetic preferences, historical styles and market availability, specific pigments have properties that determine the quality of a building's relation with the environment and with other-than-human beings. The choice of color ultimately affects its long-term preservation. For instance on exterior surfaces, darker colors suppress the growth of microorganisms, and red wooden façades that absorb more energy from sunlight than white coatings, also dry up faster after a rainy day (Sjökvist and Blom 2019). Color has a function beyond the giving buildings a desired finish, signifying the historical identities of humans, it also primes specific relations in the environment. This is why color in certain respects travels across the deep divide between function and form in architecture. It engenders a range of effects that makes us recognize that surfaces matter and that the color of walls structures its specific way of being in the world. The effect of color is not an ancillary phenomenal aspect, inferior to the function of architecture, rather it can be treated as a form of 'mattering' which is both representational and material (Dolphijn et al. 2012, p. 96).

The oil in oil-based paint is called a medium, or a vehicle, and the purpose of binding mediums like linseed oil, alkyd resins or acryl or egg tempera used in older art paintings, is to hold the particles of pigments together and produce a coherent film without affecting the color. Studies have shown that the behavior of drying pant and crawling of cells are quite similar with regards to the mechanical exchange between the binding agent and the surrounding substrate (Tsoi 2011). By absorbing oxygen from the outside environment (in some cases increasing the weight of the film by more than 15%), and releasing volatile solvents into the air, the paint expands before it eventually regains its original weight.

Paint is understood as a complex 'system.' The term refers to the interaction between the material substrate and the paint and the coherence of the system depends on the chemical composition as well as the properties of the material; its flexibility, porosity, saturation and density. The chemical process of hardening through oxidation may continue for a long time, and certainly for years after the oil paint is dry to the touch. In cases where paint systems fail, like the brittle cracking pink wall paint in the Olderfjord house, it is often caused by the application of a less flexible, hard paint coating on top of a relatively soft, underlying layer. This volatile interaction between a whole range of elements plays out in front of us, albeit imperceptibly slow, on the surface of an ordinary bedroom wall.

The surface in this rendition may be related to the John Ruskin's concept of the 'Wall Veil' which according to Lars Spuybroek is one of the rare theories that 'successfully relate massing to texture through interdependence' (Spuybroek 2011, p. 80). For Ruskin, the wall veil was a way of understanding the geological surface composition of Matterhorn in Switzerland and extending this insight to architectural edifices that similarly articulate forces 'gathering and converging onto a shape' (Spuybroek, 2010, p. 235). Relating the wall veil to his ontology of things,

Spuybroek stress that both buildings and mountains have 'faces' with which they orient themselves in the environment, and through which they articulate the mutual dependency of matter and ornament (Spuybroek 2011, pp. 77–9). The wall veil is formed constitutively from the inside out, and erosively from the outside in (Spuybroek 2011, p. 80).

The surface, the slopes of the rock face of the Matterhorn – the profile of stone courses, breaks and fractures – channels the forces of sedimentation, it 'completely structures the generation of form' (Spuybroek 2011, p. 81). The Ruskian wall veil is a surface 'limitless in the extent of its outpouring into the surroundings' (Ingold 2017, p. 104). Together, the geological processes of erosion and uplifting form an imbricated surface, a form of 'self-adornment' (Spuybroek 2011, p. 80), and like a dress which does not erase the trace of the body, it outlines as it covers, and allows us to sense the depth in the surface (Ingold 2017, p. 104).

The promise of this particular way of approaching surfaces, is that by acknowledging the dual composition of inside and outside, erosion and sedimentation, it seems difficult to clearly distinguish boundaries from substance. If we consider the physical composition of walls, the same logic applies. Any attempt to establish an unambiguous, physical threshold separating surface from substrate is complicated by the indistinct edges of different materials. For example, what looks like a metal surface is often impure, tainted and intriguingly-rarely strictly metallic. Due to contamination from the elements that are *on*, but not *of* the surface, its exterior, its fringe, is really more like an oxide layer. Surfaces, in short, 'are seldom what they seem' (Lambourne 1999, p. 5). This claim does not have to imply that surfaces hide, conceal or cover up something else, but rather that surfaces are fundamentally ambiguous in themselves, an exhilarating region of indistinction.

The clear distinction between substance and surface, or between depth and surface has, moreover, been problematized by relationalist approaches that emphasize the inherent leakiness of things, the sense in which both materials and living bodies discharge into the environment and similarly absorb elements from the environment (Ingold 2012). If this membranous notion of surfaces is employed with regard to the pink wall in the Olderfjord, it seems that the surface in this case is less the finite boundary which separates past from present in the material's inside and outside. Slow processes of paint cracking are integral parts of the vibrancy of materials and the articulation of forces that converge on the surface in a form which makes it difficult to clearly determine the boundaries between texture and mass, ornament and structure. In this scheme of things, texture has a structuring capacity, and colour has a function in conditioning the relation between the material and the environment. The surface is not the extraneous layers that conceal some more privileged origin. A painted wall may well expose the different strata of cultural history, the sedimented traces of changes in style, income or individual taste, but this successional history is constantly intertwined with the material story of surfaces relating and shaping each other over time.

Summary

Sometimes the cultural and material history show a neat overlap, at other times they diverge. When surfaces decompose, they manifest the slow creaturely processes of things that are not yet, if ever, fully constituted and finite. A vertical wall, seen as a Euclidian object with four corners and a uniform, continuous surface comes across as finished, stable and at rest, but this is an object that can only be seen and not felt, according to Spuybroek: 'Sympathy can be felt only for things that are in the making or in transition, that have a life' (Spuybroek 2011, p. 129). The house from Olderfjord illustrates the slippage between cultural history and material history, at the point where stylistic evolution ceases and is superseded by material memory that evokes sympathy, that makes us relate to its surfaces differently.

A building which is no longer perfectly in synch with the technical requirements and living standards of the present day and age and no longer perfectly aligned with our time, offers the opportunity for museum conservators to work closer to the form of the building as it once was when it first came into use. A house is unlikely to end up in any museum exhibition in a state which confuses the desired temporal specificity of displays, but this friction between a spontaneous material memory and stratified cultural history attests to different ways of enabling surfaces in the construction of historical knowledge with regards to architecture. The ambition of this chapter has been to show how, in different disciplines, the surface is often perceived as discontinuous with the historical fabric of buildings. And yet the surface acts as an epistemological precondition for the historicist gesture of going deep, the architects' call for transparency and the museum conservators', recovery of buried layers.

The ability to take pleasure in the face to face encounter with things is still curtailed by a deep distrust in surface impressions if not in the veil of the earth itself. The 'real' is veiled in inverted commas and that particular gesture reinforces the fissure between exterior appearance and an inaccessible, interior realm. This makes the attempts to dwell in the surface and relate to its offerings all the more worthwhile. In this chapter, I have claimed that a vital contribution to the relational, sympathetic and agentive capacity of architecture in general and of the Olderfjord house specifically, resides in the liveliness of surfaces. More than a barrier to a historical or ontological profundity of things and buildings, the surface is a vibrant interface a literal 'between faces' (Joy 2013, p. 213) connecting human worlds, chemical worlds, geological worlds and bacterial worlds. The peeling layers of paint or wallpaper in decaying buildings resembles a form of 'self-excavation' (Olsen 2010, p. 170), but it is, importantly, also a 'self-adornment' (Spuybroek 2011, p. 80) where surfaces are encrusted with the traces of their own history of transformation. The pink alligator pattern in the Olderfjord house illustrates the textured material memory which works both from the inside and the outside, channeled by past events and their accretions, but also shaped through an ongoing re-figuration of the surface.

The agency of surfaces also extends to how some decisions in conservation practice relies on a distinct feel for the materials and their internal logic of movement

FIGURE 6.9 The reconstruction house in its new location at Bygdøy. July 2019. Photo: Torgeir Rinke Bangstad

or stubborn recalcitrance. In line with the reparative reading of the literal, the apparent, and the surficial such indistinct expressions of a feel for the surface at hand for the material at hand should be taken at face value and not be disregarded as esoteric. Architecture enables relations, it is never restricted to representing ideas (Bille and Sørensen 2016). The complex material choreography of veiling and unveiling, outlining and re-composing is made overwhelmingly apparent in abandonment contexts where surfaces crumble and gesture in directions that once seemed unlikely and fanciful. 1800 kilometres away from where it once stood by the side of the road, the house from Olderfjord has spectacularly come to life, once more (see Figure 6.9). The lesson written on its surface, however, is that it was never dead. If you ever visit Norsk Folkemuseum, look for the faint traces and residue of pink paint in the upstairs bedroom of the Olderfjord house. It is still there, in your face, like the relentless skin of the mighty alligator.

References

Aall, H., 1925. *Arbeide og ordning i kulturhistoriske museer.* Oslo: Norske museers landsforbund.

Bangstad, T. R., 2019a. Beyond presentism: Heritage and the temporality of things. *Ethnologia Europaea,* 49(2).

Bangstad, T. R., 2019b. Buildings on the move: Relational museology and the mutability of place. In: Smeds, K. and Davis, A. eds. *Museum & Place.* Paris: ICOFOM – ICOM International Committee for Museology, 87–106.

Bangstad, T. R., 2019c. Heritage and the untimely. In: Tamm, M. and Olivier, L. eds. *Rethinking Historical Time: New Approaches to Presentism.* London: Bloomsbury Academic, 147–62.

Bendix, R., 1997. *In Search of Authenticity: The Formation of Folklore Studies.* Madison, Wis: University of Wisconsin Press.

Benjamin, A., 2006. Surface effects: Borromini, Semper, Loos. *The Journal of Architecture,* 11(1), 1–36.

Bille, M. and Sørensen, T. F., 2016. Into the fog of architecture. In: Bille, M. and Sørensen, T. F. eds. *Elements of Architecture: Assembling Archaeology, Atmosphere and the Performance of Building Spaces.* London and New York: Routledge, 1–29.

Chatterjee, A., 2009. Tectonic into textile: John Ruskin and his obsession with the architectural surface. *Textile,* 7(1), 68–97.

Chatterjee, A., 2017. Between colour and pattern: Ruskin's ambivalent theory of constructional polychromy. *Interstices: Journal of Architecture and Related Arts,* 18, 11–18.

DeSilvey, C., 2006. Observed decay: Telling stories with mutable things. *Journal of Material Culture,* 11(3), 318–38.

Dolphijn, R., van der Tuin, I. and Foundation, O., 2012. *New Materialism: Interviews & Cartographies.* Ann Arbor: Open Humanities Press.

Farstadvoll, S., 2019. *A Speculative Archaeology of Excess: Exploring the Afterlife of a Derelict Landscape Garden.* Tromsø: UiT – The Arctic University of Norway, Ph.D dissertation.

Farstadvoll, S., 2020, forthcoming. Mold, weeds and plastic lanterns: Ecological aftermath in a derelict garden. In: Pétursdóttir, Þ. and Bangstad, T. R. eds. *Heritage Ecologies.* London & New York: Routledge.

Gerhardsen, E., 1946. Innsats. *Bonytt,* 6, 1.

González-Ruibal, A., 2005. The need for a decaying past: An archaeology of oblivion in contemporary Galicia (NW Spain). *Home Cultures,* 2(2), 129–52.

Gumbrecht, H. U., 2004. *Production of Presence: What Meaning Cannot Convey.* Stanford: Stanford University Press.

Hage, I., 1999. *Som fugl føniks av asken? Gjenreisingshus i Nord-Troms og Finnmark.* Oslo: Ad notam Gyldendal.

Harrison, R., 2011. Surface assemblages. Towards an archaeology in and of the present. *Archaeological Dialogues,* 18(02), 141–61.

Ingold, T., 2012. Toward an ecology of materials. *Annual Review of Anthropology,* 41(1), 427–42.

Ingold, T., 2017. Surface visions. *Theory, Culture & Society,* 34(7–8), 99–108.

Jameson, F., 1984. Postmodernism, or the cultural logic of late capitalism. *New Left Review,* (146), 53–92.

Jones, S. and Yarrow, T., 2013. Crafting authenticity: An ethnography of conservation practice. *Journal of Material Culture,* 18(1), 3–26.

Joy, E. A., 2013. Blue. In: Cohen, J. J. ed. *Prismatic Ecology: Ecotheory beyond Green.* Minneapolis & London: University of Minnesota Press, 213–32.

Krigsskadetrygdens gjenreisningsnemd 1940. Regler for gjenoppbygging etter krigsskade med støtte av Krigsskadetrygden. *Byggekunst,* 22, 18–19.

Krokann, I., 1982. *Det store hamskiftet i bondesamfunnet.* Oslo: Samlaget.

Lambourne, R., 1999. Paint composition and applications: A general introduction. In: Lambourne, R. and Strivens, T. A. eds. *Paint and Surface Coatings: Theory and Practice.* Cambridge: Woodhead Publishing, 1–18.

Maleuvre, D., 1999. *Museum Memories: History, Technology, Art.* Stanford: Stanford University Press.

Mol, A., 2003. *The Body Multiple: Ontology in Medical Practice.* Durham: Duke University Press.

Olsen, B., 2010. In Defence of Things: Archaeology and the Ontology of Objects. Alta Mira Press: Lanham.

Rigney, A., 2015. Things and the archive: Scott's materialist legacy. *Scottish Literary Review,* 7(2), 13–34.

Rigney, A., 2017. Materiality and memory: Objects to ecologies. A response to Maria Zirra. *Parallax,* 23(4), 474–8.

Roede, L., 2010. Autentisitet i friluftsmuseene. In: Rogan, B. and Amundsen, A. B. eds. *Samling og museum: Kapitler av museenes historie, praksis og ideologi.* Oslo: Novus Forlag, 167–85.

Sandvig, A., 1943. *I praksis og på samlerferd.* Oslo: Johan Grundt Tanum.

Sedgwick, E. K., 1997. Paranoid reading and reparative reading; or, you're so paranoid, you probably think this introduction is about you. In: Sedgwick, E. K. ed. *Novel Gazing: Queer Readings in Fiction.* Durham: Duke University Press, 1–37.

Shetelig, H., 1944. *Norsk museers historie: festskrift til Thor B. Kielland på 50-årsdagen 9.12.1944.* Oslo: J.W Cappelens Forlag.

Sjökvist, T. and Blom, Å., 2019. The influence of coating color, heartwood and sapwood, on moisture content and growth of microorganisms on the surface during outdoor exposure of Norway spruce boards. *Journal of Coatings Technology and Research,* 16(3), 819–26.

Spuybroek, L., 2010 The Matter of Ornament. In: Brouwer, J., Mulder. A. and Spuybroek, L. eds. *The Politics of the Impure.* Rotterdam: V2_Publishing, 233–267.

Spuybroek, L., 2011. *The Sympathy of Things: Ruskin and the Ecology of Design.* Rotterdam: V2_Publishing.

Sundt, E., 1862. *Om Bygnings-Skikken paa Landet i Norge.* Christiania: P.T. Mallings Bogtrykkeri.

Sørensen, T. F., 2016. I tidens fylde – samtidslevn og arkæologiske de/formationsprocesser. *Arkæologisk Forum,* 35, 23–30.

Sørensen, T. F., 2020, forthcoming. A gentle shock of mild surprise: Surface ecologies and the archaeological encounter. In: Pétursdóttir, Þ. and Bangstad, T. R. eds. *Heritage Ecologies.* London & New York: Routledge.

Trilling, L., 1973. *Sincerity and Authenticity: The Charles Eliot Norton Lectures, 1969–1970.* Cambridge.

Tsoi, G., 2011. Paint drying: A stressful process. *Yale Scientific,* February 13, 2011. Url: www.yalescientific.org/2011/02/paint-drying-a-stressful-process/

Witmore, C., 2014. Archaeology and the new materialisms. *Journal of Contemporary Archaeology,* 1(2), 203–46.

PART II
Affects: Sensing things

Mats Burström

'Affect,' writes Katleen Stewart,

> is the commonplace, labor-intensive process of sensing modes of living as they come into being. It hums with the background noise of obstinacies and promises, ruts and disorientations, intensities and resting points. It stretches across real and imaginary social fields and sediments, linking some kind of everything.
>
> *(Stewart 2010, p. 340)*

Stewart's words remind us how we constantly are surrounded by things and how their presence involuntary and ineffably affect us and the way we comprehend and sense the world. We encounter things with all our senses and this bodily experience is profoundly different from reading about them or otherwise experiencing them in a mediated way. Some of the sensations may of course be transmitted through text or images but something is inevitably lost in translation. A main objective of this section, thus, is to explore ways to include, account for, and disseminate the ineffable, immediate and corporal experiences involved in our encounters with things. An unescapable dilemma, of course, is that we have few other means for scholarly articulations than words and pictures. Still, by attending to and addressing the affects that usually are emitted from scholarly writing and discourse we hope to allow for a nearing of what may be termed an archaeological sensibility.

A central aspect of an archaeological sensibility is to acknowledge the significance of the vastly underrated field method of *being present* at a site and being exposed to its rich portfolio of material impacts. In other words, to the wealth of sensory experiences that shape one's overall understanding of the place. Despite their great influence and felt importance at the very moment of encounter, experiences of this kind are often marginalized as an ornamental excess or considered too subjective to become part of our archaeological writing. To include them is, however, the only way to account for the crucial phenomenological dimension of fieldwork which otherwise far too often is lost in translation. Another important current that runs through all the contributions to this section is the intricate interplay between knowledge and feeling, between making sense of and sensing. On one hand, knowledge of what a specific thing actually is, and its history, may generate feelings that affect you. On the other hand, you may be affected by a thing and its aura, and because of this want to know more about it. So, while knowledge is a self-evident part of scholarly writing and discourse, there is every reason to make room also for emotions and wonders and reveal their intimate relation to knowledge.

The chapters in this section report on down-to-earth experiences of how things evoke thoughts, feelings and memories. And in each their own way the cases also shed light on fieldwork as a sensory experience and a prerequisite for a deeper understanding of a site or a place. In his personal and thought-provoking chapter, 'The view from somewhere: Liquid, geologic, and queer bodies', Denis Byrne presents fieldwork carried out on a harbourside reclamation at Elizabeth Bay in Sydney, Australia. Following the rhythms of water Byrne proceeded along the non-linear trajectories of time and space that led him into the water that the reclamation reverberated into and into the sandstone seawall which the harbour waters helped erode. He followed the queer bodies that cruised the reclamation park in the 1970s and 80s and, in his pursuit of a deeper understanding of the enfoldment of sandstone and colonial history, he moved some kilometres away to examine the eroding walls of a colonial gaol. Following Haraway's critique of the 'god-trick of seeing everything from nowhere', he further insists on the situatedness of fieldwork as an embodied practice.

My own contribution, 'Stranded stones and settled species: Affect and effects of ballast', shows how the encounter with an unexpected archaeological find – a hand-axe of European origin found in Australia where it had been shipped in as ballast – may evoke an interest that sparks an explorative journey leading far away from the initial find. My newfound interest for ballast traffic in the past and the various marks it has left in the world brought me to places I otherwise never would have visited. These on-site experiences inspired not just a deeper understanding of the ballast phenomenon itself, but also gave rise to fundamental questions about what things are, how they become of archaeological concern and what is indeed their proper place.

In his chapter 'Out of the day, time and life: Phenomenology and cavescapes', Hein B. Bjerck leads readers into the dark underworld of North Norwegian caves featuring red ochre paintings. The cave paintings were probably made during a short period within the Bronze Age but as made explicit through Bjerck's prose there is something imperative in the way the caves shape our experience of them and how they affect us, seemingly irrespective of time and space. The familiar human world of life, light, motion, colours, sounds and odours are absent and most caves lack definite ends; they merely restrict the reach of human bodies, and nourish a notion of caves as corridors to realms beyond. All caves seem to lead to the same – a world out of the day, time, and life.

A video showing militants methodically smashing and shooting at selected sculptures in the desert city of Hatra in north-west Iraq in 2015 is the starting point for Saphinaz-Amal Naguib's remembering process and discussion in the chapter 'Ruins of ruins: The aura of archaeological remains'. The video triggers a flashback of a visit to the site many years earlier, the impression it made, and the interest it evoked for the history of the city. Unfortunately Hatra is just one of many examples of new ruins being made out of existing ruins that have been there for centuries. Naguib examines Hatra through the lenses of sensorial assemblages, and draws upon the notions of aura, presence and resonance to probe the affective power of ruins and archaeological fragments.

In the final chapter in this section, 'What remains? On material nostalgia', Alfredo González-Ruibal reappraises the concept of nostalgia, which for long has been the object of systematic criticism for its association with reactionary ideologies, essentialism, and misrepresentations of history. González-Ruibal argues, however, that nostalgia is a powerful feeling that enables different, critical engagements with the past and its remnants, which also can be forward-looking and utopian. His own longing for a preindustrial materiality was born through his interaction and bodily experience with the vanishing material culture of peasant Galicia. In this chapter González-Ruibal first revises critiques of nostalgia, then explores the problematic relationship between nostalgia and language, to subsequently propose material nostalgia as a sound alternative for an archaeology constructively exposed to its affective qualities.

Reference

Stewart, K., 2010. Afterword: Worlding refrains. In: M. Gregg and G.J. Seigworth, eds., *The Affect Theory Reader*. Durham: Duke University Press.

7

THE VIEW FROM SOMEWHERE

Liquid, geologic, and queer bodies

Denis Byrne

At numerous points along the world's coastlines, humans have extended their terrestrial habitat out into the sea in the form of coastal reclamations. These are formed by the deposition in the inter-tidal zone of dredged sediment, urban waste and quarried rock, among other materials, to form new platforms for human living. The 're' in the word 'reclamation' implies prior ownership and in itself is an eloquent enough statement of humanity's totalizing claim over planetary space.

While the reclaiming of littoral space, principally for agriculture, has occurred at numerous locations in Asia and Europe from around 1,000 years ago, over the last two to three centuries there has been a marked acceleration in the extent of coastline under reclamation. Vast areas of new land have been created for port facilities, industrial plants, urban residential expansion and tourism facilities. Simultaneously both an expression and a trace of the global predicament known as the Anthropocene, they form part of industrial capitalism's 'second nature' (Bonneuil and Fressoz 2016, p. 22). It is in this respect that for the last few years I have been studying coastal reclamations in the Asia-Australia region, approaching them both as archaeological objects and as Anthropocene heritage sites (Byrne 2017a, 2018). This inquiry has propelled me to the edge of the sea, to that geometric edge or striation which the reclamation imposes on the coastline. But I should also say that since I was a child I have been drawn to the sea's edge wherever it can be found. In what follow, I try to avoid distinguishing too much between this personal desire for the 'waterfront' as an affective environment and the intellectual curiosity that propels me into the same space. My concern is with giving an account of fieldwork as an embodied experience.

I am interested in the trajectories through nonlinear time and space that fieldwork on coastal reclamation entails. The first part of the chapter is set on the small late-nineteenth century reclamation at Elizabeth Bay on Sydney Harbour. Initially, I understood this reclamation as a purely terrestrial object, but as I became conscious of the ways in which it reverberated out into the sea I came to see it as a watery as well as a terrestrial thing. At the same time I was drawn into the sandstone material of the reclamation's seawall – into, for example, the varying temporalities of its Triassic formation and its present-day erosion. Any consideration of sandstone as an element of Sydney's urban infrastructure is liable to lead one into the history of the stone's enrolment in the British colonial project and this, in my case, took me from the seawall to the sandstone perimeter wall of the old Darlinghurst gaol, located more than a kilometre inland. In moving across this space, the chapter navigates a queer logic between those gay men who in the 1970s and 80s hijacked the park on the Elizabeth Bay reclamation for the purposes of cruising and those less unfortunate men who, convicted in the nineteenth century of the crime of sodomy, found themselves imprisoned with the sandstone walls of Darlinghurst gaol.

My archaeological inquiry may appear to side-track into a fascination with queer flesh and its geologic enfoldment but I maintain that an archaeological sensibility given sufficient license will naturally tend to corrupt the conventional objective framing of fieldwork. In fieldwork, as we follow the material and encounter its 'unruliness' (Olsen 2013; Olsen and Pétursdóttir 2016) we simultaneously engage the unruliness of our own inquisitiveness and the free play of our embodied propensities. We may, and usually do, attempt the kind of moral recovery in which the fieldwork experience is translated into scholarly discourse, but in responding to the challenge that *After Discourse* throws out I suggest that this translation should itself be brought under attack.

Liquid reverberation

At Elizabeth Bay, located on the south side of Sydney Harbour, the edge of the 1880s reclamation is never more than 40 metres out from the former waterline. The sea is hence a real and constant presence for anyone who happens to be in the small park that occupies the space of the reclamation. Only a quarter of a hectare in size, the reclamation was created by building a curved sandstone seawall across the intertidal zone of a minor embayment and then infilling the space behind it with urban waste material and dredged sediment.

Late in the afternoon of one of the first warm days of September 2015 I stood at the waist-high seawall at Elizabeth Bay. Rain had been falling intermittently out of a low grey sky for most of the day and the few other people in the park stood under umbrellas watching their dogs run across the sodden lawn. I imagined the reclamation to be saturated all the way down from the lawn's muddy surface to the relict beach stratified several meters below. Water seeped through the gaps between the sandstone blocks of the seawall and dribbled down the rock of the wall's seaward face. The wall seemed like a dam holding back the pond-like reclamation from the somewhat lower pond of the harbor. In the bay, small incoming waves were layered over a gentle swell, that rhythmic heaving of the harbor's body that could seem like the breathing of a great beast at rest (Figure 7.1).

FIGURE 7.1 Elizabeth Bay at high tide, dusk, May 2019. Photo: Denis Byrne

Compared to other liquids, water has great surface tension, a product of the peculiar propensity of its molecules to stick to each other, meaning the surface of the harbor is readily deformed by the agency of wind and rain. On that wet afternoon in September the raindrops falling into the bay were spaced far enough apart for me to see individual rings radiating out from where they struck the water's surface. Rings radiating out from adjacent raindrop impact-points ran into each other, creating complicated patterns of collision, continuance and reverberation. You could follow a single raindrop ring as it moved across the surface of the water and still be aware of the others around it, even though there were other patterns of movement subtending them, including the large, slow movement of the harbor swell, the ripples generated by the breeze and the other ripples running back from where small waves broke on the wall. Rallying my attention, I could momentarily encompass all the moving parts of this pattern, but the slightest distraction was enough for that intricacy to vanish. I glance sideways at a dog chasing down a ball on the lawn behind me and when I look back the pattern is gone and there is only the harbor, that more abstract marine entity barely tangible in its given-ness.

That 2015 experience recalled to mind a summer day 25 years earlier when I sat on the same seawall gazing at the sea and a moment came when the water, with all its surface mobility, seemed simultaneously to be inside me and out there in the bay. This fleeting experience, which occurred several times later, might be covered by Mathew Gandy's (2012, p. 733) term 'ecological rapture' but Maurice Merleau-Ponty's (1968) account of visuality and what he refers to as 'the chiasm' comes closer. For Merleau-Ponty, we are joined to the world in a mutually inclusive relation of folding: simultaneously touched by the world as we touch it, we look out upon it both as the seer and a participant in what we see. It may seem odd that this should occur on a reclamation, but it supports Jane Bennett's (2001) point that enchantment is as possible in manufactured settings as in those that are pristine. The fragility of reclamations, their contingency, lies in the illusion we harbor that we can wring the sea out of the land altogether and produce something purely and permanently terrestrial. From that perspective, it seems entirely unsurprising that it would be there, at the edge of a reclamation, that the sea came flooding into me.

The reclamation in the sea

Over the last few decades I have never lived more than walking distance from Elizabeth Bay and this has allowed the experience of fieldwork there to be an ongoing process of incremental discovery. In visits to the reclamation in late March 2019, early autumn in Sydney, I became attentive to those patterns of ripples created as incoming waves hit the seawall. Waves formed by the wind's energy enter the bay directly but their energy (transferred from the wind) dissipates as they approach the wall, partly because of the gradient of the floor of the bay, so they are often only several centimetres high when they hit it. One afternoon in particular, with a breeze blowing out of the northeast, I leaned over the top of the wall to watch the 'reflection ripples' bouncing back from the wall as incoming waves made contact. As they moved outward, these ripples interfered with new incoming waves, creating a complex pattern on the water's surface. Larger waves, created by a motorboat passing across the mouth of the bay, arrived at the wall in a formation that underlay both the wind-generated waves and their reflection ripples. As if things weren't already complicated enough, these boat waves hit the wall and reflected back into the pattern already there. Meanwhile, the same warm breeze that was creating waves on the harbour's surface was blowing on my surface, my skin, as if to underline the impossibility that I could ever be a disembodied observer here. Would the wind on my face create ripples that would alter the pattern of native creases that would materialize, for instance, if I smiled? Naturally, this thought, triggered by the wind and waves, made me smile.

I find Deleuze and Guattari's (1987, pp. 474–500) discussion of the two kinds of space they term the smooth and the striated a stimulating background for thinking about reclamations. In *One Thousand Plateaus* they describe the sea as 'smooth space par excellence' (Deleuze and Guattari 1987, p. 479). The Elizabeth Bay reclamation, on the other hand, can be thought of as a striation produced by the state's commodification of land and by the technology of reclamation. Smooth space is amorphous whereas striated space is geometric. The smooth and the striated correspond to other distinctions Deleuze and Guattari make between the nomadic and the sedentary and between felt and woven fabric. In the smooth, 'one distributes oneself in an open space', as in an itinerate lifestyle, whereas 'in striated space, one closes off a surface and "allocates" it according to determinate intervals, assigned breaks' (Deleuze and Guattari's 1987, p. 481). In colonial Australia indigenous land was surveyed and quickly became a tradeable commodity, creating a body of capital to underpin and fuel the colonial economy, lending impetus to the subdivision of many of the early land grants around Sydney, including that which had covered the slopes around the edges of Elizabeth Bay. Those who bought subdivided blocks of land around the shoreline were permitted to reclaim out to the low-water line and by the 1880s all had done so, space for the adjacent park being reclaimed at about the same time. The seawall marks the edge of this seaward expansion.

The smooth and the striated might seems like a binary pair but this would be to miss the way they are theorized as occurring in mixed and folded form, as in the situation of smooth maritime space which, in Deleuze and Guattari's argument (1987, p. 479), was from 1440 striated by the navigational and marine mapping technology of the Portuguese. At Elizabeth Bay, the 'smooth' space of the harbour water is striated by the interruption of the reclamation's seawall as well as by the reflection ripples moving outward from the wall. If the reclamation and its bounding seawall weren't there, the incoming waves would continue on until they ran up the former beach. The reclamation forecloses on this.

Sitting high and dry on the seawall, I might seem to be perched at the boundary of my species' natural habitat, the land. But humans are adept at operating and living out beyond the waterline, fishing from and trading with boats, for example, or living in stilt houses over the sea. At Elizabeth Bay, the yachts and motor boats moored just offshore provide mobile platforms (or decks) on which people can move about and act much as they do on land. I watch them doing this from where I sit. These platforms, or decks, endeavour to reproduce the surfaces we are used to on dry land. They are not land as such, but then neither can I any longer think of the reclamation as bona fide terra firma. Boats blur the land-sea boundary the way the pontoon connected to the end of the Elizabeth Bay boathouse does. The instant I set foot on the pontoon the liquid mobility of the sea's surface, which a moment ago I had been observing from the land, extends into my body. Caught off-guard by the pontoon's multi-dimensional tilting, my legs, torso and arms make rapid and minutely coordinated movements as they hurry to stabilize a body, too long accustomed to terra firma, on this surface where the terrestrial and the marine overlap.

Another seaward projection of the land takes the form of the reflections which you see when looking landward across the sea's surface. If, for example, I stand at the seawall at the eastern end of the bay's crescent and look back across the water to where Ithaca Road descends the slope and ends at the reclamation park I see the reflection on the water of the apartment buildings which were mostly erected in the first half of the twentieth century and cluster on the bay's sloping amphitheater. If the surface of the bay were perfectly still (which it never is) then I might see an actual image of these buildings. Instead, the agitated, rippled surface of the bay shatters the buildings into many hundreds of gyrating fragments of colour. In this way, and in the eye of the beholder, the things of the land spill out into the sea and the idea of a hard land-sea binary is further undermined. The broadcasting of the buildings over the water – I imagine a hand releasing particles of them over the bay with the sweeping motion of a sower of grain – reminds me not to put quite so much faith in the stability and dependability of these objects. When caught in the sunlight, the seawall also extends itself as an optical reflection, reminding me not to slip into thinking of the reclamation itself as too stationary an object.

We might turn from the land's extension into the sea to consider the sea's presence onshore. There is, for example, a real sense in which we, who are mostly habitual land dwellers, are a projection of marine space onto terrestrial space. Drawing on Rachel Carson's (1950) *The Sea Around Us* and alluding to our evolutionary history as sea-dwellers, a history that is inscribed in our biology, Stacy Alaimo notes that 'the sea surges through the bodies of all terrestrial animals, including humans – in our blood, skeletons, and cellular structure' (Alaimo 2012, p. 482). Carson had observed that, in our blood, 'the elements of sodium, potassium, and calcium are combined in almost the same proportions as in sea water' (Carson 1950, p. 14). In her 1955 book, *The Edge of the Sea*, Carson, with her unique blend of poetry and science, describes a number of 'pioneering' marine species which are at various points along the transition to terrestrial life. Some of them, like barnacles and sea snails, occupy the intertidal zone where they are alternately covered by sea and exposed to air; for others, including some periwinkles, their only contact with the sea is in the form of the spray of breaking waves (Carson 1998, pp. 50–1). The coastal reclamations which we build at an increasing pace in regions like East and Southeast Asia might seem a kind of seaward migration, evincing a primal nostalgia for the sea, but for the most part they are simply representative of capitalist material accumulation. Curiously, the concrete tetrapods which defend the edge of many coastal reclamations against the sea derive their name from the first four-legged creatures who transitioned from the sea to the land around 390 million years ago (Figure 7.2).

Carson (1998, p. 136) writes of a beach on one of the sea islands of Georgia in the United States where the retreating tide leaves behind ripple marks in the sand that 'look like a miniature model of the sea's waves'. As sea water left by the high tide drains back down this gently sloping beach it creates 'winding gullies' that 'wander across it like creeks across the land' (Carson 1998, p. 136). Reading this passage provokes me to wonder whether, when the sea drained off the runways of Kansai Airport (built on a reclaimed island in Osaka Bay) after the airport was inundated by Typhoon Jebi in September 2018, it left similar markings in the layers of sand left behind.[1] The Typhoon Jebi event points to the nature of the reclamation's relationship with the sea as one of overlap rather than dichotomy. A land-sea overlap of a different kind was encountered by Þóra Pétursdóttir (2017, 2018) on a drift beach in northern Norway where, in the course of a study of stranded matter (including driftwood, plastic bottles and shoe soles, synthetic rope and net floats) she found fossilized ridges of drift matter onshore: 'Walking this plane of temporal ridges folded against each other, rising and falling simultaneously, like waves in water,

FIGURE 7.2 Concrete tetrapods at the edge of a reclamation on Jakarta Bay, 2017. Photo: Denis Byrne

generates a different notion of time and event' (Pétursdóttir 2018, p. 90). In the next few pages I turn to the way the Elizabeth Bay, which at first sight appears to draw a hard line between land and sea, is itself a zone of interpenetration.

The folding of the seawall

When the tide goes out at Elizabeth Bay a slither of beach is exposed below a section of the seawall, a remnant and a reminder of the beach that vanished with the creation of the reclamation. A set of concrete stairs next to the boathouse makes the remnant beach accessible and from there at low tide it is possible to make a close inspection of the outer surface of the wall. The sandstone blocks of the wall that are positioned in the splash zone and above it are revealed to be eroding at a surprising rate – you only need to reach out and brush their surface with your fingers to see a sprinkling of sand grains fall. The Hawkesbury Sandstone that was quarried for the wall is a sedimentary rock formed during the Triassic Period between 200 and 400 million years ago. Sand washed down a river system from far inland was deposited to form a floodplain in the present-day Sydney region and over millions of years the sand compacted to form the Hawkesbury Sandstone that is Sydney's bedrock. Although it has great compressive strength, the stone erodes relatively quickly in a process of disaggregation in which the clays and other minerals that bind together the silica grains (sand) in the stone dissolve, leaving the affected grains to fall away (Swan 2011). At Elizabeth Bay, as the sandstone blocks of the seawall erode they drop quartz grains onto the beach which itself, like all Sydney beaches, is composed of sandstone-derived quartz grains.

In eroding, the sandstone blocks of the seawall lose mass and allow the sea to advance inland a millimetre at a time. If we concede that the waves hitting the wall 'intend' not to end there but to run up the sandy surface of the former beach, just as they did in the days before the wall was built, then it follows that the eroding wall is responding to the sea's intentions as much as it is to our intention that it keep the sea out of the reclamation. The Elizabeth Bay reclamation is a cultural artefact in the creation of which sandstone blocks were enlisted to keep the sea 'at bay'. But the word 'enlisted' should not be understood to mean its geologic agency has been subsumed by human agency. Stone, as Jeffrey Jerome Cohen (2015, p. 4) observes, can be a 'collaborative force' but it can equally be 'bluntly impedimental'. Its collaboration can, of course, be with agents other than ourselves (with the sea, for example), or simultaneously with ourselves and such others (therein assuming the guise of that most anxiety-inducing entity, the double agent). The sandstone blocks of the seawall, upon which incoming waves and ripples break, are deployed by us against the harbour's water – they are *positioned* as antithetical to it – but we know that the sandstone is no stranger to water. It was formed in the medium of water, water flows through it geologically. Ripple marks that are visible in the sandstone today are an embodiment of water currents flowing through the freshwater delta in which the sediments making up the stone were deposited.

Nor should we understand the present form of the seawall to be anything but temporary, even momentary. In the process of eroding, the sandstone blocks slough off the rectangular dressing given to them by the nineteenth-century quarrymen

FIGURE 7.3 Eroded sandstone blocks in the seawall at Elizabeth Bay, 2015. Photo: Denis Byrne

and take on the sinuous shapes congenial to their matter and to their character-istic mode of decay. The folded surface of the eroding sandstone of the seawall is a reflection of the stone's history of sedimentation, re-enacting the way sediments settled into a pattern of ripples on the bottom of the lake that occupied the space of the Sydney region in the Triassic. The time of the lake bed loops up into the present and undoes the rectilinear, striated shape given to the stone in recent time. The curvaceous form of the eroding stone (Figure 7.3) suggests the metaphor of the fold in Merleau-Ponty's (1968) phenomenology and, inspired by mathematical topology, Deleuze's (1993) examination of folded matter in Leibniz, the Baroque and the world at large. In 1969 the landscape artists Christo and Jeanne-Claude wrapped the sandstone cliffs along a 2.4 kilometre stretch of Sydney's coastline using woven synthetic fabric and rope.[2] There, the folds of fabric simultaneously covered and revealed the stone's form in a manner similar to the way fabric draped over the human body in Baroque art reveals the body in the act of hiding it (the fabric, for example, takes on the curves of a shoulder or thigh).

The sandstone's erosion prompts me to reflect upon my own temporality, the processes of decay acting on and in me, and upon my geosubjectivity (Byrne 2018). Kathryn Yusoff (2016, p. 22) writes that, 'as human history gives way to geologic horizons, the matter of human subjectivity must change and reach beyond life and the organism to think its way through the stratified layers of the earth's formation. It must abandon its anthropogenesis – in order, ironically, that it can say something about how to live beyond the material erasure of the Holocene'. Yusoff's writing, washing up on the shores of Australia as I was immersed in fieldwork at Elizabeth Bay, changed the way I thought about sandstone and the materiality of the reclam-ation more generally.

The numerous visits I have made to the Elizabeth Bay reclamation, spaced out over years and decades, form a series that connects me to the time of the reclamation's creation in the 1880s and, further back, the time of the sandstone's formation. In fieldwork, the events of this series are, however, experienced not in terms of linear continuity but as the kind of temporal folding that Michel Serres (1997) depicts in his account of folded time. For Serres (1997, p. 60), events from different eras bend toward each other, becoming adjacent or coexistent and evoking the figure of a 'crumpled handkerchief'. In Steven Connor's (2004) words, this gives us an image 'not of time moving on and dissipating, but of endlessly regathering itself', words that evoke for me the harbour waves that regather themselves to break just behind me where I stand on the remnant beach. The history of the reclamation is a matter of rhythms and repetitions rather than linear progression. Included here are the rhythmic movements of the waterline in response to diurnal and monthly tide cycles, the spring and neap tide cycle, and the much more stretched-out rhythm of the glacial and interglacial cycle of the Quaternary Period we were born into, a rhythm that has its origin principally in the Earth's orbital eccentricity.

If the sea surges in the bodies of all terrestrial creatures it also surges in the reclamation. Many coastal reclamations were won from the sea in a time, the late Holocene, when sea level had long been stable. Others date from the Anthropocene, with its current reality of rising seas and its promise of more to come. This surge is prefigured in the extra metre of concrete added to seawalls in parts of Japan (Byrne 2017b) and in the spectre of additional tiers of sandstone blocks that at some point will need to be added to the top of the wall at Elizabeth Bay. I turn now from surging to cruising, both of which are resonant with the marine and the smooth.

The queer reclamation

During the 1970s and 80s the park at Elizabeth Bay became a well-known gay cruising site. Kane Race (2017, p. 153) describes how certain parks, streets and washrooms provided the only spaces where in the early twentieth century it was possible for many gay men to have sexual liaisons, but also how they were actively favoured by men who were seeking anonymity and no-strings convenience in their sexual encounters (at least at certain times), thus lending these spaces a similarity with such elements of the infrastructure of gay life as saunas and sex clubs. But I think we need to be wary of seeing such spaces as simply containers for practices of pleasure.

Mathew Gandy's (2012) essay on gay cruising in a North London cemetery dwells on the relationality between the act of cruising and the environment in which it takes place.

> If cruising is understood as a complex interplay between bodies and space then a queer reading of space reveals a distributed agency of desire that extends beyond individuals or even multiple human bodies to incorporate nonhuman nature, inanimate objects, surfaces and smells.
>
> *(Gandy 2012, p. 738)*

At Elizabeth Bay I propose that it extended to include the seawall as an agentic entity that not only projects its affects and substance seawards but also landward to engage the bodies of those who lean against it, sit on it, or, to invoke a watery metaphor, cruise along it. Gandy (2012, p. 733) also draws our attention to the way that the *time* of public sex tends very much to be the time of the here and now: 'The sense of stilled time experienced through encounters with gardens, cemeteries, or nature itself links with modes of sensory experience that heighten not only the experience of the present but also an existential awareness of human finitude'.

Back in the 1970s and 80s, the Elizabeth Bay park's promise of 'ecological rapture' (Gandy 2012, p. 733) put it on the gay map of Sydney, a map which existed not on paper (as far as I can recall) but in the minds of many gay men. In a similar way, the park was inscribed on the mental maps kept by dog walkers, sunbathers and picnickers, interest groups whose membership was not mutually exclusive. But the cruising map had an underground quality peculiar to it and was necessitated partly because gay sex was illegal in New South Wales until 1984 (Wotherspoon 2016). To say the park had never been intended for gay cruising by the reclamation's creators is to underplay the social and institutional sanctions that existed against this activity, an activity that fits what the French Situationalists of the 1960s called *détournement*, meaning an appropriation of 'the elements or terrain of the dominant social order to one's own end, for a transformed purpose' (Ross 1987, p. 116). It also clearly fits within the concept of 'poaching' developed by Michel de Certeau (1984) to refer to the way everyday practices such as reading and walking can inscribe new meaning in texts and spaces. The cruiser might be compared to the readers whom de Certeau (1984, p. 174) describes as 'travellers': they move across lands belonging to someone else, like 'nomads poaching their way across fields they did not write, despoiling the wealth of Egypt to enjoy it themselves'. Is there, I wonder, a sense in which archaeological fieldwork is a form of poaching? Presumably that would depend on whose interests it serves and on its openness to the affectivity of its setting.

Geologic propensities and prisoners of love

Having been drawn to – perhaps I should say drawn *into* – the sandstone of the seawall, I soon I found I was looking differently at sandstone encountered further afield, including the sandstone curb stones and retaining walls, the sandstone court houses, hospitals terrace houses, stairways and steeples that populate the square kilometres of terrain which I roam in the course of everyday life. My awareness of the stone's sedimentary history, its potentialities and affordances, spilled out from Elizabeth Bay across this larger area and it was in this context that I found myself confronting the boundary wall of the old Darlinghurst gaol (Figure 7.4).

A number of penitentiary structures had been erected in Sydney during the colonial era, which begins with the arrival of the British 'first fleet' in 1788 and ends with Australia's 1901 Act of Federation. One of the many tasks colonial-era convicts in Sydney were forced to labour on was the quarrying of sandstone to produce building blocks such as those used in the construction of the perimeter wall of the 1819 Hyde Park Barracks in what is today the city's CBD.[3] The construction of the Darlinghurst gaol began in 1822, its sandstone perimeter wall was erected first, using convict labour. Internal buildings, including cell blocks and a hospital ward, were then erected by professional stonemasons aided by those prisoners in the gaol convicted to 'hard labour'.[4] Only those convicted of crimes within the colony were incarcerated in the gaol.

There is a systemic continuity between the British cadastral grid of property boundaries, which spread outward in the first decades of the nineteenth century from the early settlement at Sydney Cove, and a place like Darlinghurst Gaol which was designed for confinement within one of the grid's rectangles. The rapid spread of the cadastral grid represents a form of spatial liberty enabled by the wholesale dispossession of Aboriginal people of their land. The gaol represents the opposite, a carceral regime of strict confinement. Like the sandstone of the seawall, the stone blocks for the prison walls were cut from quarries just a few kilometres away from where they would be used. To again invoke Deleuze and Guattari's (1987) concept of smooth/striated space, the living bedrock of the city represents a spatial

FIGURE 7.4 The perimeter wall of the old Darlinghurst Gaol, 2019. Photo: Denis Byrne

smoothness striated by the quarryman's pegs and saws, instruments which effectively project a rectangular grid down into the bedrock, anticipating the rectangular blocks that will come out of it. To refer to the bedrock as smooth is not to imply that it lacks internal organization – its framework grains and mineral cement form regular patterns and it possesses a complexity of bedding layers. In Arun Saldanha's words (2017, p. 109), 'smooth space is definitely organized but in a dynamic non-Euclidian way, based on its physicality and not on flat formal coordinates imposed on it from outside'. Once quarried and 'finished' into rectangular blocks, the sandstone was then rearranged into the stacked formation of the prison wall. The rearrangement is evident in the way the internal bedding lines in one block will be out of alignment with those of its neighbor. It is evident also in the variation in the colouring of adjacent blocks and in the propensity of one block to erode more rapidly than its neighbor.

Those incarcerated within the sandstone walls of the Darlinghurst included men convicted of sodomy or attempted sodomy, for which, in the late 1900s, typical sentences were two years with hard labour, although death sentences for sodomy were also not uncommon in New South Wales prior to the twentieth century.[5]

Ironically and fittingly, the gaol is now located in the epicentre of gay Sydney (Faro and Wotherspoon 2000). In 1921, the gaol was repurposed as a technical college, subsequently becoming an art school with the cells serving as studios for individual students.

At the very moment in the 1970s when the gaol was scheduled as a heritage object for its convict past, the outside of its boundary wall on Darlinghurst Road was being informally repurposed as a gay cruising strip, a kind of erotically charged queer promenade. The sandstone blocks of the wall, quarried and shaped by convict hands to imprison themselves with, now radiated heat stored from the afternoon sun into the bodies of those leaning against it in the cool of the evening. The same wall that had earlier imprisoned recalcitrant queers and others now, for those cruising it's outside perimeter, had become a 'line of flight' (*ligne de fuite*) for the liberated (Deleuze and Guattari 1987, p. 3).

Stone can be shaped to fit human purposes but it cannot be *encompassed* by human projects, however seduced we may be by the drama of our marshalling of the geologic – of coal and iron ore, for example – for human purposes. According to Jeffrey Jerome Cohen (2015, p. 11), 'The lithic has for too long served as an allegory for nature stilled into resource'. The sandstone can be enlisted but never stilled.

Bjørnar J. Olsen calls for a 'recognition of things in their thingly difference' (2013, p. 293) and their 'wildness' (2013, p. 295). The term 'dressed stone', stone that has been shaped and surfaced, harbours the implication of undressed stone, of stone going its own way in the act of erosion. It also carries erotic intimations, suggesting to me the soon-to-be-undressed state of the bodies leaning against the gaol wall in the 1970s and 80s. The two converge in the thought that grains of sand will inevitably have stuck to the skin and clothes of those leaning, desiring bodies (such is the friability of the sandstone's surface). We are conscious of the way heritage, as a discourse and practice, dresses things up to convey particular messages – heritage in this sense is a form of drag – but we are equally alert to the ways heritage objects, in their wildness, wriggle out of these raiments, scattering them on the bedroom floor of the public sphere of heritage's enactment, just as the clothes of those wall-cruisers will soon drop to a bedroom floor somewhere, along with the sand grains picked up from the wall.

Fieldwork: The view of somewhere

One of the ways sexuality can be understood, according to Elizabeth Grosz (1994, p. viii), is as 'an impulse or form of propulsion, directing a subject towards an object'. It can propel a subject not only towards other bodies but towards things. This understanding resonates with the history of the Elizabeth Bay reclamation and the wall of Darlinghurst gaol, objects which gay men in the 1970s and 80s were mobilized towards. This propulsion towards things does not leave us unmarked or unchanged. Rather, as Susanna Paasonen (2018, p. 132), following Lauren Berlant, maintains, 'As sexual desire moves toward and becomes attached to different scenes and objects, its forms are reorganised, and so is one's sense of self.' Desire sets up what are often long-term associations of attachment between people and things, associations which, as in the case of landscapes of lost love, can be as painful as they are compulsive (Byrne 2013).

We might think of fieldwork in terms of propulsion. Our encounters with things 'in the field' set us in motion in various ways, engendering trains of feeling and thought which mobilize our bodies through space and time such that the process of archaeological fieldwork produces its own archaeological traces and trails. The palimpsest idea in archaeology (Olivier 2011, pp. 129–34) and Olsen's (2010, pp. 123–5) discussion of the material corelates of 'habit memory' are helpful in conceptualizing this.

All of this seems in line with one of the stated objectives of this section of the present volume, namely to 'explore ways to include, account for, and disseminate the ineffable, immediate and corporal experiences involved in our encounters with things' (Introduction to Part II). Clearly the process of writing is central here. The standard academic style of reporting on fieldwork in archaeology tends to iron out the temporal loops, the happenstance, the intuitive moves, and the bodily-cerebral lurches which can occur when, for example, we become aware that rather than encompassing the object of study we have been encompassed by it. The actual experience of fieldwork is evacuated from the standard text, as in a sense is the author, in order to produce the 'author-evacuated' style of ethnographic writing that Clifford Geertz (1988, p. 140) wrote against.

Rather than accounting for the intimacy of our encounter with particular things and materials in 'the field', standard academic writing pulls back to produce a more distant view. I do not mean a distance that erases intricacy – the archaeological literature is replete with minutely detailed accounts of objects and sites under study – but rather of conjuring what Donna Haraway (1988, p. 581) refers to us as 'the view from nowhere' in her critique of what she sees as the masculinist and exploitative approach to the world enacted with the aid of such visual technologies as satellite cameras and electron microscopes. The 'god-trick of seeing everything from nowhere' (Haraway 1988, p. 581 seems alien to the whole spirit of the new materialism and of the posthumanities more generally. Implicitly they call for a view from *somewhere*.

Notes

1 Dramatic aerial photos of Kansai Airport immediately after its inundation are available on The Mainichi newspaper website: https://mainichi.jp/english/graphs/20180905/hpe/00m/0na/001000g/3

2 For Christo and Jeanne-Claude's 'wrapped coast', see https://christojeanneclaude.net/projects/wrapped-coast?view=info

3 For further information on the Hyde Park Barracks see Sydney Living Museums: https://sydneylivingmuseums.com.au/hyde-park-barracks-museum

4 See articles on Darlinghurst gaol in the *Sydney Morning Herald*, 1841, 1866, 1886 and 1899.

5 For convictions for sodomy in New South Wales see 'Criminal indictments, 1863–1919', NSW State Archives and Records.

References

Alaimo, S., 2012. State of suspension: Trans-corporeality at sea. *Interdisciplinary Studies in Literature and Environment*, 19(3), 476–93.

Bennett, J., 2001. *The Enchantment of Modern Life: Attachments, Crossings, and Ethics.* Princeton, NJ: Princeton University Press.

Bonneuil, C. and Fressoz, J-B., 2016. *The Shock of the Anthropocene.* London: Verso.

Byrne, D., 2013. Love and loss in the 1960s. *International Journal of Heritage* Studies, 19(6), 596–609.

Byrne, D., 2017a. Remembering the Elizabeth Bay reclamation and the Holocene sunset in Sydney Harbour. *Environmental Humanities*, 9(1), 40–59.

Byrne, D., 2017b. Raising seawalls in Japan. *The Seed Box Blog.* Available from: https://theseedboxblog.wordpress.com/2017/01/24/raising-seawalls-in-japan/

Byrne, D., 2018. Time on the waterline: Coastal reclamations and seawalls in Sydney and Japan. *Journal of Contemporary Archaeology*, 5(1), 53–65.

Carson, R., 1950. *The Sea Around Us.* Oxford: Oxford University Press.

Carson, R., 1998. *The Edge of the Sea.* Originally published 1955. New York: Mariner.

Certeau, M., de. 1984. *The Practice of Everyday Life.* Translated from the French by S. Randall. Berkeley: University of California Press.

Cohen, J. J., 2015. *Stone: An Ecology of the Inhuman.* Minneapolis: University of Minnesota Press.

Connor, S., 2004. Topologies: Michel Serres and the shapes of thought. *Anglistik*, 15, 105–17. Available from: www.stevenconnor.com/topologies/

Deleuze, G., 1993. *The Fold: Leibniz and the Baroque.* Translated from the French by Tom Conley. London: Continuum.

Deleuze, G. and Guattari, F., 1987. *A Thousand Plateaus: Capitalism and Schizophrenia.* Translated from the French by Massumi, B. Minneapolis: University of Minnesota Press.

Faro, C. and Wotherspoon, G., 2000. *Street Seen: A History of Oxford Street.* Melbourne: University of Melbourne Press.

Gandy, M., 2012. Queer ecology: Nature, sexuality, and heterotopic alliances. *Environment and Planning D*, 30, 727–47.

Geertz, C., 1988. *Works and Lives: The Anthropologist as Author.* Stanford, CA: Stanford University Press.

Grosz, E., 1994. *Volatile Bodies: Toward a Corporeal Feminism.* Sydney: Allen and Unwin.

Haraway, D., 1988. Situated knowledges: The science question in feminism and the privilege of partial perspective. *Feminist Studies* 14, 3: 575–99.

Merleau-Ponty, M., 1968. *The Visible and the Invisible.* Translated from the French by Lingis, A. Originally published 1964. Evanston, IL: Northwestern University Press.

Olivier, L., 2011. *The Dark Abyss of Time: Archaeology and Memory.* Lanham, MD: AltaMira.

Olsen, B., 2010. *In Defense of Things: Archaeology and the Ontology of Objects.* Lanham, MD: AltaMira.

Olsen, B., 2013. The return of what? In: González-Ruibal, ed., *Reclaiming Archaeology: Beyond the Tropes of Modernit.* London: Routledge, 289–97.

Olsen, B. and Pétursdóttir, Þ., 2016. Unruly heritage: Tracing legacies in the Anthropocene, *Arkæologisk Forum*, 35, 38–45.

Paasonen, S., 2018. *Many Splendored Things: Thinking Sex and Play.* London: Goldsmiths.

Pétursdóttir, Þ., 2017. Climate change? Archaeology and the Anthropocene, *Archaeological Dialogues* 24(2), 175–205.

Pétursdóttir, Þ., 2018. Drift. In: S. E. P. Birch, ed., *Multispecies Archaeology.* London: Routledge, 85–102.

Race, K., 2017. *The Gay Science: Intimate Experiments with the Problem of HIV.* London: Routledge.

Ross, K., 1987. Rimbaud and the transformation of social space. *Yale French Studies* 7, 104–20.

Saldanha, A., 2017. *Space After Deleuze*. London: Bloomsbury.

Serres, M., 1997. *Genesis*. Translated from the French by James, G. and Nielson, J. Ann Arbor: University of Michigan Press.

Swan, J., 2011. Modes of decay. *Discovering Stone*, 10(20), 24–9. Available from www.jasperswann.com.au/stonemason/wp-content/uploads/2017/04/Modes-of-Decay.pdf [Accessed April 17, 2019].

Wotherspoon, G., 2016. *Gay Sydney: A History*. Sydney: Newsouth Books.

Yusoff, K., 2016. Anthropogenesis: Origins and endings in the Anthropocene. *Theory, Culture and Society*, 33(2), 3–28.

8

STRANDED STONES AND SETTLED SPECIES

Affect and effects of ballast

Mats Burström

Standing at seashore, watching and listening to the waves coming in, smelling the salt seawater, there is a feeling of timelessness. The waves arrive to shore just as they always have and always will. There is something meditative about their repetitive sound; an impression strengthened by the realization that although you are experiencing it right now, it is a sound that transcends time. Waves were here before any human were, and they will certainly be here also when you are gone. It is a reminder of all the natural phenomena that have an independent existence beyond human control.

There are also things that appear natural, but in fact are a kind of culture in disguise as they are the results of human actions in the past. Standing on a shore in Newfoundland my eyes fall on stones that look most familiar, but at the same time seem to be out of context. They are of flint, which is a well-known material for an archaeologist, but as flint stones do not naturally occur here you realize they must one way or the other have been brought here. Tracing the background of these stranded stones leads to more general reflections concerning the 'correct' place of things as well as what kind of objects may be of archaeological concern.

Piquing an interest

My way to the Newfoundland shore started on another continent a few years before. During a stay in Melbourne, Australia, a colleague told me about a Palaeolithic hand-axe that had been found at an excavation in the city. The tool had been found in a flint filling layer, and the archaeologists had immediately realized that it was not native to Australia, but must have been shipped in from Europe with the rest of the flint as ballast. I was affected by the story and the find piqued my interest. I found it fascinating that an object so many thousands years old could move from one continent to another in this way and turn up in such an unexpected archaeological context.

Disappointingly, it proved impossible to find out more about the find. Nothing about it made it into print, and the excavation's directors did not answer the questions passed on for me by my colleague. Yet nevertheless it raised questions. Were there other examples of ancient objects that had criss-crossed the oceans as ballast and turned up in surprising places? And what other physical traces were there of ship ballast? Until that point I had no real interest in ballast in archaeological terms, but now I found I wanted to know more. It was this quest that brought me to that Newfoundland shore, listening to the waves, collecting impressions and facts about ballast traffic in the past.

Ballast basics

Ballast is what gives ship stability, preventing it from capsizing when it is not sufficiently laden with cargo. Nowadays water is used, pumped into large ballast tanks in the hold of the ship, but for most of the Age of Sail, which is from the sixteenth to the early twentieth century, ballast was solid. Materials used were sand, gravel, or stone, sometimes iron or brick, or anything else that could be sold on, but traditionally whatever material was readily available where the ship had put in. Often the ballast was collected from a nearby beach (Figure 8.1). When loading cargo at the destination, any ballast that was no longer needed was simply discarded. Sometimes it was dumped into the sea, sometimes it was offloaded on land. If a boat deballasted onto land, it could be reused, either as ballast or for something completely different. Ballast dumping into the sea soon became a problem because it silted up harbours and channels, with the result that in many places it was regulated from an early date. Ports often had special inspectors or ballast masters to ensure boats took on and discharged ballast according to the regulations, and strict fines were imposed on skippers who broke the rules.

The amount of ballast needed to give a boat the necessary stability depended on its size, its freeboard (the height of the ship's side between the waterline and the deck), and the height of its masts. The greater the surface above the waterline and the higher the masts, the greater the quantity of ballast needed. For the big sailing ships that crossed the Atlantic, ballast is estimated to have amounted to about a quarter of their total weight (Riebe 2002, p. 78). An eighteenth-century East Indiaman could be anything from 400 to 1,200 tonnes in size, and thus by this reckoning would have needed between 100 and 300 tonnes of ballast (Parham et al. 2013, p. 147). These were the largest of all vessels in the heyday of the Age of Sail, of course; smaller ships required less ballast.

There were several considerations when choosing ballast. It had to serve its purpose once at sea, it had to be as easy as possible to load and unload, it had to be readily available, and it had to be cheap, and preferably free. Or, even better, something which had a market at the port of arrival. There were therefore several factors to be weighed up when choosing ballast, and know-how was crucial. The written

FIGURE 8.1 Ballasting boats with sand and gravel at low water in North Devon, England, in about 1900. Photo: National Maritime Museum, Greenwich

sources are, however, silent when it comes to more practical aspects of ballasting ships. Plainly this was implicit knowledge – essential, but instead of committing it to paper it was communicated by word to mouth from skipper to skipper, and adapted according to circumstance.

What can be found in the written sources apart from the official regulations governing where ship could deballast, is typically records from individual ports about the number of ships arriving or departing 'in ballast' – laden only with ballast. Occasionally, the quantity of ballast handled in a year is recorded. Registers from Poole on the south coast of England show that the amount of outbound ballast in 1823 varied between 100 and 700 tonnes a month, while for the year the total was about 4,300 tonnes (Lindroth 1957, p. 165). There are too many unknowns – the number of ships, the number of voyages, the quantity of ballast – for it to be possible to calculate the exact amount of ballast the crossed the oceans over the four centuries when tall ships dominated global trade. It would, however, seem that the figure most probably was in the millions of tonnes.

Previous archaeological research

Considering the huge amount of material that has been transported to new places as ballast in the past, it is somewhat surprising that it has not received more archaeological interest (for an overview of previous studies, see Buckland and Sadler 1990; Burström 2017, pp. 21–5). When archaeologists have taken note of ballast it has usually been because they have wanted to establish its geographical origin in order to reconstruct ancient trade routes. While an interesting question, the method is problematic, because ballast was often reused. Ballast from a single wreck or in a ballast mound could thus be a mix that had previously been used by several different ships. Nor is it easy to gauge where ballast stone came from in geological terms, because it could well have moved from its place of origin thanks to the action of ice or glaciers. For example, flint frozen on the flint beaches of southern Scandinavia is known to move north with the drift ice, carried by the wind and currents up to the Swedish west coast and on to eastern Norway (Johansen 1956).

The geology of ballast stone that was reused as building material has also been studied in order to map old trade routes. One investigation concerns the city walls of King's Lynn on the English east coast (Figure 8.2). It is reckoned that work on the walls began in 1266, and took about a century and 55,000 stones to complete, of which some 3,000 are thought to be reused ballast stones. These stones are usually rounded and much the same size. The geological analysis shows that most had been collected from Baltic Sea beaches. While accepting the difficulty in determining the origin of individual stones, there is every indication that King's Lynn had particularly strong trading links with Estonia (Hoare et al. 2002).

Ballast stones from ships wrecked close to land were brought ashore by the waves and currents once the hull had broken up. A shoreline with stones that do not naturally occur there is one indication that there is a wreck nearby (Emery et al. 1968, p. 1227). It has also been suggested that ballast can be used to determine the nationality of wrecks. If so, it would largely be true of warships, which did not change their ballast as often as merchant vessels. For example, for much of the eighteenth century British naval ships used iron ballast, while Spanish warships used stone (Peterson 1965, pp. 128–9). Until that point, the Royal Navy had used sand, gravel, and beach stones as ballast, but over the course of the seventeenth century had switched to larger and larger material. This improved the ventilation in the holds where the ballast was stored, and where the bilge water – the dirty water from the upper decks – collected. With better air flow, the health situation improved on board because it became more difficult for bacteria to grow (Simmons 1998[1991], p. 7).

Despite centuries as an essential prerequisite for shipping, and despite the huge quantities involved, why then has ballast not attracted greater archaeological interest? One reason is that most of the material used as ballast were not artefacts – objects made by people – but instead consisted of sand, gravel, and stone. As natural objects, such material may seem to fall outside the scope of archaeology. Another reason is that it is thought to have been secondary to the actual cargo, and therefore less important. But unlike cargo such as cereals, coffee, cotton, tea, and tobacco, all of which were consumed long ago, ballast often survives and can be studied.

FIGURE 8.2 The city walls of King's Lynn, with rounded beach stones once used as ballast. Photo: Peter G. Hoare

Ancient artefacts in the ballast

My interest for ballast started, as mentioned, with the hand-axe found seemingly out of context in Australia. Given the huge amount of material shipped around as ballast, it is not surprising that it sometimes included ancient artefacts. This was especially true of ballast collected in long-settled areas, as was common in the British Isles and France for example. There are several known cases of prehistoric artefacts transported as ballast to new areas, but unfortunately most are poorly documented. The reason is probably that the objects were not found in their original contexts, and were thus considered anomalies of minor importance. In the case of flint items, there can also be some confusion over whether they were shaped by human hand or by nature (e.g. Emery et al. 1968; Rose 1968). Often, findings are merely mentioned in passing in the archaeological literature, and some are only known anecdotally. For example, Canadian archaeologists talk of a researcher in the fifties or sixties who found a Palaeolithic flint tool among flint ballast near St. John's, the provincial capital of Newfoundland and Labrador (personal communication B. Gaulton and P.E. Pope, August 4–5, 2015). Nothing has been published about the find, however, and no one today knows what kind of tool it was, exactly where it was found, and where it is now. However, as we will see, there were other flint items found in Newfoundland that were likely to have been European Palaeolithic in origin and had crossed the Atlantic as ballast.

Similarly, in Port Lincoln in southern Australia, Palaeolithic flint tools have been found among ballast dumped in the harbour by British ships. According to a report from 1978, the items were exhibited by the South Australian Museum in Adelaide (Glover et al. 1978, p. 48; Dortch and Glover 1983, p. 330). Today they are stashed away somewhere with the other millions of stone objects in the museum's collections, and cannot be traced (email P. Jones, March 7, 2017). Prehistoric flint tools have also been found among ballast discarded by British ships at Point Gellibrand in Melbourne and used as beach backfill (Lawrence and Davies 2010, p. 254). Unfortunately, there is no further information to be had about these finds, and most seem to have been regarded as curiosities.

One find that has received attention is the so-called Scaddan implement. Named for the place in south-western Australia where it was found by a private person on a road construction site in around 1930, it has a pointed tip and looks a lot like a Palaeolithic hand-axe from Europe. The question was whether it was brought to Australia or whether it was made locally by Aborigines. An extensive archaeological and geological analysis concluded that it was indeed a Palaeolithic hand-axe (Dortch and Glover 1983). It resembles English flint, and certain details are typical of hand-axes from the Thames Valley. Most likely, it was shipped in a load of ballast from the UK to Australia and dumped there.

Meanwhile, in North America a Palaeolithic hand-axe was found which is believed to have arrived there with ballast from Europe (Newell et al. 1991). The discovery was made in 1988 during an archaeological investigation of a lock in Santee Canal in South Carolina. There had been speculation about the chances of finding such items in the US, but this was the first find to be archaeologically documented. A petrological analysis of the flint's composition established that it was European in origin. The general impression of the tool, along with its type and manufacture, led experts to conclude that it was an Early Palaeolithic hand-axe from the west of France. The tool probably arrived in North America among ballast unloaded in Charleston, a nearby port where it was later reused as ballast for a small canal boat. For unknown reasons, the hand-axe was dropped into the canal lock, probably at some point when the lock was in operation between 1800 and about 1860.

Some finds made in the past by private individuals were never fully studied or documented, but nevertheless caused something of a stir, especially in the newspapers. A Swedish local paper reported in 1908 that Roman coins had been found the year before in Nyland at the mouth of the river Ångermanälven in northern Sweden. Nyland was one of Sweden's major timber ports, and ships unloaded large amounts of ballast there. It was in a delivery of gravel ballast there that eleven heavily corroded bronze coins were found. According to the newspaper, 'on closer inspection by an expert on ancient relics' the coins were found to date to the Roman Empire. The coins were believed to have arrived at the site with ballast collected 'on any southern European coast or the coast of any sea sailed by the Romans' (Malmer and Wiséhn 1983, p. 44).

Another Roman bronze coin was found under similar circumstances in the US too, this time at Bennett's Point in Maryland on the East Coast. A find of a much worn copper coin from Greece or southern Italy dating from the third or second century BC was made on a riverbank outside the city of Woodstock, North Carolina. In Virginia, on the James River, two coins were found that appeared to be Roman silver coins from the first century BC; however, they were fakes, probably from the eighteenth century. Common to all these genuine and counterfeit antique coins is that they were found close to estuaries – places where boats were likely to deballast and reballast. The archaeologist Ivor Noël Hume has pointed out that similar finds of genuine and counterfeit coins have been made along the River Thames in England, his suggestion being that the coins found in the US had arrived there in ballast taken from the banks of the Thames (Noël Hume 1974, pp. 121–3). Yet another find of a Roman bronze coin in the US has been reported from Seattle's harbour in Washington State on the West Coast (Wilkinson 2020).

The Åland Islands in the Baltic Sea offer an unusually well-documented ancient artefact that had been shipped in a load of ballast (Burström 2017, p. 32–3). The object in question is the islands' only Late Neolithic flint dagger. Some four thousand years old, the dagger is in the collections of the Åland Museum, with an informative catalogue entry:

> The item was found in 1910 by a farmer's son, Valfrid Karlsson of Laby, Saltvik, when unloading the ballast from the barque Jonstorp in Verkviken, Saltvik. The ballast had been taken on at Aarhus, Denmark. Presented in 1911 by J. A. Bergenroth.

In this case, it is quite clear that the dagger had crossed the Baltic Sea in the ship's ballast. Flint daggers of this type are relatively common in Jutland, of which Aarhus was the largest city, so it seems entirely plausible that it originated there.

There are more examples of ancient artefacts that have moved from place to place in ship ballast, and turned up by both archaeologists and members of the public alike (Burström 2017, pp. 27–38). Unfortunately, most of them are poorly documented and there are no doubt a large number of unrecorded cases.

The Newfoundland case

Let us return to my Newfoundland experience mentioned in the beginning. Here and there along the shores of the island there are large amounts of flint. Since flint does not occur naturally in the area, we know that it was once ballast. This is remains of the vast seasonal Grand Banks fisheries, so important from the early sixteenth to the early twentieth centuries.

In Eurocentric terms, Newfoundland was discovered in 1497 by John Cabot, a Venetian-born navigator sponsored by King Henry VII of England and a group of Bristol merchants. By that point, of course, there had been people living in

Newfoundland for a good nine thousand years, and we also know that around AD 1000 there was a short-lived Viking settlement at L'Anse aux Meadows at the northernmost tip of Newfoundland (Rankin 2008). Cabot's 'discovery' of Newfoundland and the huge stocks of cod in the waters of the Grand Banks had a direct impact on Europe for centuries to come. The demand for dried or salt fish in the Catholic countries of Europe made cod a valuable commodity. This rich resource was exploited first by the French, Spanish, and Portuguese, and later mostly by fishermen from the British Isles. About 350 ships are believed to have joined in the seasonal fisheries in the sixteenth century, although there are contemporary data that indicate a much larger number (Pope 2004, pp. 19–20). The fishing fleet arrived in Newfoundland in April or May and sailed home to Europe in October. With the exception of a small number of people who were left behind to look after the fishermen's investment in the shape of jetties and fish flakes, or racks for drying fish, Newfoundland was left largely uninhabited by Europeans in the winter months, and it was only in the early seventeenth century that the first permanent settlements were established. This meant that the fishing fleets that arrived from Europe had no local markets to supply with merchandise, and as the crews' stores did not make up a full load, the ships had to sail in ballast. When the ships returned home in the autumn, they were laden with fish and had little need for ballast. As a rule they did not sail straight to their home ports, but instead made first for the Catholic countries of southern Europe, where the demand for dried or salt fish was greatest. From there they returned then to their home ports having taken on wine and salt and other marketable goods – and perhaps new ballast (Lindroth 1957, p. 156). This triangular trade has been neatly summarized as turning fish into wine (Pope 2004).

The size of the fishing boats increased from an average of 50–100 tonnes in the sixteenth century to double that or more in subsequent centuries (Pope 2004). In the early nineteenth century, the ships that left Britain for the Grand Banks fisheries carried an average of 50–70 tonnes of ballast (Lindroth 1957, pp. 161–2). Given the number of vessels involved in the cod fishing over those four centuries, it is evident that very large amounts of ballast crossed the Atlantic. An accurate figure is impossible, but suppose for a moment that 350 ships each offloaded 25 tonnes of ballast every year for 400 years, and 3.5 million tonnes is a not unreasonable number. Whether this is a high estimate or a low one cannot be said with any certainty, but either way the sheer quantity of ballast must have left its mark on Newfoundland.

Large quantities of ballast flint have been found at archaeological excavations across Newfoundland, including in Ferryland, a British settlement dating from 1621, where an extensive study has been underway since 1992 (Figure 8.3). On excavating a wharf-like structure, oak barrels of flint gravel and sand were found to have been used as landfill. Among this was found what is thought to have been the tip of a Palaeolithic tool, which would have arrived in the ballast from Europe (personal communication B. Gaulton, August 4, 2015). In Ferryland, as at other

FIGURE 8.3 Ballast flint from excavations in Ferryland, Newfoundland, with centimetre scale. Photo: Mats Burström

sites in Newfoundland, ballast flint had been used as fire strikers and gunflints. Both types of object were essential to everyday life in the early modern period, and even though finished gunflints were imported from Europe, ballast flint was still a welcome addition (Figure 8.4). There is also a find of an arrowhead that is thought to have been made from flint ballast by the Beothuk, an indigenous people based in Newfoundland (Gaulton 2001, pp. 36–7).

A flint scraper found on a beach at Grandois in northern Newfoundland during an archaeological survey hints at some interesting possibilities (Figure 8.5). It is believed to have been made by the Beothuk from European ballast flint. If that assumption is correct, then it dates to between 1500, when the European fishing fleets first arrived – in ballast – in Newfoundland, and 1650, when the Beothuk switched to using tools made of reworked European iron (Pope 2007, pp. 38–9). The iron was taken from the Europeans' fishing camps when they were left unoccupied in the winter months. An alternative reading by Peter E. Pope, the archaeologist who found the scraper, is that it was instead a Palaeolithic artefact that had arrived with the ballast from Europe (personal communication P.E. Pope, August 5, 2015). Whichever interpretation is correct, the scraper is silent testimony to the way ship ballast can challenge all the stereotypes of an object's 'proper place'.

In Newfoundland, as elsewhere, it has been assumed that the colour of the flint is an indication of its origin. The suggested line is that grey or black flint comes from England, pale brown or honey-coloured flint from France, but this is in fact not reliable. However, there are other, more surprising ways to track ballast's origin. The Swedish entomologist Carl Lindroth (1957) studied the spread in North America of plant and animal species that originated in Europe, and found that Newfoundland is the part of North America that has by far the largest proportion of introduced species. The nineteen species of ground beetle (*Carabidae*) are

FIGURE 8.4 Gunflints made of flint ballast, found in Ferryland. Photo: Barry Gaulton

FIGURE 8.5 A flint scraper from Grandois, either made by the Beothuk from ballast flint, or a Palaeolithic artefact from Europe that happened to be included in a load of ballast. Photo: Peter E. Pope

a case in point (Figure 8.6). They are especially prevalent in the Avalon peninsula on the east coast of Newfoundland – which is where the seasonal fisheries were concentrated. Subsequent studies have confirmed Linderoth's findings (Larson and Langor 1982). The same has also been found to be true of plants with a European origin – they mainly occur around the harbours used for the seasonal fisheries (Cooper 1981, pp. 252, 261–3).

FIGURE 8.6 *Notiophilus biguttatus*, the spotted ground beetle, one of the species whose distribution in North America bears witness of the European ballast deposited in Newfoundland. Photo: James Lindsey

Lindroth was intrigued by the fact that the same species of ground beetle can produce both short- and long-winged individuals. The latter spread more readily, which means that the greater proportion of short-winged ground beetles, the greater the likelihood that they had been there a long time. Again, it transpired that short-winged ground beetles predominated in the eastern part of the Avalon peninsula. This distribution pattern coincided with the sites which the European fishing fleets had used the most. This realization led Lindroth to study the historical record of the European trade with Newfoundland in considerable detail. He demonstrated that huge amounts of ballast were shipped across the Atlantic and then disposed of. As early as 1611 there were regulations prohibiting the dumping of ballast in a way that could obstruct harbours. The ban was reiterated in a succession of seventeenth- and eighteenth-century regulations, which required that ballast be taken ashore and left where it could not do any harm (Lindroth 1957, pp. 157–8). Lindroth concluded that it was the transatlantic movement of ballast that explained the presence in Newfoundland of a large number of animal and plant species of European origin.

To better understand ballast's part in the introduction of new species to Newfoundland, Lindroth broadened his study to include the coastal regions of south-west England, where most of the European fishing fleet was based. While he did not hazard a guess as to the total volume of traffic, Lindroth gathered information from a variety of sources. Thus of a list of ships that used Poole in England over a twelve-month period in 1813–1814, fully 38 were bound for Newfoundland, of which 21 were partially or fully loaded with ballast, with the total amount of ballast exceeding 1,100 tonnes. These ships were thus ballasted with roughly 52 tonnes on average. Given that Poole was then only one of nine major ports in south-west England, and that the data concerns a single one-year period, it can safely be said to bear out the vast scale of ballast operations. Not long after, in 1823, the total amount of ballast that left Poole for all destinations – not only Newfoundland, in other words – was 4,298 tonnes. The ballast consisted of sand, gravel, stone, or rubble (Lindroth 1957, pp. 160–5).

Lindroth examined the spread in Europe of the species of ground beetle that were introduced to Newfoundland in ship ballast. He found that all species were present in the places where ballast was taken in south-west England, and therefore they probably also originated from the region (Lindroth 1957, p. 143). It would seem that beetles are a better indicator of the origins of the ballast found in Newfoundland than is the colour of flint. The fact that the presence of so many animal and plant species is the result of the past movement of ballast begs the question of what qualifies as archaeological source material in the first place. Animals and plants are in any sense not artefacts – they are not created by people – but nevertheless their presence is a direct consequence of human action in the past.

Plants and people

In amongst the ship ballast there were in most cases seeds from plants that grew where the ship had been ballasted. These seeds could well, as the Newfoundland case shows, germinate and take root in the places where the ballast was offloaded. In this way, many species of plant spread to new areas where, if conditions were favourable, they became settled. It was fears about the risk of an invasion of non-native plants that led New Zealand to ban deballasting onto its beaches (Ridley 1930, p. 645). But to this day, there is a wealth of flora that testifies to the shipping – and ship ballast – of the past. Thus, for example, the island of Reposaari, off Pori in Finland, has 135 species of so-called ballast plants, of which 75 are now permanent. In the late nineteenth century, Reposaari was Finland's timber port bar none, and ballast from arriving ships was dumped over an area almost 50 hectares in size (Kalinainen and Lampolahti 1994). In the early twentieth century, timber operations were moved away from Reposaari, and the subsequent absence of ground disturbance in the shape of metalled roads and the like has been kind to the ballast flora. The most exotic species originate from South America, but most come from central and southern Europe (Laine 1981, after Jutila 1996, pp. 166–7). A recent botanical survey of Reposaari to look at the dormant seeds of ballast plants (Jutila 1996) inspired the Brazilian artist Maria Thereza Alves, who was struck by the length of time seeds can lie dormant in the ground in so-called soil seed banks, only to germinate and grow into new plants when the opportunity presents itself. On Reposaari the moment came in 1992, when there were major works in order to put in a new water main. The following summer was a bumper year for ballast plants, a few of which had not been seen since the turn of the century. Some were only seen that one summer, but there is always a chance that they set seed – which is lying dormant, waiting for the next opportunity (Jutila 1996, pp. 176–7).

In response to Reposaari, Alves embarked on *Seeds of Change*, in which she explores ballast flora in a number of ports across Europe, including Bristol, Exeter, and Liverpool in the UK, Dunkirk and Marseille in France, and Rotterdam in the Netherlands (Fisher 2012; Lozano 2012). Using archival material and charts, Alves mapped out the sites where ballast had been dumped in past centuries. She then took soil samples from each site to determine whether they contained the seeds of ballast plants, and whether it would be possible to propagate them.

In 2007, Alves was invited to participate in a group exhibition about ports, 'Port City', in Bristol. Having dug up soil samples from ballast sites in the city's docks and along its riverbanks, she made a public appeal for help cultivating the dormant seeds of ballast plants (Figure 8.7).

The result was a collection of plants that embodied Bristol's leading role in long-distance trade. It was also a very dark chapter in the city's history, as it was central to the Atlantic triangular trade in slaves. When the ships that took part in this trade returned to Bristol, they were carrying in their ballast the seeds that Alves would find

FIGURE 8.7 Proud Bristolians with some of the ballast plants they grew from dormant seed. Photo: Max McClure

a couple of centuries later, and which with the city community's help she coaxed into growing. Many Bristol residents have family roots that go back to the ballast plants' places of origin. By linking botany and history, Alves addressed the wider issues of diversity and cultural identity. Although ballast plants might well count as 'illegal immigrants', over time many have settled and become a natural part of the British landscape. Alves' project affected many and generated reflections about the past as well as the present and the interplay between these. In the summer of 2012, Alves took her project one step further: in collaboration with a number of Bristol institutions she created a floating garden full of ballast plants, *The Floating Ballast Seed Garden*. The garden was planted on an old grain barge, refitted to a design by the German designer Gitta Gschwendtner. The barge, a piece of living history, was moored on the River Avon in Bristol city centre. The garden has been replanted every year since its inauguration and is proving a popular tourist attraction.

That ballast plants feature in the flora of many regions of the world is common knowledge, but has so far mostly caught the interest of botanists. Ballast plants are a prime example of the fact that much of what we regard as natural is actually the result of human action in the past; they are living testimony to the close relationship between natural history and cultural history.

From affect to insight

The initial affect the story about the Palaeolithic hand-axe brought to Australia as ballast had on me soon gave way to astonishment at the enormous quantities of material that had criss-crossed the oceans as ballast, and the lasting effects it had made in the world. The sheer variety makes it difficult to get a sense of the scale. Ballast stones on a beach will look just like any old stones to the untutored eye, and an island made up of tipped ballast will look like any other island. As stonework or cobbles, ballast melts into the urban environment; as landfill it is invisible until you start digging. Despite its very substantial nature – it is nothing if not bulky – ballast has never made it onto most archaeologists' radar.

The lack of interest in ballast may well reflect the fact that most ballast cannot be defined as an artefact in the conventional sense. In other words, it is not made by people. Instead, it consists of raw materials such as sand, gravel, and stone, which traditionally are not something archaeologists concern themselves with. Yet even if ballast is not human-made, it has still been put to human use, which explains why it is found in such quantities today, and where. For a single stone, its lifetime as ballast may have been brief in the extreme, but it can still have made a lasting difference. As archaeological material, ballast transcends the boundary between nature and culture.

Ballast's impact also extends to living organisms. With ballast came non-native plants and animals, which sometimes settled and became established in their new habitats. In many places, today's flora and fauna are an effect of the movement of ship ballast. That the presence of animals and plants is proof of human activity merely adds to the blurring of the boundaries between nature and culture. Its very transnationality is what inspires the artist, who sees in ballast an opportunity to explore the major issues of the day from an oblique and seemingly trivial angle. Stones and plants, presented in new contexts, can interrogate cultural identity and historical change. For the archaeologist, ballast, once the ultimate stabilizer, now serves to destabilize the standard notions of the 'correct' place of things, and indeed of what kind of objects may be of archaeological concern.

Ballast has long seemed to be of little or no archaeological interest; yes, it may indeed have been important for shipping in the past, but now it is essentially irrelevant. Ballast does not make for strikingly conspicuous monuments; wherever it fetches up, it blends in, unnoticed, in its new setting. And that perhaps is what ballast can teach us. It reminds us that we are constantly surrounded by the past, whether we are aware of it or not. In some cases, as with flint on a shore, it is not immediately obvious that it is a result of human actions in the past; you need some basic knowledge about flint to realize it. In other cases, as with some ballast plants, they may be hidden in the ground as seeds for quite a long time, but they are nevertheless there and when the time is right they will turn up, just like archaeological artefacts.

Ship ballast shares correspondences with the generations upon generations of people who have preceded us, but whose names we do not know and whose existence seems unimaginably distant from ours. It is the grand monuments and famous names that catch the light, but in their long shadow is the great generality of the past. Ready and waiting to be discovered by anyone prepared to take a wider view.

References

Buckland, P. C. and Sadler, J., 1990. Ballast and building stone: A discussion. In: D. Parson, ed. *Stone: Quarrying and Building in England AD 43–1525*. Chichester: Phillimore, 114–25.

Burström, M., 2017. *Ballast. Laden with History*. Lund: Nordic Academic Press.

Cooper, K., 1981. Alien anthropophytic vegetation of the Avalon Peninsula. In: Macpherson, A.G. and Macpherson, J.B., eds., *The Natural Environment of Newfoundland, Past and Present*. St John's: Memorial University of Newfoundland, 251–65.

Dortch, C. E. and Glover, J. E., 1983. The Scaddan implement: A re-analysis of a probable Acheulian handaxe found in western Australia. *Records of the Western Australian Museum*, 10 (4), 319–334.

Emery, K. O., Kaye, C. A., Loring, D. H. and Nota, D. J. G., 1968. European Cretaceous flints on the coast of North America. *Science*, 160, 1225–8.

Fisher, J., 2012. The importance of words and actions [online]. Available from: www. mariatherezaalves.org/assets/files/fisher_the-importance_web.pdf [Accessed Feb 27, 2019].

Gaulton, R., 2001. An early historic Beothuk occupation at Ferryland, Newfoundland. *Avalon Chronicles*, 6, 19–55.

Glover, J. E., Dortch, C. E. and Balme, B. E., 1978. The Dunsborough implement: An Aboriginal biface from southwestern Australia. *Journal of the Royal Society of Western Australia*, 60 (2), 41–7.

Hoare, P. G., Vinx, R., Stevenson, R. C. and Ehlers, J., 2002. Re-used bedrock ballast in King's Lynn's 'Town Wall' and the Norfolk Port's medieval trading links. *Medieval Archaeology*, 46 (1), 91–105.

Johansen, E., 1956. Tilgangen på local flint i Øst-Norge under yngre steinalder. Et nytt syn på et gammelt problem. *Stavanger Museum Årbok*, 1955, 87–94.

Jutila, H. M., 1996. Seed bank and emergent vascular flora of ballast areas in Reposaari. Finland. *Annales Botanici Fennici*, 33, 165–82.

Kalinainen, P. and Lampolahti, J., 1994. Porin Reposaaren painolastikasvit – kulttuuriaarre merten ja aikojen taka [The ballast flora of the Island Reposaari (Räfsö), off Pori, SW Finland]. *Lutukka*, 10 (1), 3–12.

Laine, U., 1981. Painolastikasvit. In: P. Kallio and A. Rousi, eds., *Kasvien Maailma*. Helsingfors: Otava, pp. 1480–1.

Larson, D. J. and Langor, D. W., 1982. The carabid beetles of insular Newfoundland (Coleoptera: Carabidae: Cicindellidae) – 30 years after Lindroth. *Canadian Entomologist*, 114, 591–7.

Lawrence, S. and Davies, P., 2010. *An Archaeology of Australia since 1788*. New York: Springer.

Lindroth, C. H., 1957. *The Faunal Connections between Europe and North America*. Stockholm: Almqvist & Wiksell.

Lozano, C., 2012. *Stubborn Waste* [online]. Available at: www.mariatherezaalves.org/assets/files/lozano_stubborn-waste_web.pdf [Accessed Feb 27, 2019].

Malmer, B. and Wiséhn, I., 1983. *Myntfynd från Ångermanland*. Stockholm: Kungl. Myntkabinettet.

Newell, M. M., Upchurch, S. B. and Goodyear, A. C., 1991. Tide-lock chopper-core: Discovery and analysis of a cultural anomaly in the southern terminus of the Santee Canal. *Archaeology of Eastern North America*, 19, 43–50.

Nöel Hume, I., 1974. *All the Best Rubbish*. New York: Harper & Row.

Parham, D., Rundell, E. and Merwe, van der P., 2013. A late eighteenth-century merchantman wrecked in the South Edinburgh Channel, Thames Estuary, England. *International Journal of Nautical Archaeology*, 42 (1), 137–49.

Peterson, M., 1965. *History under the Sea: A Handbook for Underwater Exploration*. Washington DC: Smithsonian Institution Press.

Pope, P. E., 2004. *Fish into Wine: The Newfoundland Plantation in the Seventeenth Century*. Chapel Hill: University of North Carolina Press.

Pope, P. E., 2007. *Petit Nord Survey 2004: An Archaeological Reconnaissance of Historic Sites in Conche, Crouse, Croque and Grandois-St Julians, Newfoundland. Final Report to Archaeology Office, Newfoundland and Labrador*. Archaeology Unit, Memorial University, St. John's Newfoundland. A1C5S7. Unpublished Report.

Rankin, L., 2008. Native peoples from the Ice Age to the extinction of the Beothuk (c. 9,000 years ago to AD 1829). In: S. Lewis-Simpson, ed., *A Short History of Newfoundland and Labrador*. Portugal Cove-St Philip's: Boulder Publications, 1–19.

Ridley, H. D., 1930. *The Dispersal of Plants throughout the World*. Ashford: L. Reeve.

Riebe, A. R., 2002. *Chronicle of Shipwrecks and Sunken Treasure, 900–1900 AD: A Guide for Undersea Explorers*. Beaufort: Seven Seas.

Rose, P. F., 1968. A flint ballast station in New Rochelle, New York. *American Antiquity*, 33 (2), 240–3.

Simmons, J. J., 1998 [1991]. *Those Vulgar Tubes: External Sanitary Accommodations aboard European Ships of the Fifteenth through Seventeenth Centuries*. London: Chatham.

Wilkinson, R., 2020. Identifying ancient coins deposited with modern ships' ballast: A problem for distribution studies? *American Journal of Numismatics*, 32: forthcoming.

9

OUT OF THE DAY, TIME AND LIFE

Phenomenology and cavescapes

Hein B. Bjerck

> Into the underland we have long placed that which we fear and wish to lose, and that which we love and wish to save
>
> *(Macfarlane 2019, p. 8)*

Affects of cavescapes – an introduction

It is a paradox; perhaps our confidence in a scientific approach sometimes make us miss the point. Archaeologists cherish caves as a place for fortunate discoveries – they are containers of well-preserved things from the deep past; the scarceness of weathering and microorganisms in caves are a good thing. The result is that caves may produce unexpected and wonderful things, fragile paintings that still retain their colours, delicate artefacts, faunal remains that may be classified, negative imprints of human hands, arrangements of things, burials, and even ancient human barefoot imprints and finger marks. We bring sharp instruments to retrieve objects and document contexts, electrical torches, lasers to measure distances, sensors to explore sounds and temperature – still, perhaps the essence of the situation escapes us.

Very likely, the past people that ventured into the dark spaces saw it differently. They did not enter caves to retrieve well-preserved things – they probably were drawn to a wider range of what we may label cave affects – they probably came to visit the cave itself. At best, they came with flickering torches, and had little other instruments to record what was in here, except their own bodily sensing organs. They lacked the instruments that could separate soundscapes from fragrances, and temperatures form visions – but had to take it all-in at the same instant. The electric light and specialized recording facilities we bring along to explore the darkened enclosures may very well counteract our ability to sense what was at centre for past people's reasons to visit the cave. In this chapter, I will explore how caves as landscapes are sensed by human visitors (Clottes 2003) – the affects of *cavescapes*:

> Emphasizing involuntary material memory and the significance of experience also connects to [...] the *affective aspects of material encounters*. The preferred academic conception is that things, monuments, and places are interpreted – in other words, made sense of rather than sensed – whereby significance is rendered humanly inscribed rather than released from encounters with things themselves.
>
> *(Olsen and Pétursdóttir n.d.)*

My fascination of caves emerged by coincidence back in 1992. My geologist college Jacob Møller had invited me to a cave in the outer parts of the Lofoten islands in North Norway. In the ancient beach sediment in the floor of the cave named 'Helvete' (Hell) he had collected shell fragments that was dated to 33.000 BP, i.e., from an interstadial during the last Ice Age (Møller et al. 1992). This implied that the cave had been open to 'whatever' that might have happened since then. In theory, the cave could host remains from Neanderthals as well as Hipsters, and all that was between. Now, we intended to check out things in more detail, and aimed at test pits in the gravel floor of the inner part of the cave. Remembering a recent discovery of paintings in a nearby cave (Hauglid et al. 1991), I entered the cave with one eye on the floor – the other on the walls. Very soon after arrival, my flashlight revealed faint red lines on the wall – the same stick-men as was found in a few other caves. The discovery was like a shooting star, sudden, unexpected and undeserved, that immediately turned into addiction, an urge to find more. For years I used every opportunity to check out caves. In the next few years, my archaeologist colleague Martinus Hauglid and I discovered three more caves with paintings – and also visited many other caves, with or without paintings (Bjerck 1995; 2012). The anticipation of looking into the dark from the mouth of a new unexplored cave, feeling the cave's timeless chill to your face, the mouldy scent of a possible successful finding – it was as exciting as exploring can be.

In my study of earlier publications on cave paintings discoveries in Norway since the first case was reported in 1913, I was startled to find that the affective aspects of caves were hardly mentioned prior to the careful hints in the works of Johansen (1988) and Hesjedal (1994). The sequence of papers that presented and discussed new findings was clearly biased towards what was the current research focus at the time of publication. Each paper hosts the hallmarks of popular research in their time of publication, and in sum they reveal interesting trends in archaeological research history. Normally, the documentation of the caves is sketchy, the profile of floor and roof, and a plan drawing with lines where floor meets walls, its basic measurements. The affects of caves are for the most part reduced to the drop line, the 'beginning' of the cave as out of the rain (Bjerck 1995; 2012).

Anybody that has visited caves knows that there are more than this. But most 'other things' are soft data that are perceptible, but positions are intangible, they are hard to document with pencil lines on millimetre paper, they are impossible to bag – as this 'otherness' is basically found in your own experience from being here – things that had no space in the trustworthy format of a traditional, decent archaeological report. Within the positivist theoretical regime that many of us come from, we were plainly warned about this – our own references to being-in-the-world was straightforwardly 'harmful' to our ability to an 'uncontaminated' understanding of the past, the present was an unescapable burden that we could not be relieved of. Thus, perhaps the most important phenomena that caves offed to past human visitors escaped any further inspection. Ironically, all archaeologists that have worked in darkness of caves have experienced to fumble around to retrieve pencil, eraser and folding rule – but it seems that none of them actually saw the relevance of the darkness itself (Bjerck 2012).

In Bjørnar J. Olsen's words 'Phenomenology is […] concerned with the world as it manifests itself to those who take part in it' (Olsen 2010, p. 66). He proceeds to point out that

> the phenomenological approach to human perception imply two important insights:
>
> • Our relatedness to the world. We are entangled beings fundamentally involved in networks of human and nonhuman beings
> • We relate to the world not (only) as thinking subjects but also as bodily objects – our being in the world.
>
> *(ibid.)*

In a 'presentism' perspective (e.g. Olivier 2004; 2011), the same repertoire of sensible cave properties that the caves offered people in the past, are also *here and now*, and always ready to be sensed and explored. Evidently, some 2–3000 years ago, past peoples entered a set of caves, and inscribed paintings on the walls, paintings that for the most part depict human beings. One might assume their reasons for entering the caves and what they did in here were related to what they sensed in cavescapes. Past peoples, as they were humans like us, encountered the same cave affects that are available for humans today.

Thus, the meeting points between cave properties and the things the cave painters added to cavescapes, embrace memories of events that took place here, events that hold strong relations to how caves were sensed and understood. What we may not know, are how experiences from the caves mixed in with the cave painters' worldview and past peoples' relatedness to the world (Jackson 1986). The ontological depths of past phenomenological relations have probably evaporated for good. Nonetheless, and well aware of the critical stances (e.g. Brück 2005; Hamilton et al. 2006), I share Tilley's (1994; 2004) basic phenomenological assumption that we and the peoples of the past share 'carnal bodies', size, shape, and sensory organs – that we engage with the same physical world and the same repertoire of phenomena – and that these factors may serve as 'guidelines' in the understanding of past actions, praxis and beliefs.

Nevertheless, I think it is a worthwhile endeavour to bring you along on a tour to the affective aspects from my embodied encounters of caves, that eventually will end up in exploring the placements of cavescape paintings. In Robert Macfarlane's words, these meeting points are '*thin places* [...] where borders between worlds or epochs feel at their most fragile' (2019, p. 270, italics added).

Actually, in line with a presentism perspective, 'thin places' may be studied as part of the contemporary, just as much as exploring an abandoned post-war mining town or derelict industrial areas. 'There is no archaeology of the twenty-first century

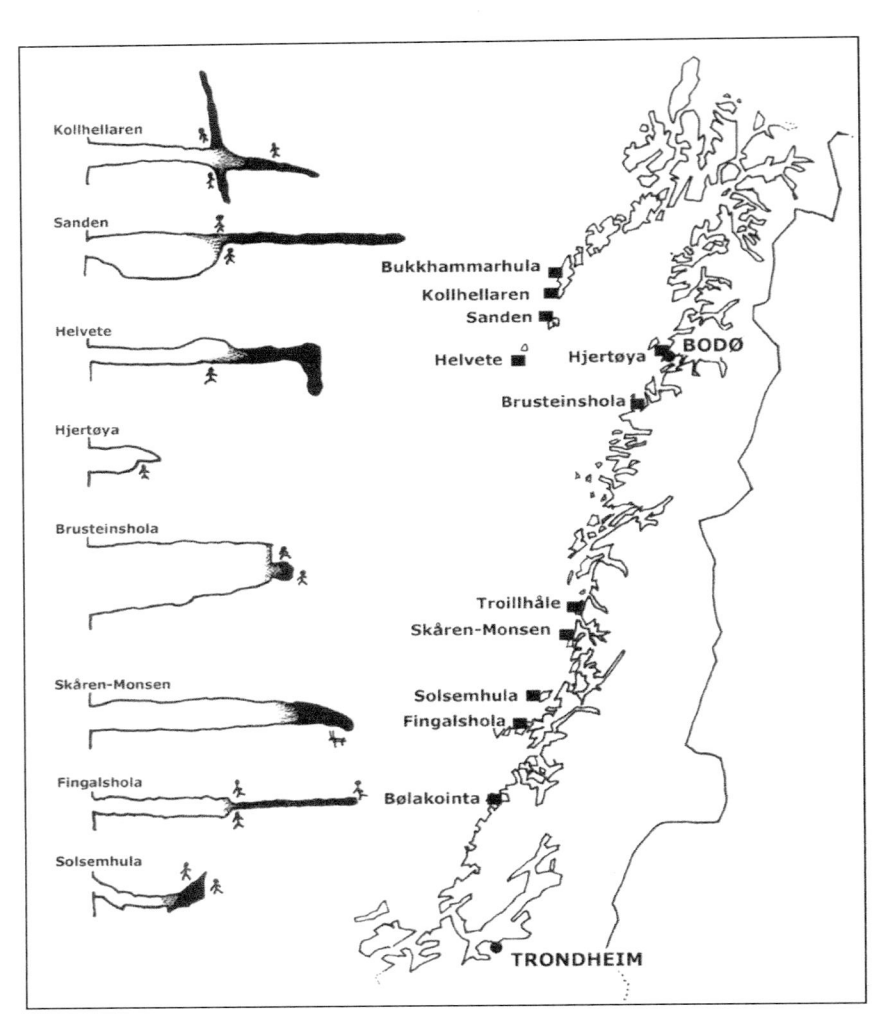

FIGURE 9.1 The Norwegian cave paintings are situated in a c. 500 km long coastal area in Northern Norway. To the left, a schematic sketch of caves, the darkness within, and proximate location of paintings. Map: Hein B. Bjerck

but only an archaeology of the twenty-first and all its pasts, mixed and entangled' (González-Ruibal 2008, p. 262).

Cavescapes and paintings

Basic information on the findings is needed before exploring cavescape affects. Paintings are documented in 12 caves, with a total of less than *c.* 150 individual figures (Figure 9.1) (Bjerck 2012; Norsted 2013). They are all found in big caves exposed to open sea, costal caves produced by marine erosion during the Pleistocene Ice Ages (Møller 1985; Møller et al. 1992). Most caves are situated near the marine limit at raised shorelines and are accordingly located in various elevations, in line with differences in isostatic uplift. The majority are deep, proper caves that reach into dark chambers, up to 200 meters deep. From floor to ceiling there may be as much as 20–50 meters, and the formations may be seen from great distance (Figure 9.2). In their back parts, signs of wave erosion are still evident – slick walls and round beach cobbles/gravel cover the floor. After the freezing ocean waves, gravity took over: in and around cave mouths frequent rock falls added up to a wall of talus scree that block the cave entrance. In some cases, ropes or ladders are needed to overcome huge rock downfalls. Probably, numerous caves are presently totally sealed off by scree formations.

The context of cave paintings may indicate a shared ritual tradition. This is also reflected in the very paintings, that are remarkably similar in shape, colour and size. The painted rock art found in open rock faces include a far wider range of motifs and time (Gjessing 1936; Slinning 2005; Andreassen 2008; Helberg 2016). Most cave paintings are *en face* 'stick men' around 25–40 cm tall: a round head, a body line, arms and legs splayed to the sides (Figures 9.3 and 9.4). 'Red dancers' could very well be a better term, which certainly is closer to how the paintings are sensed:

> Their red is rough at its edges, fading back into the rock that made it, blurred by water and condensation, and all of these circumstances – the blur, the low light, my exhaustion, my blinks – are what give the figures their life, make them shift shapes on this volatile canvas in which shadow and water and rock and fatigue are all artists together, and for once the old notion of ghosts seem new and true in this space. These figures are *ghosts* all dancing together, and I am a ghost too, and there is a conviviality to them, to *us*, to the thousands of years for which they have been dancing here together.
>
> *(Macfarlane 2019, p. 278)*

In spite of obvious similarities, details demonstrate that the uniformity is more prominent within caves than between panels in different caves (size, proportions, how arms/legs are splayed), suggesting local variations within a wider, communal tradition (Bjerck 2012). Nonetheless, there are exceptions from the anthropomorphs motifs – like the big cross in the Solsem cave (Petersen 1914). A long horizontal line below the panel is reported from Helvete in Lofoten (Norsted 2006, pp. 32–3),

FIGURE 9.2 The Sanden caves are found in the northwest coast of Værøy in Lofoten, wide-open to the marine erosion that excavated the coastal caves during the Pleistocene Ice Ages. Two of them are showing in the cliff by the fishing boat. The cave with paintings is nearly sealed off by the rock fall fan to the left of the open caves. Behind the scree, a big chamber leads to a narrow corridor that extends into the deep dark. The red 'stick men' are painted in the innermost part of the dusk, outer chamber, on both sides of the mouth of the pitch black corridor (Figure 9.1). According to a local myth, a dog that once disappeared in the deep part of the cave resurfaced at the other side of the mountain. Photo: Hein B. Bjerck

FIGURE 9.3 'Red dancers', a section of the painted panel in 'Kollhellarn', Moskenes. Drawing: Hein B. Bjerck

where there also is a considerable larger human figure with open hands, legs with bent knees, and feet with soles. Some caves have a few crosses and undefinable lines (Johansen 1988). The Skåren-Monsen cave is the only one without human figures – the long-horned animal here is unique among cave paintings (Sognnes 1983). About 20 other large coastal caves in the region (there are many) have been searched with no result (Bjerck 2012).

Cultural deposits are frequent in rock shelters – but caves are rarely used for habitation. Nevertheless, a Bronze Age cultural layer was excavated in the Solsem cave, that contained a few bone artefacts, shells, and c. 2000 animal bones (fish, birds, seal, goat/sheep, ox, horse), and some human bones, datings from range from *c.* 1700 to 200 cal BC (Petersen 1914; Sognnes 1983; 2009). The location of the cultural layer was in the near-dark part of the cave, which in addition to the absence of lithic waste indicate non-residential activity. In Helvete, there were bones from a big gray seal (*Halichoerus gryphus*) in the innermost part of the cave; samples demonstrate cut marks from butchering. The remains seem to represent a complete animal – big bones, scull fragments, teeth, claws from flippers, and date to 1600–1400 cal BC (Bjerck 2012). The closest associated artefacts to the images are the

FIGURE 9.4 Human figure painted on the calcite crust in the roof of 'Brusteinshola', arms and legs splayed, drenched by condensed water. Photo: Hein B. Bjerck

'palette slabs' and lumps of pigment that Marstrander (1965, p. 159) reported from the floor below the panels in the innermost Finngal's cave. Unfortunately, these artefacts are not found today (Norsted 2008). Until a direct dating of the very painting is presented (which seems possible), I guess the exact age of the tradition will be unclear.

Sensing cavescapes

From a distance, most caves stick out as unfamiliar formations – big openings in the normal world of mountains and gigantic, steep rock faces leaning towards the forces of open sea. On coming closer, the breath-taking dimensions evoke a feeling of being small and inferior, you are reminded of the many things that are bigger than a human in the world. Very often a fissure, a fault or a bedrock vein may be spotted in the rock directly above the opening. To the modern human, a weakness that permitted frost and the abiding pounding from icy ocean waves to excavate ever deeper, accelerating as the cave itself funnelled the forces. To others that saw the world differently, fissures and bedrock alterations perhaps revealed why this door opened precisely here.

... losing colours and light

Standing on the huge wall of rock falls that normally is in cave mouths, you may look down and into the eerie cavescape. Sometimes, the outward wall side may be covered with soil and vegetation, on the inside the guts of the formation is revealed; open scree and gigantic rock falls, dusted and unstable. The mouth of the cave is surprisingly green with lush ferns, wide-bladed grass and wet moss. Inside there is a dim interplay of hues, with alternating stripes of rock and mineral precipitates – white, yellow, red, brown, black, and grey. As you enter the proper cave, you very soon lose the light. Further in, there are only the wet and smooth rock surfaces that shine faintly. The full 'effect' of the cave is not experienced before you have reached the point where the light fades and shifts to darkness. You have moved from broad daylight to muted reflections from lustreless rock walls.

The last you will see is that colours vanish, except for a patchy cover of green lichen, nothing grows, nothing moves. You are as blind were it not for the light you brought with you (Figure 9.5). Even with a reasonable flashlight, you need to take extra care as you move around – even more if the light you brought was a flickering, flaming torch, as most past visitors had to manage by.[1] Perhaps you need to climb huge rocks that have fallen from the roof. Do not trust the shadows in-between, you never know if there is five centimetres or two meters down.

... there is no ending

You may think that you are surrounded by surfaces of solid rock. If you look closer, you can see that this is not true. There is no definite ending, only an entanglement

FIGURE 9.5 Jacob Møller and my son Trygve during a break in 'Helvete'. The paintings are found in the wave abraded wall to the left, in the outer part of the darkened cave. Photo: Hein B. Bjerck

of solid rock and deep shadows. In the roof, where your little light can barely reach there are just darkness, in the floor there are openings below large rocks everywhere. Cracks and openings in walls and floor – they do not end, they just bend. Not in long, you realize that the cave is not a confined space – there are passages beyond in so many places. The sensation of being diminutive on entering is suddenly revolved, now size is your problem. Your over-sized human body are unable to pass any further. Even if you could persuade someone smaller to go deeper, you know that this creature too, due to its bodily size soon would be stopped. You may think that sooner or later the cave will end, completely enclosed by faces of solid rock. More likely, a smaller body would discover even more openings that could not be entered, more forking cracks and fissures, and instead of getting closer to the end of the cave – you would expand the mystery. The ending of the cave is nowhere to be seen, nowhere to be felt. How do you know where the cave ends? How do you know that there *is* an ending?

... the evil of narrow spaces

If you venture deeper through the narrow parts in your search for the cave's end, in the limits of how far the size of your body permits you to pass, you may experience a sudden, paralyzing anxiety. In our time, we have learned this phenomenon by the name 'claustrophobia'. Each time (many) I have encountered claustrophobia it strikes very suddenly, each time I am likewise unprepared. It is very unpleasant. As you crawl, and see that you cannot advance any longer, and it is impossible to turn around, you have to crawl backwards. When you find yourself in a light squeeze between the floor and the rock roof, and you feel the weight of the many hundred meters of rock above you. One time, I was leading a group of people through a narrow passage. Right around the next bend, I realized that it was the end of the cave for my bodily measurements. The rest of the party blocked my retreat in the narrow passage. Each time, I know that I will survive, that I will be back in the open in due time. Nevertheless, this panicky feeling always strikes me hard.

In my normal being-in-the-world, I am told that claustrophobia is something coming from within me, a panicky feeling triggered by narrow spaces, a notion of being trapped, and I believe this is true. But how can I know for sure? Each time I have experienced claustrophobia this scary feeling could just as well have been from encountering some evil, invisible force that percolate from the dark and narrow, something that resides or is emitted by the cave, a thing that grabs me, a warning that this is far enough. How can I know the difference? I acknowledge that this uncanny feeling is not universal. Some people are not prone to claustrophobia, and you may lose this feeling by training. Nevertheless, I am confident that I am not alone in the world through the times to have bumped into this scary experience. The traditional Norwegian beliefs that gruesome (but stupid) trolls resides inside mountains, and the possibility of being 'bergtatt', literally locked into the rock in the home of a troll, has to come from somewhere.

... chill, sounds and scents

Closer to the mouth of the cave, you may hear faint sounds from the outside, birds, the ocean surfs, that the cave transform by adding reverb and echo, sounds that have lost their direction. Approximately where you enter the dark, there are simply no other sounds apart for your own, the rattle from pebbles and stone as you move. If you stop, there is your breath, and a steady switch you do not hear very often. The sound of silence, the sound of your own heart beats doing something to your eardrums. A rhythmic swish from the blood pumping through your inner ear. Perhaps there is the sound from a falling drop of water. Sometimes there is a long wait until the next one. Long enough for you to start wondering ... was it really a falling drop of water you heard?

The cave emits a steady odour that you may recognize from a fridge that has not been opened for a long time, or perhaps the cellar of an old house. But unlike the normal world, where you constantly sense whiffs of different smells with changing intensities as you move about, the cave offers no olfactory variation, just this steady, musty odour. Soon, the lack of variation makes your olfaction dormant. All in all, in a way, you are deprived of most senses that make you engage with the normal world.

By now, you would surely notice the chill. If the climb to the cave made you sweat, the wet cold shirt would stick to your back. Your slow movements in here are not sufficient to maintain the normal body heat, not in long you start to get cold. Cold, the temperature of what is below, things left by life – along with everything else in here, it adds up on you.

... *nothingness and the tentacle of fear*

It is normal practice among cave travellers in our time: to sit down, be totally quiet, and put out the light. This weird feeling of nothingness, like weightless floating in space. You may feel like very big, or perhaps tiny – there is no scale in the dark. Like being on the outside of everything, or perhaps in the very middle of it. Sometimes, when I have done this in solitude, this exercise is accompanied with a sneaking feeling of insecurity. Some kind of uncertainty, slightly scary – even if I know that I am in a safe place, there is this growing anxiety in the depths of my disrupted senses. You may feel an urge to light your torch. Unfortunately, it does not help much – as the light reveals the many dark spaces between the rock surfaces to the left, right, above and below. And even worse, wherever you turn the beam of light, there is the big darkness right behind you. How can you know for sure what darkness is and what resides there? Soon after, the feeling that the light you just lit to counteract anxiety made you very visible, vulnerable, a highlighted eye-catcher for all nameless beings that surround you. Light, or no light – once you are touched by the gentle tentacle of fear, safety is hard to reclaim.

... *beyond time*

All in all, it is the absence of everything that hits you – the lack of movement, colours, scents, and noise which we are used to in the life and day outside. The cave is monotonous, silent, unmoving and evasive, cold and unseen – the very opposite of the living world. There is no day, no winter, no summer, and nothing that grows. The cave extends beyond life, and beyond time.

In our normal being-in-the-world we experience 'time' in movements and changes. The sun moves across the sky during the day, leaving the scene for the night as soon as it sinks below the horizon, leaving the sky to the slow movement of stars and moon, the sequence of seasons. In some caves, sometimes, the sun may shine directly into the cave mouth, a brief moment of light and movement, that

FIGURE 9.6 Leaning against the cold wall in 'Helvete' is a young bird, still in its pose of a living creature. Life has left it, but it is still sitting there. How long has it sat there? It is not easy to tell, because time does not seem to exist here in the conspicuous absence of life. Photo: Hein B. Bjerck

still rarely reach to the inner part of the cave; nothingness prevails in spite of brief moments of life.

Cavescapes hold very few visible signs of 'time'. Weather is absent. Storms, snow, rain, cold, warm – all these familiar phenomena seem indifferent to caves. Living things move around or grow – dead things decay and vanish. Nothing of this is in cave. On the floor there are remains of dead animals and birds, cadavers with hair and feathers, but without swarms of flies or crawling maggots. Leaning against the cold wall is a young bird, with its upward pointing beak optimistically open, still in its pose of a living creature, in contrast to its matt black eyes without the brightness of life (Figure 9.6). Life has left it, but it is still sitting there. How long has it sat there? It is not easy to tell, because time does not seem to exist here in the conspicuous absence of life. What is present is a kind of baseline for being, including what is beyond life, before and after. As archaeologists, we are perhaps blinded by the prospects of exceptional condition for preservation. For past people, perhaps the lack of decay in here was just another sign of a space outside life and time.

In the deepest part of 'Helvete', scattered around a large rock, there was collection of fresh-looking bones from a grey seal, cut marks proved that it was put here by humans. A radiocarbon date reveal that it has been here for 3600 years. That is, 120 generations have had the opportunity to see this thing from the past in their present, the rate of decay so slow that everyone have seen the remains just as they saw it on their last visit.

FIGURE 9.7 View from the mouth of 'Helvete'. Perhaps the most profound embodied cave experience is when you re-enter the life and light outside the cave: your more or less dormant senses from the time you spent in lifeless silence below are suddenly bombarded with movement, sounds, scents and colours; the familiar world, now estranged. Photo: Hein B. Bjerck

... returning to the day

However, you may still have the greatest surprise from being-in-the-cave in reserve. Perhaps the most profound embodied experience is when you re-enter life and light outside the cave: your more or less dormant senses from the time you spent in lifeless silence below, are suddenly bombarded (Figure 9.7).

It is a strange feeling to be surprised by all familiar things, to encounter your own world with amplified alertness, almost as coming to a new world. Or perhaps a sense of yourself as being new to the world. The affect of a warm whiff of wind, the blue sky above you, the moving clouds. The sudden attention to the sound of lazy bumble bees and busy birds, the scent of the sea and bird excrements, grass and flowers in bright red and yellow, the abundance of life, movement and colour. Straws that nod in the wind, the blinking reflections of sunlight from the ever-moving surface of deep blue sea – the living everyday things we always see, but hardly notice.

Discussion and conclusions: Cavescapes and the Underworld

Sensing cavespaces – how can this be relevant for understanding past people's rationale for visiting here and add painted human figures to darkened rock faces? Are not the unlimited possibilities for how *affects of cavescapes* were influenced by past people's personal experience and worldview just too farfetched, too mingled and folded to be handled in the archaeological discourse? Perhaps this is the problem – that we are better off by analyzing cave paintings as *human beings in the world* than scholarly archaeologists, to have faith in things that affect us as human rather than scientists.

Leaving out details in the paintings – the fact that more than 90% of the figures are anthropomorphic must be an imperative observation. The similarity in context, style and size indicate a common tradition. In addition, there may be clues in the *placement of paintings* in these cavescapes. A rough overview of cave plan drawings reveal that paintings are placed differently (Figure 9.1). In a strict, objective sense there seem to be no order. Paintings tend to be grouped – but single figures are also found. Distances from panels to cave mouths and deep 'ends' vary. In some caves, paintings are found by distinct narrowings within. Others have paintings in their dark depths. There are paintings in large chambers where they could be displayed to many – as well as in narrow chambers that limited viewing. Several caves are painted in the twilight zone between light and dark. The single sure fact is that no caves have paintings close to their mouths.

However, and this is my main point, if paintings are included in *how cavescapes are sensed*, and not tri-dimensionally measured, there is perhaps a more distinguishable pattern. Paintings may reveal the importance of borders; as paintings are placed near positions where a human being would sense that he or she is departing from the human world, and sense the border of entering something else, a world outside the day, beyond weather and life, movement and time. These borders may be conceived differently – where the light fades, by narrow passages, in places where your body restrains further movement, or where claustrophobia hits you. Thus, there may be a structure in what appears unstructured. A panel in Brusteinshola in Gildeskål is particularly interesting (Bjerck 2012, p. 53). Here, the painters seem to have erected a flat rock to paint three human figures adjacent to a wide horizontal fissure that delimit any further human reach. As the 'canvas' of the panel seems artificial, it is reason to believe that this exact spot, evidently not an ending, but the outer limit for humans, was imperative.

This is perhaps where phenomenology departs from traditional archaeology. You may measure exact positions, if openings face north or south, distances between caves, calculate means and average values in the relations of paintings, walls, roofs, floors, opening and end – and yet never get closer to understanding. To change the scale from meters to millimetres will not bring you further. You can add complex lux-values, sound recordings measured in hertz with decimals, document relative humidity values, and yet nothing will come out as clear patterns in diagrams and tables. The way towards knowledge is not found in minute details prehistoric people had no capacities to know.

Why? It is because the answer is too complex, and at the same time too simple. The human body is a fine tuned sensory instrument that constantly records, compare and convey, probably without even knowing. The human mind mingles all this with experiences and worldviews embedded in the depth of their cognitive systems – that aggregate in sentiments. The human body do not separate sounds from vision in different tables, do not analyze fragrances separate from temperatures, and do not make calculations where answers have decimals. On the contrary, all this is intermingled in the same instant, and condensed in a notion that tells you when things are right.

With respect to the engagement with caves, cave painters probably experienced and ascribed affective meaning to the overall sense of caves as opposites to the human world; that caves lack colours, sounds, smells, movement, life and time. Very likely, visitors would have sensed the elusive termination of chambers and passages, which evokes a feeling that there is more – which is beyond the reach of humans.

I addition to fascination, I believe that engaging with caves induce a certain level of apprehension on a scale ranging from uneasiness to fear. The loss of sensory control in here – when eyes fail to provide the information you need to move and detect things (and threats) that surround you, ears failing to detect the directions and provenience of sounds, not being able to see what is making sounds, and your nose filled is with an all-encompassing smell of chilled decay – death, nothingness and eternity. The phenomenon 'claustrophobia' – the strange and paralyzing feeling triggered by narrow spaces, simultaneously coming from within and outside – may also have evoked a feeling of being overpowered and out of place. The level of uneasiness may vary – but still, enough people are likely to have experienced anxiety to define and mediate the phenomenon.

Finally, there is the dichotomy between the caves' realm of absence and the reinforced awareness of all 'normal' things in the world on returning from caves, a profound wakefulness of life, a joyful reunion with movements and soundscape, colours and scents – familiar and abnormal simultaneously. I daresay that it is an overall joyful sensation, a sense of coming back, a sense of belonging.

Very likely, some of these facts have been engaged in the much wider array of rationales that constructed the reasons for painting red 'stick men' in Norwegian caves. With or without paintings, and far beyond Bronze Age North Norway in time and space, caves may very well have been imperative in constructing the widespread notion of *axis mundi* and the three-tier universe that are found in many cosmologies around the world (e.g. Anisimov 1963). The very tangible sensuous world of caves, the affects that caves offer to humans, are a places one may see for oneself. Step by step the living world vanishes before your eyes to be replaced by nothingness – a dead world that may actually be seen and sensed by the living, spaces that also witness a continuum to realms beyond humans.

Caves appear in a myriad of shapes, sizes, hardships in how to enter them, if they face north or south. Nevertheless, all these variation melts into one when you reach the cave proper – details conger in a kind of sensed sameness. Thus, caves are more than individual, confined holes in the surface. In fact, as you encounter the very same wherever or whenever you enter these cracks in the human world. Consequently, cavescapes are material witnesses that nourish a belief of a world-encompassing and eternal Underworld through the times.

The phenomenological conclusion is that the affects of cavescapes probably are imperative for the widespread notion of an underworld. The unreachable underneath is a realm tilted towards fear and evil – the opposite of the likewise inaccessible Heaven above us, the home of harmony, hope and the noble.

Acknowledgements

Thanks to Bjørnar J. Olsen and the 'After Discourse' research group at Centre for Advanced Studies, Knut Andreas Bergsvik, Terje Brattli, Jo Sindre Eidshaug, Martinus Hauglid and Robert Macfarlane for input and encouraging discussions.

Note

1. A flaming torch is said to emit about 10 watts / 1850 kelvin of light, quite less than our electrical torches (Pettitt 2016, p. 15).

References

Andreassen, R. L., 2008. Malerier og ristninger – bergkunst i Fennoskandia. *Viking* 71, 39–60.

Anisimov, A., 1963. Cosmological concept of the people in the north. In: Michael, H., ed., *Studies in Siberian Shamanism.* Toronto: University of Toronto Press, 157–229.

Bjerck, H. B., 1995. Malte menneskebilder i 'Helvete'. Betraktninger om en nyoppdaget hulemaling på Trenyken, Røst, Nordland. *Universitetets Oldsaksamling Årbok* 1993/1994, 121–50.

Bjerck, H. B., 2012. In the outer fringe of the human world: Phenomenological perspectives on anthropomorphic cave paintings in Norway. In: Bergsvik, K. A. and Skeates, R., eds., *Caves in Context. The Cultural Significance of Caves and Rockshelters in Europe.* Oxford: Oxbow Books, 48–78.

Brück, J., 2005. Experiencing the past? The development of a phenomenological archaeology in British Prehistory. *Archaeological Dialogues* 12 (1), 45–67.

Clottes, J., 2003. Caves as landscapes. In: Sognnes, K., ed., *Rock Art in Landscapes – Landscapes in Rock Art.* Det Kongelige Norske Videnskabers Selskabs Skrifter 4. Trondheim: Tapir Academic Press, 9–30.

Gjessing, G., 1936. *Nordenfjelske ristninger og malinger av den arktiske gruppe.* Instituttet for sammenlignende kulturforskning Serie B. Oslo: Aschehoug.

González-Ruibal, A., 2008. Time to destroy. An archaeology of supermodernity. *Current Anthropology* 49 (2), 247–79.

Hamilton, S., Whitehouse, R., Brown, K., Combes, P., Herring, E. and Thomas, M. S., 2006. Phenomenology in practice: Towards a methodology for a 'subjective approach'. *European Journal of Archaeology* 9 (1), 31–71.

Hauglid, M. A., Helberg, B. and Hesjedal, A., 1991. *Strekfigurene i Kollhellaren på Moskenesøya, Vest-Lofoten.* Tromura, Kulturhistorie 19, 157–69.

Helberg, B., 2016. *Bergkunst nord for Polarsirkelen.* Tromsø museums skrifter 36. Tromsø: Orkana Akademisk.

Hesjedal, A., 1994. The hunters' rock art in Northern Norway. Problems of chronology and interpretation. *Norwegian Archaeological Review* 27 (1), 1–28.

Jackson, F., 1986. What Mary didn't know. *The Journal of Philosophy* 83 (5), 291–5.

Johansen, A. B., 1988. Bildene i Troillhåle. *Årbok for Helgeland* 1988, 29–32.

Macfarlane, R., 2019. *Underland. A Deep Time Journey.* UK: Hamish Hamilton.

Marstrander, S., 1965. Fingalshulen i Gravvik, Nord-Trøndelag. *Viking* 29, 147–65.

Møller, J., 1985. Coastal caves and their relation to early postglacial shore levels in Lofoten and Vesterålen, North Norway. *Norges geografiske undersøkelser, Bulletin* 400, 51–65.

Møller, J., Danielsen, T. K. and Fjalstad, A., 1992. Late Weichselian glacial maximum on Andøya, North Norway. *Boreas* 21(1), 1–15.

Norsted, T., 2006. Hulemaleriene i Norge. Egenart, kontekst, mening og konservering. In: Egenberg, I. M., Skar, B. and Swensen, G., eds., *Kultur – minner og miljøer. Strategiske instituttprogrammer 2001–2005.* NIKU-Tema 18, 11–46. Oslo: NIKU.

Norsted, T., 2008. *Maleriene i Fingalshula, Gravvik i Nærøy.* – NIKU Rapport 23. Oslo: NIKU.

Norsted, T., 2013. The cave paintings of Norway. *Adoranten*, 5–24. www.rockartscandinavia.com/images/articles/a13norstedt.pdf (accessed April 2019).

Olivier, L., 2004. The past in the present. Archaeological memory and time. *Archaeological Dialogues* 10 (2), 204–13.

Olivier, L., 2011. *The Dark Abyss of Time: Archaeology and Memory.* Lanham: Alta Mira Press.

Olsen, B., 2010. *In Defense of Things. Archaeology and the Ontology of Objects.* Lanham: Altamira Press.

Olsen, B. and Pétursdóttir, Þ., n.d. *After discourse: Things, archaeology, and heritage in the 21st century.* Unpublished project description, Centre for Advanced Study at the Norwegian Academy of Science and Letters, Oslo.

Petersen, Th., 1914. Solsemhulen paa Leka. En boplads fra arktisk stenalder. Foreløpig meddelelse. *Oldtiden* IV, 25–41.

Pettitt, P., 2016. Darkness visible. Shadows, art and the ritual experience of caves in Upper Palaeolithic Europe. In: Dowd, M., and Hensey, R., eds., *The Archaeology of Darkness.* Oxford: Oxbow Books, 11–23.

Slinning, T., 2005. Antropomorfe klippeformasjoner og fangstfolks kultsted. In: Goldhahn, J., ed., *Mellan sten och järn.* Gothenburg: Gotarc Serie C. Arkeologiska Skrifter No. 59, 489–502.

Sognnes, K., 1983. Prehistoric cave paintings in Norway. *Acta Archaeologica* 53, 101–18.

Sognnes, K., 2009. Art and humans in confined space: Reconsidering Solsem Cave, Norway. *Rock Art Research* 26 (1), 83–94.

Tilley, C., 1994. *A Phenomenology of Landscape. Places, Paths and Monuments.* Oxford: Berg.

Tilley, C., 2004. *The Materiality of Stone. Explorations in Landscape Phenomenology.* Oxford: Berg.

10

RUINS OF RUINS

The aura of archaeological remains

Saphinaz-Amal Naguib

Flashback

On 3 April 2015, militants of the Islamic State of Iraq and the Levant (ISIL; Da'esh in Arabic)[1] posted a video on YouTube showing some of their men methodically smashing and shooting at selected sculptures at the archaeological site of Hatra in north-west Iraq. The rhythm of the men breaking the artefacts sets the tempo of the three-minute-long film. The musical background to the action all along the film consists of a men's choir singing a hymn or *nashid* composed in the genre of nationalistic, military songs that were popular in many Arab countries during the 1960s. This 'spectacle of destruction' deeply affected me, and took me back to my first encounter with Hatra in the mid-1980s. I had no previous knowledge of the place, and my own research interests have taken me towards different fields. Eventually, Hatra became (or so I thought) a hazy memory, supported by some slightly faded pictures my husband had taken. Yet, when I saw the video of its demolition I realized the deep impression Hatra had left on my mind and feelings.

At the time of our visit, the Iran–Iraq war was at its height. We had left Baghdad early that morning, and passing through the many security checkpoints that controlled the roads, a stop at the Great Mosque of Samarra and its spiralling cone-shaped minaret, we were on our way to Jebel Sinjar and Mosul. Suddenly, some remarkable monuments appeared in the wide horizon of the steppe landscape that surrounded us. They stood proudly in splendid isolation inviting us to come nearer. (Figure 10.1) There were no other visitors at the site, just some bored guards at the entrance. I remember entering the wide *temenos* and seeing the tall statue of Abu bint Damyōn dressed up in her fine attires. She was standing in front of the remains of a big temple, and seemed to have been waiting for us. She was greeting us with her raised right hand as we approached (Figure 10.2).[2]

FIGURE 10.1 Arrival at Hatra, February 1985. Photo: Robert W. Vaagan

FIGURE 10.2 Hatra: Abu bint Damyōn greeting the visitors, February 1985. Photo: Robert W. Vaagan

FIGURE 10.3 Hatra: the male Gorgon, February 1985. Photo: Robert W. Vaagan

I can still feel the overwhelming sense of wonder and reverence that hit me when my travel companions and I entered the towering *iwan* and ambled amid the imposing ruins. I recall the emotion I experienced looking up at the face of the male Gorgon with his full beard made of acanthus leaves and snakes in his hair watching over the place and protecting his territory (Figure 10.3). The masks in high relief and the sculpted busts intensified the feeling of being continuously observed, while the relief of the camel cow feeding her calf conveyed tenderness. I see myself staring at the head of a woman protruding out of the wall just under the arch of the *iwan* as if she was leaning out of a window calling out at someone in the street (Figure 10.4). In the video circulated by Da'esh, one of the men is pounding furiously at this piece with his sledgehammer until he breaks it off the wall. Why would anyone want to destroy these beautiful ruins? What covert meaning and memories do they bear that trigger such fierce brutality?

Aesthetics of destruction

The turn of this millennium has witnessed a wave of systematic destruction and organized looting of ancient buildings, monuments, archaeological sites and artefacts in the Middle East. War has been taking its toll. Towns and villages are suddenly turned into ruins, and their inhabitants endure all kinds of hardship and losses. Existing ancient ruins that have stood in the same places for centuries, and for centuries made the admiration of innumerable visitors from different parts of the world are being even more fragmented. Among the most salient examples of recent destructions are the ancient towns, archaeological sites and monuments in Iraq, Syria and Yemen. Museums are looted; statues are smashed; monuments are demolished; blocs from ancient buildings are re-used to rebuild people's destroyed homes; artefacts are sold through more or less shady international networks trading in antiquities. One of the places that have recently suffered the wounds of war is Hatra in northwest Iraq.

Hatra is an ancient Parthian city that has been listed as a UNESCO World Heritage Site since 1985.[3] The site was looted after the Gulf War in the 1990s and again during the USA led war in 2003. In 2014, members of Da'esh occupied the area. They used the ruins to train in urban warfare well aware, in my opinion, that the coalition forces would not bomb the site. In early 2015, militants from Da'esh announced their intention to obliterate what they proclaimed to be 'un-Islamic' artefacts and images. As mentioned above, at the beginning of April 2015, they posted a video on YouTube, showing how they went about systematically breaking and ruining sculptures, reliefs, wall paintings and monuments at Hatra. This 'spectacle of destruction' as Ömür Harmanşah (2015) calls it, is part of a thoroughly staged performance addressed mostly towards an international audience (Harmanşah 2015; De Cesari 2015, pp. 22–3). That same year (2015), the UNESCO put Hatra on the list of World Heritage in danger. The pro-Iraqi government Popular Mobilization Forces (PMF) regained control over Hatra on 26 April 2017. The reports of the damage endured by the site are somehow vague and contradictory. A journalist of the Spanish news agency EFE reported finding many broken statues, defaced reliefs and wall-paintings, burnt buildings as well as signs of looting. A spokesperson for the PMF stated that Da'esh had destroyed the sculptures and reliefs, and that the walls and towers still standing contained holes and scratches from Da'esh's bullets. In addition, Da'esh had left mines at the eastern gates of Hatra, thus preventing archaeologists and heritage professionals from assessing the damages. According to official sources and the head of antiquities for Nineveh Governorate, Layla Salih, the site had suffered less damage than feared and most buildings were intact.[4]

Several scholars have in recent years discussed the ambiguity of 'embedded archaeology', and denounced the destruction of Iraq's cultural heritage in the

FIGURE 10.4 Hatra: head of a woman looking out, February 1985. Photo: Robert W. Vaagan

aftermath of the Gulf War in 1991 and the USA and British coalition in 2003. These acts were condoned as accidental 'collateral damage,' and steps were taken to educate the military on local cultures and heritage before sending them to the field (Gerstenblith 2009; Hamilakis 2009; Kila 2013; Stone and Bajjaly eds., 2008). The demolition of Hatra's ruins and the organized breaking of the reliefs and statues by Da'esh were not merely acts of senseless violence. On the contrary, they were, as mentioned earlier, well prepared, intentional actions framed in what I consider an aesthetics of destruction. Pictures and videos showing members of Da'esh at work against the monuments and sculptures have been mediated, remediated, and gone viral on various news agencies and a plethora of social media. They have triggered a wave of outraged reactions internationally, and have been condemned as 'acts of barbarism', 'iconoclasm', 'crimes of war', 'cultural cleansing' and 'cultural genocide'.[5] In contrast, the PMF and coalition forces taking over Hatra have been regarded as the 'saviours' and 'liberators' of the ancient city, freeing it from the shackles of a cruel, ignorant enemy. Both events – the attack on the monuments and their subsequent salvage – pertain, in my view, to forms of affective practices of violence that have deeply marked the perception of the place's aura.

Studying Near Eastern archaeology, heritage and material cultures entails, among other things, to take into consideration which past has been used in the formation of modern nation-states and national identities. One has to be aware of a long history of complex relations between nomadic and sedentary populations, of ethnic, tribal and sectarian divides and shifting allegiances, the significance of city-states, incessant power struggling among rulers in the region as well as foreign, colonial and post-colonial interests, and take into account the dissonant, often silenced and forgotten voices of various ethnic and religious communities. Mobile populations and minorities have regularly been considered as disruptive elements in the geo-political landscape of the region. Their history has been disregarded; their material culture has been overlooked and often gone unrecorded in official archives or simply destroyed; their discordant voices have been toned down and are rarely listened to. Nevertheless, much has been kept alive in their own cultural memory and intangible heritage. Generally speaking, nation-states have not been fair to their minorities, especially if they are nomads. Iraq is no exception to this rule. With their apparent freedom from fixed territorial borders and bonds, nomads and semi-nomad pastoralists have been considered as threats to the unity of the Iraqi nation-state. Nomads, however, do not normally roam around aimlessly. They are not wanderers swinging between freedom, displacement and exclusion. Nomads whether they are land-nomads or seafarers have complex social and cultural organizations and worldviews. Their ways of life are highly structured. They may be tied to seasonal cycles and the natural environment or to trade routes. In the Middle East, North Africa and Central Asia, nomads have for centuries followed known routes, stopped at the same oases, markets or religious centres where they refurbished their caravans, exchanged goods and built extended networks. For centuries, nomads have acted as cultural brokers carrying merchandises and ideas from one place to another. The history and material culture of Hatra and its ruins reflect much of the interaction between central authorities, city-dwellers, nomads and different ethnic and religious groups.

This chapter is about the politics and poetics of archaeological remains in borderlands. In my use of the term, borderlands denotes in-between geographical territories, which provide prolific grounds for various forms of cultural, religious and social encounters, some peaceful others more confrontational. Before the establishment of nation-states, borderlands were not delimited by clearly defined frontiers and were open to varied transcultural flows. In Hatra, these cultural contacts are clearly expressed in the figurative art and architecture where Hellenistic and Roman influences merge with Mesopotamian and Parthian motives, and in the religious life of this ancient city (Figures 10.5, 10.6). In the following, I make use of a combined archaeological and culture historical approach to explore the place of emotion in

FIGURE 10.5 Frieze of busts on the arcade of an *iwan* (detail), February 1985. Photo: Robert W. Vaagan

FIGURE 10.6 Masks on the wall watching, February 1985. Photo: Robert W. Vaagan

contemporary engagements with the past in areas that have recently been exposed to armed conflicts. I examine Hatra through the lenses of sensorial assemblages (Hamilakis 2017) where the tangible, the intangible, affect, politics, mnemonics and multi-temporalities are central interconnected elements. Such an approach opens up for a perception of time that is non-linear and non-chronometric. It also brings forth the polyphony of a place. Relying on the accounts of travellers who have visited Hatra at different periods, I probe the concepts of aura, presence and resonance to analyze the enchantment of ruins and archaeological fragments. How they can reach our feelings and move us in unexpected ways. As Mats Burström (2013, p. 319) explicates, fragments are metonymies that point to something beyond the original larger whole of which they were part. Things, in his view, may gain rather than loose meaning through fragmentation. To perceive their many layered meanings one has to delve into the historical, social and political contexts that shaped them as well as the cultural memory of a diverse population. As analytical tools, the notions of aura, presence and resonance may help to shed new light on the substance and character of Hatra, on the entanglement between different populations and material culture, their intertwined histories and conflicting experiences.

The city of the Sun God

Hatra is situated between the Tigris and the Euphrates in the steppe landscape of the Jazirah desert at 200m above sea level, and at about 100km south of Mosul and 290km north of Baghdad. There are several water points in the area, but the water is brackish and the supply depends mostly on underground water, the occasional winter rains and the Tharthar river. The name Hatra (Arabic الحضر *al-Ḥaḍr*; Aramaic: *Hatera*; Latin: *Atraï*) means 'enclosure' in Aramaic and Arabic, with the added meanings of 'city' and 'holy place' in Arabic (Ibrahim 1986, p. 91, nn. 123, 139). Hatra's population consisted of sedentary urban dwellers interacting closely with semi-nomad pastoralists, and comprised different ethnic and religious communities (Dijkstra 1990). The common language was Hatrean, a local dialect of Aramaic. Hatra had a circular plan with a circumference of about 6 km, and was protected by concentric solid inner and outer walls that were supported by more than 120 towers. There was a gate at each of the cardinal points (Foietta 2016). In the centre of the city, there was a large rectangular *temenos* or sacred area of about 440m x 320m, where the main temples were situated (Figure 10.7). The major temples inside the temenos are characterized by the *iwan*, an architectural feature that was introduced during the Parthian period in the 1st century BCE in Mesopotamia. It consists of rectangular halls walled on three sides with an open vaulted façade and roofed with high barrel vaults (Figure 10.8). The main building materials used at Hatra were local limestone and sun-dried mudbricks (Safar and Mustafa 1974, p. 51). The history of Hatra is one of resilience. It entails the capacity of 'bouncing forward', of absorbing adversity, changing and continuing to exist (Holtorf 2018, pp. 639–40). The history of Hatra is also that borderlands open for various forms of cultural contacts. In Antiquity, the city stood as both a buffer state and a battle field between the Roman and Parthian empires.

Hatra, has attracted considerable academic interest, and in spite of the recurrent tense political situations in the country and the limited access to the site, much has been written about the city's archaeological remains, architecture and

FIGURE 10.7 The circular city. https://hatrasite.com/la-citta/. Courtesy dr. Roberta Ricciardi Venco, original in: Stierlin 1987, fig. 163. Accessed February 13, 2018

artworks, religious life and juridical documents (Andrae 1908; 1975[1912]; Bahrani 2017, 340–51; Dirven 2006–2007, 2013; Drijivers 1977; Fukai 1960; Hauser 2013; Herzfeld 1914; Ibrahim 1986; Kaizer 2000, 2013; Safar and Mustafa 1974; Sommer 2003, 2013; Venco Ricciardi 2000). To go into the details of these studies will largely exceed the scope of this chapter. Suffice to say that scholars have quite divergent interpretations of the remains of this ancient city. According to the Iraqi archaeologists, Fuad Safar and Muhammad Mustafa (1974, p. 18) who led the excavations from 1951 through the 1960s, Hatra was at first a small Assyrian settlement located near water points. It grew in importance during the Seleucid Hellenistic period and developed into the wealthy capital of a semi-autonomous Arab kingdom under Parthian rule, and withstood several attacks by the Roman armies. European archaeologists who have worked on the site more recently contend the long chronology proposed by their Iraqi colleagues, and argue for a later development of Hatra. They posit that the place was first occupied by the Parthians in the second century BCE, and that by the first century BCE it had developed into an important fortified city of the Syrian-Mesopotamian desert.[6] These views seem to corroborate the account by the Roman historian, Cassius Dio who described Hatra at the time of the attack by the Roman emperor, Trajan in 117 CE, as an insignificant town 'neither large nor prosperous, and the surrounding country is mostly desert and has neither water (save a small amount, poor in quality), nor timber nor fodder' (Cassius Dio, LXVIII, 31). Eighty years later when Septimius Severus tried

FIGURE 10.8 Hatra: entering the *iwan*, February 1985. Photo: Robert W. Vaagan

to conquer the city, Hatra had according to the same Cassius Dio become a vibrant, rich city: 'The fame of the place was great, since it contained enormous offerings to the Sun God and vast stores of valuables' (Cassius Dio, LXXVI, 12).

Most archaeologists and historians agree, however, that Hatra's growth was due to three main factors. The first was the city's strategic geopolitical position on the edges of two big empires, the Roman and the Parthian, and its role as a military stronghold. The size, material and structure of the concentric walls encircling the city emphasize its function as a fortress (Foietta 2016).

The second main factor was the significant economic role played by Hatra in the region and its importance in caravan trade. It was well placed at the crossroad of different trade routes between Asia, the Mediterranean, the Arab/Persian Gulf and Africa, and was included as an important station for caravans in a medieval copy of the late Roman road map, *Tabula Peutingeriana* (Altaweel and Hauser 2004, pp. 72–5). However, unlike Dura Europos, Palmyra, Baalbek and Petra, Hatra was not a 'caravan city' that depended mainly on long-distance trade of luxury products such as silk and spices (Sommer 2003 pp. 44–6). Satellite imagery has shown that the city was situated in an area with many agricultural and pastoralist settlements. It grew within an interdependent relation between semi-nomad pastoralists, urban sedentary populations and the regular sojourns of caravans (Altaweel and Hauser 2004; Ibrahim 1986, p. 133; Kaizer 2013, pp. 59–70; Safar and Mustafa 1974, p. 11).

The third, and probably most important factor was the role of Hatra as a religious centre for diverse populations. A number of scholars postulate that at its beginnings Hatra served as a kind of 'pre-Islamic Mecca,' that is a sacred enclosure with temples reflecting the religious diversity of people that lived in the region and of those who passed through it. Such places of pilgrimage provided the various tribes and the passing caravans with neutral and fruitful grounds for trade, various forms of cultural exchanges and religious contacts (Drijvers 1977; Dirven 2006–2007; Ibrahim 1986, p. 139; Kaizer 2013, p. 58).

In Aramaic, Hatra was known as the 'House of God' (*Beit̠ Ĕlāhā*). It was famous for its varied pantheons encompassing Mesopotamian, Canaanite, Greek, Aramean and Arabian deities (Kaizer 2000; Safar and Mustafa 1974, pp. 13–18, 41–7). Hatrene coins bear the Aramaic inscription *enclosure of Shamash*, which indicates that the Babylonian sun god and god of justice, Shamash was the chief god of Hatra. In addition, there were temples dedicated to the triade of the city Maren (*Māran*: 'Our Lord'), who was probably identified with Shamash, his wife Marten (*Mārtan*; 'Our Lady'), and their son Bar-Maren ('the Son of Our Lord and Lady'; Tubach 2013, pp. 203–4). Other prominent deities were the Sumerian-Akkadian god Nergal, the Greek god Hermes, the Aramean god Atargatis; and the Arabian goddesses Allāt and Shāmiyyah. Allāt was most likely the protective goddess of Hatra; she was identified with Marten and the camel cow was her symbolic animal. In addition, at least fourteen smaller shrines dedicated to various other deities have been located in different parts of the domestic quarters of the city.

In 117 CE, the Roman emperor, Trajan tried to conquer the city, and later in 198/99 CE emperor Septimius Severus tried again. Both failed, and Hatra continued to grow and prosper. After a siege that lasted two years, it fell in 241 CE to the attacks of the Sasanian armies led by Ardashir and his son Shapur I. The city was plundered and abandoned; its population dispersed. Hatra was left to a slow process of ruination for centuries to come.

Ruins and their aura

Ruins have a special aesthetic and emotional appeal. They have the faculty of bringing to mind visions of 'enchanted, desolate spaces, large-scale monumental structures abandoned and grown over' (Stoler 2008, p. 194). In his essay *Die Ruine*, Georg Simmel (1958 [1911]) took a Romantic view of decaying buildings and monuments. To him, ruins denote the harmonization between nature and culture as they merge within the surrounding landscape. Walter Benjamin perceived the ruin as 'petrified' history; an allegory of the briefness of life and the ephemerality of material culture. He saw ruins as traces from the past that underscore the sense of transience and vulnerability (Benjamin 1977, pp. 177–8). Reflecting on the writings of architects, painters, novelists and various writers Christopher Woodward (2001) suggests that the attraction of ruins and their lasting hold on the imagination of people lies in the feeling of stillness that emanates from them. This stillness is not, however, synonymous to absolute immobility and demise. Rather, it carries in it the promise of a new life, a new beginning that takes form in ruins and rubbles. It is, in my view, this sense of constant ephemerality mixed with continual renewal that imbues ruins with aura.

For many, ruins glow with an aura that even when well-prepared often takes one by surprise. The word aura stems from the ancient Greek and Latin *aura* meaning breeze, wind, breath of air. It has four main semantic values. The first expresses a distinctive atmosphere surrounding a person or thing; it denotes a subtle sensory stimulus like, for instance, an aroma. The second indicates a luminous radiation such as a nimbus or luminous cloud, a halo. Aura is also used in medicine to designate perceptual disturbances that some people experience with migraines or flashes of light that precede a seizure, most often related to epilepsy. In esoteric terminology, aura signifies an energy field that seems to emanate from a person or an object[7]. Walter Benjamin (2008[1936], p. 23) explicates that the 'aura of objects' is a mystifying experience of 'a strange tissue of space and time: the unique apparition of a distance, however near it may be.' The sense of distance is related to the originality and authenticity of the work of art, the tradition on which it is shaped, and the immediateness of the experience in encountering it:

> [T]he here and now of the work of art – its unique existence in a particular place. … The here and now of the original underlies the concept of its authenticity, and on the latter in turn is founded the idea of a tradition which has passed down the object as the same, identical thing to the present day.
>
> *(Benjamin 2008[1936], p. 21)*

Thus, aura is contingent to a sensory experience of a fleeting moment, an atmosphere that emanates from the thing itself and its surroundings. Distance, authenticity and tradition are main elements in Benjamin's understanding of aura. In the *Arcades Project* he includes the idea of the reciprocity of the gaze and explains it as 'the look that awakens in an object perceived.' (Benjamin 2002[1999], p. 314) Further, he contrasts the notion of aura with that of trace (*Spur*):

> Trace and aura. The trace is the appearance of a nearness, however far removed the thing that left it behind may be. The aura is the appearance of a distance; however close the thing that calls it forth. In the trace, we gain possession of the thing; in the aura, it takes possession of us.
>
> *(Benjamin 2002 [1999], 447)*

In my understanding of Benjamin's definition of aura, the sense of distance pertains to both the physical space and the span of time that separate the beholder from the object of her gaze. We may infer that the aura of ruins such as those of Hatra expresses an ethereal quality that radiates through the interplay between the landscape and physical environment, multiple temporalities, the material culture, the senses and knowledge about the biographies of the heterogeneous assemblages as well as the ideas they bear. It represents an intangible distinctive quality, an atmosphere that surrounds the site, and brings forth its uniqueness and authenticity. The experience of aura emanating from the material traces of bygone cultures draws attention to the presence of things and their resonance. Eelco Runia (2006, p. 5) defines presence as 'being in touch.' For him, the notion of presence helps understanding how the past is present in the present, albeit all the gaps and discontinuities, and how we feel about it. In the case of ruins as the ones in Hatra, it is very much tied to their materiality, the structure and aesthetics of the remains and how they are preserved, restored and exhibited. It entails upholding the continuity of the place in the surrounding landscape despite the political and social changes and upheavals. As for resonance, it suggests an echo, a multi-temporal, mnemonic lingering of the site and the changes it has undergone. Used figuratively it triggers images, memories and emotions and, concurrently, brings forth the historical, geopolitical and cultural contexts (Greenblatt 1990). Further, resonance implies the interaction between two separate entities, one located in the foreground and the other in the background, that respond to each other. The elements in the foreground relate to the present while those in the background pertain to the past and to cultural memory. Resonance refers to ways of awakening and intensifying the affective impact of the past in the present and passing it on to the future (Assmann 2015, p. 45). The feelings of aura, presence and resonance are often experienced in relation to the knowledge one has about the place and things contemplated and marvelled at.

Musing about the 'cradle of civilization'

I have argued elsewhere (Naguib 2015, 2018) that archaeology, heritage and politics are often tightly entangled matters. The history of Middle Eastern archaeology is very much tied to colonial domination and post-colonial interests in the region. From the 19th century to the end of WWII it was greatly subject to the rivalry between the two big colonial powers, Britain and France, the decisions of the Ottoman sovereigns and local governors, as well as to the presence of other players in the region such as Germany and the USA. The relation between nationalistic feelings, independence movements, archaeology and cultural heritage has been particularly sensitive during that time. Mesopotamia has repeatedly been defined as the 'cradle of civilization' (Bahrani 1998, pp. 162–4; 2017, pp. 17–25; Bernhardsson 2005, pp. 24–5; Al-Hussainy and Matthews 2008). This is where writing was invented, where the first code of laws was compiled, where city-states and urbanization developed, and where, according to many, the supposed location of the

Gardens of Eden was situated at Shatt al-Arab at the confluence of the two rivers, the Tigris and the Euphrates. Reading about archaeological surveys and excavations in Iraq, the discovery of Mesopotamian monuments, and the conditions of their hasty shipments abroad, one is overwhelmed by an atmosphere of urgency and competition. Western archaeologists competed with one another in who would assure the most prestigious finds to their countries, museums and universities. The main objective of the Ottoman Antiquity Laws from 1874 and 1884 was hence to regulate the movements of antiquities and archaeological material, and fight the looting of archaeological sites.

The British controlled the majority of archaeological sites in Iraq after the Mesopotamian Campaign (1914–1918), the dissolution of the Ottoman Empire in 1922, and until the end of the British Mandate in 1932. In his book, *Reclaiming a Plundered Past*, Magnus Torkell Bernhardsson (2005) investigates the history of archaeology in Iraq until the 1950s. He distinguishes three major phases. The first one is that of removal. From the 1830s to WW1, European archaeologists and institutions considered Mesopotamian antiquities to be 'international,' and thus, part of their own cultural heritage. They argued that they would take better care of the monuments and artefacts than local populations had done so far. During this first period, the British archaeologist, Austen Henry Layard led the excavations at Assur in north-west Iraq; the French consul, Paul-Émile Botta, later followed by Victor Place excavated the site of Khorsabad in the northeast of the country; the Germans under the direction of Robert Koldewey worked on the site of Babylon. Another German archaeologist, Walter Andrae was leading the excavations at Assur. Together with members of his team he made several brief visits to Hatra, and was the first to map and document photographically the site between 1906 and 1911 (Andrae 1908, 1975[1912]).

The second phase, according to Bernhardsson, is that of the interwar years from 1921–1941, which corresponds with the creation of Iraq as a nation-state (1921), and the implementation of the British Mandate (1921–1932). It marked the beginning of a 'national' phase for Iraqi archaeology and heritage which, however, remained under British supervision. Antiquities became the national property of Iraq, and it became more difficult to take them out of the country. This change of policy was greatly due to the efforts and influence of the 'woman who invented Iraq' (Irving 2014), the British political officer, administrator and archaeologist, Gertrude Bell (1868–1926). She played a central role in the creation of Iraq as a new nation-state in the Middle East. Moreover, Bell set up the Antiquities Department and became the first Director General of Antiquities. She put archaeological excavations under state supervision, and pushed for the creation of the Iraq Museum in Baghdad.

The third phase in the history of Iraqi archaeology started in 1941. Since then, Iraq has had full control of its archaeology, at least until the sanctions imposed on the country in the 1990s followed by the successive attacks on and looting of archaeological and heritage sites and museums since 2003.

In their endeavour to carve a unified national identity from an existing very diverse population, the different political regimes that succeeded each other in Iraq's contemporary history adopted the melting pot model (Naguib 2015, pp. 230–1). They constructed a common heritage by drawing mainly upon the pre-Islamic heritage and the Islamic golden age (Abdi 2008; Baram 1983). The Code of laws of Hammurabi, the military valour and competence of the Assyrians and of Saladin and his armies fighting the Crusaders, the splendour of Mesopotamian city-states, the architecture and scientific knowledge of the Abbasids, have been favourite motives in political campaigns. During the 1980s, one could, for example, see gigantic murals and posters picturing Saddam Hussein as a modern day Nebuchadnezzar, Sargon or Saladin, or receiving the code of laws from the hands of Hammurabi, strategically placed at the entrance of towns, on the external walls of official buildings and along the major highways (Figure 10.9). Other pasts, as for instance, the ones of the Sabeans from the Marshes in the south, the Kurdish, the Assyrians, the Yazidis or that of semi-nomad pastoralist tribes that live in northern Iraq have suffered from enforced amnesia. In the 1970s and 1980s, the ruling Baath party in Iraq allocated large amounts of oil-derived resources into archaeological excavations, the restoration and preservation of archaeological sites such as Babylon, Hatra, Assur and Nineveh, as well as the creation and upkeep of several new museums (Baram 1983, p. 428; Bernhardsson 2005, pp. 164–216; de Cesari 2015, p. 24).

The projects and their implementation were all top-down decisions; local communities were not consulted during the process. The Iraqi led excavations and

FIGURE 10.9 Poster at the entrance of the city of Kirkuk, north-east Irak. It shows Saddam Hussein as the heir of both king Sargon of Akkad (top left corner) and Saladin (top right corner), February 1985. Photo: Robert W. Vaagan

restoration works at Hatra started in 1951 and lasted until the mid-1970s (Safar and Mustafa 1974, p. 12). Most of the statues and smaller artefacts that were found were moved to the newly established museum in Mosul, some also to the museum in Baghdad. The restoration of Hatra involved cleaning the area from all sorts of débris and a good deal of 'reconstruction' in three meanings of the word, namely, repairing, remaking and modifying. Hatra was reconstructed as a unique model of Parthian city. The results of the works produced what the British journalist and travel writer, Gavin Young (1980, p. 98) described as *the perfect ruin*, namely, a pristine place frozen in time, and worthy to be included in UNESCO's World Heritage List. A number of archaeologists, conservators, historians and heritage professionals have strongly criticized the methods and materials used during the restoration works at Hatra judging them to be irreversible, and to have tampered with the authenticity of the site (Dirven 2013, p. 10).

Echoes in ruins and their mnemonics

Hatra was left to a process of ruination since the third century, CE. The Roman historian, Ammianus Marcellinus (Book XXV, chap. 8, 5) who accompanied emperor, Julian during his campaign against the Sasanians in 363 CE described Hatra as 'an ancient town in the middle of a desert, which had been long since abandoned.' Abandonment, however, does not mean complete void. Hatra was never really deserted in the centuries that followed its abandonment. The heaps of rubble did not stand still; life did go on there and with it small almost invisible changes came about. Traces of mobile populations and their temporary camps, inscriptions, graffiti, coins and layers of ashes indicate that the site has been used continuously (Ibrahim 1986, pp. 93, 140; Venco-Ricciardi 2000, p. 89, n. 15). Several Arab tribes had settlements within and outside the remains of the ancient city; other more sedentary groups such as the Kurds and the Yazidis inhabited the surrounding region. During their surveys, excavations and restoration works in the 1950s–1970s, Iraqi archaeologists witnessed groups of Yazidis using the premises of the great temple to perform some of their rituals, and also taking away stone blocks from the site to re-use in the construction of their own newer buildings (Safar and Mustafa 1974, p. 35). Further, the various narratives about Hatra disclose the disconcerting resonance the place has kept in peoples' cultural memory. The stories convey polyphonic understandings to the notions of belonging and identity as well as they reveal various political strategies and interests.

　　Arab historians and poets such as al-Tabari (9th century CE), Abu Dawud al-Aijadi (9th century CE) and Ibn Umran bin al-Haf bin Qudamah (10th century CE), bestowed Hatra with a tragic aura. They adopted the Arabic poetic trope known as 'stopping or standing by the ruins' (al-wuquf 'ala al-atlal, الوقوف على الأطلال),[8] and depicted the ruins with metaphors of desolation, stillness and death, but also of grandiosity and beauty. The literary theme was developed in pre-Islamic times and continued to be used extensively to express loss and longing. In their accounts, Arab authors relate the disastrous fall of Hatra, which according to legend, was caused by the betrayal of the daughter of the Hatrene king, princess al-Nadirah, who had fallen in love with the enemy, the handsome Sasanian prince, Shapur I (Herzfeld 1914, pp. 657–8; Ibrahim 1986, pp. 217–19; Zakeri 1998). Further, the writers describe how Arab tribes fought the Persian 'fire-worshippers' and exterminated them (Ibrahim 1986, p. 217). The allusion to 'fire-worshippers' may be a reference to the religious practices of the Parthians and the Sasanians and to Zoroastric rituals. It may also be related to the natural environment, and echo the Roman historian, Cassius Dio (LXXVI, 11) mention of balls of 'hatrene fire', the 'bitiminous naphta', that the Hatreans threw on Roman armies during the sieges of the city.

Epigraphic studies suggest that there probably was a military station combined with a trading post at Hatra during the Middle-Ages (Ibrahim 1986, p. 34). Two inscriptions dating from the Atabec dynasty in Mosul (1127–1261) inform of restoration works having been done in the higher levels of the main temple that had collapsed (Safar and Mustafa 1974, p. 35). Under the Ottoman rule (16th–20th centuries), Hatra continued to serve as a military station in order to monitor the different semi-nomadic, pastoralist tribes, and to lead operations towards 'the pacification of the desert.' In a letter to her stepmother, Gertrude Bell gives a vivid description of one of her visits there:

> The modern conditions at Hatra were this year almost as exciting as the ancient. It had been the centre of comprehensive and entirely successful operations for the pacification of the desert and about 300 of the 1500 men who had been sent up from Baghdad in January were still there when I arrived. The object of the expedition had been to bring the Shammar to order, and the Shammar are the most important of the N. Mesopotamian tribes.[9]

Bell is, however, more critical of the living conditions the soldiers had to endure:

> The only criticism one can make is that the whole camp was absolutely innocent of sanitary arrangements; the ruins were unspeakably dirty and even the dead horses lay half buried (if buried at all) in close proximity to the tents.[10]

Distrust of nomads and semi-nomad pastoralists persisted under the British Mandate and also after the creation of Iraq as a nation-state. In 1946, a permanent police station was set up in the area in order to control the movements of the different Arab tribes that inhabited the region, as well as the Kurds and the Yazidis. This led to the development of a village in the 1950s with a settled population, its own administrative infrastructure, schools and even a hotel to receive prospective tourists (Safar and Mustafa 1974, p. 13). The expansion and transformation of temporary military camps into a permanent village has tampered with the archaeological site and made it difficult to piece together the heterogeneous assemblages and to reconstruct a whole picture of the place and its diversity.

In contrast to other ancient desert cities like Palmyra and Petra, Hatra has never attracted large numbers of tourists. Visitors are normally requested to have an official authorization and to be accompanied by official guides at the site. European travellers who visited Hatra in the 19th century adopted a poetic style to convey a sense of wonder, awe and melancholia in their descriptions of this ancient city and its ruins. Somehow, in my mind, their accounts resonate the Arabic literary motif of 'stopping or standing by the ruins' (al-wuquf 'ala al-atlal) mentioned earlier. The art historian and archaeologist, Austen Henry Layard wrote:

> The sun, still throwing its rays upon the walls and palaces, lighted up the yellow stones until they shined like gold ... They (the ruins) rose in solitary grandeur in the midst of a desert, '*in media solitudine positae*,' as they stood fifteen centuries before, when described by the Roman historian.[11]
>
> *(Layard 1849, vol. 1, 108–9; emphasized by the author)*

From her letters and diaries we know that Gertrude Bell visited Hatra twice. Once in 1911 when the Ottoman were controlling the place, and again under the British Mandate in 1922. In letters to her family she describes the site and its ruins and how they affected her:

> one can't be heavy hearted at Hatra; it is too wonderfully interesting ... It was never reinhabited and it lies out on the stretching downs like the great ground plan of a city, grass grown walls and mounds marking the line of fortification, street and market. In the centre stands the palace – you can see it for 5 hours away on every side – immense stone built halls, roofed with huge vaults and decorated with the strangest carved ornaments that have ever grown out under oriental chisels ...[12]
>
> At sunset I lay on the highest wall under the shadow of the Arab flag and watched the light fall and fade across a universe of desert. Bellow me the camels and horses of 'Ajil's bairak strayed through the court and beyond the city wall the blue smoke rose among the tents of a Shammar camp. It was a scene in which past and present were so bewilderingly mingled that you might have looked down upon its like any evening for twenty centuries.[13]

More recently, the Swiss journalist Liesl Graz who travelled in Iraq during the late 1970s described Hatra as a golden city: 'What is left of its golden monuments shows a style combining grandiosity – not to say gigantism – that reminds of Rome with free forms that sing like the music of a wild dance.' (Graz 1979, p. 27).[14]

The same Gavin Young referred to above was also taken by Hatra's aura:

> I say 'perfect ruin' because of Hatra's stunning beauty – you don't have to be a ruin-lover to appreciate *that* – and its most satisfactory size; there is plenty

of it to look at but not too much ... Hatra will be loved unreservedly, and at first sight, ... you drive up a good road and suddenly see honey-coloured wall and columns and arches. You are inclined to stop the car and sit, looking at this wonderful sight ... It is good to take one's time in Hatra. There is so much to look at and the compulsion is to go on looking.

(Young 1980, pp. 98, 100; emphasized by the author)

Safar and Mustafa (1974, p. 12) stated that whether they were professional archaeologists or occasional tourists, visitors to Hatra were struck by the place's magic (*siḥr*) and atmosphere, and were deeply moved by the experience. The style used in the descriptions of the site is rather poetic. Henri Stierlin (1987, p. 183) calls it 'cité libre' or free city. The epithets 'golden' and 'honey-coloured' are recurrent in most of the accounts by European visitors as well as a sense of distance, authenticity and splendour that recall Walter Benjamin's explanation of aura as an interwoven web of space and time, a feeling of distance despite the nearness of the object that is contemplated. The aura enveloping places and things is not, however, always harmonious and beautiful. Quite the opposite, powerful emotions, devastating experiences and painful memories may very well permeate the aura of ruins. Hatra is an example of that. In the memory of local populations whose movements have been harshly controlled and whose voices have been subdued, Hatra has a more eerie, oppressive aura. For many, the presence of Hatra's ruins echo memories of strife, distressing past events, and of people who have been constrained to comply by the idealized national narrative of modern Iraq. The place is covered with a patina of what Lynn Meskell (2002, p. 561) calls the 'gloominess of "negative heritage",' and hence has become a site of 'negative memories'.

The British surgeon John Ross (1839, pp. 443, 453, 467) gives an intimation of the kind of sinister atmosphere surrounding Hatra in the accounts of his visits to the place in 1836 and 1837. He mentions that it took him almost two years of negotiations before his Arab contacts agreed to accompany him on his trips to Hatra, and help him with the necessary arrangements. They had, he says, strongly advised him against visiting such an 'evil' place whose inhabitants were the 'worshippers of fire'. Evilness may be related to the many statues or 'idols' ('*asnām*) scattered in different locations of the site, and also the nearby presence of the Yazidis of Jebel Sinjar. In local folklore, the latter are known as the 'worshippers of the Devil' ('*Iblis*); a label that both Layard (1849) and Bell (letter of 14 April 1911) reiterated in their writings. As stated earlier, Safar and Mustafa (1974, p. 35) relate that during the excavation seasons they saw groups of Yazidis performing old Parthian rituals in the area of the great temple at Hatra. The sense of evilness permeating the site has fuelled the imaginations of a number of people. It was taken up in the film *The Exorcist* (1973) directed by William Friedkim where the opening scene is set in the midst of ongoing excavations at Hatra.[15] One may speculate whether the presence of Da'esh's warriors at Hatra and their rampage of its ruins will increase the negative resonance of the site in future memories.

Post-conflict mending

Ancient and recent ruins resonate differently and trigger different reactions and feelings. In their introductory chapter to *Ruin Memories*, Bjørnar J. Olsen and Thora Pétursdóttir (2014, p. 7) explicate that an ancient ruin is 'clean, fossilized and terminated; it is somehow ready-ruined. And it is this stable "finalized" state that it is cared for, preserved, and admired as heritage.' Conversely, 'the ruins of the recent past, … display themselves in the ongoing process of ruining … They are caught in a state of "unfinished disposal" ' (Olsen and Pétursdóttir 2014, p. 7). However, in areas of long standing political and social strife as well as current armed conflicts, people, places and things are victims of 'collateral damage,' and subjected to deliberate acts of destitution and destruction, the categories ancient and recent ruins become blurred. Ancient ruins continue to go through a process of ruination.

A number of scholars have in recent years been concerned with ways of dealing with post conflict issues in archaeology and heritage. How to engage with healing processes, how to deal with painful memories and how to forget, how and what to save and to rebuilt, how to trigger renewal (Harrison 2013, pp. 166–203; Newson and Young 2018; Woodward 2001, pp. 208–25). Heritage is primarily based on the idea of possessions – both material and immaterial – to preserve, manage and transmit in their integrity to following generations. Tangible heritage is above all an economic, historical, cultural and natural legacy that is delineated by the concrete things, their economic value, their spiritual and their documentary importance, as well as by their affective significance. So much so that it may be used as a therapeutic tool in trying to mend the wounds after disruptive situations such as colonialism, occupation, wars and civil wars. In the case of Hatra and its ruins, the healing process and restoration procedures will need to address ways of upholding the spirit of place without erasing the recent scars that have been inflicted on people, monuments, reliefs and artefacts. As Cornelius Holtorf (2018, p. 645) argues it requires systematic efforts 'to increase people's capability to absorb adversity.' A main prerequisite will be to empower the various ethnic and religious groups living in the area and to establish a politics of trust between governmental authorities, cultural institutions, archaeologists and heritage professionals and local communities. The fragments recovered in the recent debris will add new sides to the meaning of Hatra's ruins. The inclusion of contrapuntal voices, their narratives and memories may then give another, more faceted kind of aura to the site (Naguib 2007, p. 14; 2018, pp. 44–5).

The ruins of Hatra have an enduring presence and a special composite aura. They have been fixed features in the landscape of this borderland long before archaeologists surveyed, documented, excavated and reconstructed the site. Before it was listed as a UNESCO World Heritage Site; before Da'esh attacked it and before the PMF and the coalition forces liberated it. Pastoralists and different Arab tribes had nearby settlements, caravans stopped regularly, military camps and police stations were set up to 'pacify' the desert and control peoples' movements. The rivalries between empires in the East and in the West continue to resonate in the region surrounding Hatra. They have taken new forms, and the consequences of their disputes weigh heavily on the local populations. One has to hope for sustainable solutions to take effect soon.

Acknowledgements

I began working on this chapter during my stay as member of the research group *After Discourse: Things, Archaeology, and Heritage in the 21st Century*, at the Centre for Advanced Study (CAS), the Norwegian Academy of Science and Letters, Oslo during the academic year 2016–2017. Early drafts have been presented at workshops organized by the wider project *Object Matters: Archaeology and Heritage in the 21st Century*, http://objectmatters.ruinmemories.org/. I am grateful for all the comments received during these venues. I thank Professor Janet Johnson and Professor Christopher Woods and their colleagues at The Oriental Institute Chicago for giving me the opportunity of consulting the Research Archives of the OIC during the summer 2018. This was an inspiring stay! I am greatly thankful to Dr. Roberta Ricciardi Venco, director of the Hatra–Italian Archaological Expedition, University of Turin, to have granted the permission to publish the picture of 'The circular city' used on the website of their project.

My husband, Robert Wallace Vaagan and I lived in Iraq in the mid-1980s when he was stationed at the Royal Norwegian Embassy in Baghdad. I have used some of his old photographs to illustrate parts of the text. While writing this article I have had in mind the people we met and their hospitality. Sadly, many have seen their lives completely disrupted and have endured tragic losses and hardship. Several of the places we visited are today in total ruin and wait to be given renewed life.

Notes

1 ISIS-DELETING HISTORY (Hatra) – https://youtube/dn8fJBIKAc4 (Accessed 16. 1. 2017). I shall use the Arabic name Da'esh hereafter.
2 Queen Abu bint Damyōn, (meaning: Abu daughter of Damyōn), was the wife of the last Arab king of Hatra, Sanatruq II who reigned from 200–240/241 CE. The statue is 2.10m high; Abu is wearing a long pleated chiton and a himation over it, elaborate jewellery, the high diadem on her head is covered with a veil that falls down on her back, cf. Safar and Mustafa, 1974, pp. 70–1.
3 https://whc.unesco.org/en/list/277
4 www.bbc.com/news/world-middle-east-39770395 (accessed 27 February 2018).
5 UNESCO and the Islamic Educational, Scientific and Cultural Organization (ISESCO) issued a joint statement saying "With this latest act of barbarism against Hatra, (the IS group) shows the contempt in which it holds the history and heritage of Arab people."
6 Two foreign missions have been excavating at Hatra. One led by the Italians Roberta Ricciardi Venco and Alexandra Peruzzetto from the University of Turin worked several seasons in Hatra between 1987 and 2002. The other foreign mission was led by Michel Gawlikowski from the University of Warsaw, and worked on the site for one year (1990).
7 www.merriam-webster.com/dictionary/aura (Accessed on 17 September 2017).

8 *Al wuquf 'ala al-atlal*; Paul Cooper, *The Ancient Poems that Explain Today*.www.bbc.com/culture/story/20180820-the-6th-century-poems-making-a-comeback (accessed on 21/08/2018).

9 Gertrude Bell Archive, Newcastle University, letter 14 April 1911, http://gertrudebell.ncl.ac.uk/letter_details.php?letter_id=1814

10 Gertrude Bell Archive, Newcastle University, letter 14 April 1911, www.gerty.ncl.ac.uk/letter_details.php?letter_id=1814

11 The Roman historian in question was Ammianus Marcellinus, lib. 25, chap. 8, 5.

12 Gertrude Bell Archive, Newcastle University, letter 14 April 1911, http://gertrudebell.ncl.ac.uk/letter_details.php?letter_id=1814

13 Gertrude Bell Archive, Newcastle University, letter 10 November 1922, http://gertrudebell.ncl.ac.uk/letter_details.php?letter_id=593

14 My translation. "Ce qui reste de ses monuments dorés montre un style où se mèlent étrangement une grandeur – pour ne pas dire un gigantisme – qui rappelle Rome et de formes libres qui chantent comme la musique d'une danse sauvage."

15 www.youtube.com/watch?v=Qpw-GbEpjR4 (accessed 12 October 2018).

References

Abdi, K., 2008. From Pan-Arabism to Saddam Hussein's Cult of Personality. Ancient Mesopotamia and Iraqi National Ideology. *Social Archaeology* 8(1): 3–36.

Al-Hussainy, A. and R. Matthews, 2008. The Archaeological Heritage of Iraq in Historical Perspective. *Public Archaeology* 7(2): 91–100.

Altaweel, M. R. and S. R. Hauser, 2004. Travelling via Hatra: Trade Routes in the Eastern Jazira According to Evidence from Ancient Sources and Modern Satellite Imagery. *Baghdader Mitteilungen* 35: 57–84.

Andrae, W., 1908, *Hatra. Nach Aufnahmen von Mitgliedern der Assur-Expedition der deutschen Orient-Gesellschaft*, vol. 1, Allgemeine Beschreibung der Ruinen. Leipzig: Hinrichs.

Andrae, W., 1975[1912]. *Hatra nach Aufnahmen von Mitglieden der Assur Expedition der Deutschen Orient-Gesellschaft*. Vol. 2. Osnabrück: Otto Zeller Verlag.

Assmann, A., 2015. Impact and Resonance – Towards a Theory of Emotions in Cultural Memory. In: Stordalen, T. and Naguib, S.-A., eds., *The Formative Past and the Formation of the Future*. Oslo: Novus Press, 41–69.

Bahrani, Z., 1998. Conjuring Mesopotamia. Imaginative Geography and a World Past. In: L. Meskell, ed., *Archaeology under Fire. Nationalism, politics and heritage in the Eastern Mediterranean and Middle East*. London: Routledge, 159–74.

Bahrani, Z., 2017. *Mesopotamia. Ancient Art and Architecture*. London: Thames & Hudson

Baram, A., 1983. Mesopotamian Identity in Ba'athi Iraq. *Middle Eastern Studies* 19(4): 426–55.

Benjamin, W., 1977. *The Origin of the German Tragic Drama*. Translated by J. Osborne. London: Verso.

Benjamin, W., 2002 [1999]. *The Arcades Project*. Translated by H. Eiland and K. McLaughlin. Cambridge Mass.: The Belknap Press of Harvard University Press. Available from: https://monoskop.org/images/e/e4/Benjamin_Walter_The_Arcades_Project.pdf (accessed 20 February 2017).

Benjamin, W., 2008 [1936]. *The Work of Art in the Age of Mechanical Reproduction*. (Second Version) translated by J.A. Underwood. London: Penguin Books Ltd. Available from: https://monoskop.org/images/6/6d/Benjamin_Walter_1936_2008_The_Work_of_Art_in_the_Age_of_Its_Technological_Reproducibility_Second_Version.pdf (accessed September 1, 2017).

Bernhardsson, M. T., 2005. *Reclaiming a Plundered Past: Archaeology and Nation Building in Modern Iraq*. Austin: University of Texas Press.

Burström, M., 2013. Fragments as Something More. Archaeological Experience and Reflection. In: A. Gonzales-Ruibal, ed., *Reclaiming Archaeology. Beyond the Tropes of Modernity*. London: Routledge, 311–22.

Cesari, C. de, 2015. Post-Colonial Ruins. *Anthropology Today* 31(6): 22–6.

Dijkstra, K., 1990. State and Steppe. The Socio-Political Implications of Hatra Inscription 79. *Journal of Semitic Studies* 35(1): 81–98.

Dirven, L., 2006–2007. Hatra: A 'Pre-Islamic Mecca' in the Eastern Jazirah. *ARAM* 18–19: 363–80.

Dirven, L., ed., 2013. *Hatra. Politics, Culture and Religion between Parthia and Rome*. Oriens e Occident bd. 21. Stuttgart: Franz Steiner Verlag.

Drijvers, H.J.W., 1977. Hatra, Palmyra und Edessa. Die Städte der syrisch- mesopotamischen Wüstein politischer, kulturgeschichtlicher und religionsgeschichtelicher Bedeutung. *Aufstieg und Niedergang der römischen Welt* II (8): 799–906.

Foietta, E., 2016. The Complex System of the Fortifications of Hatra: Defence, Chronology and Secondary Functions. *ARAM* 28 (1 & 2): 237–63.

Fukai, S., 1960. The Artifacts of Hatra and Parthian Art. *East and West* 11(2/3): 135–81.

Gerstenblith, P., 2009. Archaeology in the Context of War: Legal Frameworks for Protecting Cultural Heritage during Armed Conflicts. *Archaeologies* 5(1): 18–31.

Graz, L., 1979. *L'Irak au présent*. Lausanne: Éditions des Trois Continents.

Greenblatt, S., 1990, Resonance and Wonder. In: Lavine, S. and Karp, I., eds., *Exhibiting Cultures: The Poetics and Politics of Museum Display*, Washington D.C.: Smithsonian Institution Press, 42–56.

Hamilakis, Y., 2009. The "War on Terror" and the Military–Archaeology Complex: Iraq, Ethics, and Neo-Colonialism. *Archaeologies*, 5(1): 39–65.

Hamilakis, Y., 2017. Sensorial Assemblages: Affect, Memory and Temporality in Assemblage Thinking. *Cambridge Archaeological Journal* 27(1): 169–82.

Harmanah, Ö., 2015. ISIS, Heritage, and the Spectacles of Destruction in the Global Media. *Near Eastern Archaeology* 78(3): 170–7.

Harrison, R., 2013. *Heritage. Critical Approaches*. New York: Routledge.

Hauser, S.R., 2013. Where Is the Man from Hadr Who Once Built It and Taxed the Land by the Tigris and Chaboras? On the Significance of the Final Siege of Hatra. In: L. Dirven, ed. *Hatra. Politics, Culture and Religion between Parthia and Rome*. Oriens e Occident bd. 21. Stuttgart: Franz Steiner Verlag, 119–39.

Herzfeld, E., 1914. Hatra. *Zeitschrift der Deutschen Morgenländischen Gesellschaft* 68: 655–77.

Holtorf, C., 2018. Embracing Change: How Cultural Resilience is Increased through Cultural Heritage. *World Archaeology* 50(4): 639–50.

Ibrahim, J. K., 1986. *Pre-Islamic Settlement in Jazirah*. Baghdad: Ministry of Culture & Information. State Organization of Antiquities & Heritage.

Kaizer, T., 2000. Some Remarks about the Religious Life of Hatra. *Topoi: Orient-Occident* 10(1): 229–52.

Kaizer, T., 2013. Questions and Problems Concerning the Sudden Appearance of the Material Culture of Hatra in the First Centuries CE. In: L. Dirven, ed., *Hatra. Politics, Culture and Religion between Parthia and Rome*. Oriens e Occident bd. 21. Stuttgart: Franz Steiner Verlag, 57–71.

Kila, J. D., 2013. Inactive, Reactive, or Pro-Active?: Cultural Property Crimes in the Context of Contemporary Armed Conflicts. *Journal of Eastern Mediterranean Archaeology and Heritage Studies* 1(4): 319–42.

Layard, A. H., 1849. *Nineveh and its Remains with an Account of a Visit to the Chaldaen Christians of Kurdistan, and the Yezidis, or Devil-Worshippers*. London: John Murray, 2 vols.

Meskell, L., 2002. Negative Heritage and Past Mastering in Archaeology. *Anthropological Quarterly* 75(3): 57–74.

Naguib, S.-A., 2007. The One, the Many and the Other: Revisiting Cultural Diversity in Museums of Cultural History. *National Museums in a Global World. NaMu III*. Linköping University Electronic Press www.ep.liu.se/ecp/031/index.html

Naguib, S.-A., 2015. The Articulation of Cultural Memory and Heritage in Plural Societies. In: Stordalen, T. and Naguib, S.-A., eds., *The Formative Past and the Formation of the Future*. Oslo: Novus Press, 2015, 221–46.

Naguib, S.-A., 2018. Bridging Gaps: Archaeological Sources and Resources in Museums. In: Steiner, P., Tsakos, A. and Seland, E.H., eds., *From the Fjords to the Nile: Essays in Honour of Richard Holton Pierce on His 80th Birthday*. Archaeopress, 41–7 (open access e-book).

Newson, P. and Young, R., eds., 2018. *Post-Conflict Archaeology and Cultural Heritage. Rebuilding Knowledge, Memory and Community from War-Damaged Material Culture*. London: Routledge.

Olsen, B. and Pétursdottir, Th., eds., 2014. *Ruin Memories. Materialities, Aesthetics and the Archaeology of the Recent Past*. London: Routledge.

Ricciardi, R.V., 2000. Hatra- Presentazione del Sito. *Topoi: Orient-Occident* 10(1) 87–110.

Ross, J., 1839. Notes on Two Journeys from Baghdad to Al Hadhr, in Mesopotamia in 1836 and 1837. *The Journal of the Royal Geographical Society of London*, 9: 443–70.

Runia, E., 2006. Presence. *History and Theory* 45: 1–29.

Safar, F. and M. A. Mustafa, 1974. *Al-Ḥaḍar: Madinat al-shams* (Hatra. The City of the Sun God; in Arabic). Baghdad: Directory of Antiquities.

Simmel, G., 1958[1911]. Two Essays. *The Hudson Review* 11 (3): 371–85. The Ruin, translated by David Kettler, 379–85.

Sommer, M., 2003. *Hatra. Geschichte und Kulturn einer Karawanenstadt in Römischen- Partischen Mesopotamien*. Mainz am Rhein: Verlag Philipp von Zabern.

Sommer, M., 2013. In the Twilight. Hatra between Rome and Iran. In: L. Dirven, ed., *Hatra. Politics, Culture and Religion between Parthia and Rome*. Oriens e Occident bd. 21. Stuttgart: Franz Steiner Verlag, 33–42.

Stierlin, H., 1987. *Cités du desert: Pétra, Palmyre, Hatra*. L'art antique au Proche-Orient, Fribourg: Office du Livre.

Stoler, A. L., 2008. Imperial Debris. Reflections on Ruins and Ruination. *Cultural Anthropology* 23(2): 191–219.

Stone, P.G. and Bajjaly, J.F., eds., 2008. The Destruction of Cultural Heritage in Iraq. Woodbridge: Boydell.

Tubach, J., 2013. The Triad of Hatra. In: Dirven, L., ed., *Hatra. Politics, Culture and Religion between Parthia and Rome*. Oriens e Occident bd. 21. Stuttgart: Franz Steiner Verlag, 201–15.

Woodward C., 2001. *In Ruins*. London: Chatto & Windus.

Young, G., 1980. *Iraq: Land of Two Rivers*. London: Collins.

Zakeri, M., 1998. Arabic Reports on the Fall of Hatra to the Sasanids. In: S. Leder, ed., *Storytelling in the Framework of Non-Fictional Arabic Literature*. Wiesbaden: Otto Harrassowitz Verlag, 158–67.

Digital references

Ammianus Marcellinus. 1911. *The Roman History by Ammianus Marcellinus during the Reigns of the Emperors Constantius, Julian, Jovianus, Valentinian, and Valens*. translated by L.D. Yonge,

London: G. Bell and Sons Ltd. Available on: www.gutenberg.org/files/28587/28587-h/28587-h.htm Release date: April 22, 2009 [EBook #28587] (accessed October 20, 2018).

Cassius Dio. *Dio's Rome. An Historical Narrative Originally composed in Greek during the Reigns of Septimius Severus, Geta and Caracalla, Macrinus, Elagabalus and Alexander Severus.* Vol. V, Books 61–76 (AD 54–211). Translated by Foster, H.B. Available on: www.gutenberg.org/files/10890/10890-h/10890-h.htm Release date January 31, 2004 [EBook #10890] (accessed May 2, 2018).

The Gertrude Bell Archive, Newcastle University, http://gertrudebell.ncl.ac.uk/ (accessed June 10, 2018),

Irving, C., 2014. Gertrude of Arabia, the Woman who Invented Iraq. *DailyBeast* 06.17.14, Available from: www.thedailybeast.com/gertrude-of-arabia-the-woman-who-invented-iraq (Accessed 31 August 2018)

ISIS-DELETING HISTORY (Hatra) – https://youtube/dn8fJBIKAc4 (accessed April 30, 2017).

11

WHAT REMAINS?

On material nostalgia

Alfredo González-Ruibal

Introduction

In this chapter I would like to reflect on two strongly-related issues that have not enjoyed a good reputation lately: nostalgia and roots. They have been systematically associated with reactionary ideologies and the worst of identity politics. Nostalgia is often linked to a need for rootedness in a past that is more or less idealized, but that provides a ground for identity and self-explanation. Roots, however, seem anachronistic in a time of flux and change, where one can switch nationality, religion, gender and sex – at least in some parts of the world. Understandably, after so many centuries of rigid identities, this has been experienced as liberating. The large quantity of life choices is, in fact, one of the benchmarks of late modernity (Giddens 1991). Thus, it has been mobility, rather than roots, that has received all the attention for the last three decades (Marcus 1995; Clifford 1997; Tsing 2005). Mobility (spatial, biographical or both) has been often regarded as a positive phenomenon, associated with cultural creativity, freedom and the dissolution of essentialisms (Malkki 1992; Braidotti 2013). Movement, displacement, multi-sitedness, networks, connection and fluidity have been the themes and tropes that have dominated research in the social sciences, first in anthropology and sociology (Sheller and Urry 2006), and later – as often – in archaeology (Beaudry and Parno 2013; Leary 2014). Some have pointed out the asymmetries of mobility (Cresswell 2006) and the relationship between the traveling self and the identities of upper-class citizens and cosmopolitan scholars (Friedman 2002), but these voices have been in the minority, compared to celebratory ones. More recently, the harsher side of displacement has become all too obvious through mass migrations (both politically and economically motivated) and anthropologists and archaeologists are taking a more critical look at the consequences of uprootedness (cf. De León 2015; Hamilakis 2017). Nostalgia, as the need for roots, is frequently related to melancholia and vacuous idealizations.

In heritage studies, in particular, it has enjoyed a bad reputation as an index of pastiche, bourgeois ideology and conservatism (Pickering and Keightley 2006, p. 926). It also seems at odds with the current concern for the future that permeates the humanities and social sciences.

By deriding rootedness and nostalgia, however, we are leaving to right-wingers two widely-shared human emotions that are particularly relevant in times of instability and traumatic change, such as the one we are experiencing at the moment. Thus, several authors have called for a more nuanced perspective on nostalgia (Tannock 1995; Pickering and Keightley 2006; Huyssen 2006; Wilson 2014; Dawdy 2016; Tedder 2019). Fred Davis (1979), for instance, distinguished between simple, reflexive and interpreted nostalgia, the latter directing analytical questions to its purposes and significance, whereas Svetlana Boym (2001) talked about reflective nostalgia to refer to more ironical understandings of memory and the past. More recently, Victoria Tedder (2019) refers to progressive nostalgia to emphasize its critical political edge. Nostalgia is, indeed, a complex affect that defies dichotomies. Thus, against the widespread idea that nostalgics consider the past a better place, Janelle Wilson (2014, p. 115) has shown in her work with collectors that many of them acknowledge the hardships of previous generations and their collecting represents actually a way of honoring and respecting those who lived in more difficult circumstances. Nostalgia is neither just a longing for the past or an impossible desire to return to another era. It can also be a way of questioning how the past may actively engage with the present and the future and 'to recognize aspects of the past as the basis for renewal and satisfaction in the future' (Pickering and Keightley 2006, pp. 920–1). These aspects can be actively searched for and retrieved, as happens with indigenous communities that have experienced colonialism (Tannock 1995, pp. 458–9).

In this, nostalgia and archaeology come close. Archaeology is not just memory work (Shanks 2007; Olivier 2008), but also the work of nostalgia (Buchli 2010). The difference is important, because nostalgia implies the recognition of loss and lack, which are part and parcel of the experience of both modernity (Pickering and Keightley 2006, pp. 920–1) – and archaeology (Shanks 2012). Nostalgia can be melancholic, but this is not necessarily negative (when it is not pathological) or incompatible with utopian leanings (Pickering and Keightley 2006, p. 921): a sense of loss can trigger action or at least a desire for change. Andreas Huyssen argues that the modern fascination for ruins is related to the fact that we see in them 'the promise of an alternative future' (Huyssen 2006, p. 8). A good example of how the longing for a vanished past can be actively mobilized for a better present is offered by the Pataxó Indians of Brazil: this indigenous group gained consciousness of the process of cultural loss they had undergone and engaged in an active reconstruction of their identity, mainly through material culture (Grünewald 2002). This is an example of reflective or interpreted nostalgia with important repercussions in the future of the community. At the same time, the cozy feelings that are often associated with nostalgia are not necessarily universal. In some cultural traditions, this kind of emotion is more powerful and painful (Seremetakis 1994, p. 4; González-Ruibal

2019, pp. 86–8). Pain is at the etymological root of the concept – in fact, the word was originally coined by a seventeenth-century doctor to describe a disease (Cassin 2015, pp. 16–18) – and there is a measure of pain that is psychologically necessary and politically powerful. It is often in those places where the break of modernity has been felt more acutely (as with the Pataxó) that nostalgia takes more intense proportions. Poet Irma Pineda captures this feeling very well:

> Nostalgia does not turn into water under your feet
> it does not climb the back of a horse
> that takes you far away from the heart.
> It stays here
> tied
> attached to the painful flesh
> it drinks our tears
> and stirs up our blood.
>
> Nostalgia does not go away
> like river water
> it becomes a sea
> that sweeps us ruthlessly.
>
> ('*La Nostagia,*' in *Castillo 2016, p. 141,*
> *my translation*)

Irma Pineda is a writer in Zapotec and Spanish. As a member of an indigenous community in Mexico, her sense of loss cannot be associated to soft feelings of childhood memories (or not only), but a long-lasting condition of colonial expropriation. Neither can be said that film director Tarkovsky's take on nostalgia (more evident in his *Nostalghia*, but present throughout his entire work) is a simple longing for a simple past – which in the case of Russia, never was in the first place. It is rather a dark, dreamlike force, fed with fragments and traces of the past in no evident order (Tarkovsky 1989). It reminds of Derrida's (1998: 73) words: 'I finally know how not to have to distinguish any longer between promise and terror.' The element of alienation that is fundamental to the work of the philosopher should be considered seriously when trying to understand nostalgia – at least the kind of nostalgia that I am exploring here.

Nostalgia for the word

Although nostalgia and roots are commonly associated with place, the truth is that several philosophers have linked it with language. This was the case most notably with Hannah Arendt. In an interview conducted by Günther Gaus in the 1960s the philosopher was asked whether she missed that pre-Hitler Germany that would never exist again. She was also asked what remained from that lost world. Her reply was: 'The Europe of the pre-Hitler period? I do not long for that, I can tell you. What remains? The language remains' (Arendt 1994, p. 20). What survived, after the rupture created by war, genocide and totalitarianism, was language, the German language. There is no substitution for the mother tongue, she argues, and she has made every effort to preserve it. Unlike Heidegger's German, Arendt's is not linked to any metaphysical notion of soil or blood, but to the universality of being human. It is the mother tongue – as opposed to the discourse full of clichés of totalitarianism – that makes as human, at the same time singular and part of a plurality (Gaffney 2015, p. 535). Other authors have followed Arendt and vindicate the role of language in creating a sense of rootedness and belonging, which is at the same time profoundly intimate and free from the violent and patriarchal implications of the fatherland (Cassin 2015; Gaffney 2015). After all, the right to land, property and group identity tends to be transmitted by men in patrilineal societies (thus the word 'patrimony,' from the Latin 'paternal estate or inheritance'), but language is usually passed on by women (as exemplified by the concept of 'mother tongue').

Yet language is far from being an innocent, apolitical phenomenon to which one can attach her or himself without trouble. Jacques Derrida (1998) raised the point powerfully. A French-speaking Jew from Algeria, his relationship to language was more complicated than that of Arendt. French was a product of the coloniality of culture, but at the same time his only tongue. Reflecting on his personal experience, he explored the dark side of language, its 'political and historical terror' and the inevitable alienation that it entails: 'I have only one language and it is not mine; my "own" language is, for me, a language that cannot be assimilated. My language, the only one I hear myself to speak, is the language of the other' (Derrida 1998, p. 25). From here he proposes that alienation is in fact, constitutive of language as such, that no one ever masters his or her own tongue.

While not coming from a colonial context proper, I can sympathize with Derrida's ambiguous relation to his mother tongue. Mine is Castilian (Spanish), yet, as a Galician, I have a strongly ambivalent attitude to it. My grandparents' language was Galician until they dropped it, probably in their twenties, as they climbed in the social ladder and moved to the city. My father spoke fluent Galician by spending long periods in the countryside, but he did not pass on the language to me. This is a common experience among many people of my generation. The reason for the linguistic rupture has to do with the fact that, from the sixteenth century onwards, Galician has been widely regarded as a language of the poor and the peasant – this is why my grandparents stopped speaking it. I said that this is not a colonial context stricto sensu, but it is not far from it. Students at school were punished for speaking Galician during the Franco regime and Galician (Basque and Catalan, too) were considered primitive dialects, only acceptable in the domestic sphere. The colonial interdiction of the dictatorship adopted during democracy 'more subtle, peaceful, silent, and liberal ways' (Derrida 1998, p. 32). In the 1980s, I remember classmates from the countryside making every effort to speak Castilian so as not appear uncouth (their accent always betraying them), while they were being taught in a foreign tongue that they did not master. Surely, we had Galician lessons at school, but it was *explained* to us (that is the precise word) as a foreign language. So much so that even if most of us could speak it, it was still dissected in the classroom as English or French were. The situation, therefore, was not dissimilar to Arabic in colonial Algeria, taught as 'a strange kind of alien language as the language of the other' (Derrida 1998, p. 37). In our case, the language of the peasant – people from another world indeed. Despite great efforts at changing its status, an asymmetric diglossia still prevails in Galicia.

Although I can speak Galician and write it, it is not my language from a linguistic point of view. I don't speak it perfectly – too many interferences from Castilian, my 'mother' tongue, and Portuguese (which I learned later). Still, I feel that Galician is my language from an emotional point of view. This is, of course, not an unproblematic emotion. Not being a native Galician speaker, I cannot relate to it as Hannah Arendt did to German. I am not at home in Galician: I have the strange impression that I am occupying another's home – one that, however, should be mine. Galician is *unheimlich* to me, but not uncanny. Thus, I sense that I have been expelled from my own home and have not made myself comfortable elsewhere. This is because I cannot appropriate Castilian: so many of its words sound dry and alien to me. They come with their own history, which is not my history, or only partially so. Galicians lack the experience of appropriation of Castilian that people in Latin America have, despite some attempts by prominent writers such as Emilia Pardo Bazán and Ramón del Valle-Inclán. People in Latin America have subverted the language and created a new, richer and powerful one. Humberto Ak'abal, an indigenous poet from Guatemala, who wrote in Spanish and K'ich'e, the language of the colonizer and his mother tongue, expressed it beautifully:

> I did not grow up with Castilian
> when I arrived to the world.
>
> My language was born in the trees
> and has the flavor of the soil;
> the language of my grandparents is my home.
>
> If I use this language that is not mine,
> I do it as the one who uses a new key
> and opens the door to another world
> where words have another voice
> and another way of feeling the soil.
>
> This language is the memory of a pain
> and I speak it without fear and shame
> because it was bought
> with the blood of my ancestors.
>
> In this new language
> I show you the flowers of my song,
> I bring you the flavor of other pains,

> the color of other joys …
> This language is just another key
> to sing the old song of my blood.
> *(Humberto Ak'abal, 'El canto viejo de la sangre,'*
> *in Millares 2013, p. 272, my translation)*

Ak'abal's relation to Castilian, colonial as it is, is none the less easier than mine. Because his mother tongue is indeed indigenous and he uses the language of the colonizer 'as another key to sing the old song' of his people. Derrida and myself do not have this privilege. We inhabit a monolingual non-place: this double interdict – of the dominant tongue, which will never be one's own and the subaltern tongue, which we have lost – leaves one without any resource, not even that of overstepping the limits (Derrida 1998, p. 32). Still, Derrida has found a sort of redemption in a complicated but total love for the French language, which I cannot share with Castilian, for me always a foreign, colonial language that humiliated and still humiliates the language that I lost even before I was born and that fails to express the deepest intimacy of my relationship to the past. What, then, remains for me? A nostalgia, perhaps, for a lost tongue, a language that I have not inherited, except in a partial, defective way. But there is something else.

Nostalgia for the thing

The inscription of the self, wrote Derrida, 'cannot be from the space and time of a spoken mother tongue, because I had none' – except, that is, the 'forbidding-forbidden language' that we speak (Derrida 1998, p. 33). For the philosopher, however, it is still language that is at the center – and alien, complex, always-other language that cannot be mastered. Yet it is my impression that what he is looking for cannot be found in language or in language alone. His obsession for '*the truth itself* beyond memory, as the hidden other side of shadows, of images, of images of images, and of phantasms' (Derrida 1998, p. 73) seems to me irreducible to the linguistic. That truth beyond memory, located to the other side of shadows, images and phantasms, sounds rather like the Real, the traumatic kernel that is beyond symbolization (Žižek 1989, pp. 180–1). Lacan referred to this with the Freudian term *Das Ding*, the Thing, and I believe that we have to understand this literally – the Thing as material stuff – because things are excessive, irreducible to discourse or symbols (Olsen 2010). If we can never master a language, the same can be said of things.

Yet at the same time, things do not make demands of us in the way a language does. We do not have to master things to relate to them. There are other sensorial experiences that allow us to be in the proximity of the thing that is impossible with language. Things are nonverbal and, in that, they possess an element of universality. Despite the obvious (but complex) linkage between material assemblages and collective identities, materiality can avoid some of the political pitfalls of language. Language is more strongly associated with nation and ethnicity (even if the

FIGURE 11.1 An Oromo potter in Ethiopia giving post-firing treatment to her recently-made pots. Photo: Alfredo González-Ruibal

relationship is not simple either) and it has been strongly involved in the production of imperialist cultures. Arendt tried do dissociate language from people so that language could remain (Cassin 2015, pp. 109–11), but much as one wants to detach German from the Germans, it is still the language of the Germans. And in fact, attempting to dissociate them can be conducive to a more subtle and insidious form of cultural imperialism – when imperialism dresses as universalism. Besides, it is not only the language of a specific nation or nations and cultures, but also the language of Man, as any other language (Spender 1980). It is only perhaps when a subaltern group twists a tongue, corrupts it, pollutes it and makes violence to it – as with Castilian in Latin America or the Jewish people with the German and other languages that make up the Yiddish – that we can talk of a dissociation (and still the colonial, patriarchal trace would always be there). Spanish was imposed over Galician, but Castilian material culture was not forced to prevail over

Galician artefacts – when those distinctions still made sense. The most basic things, the things that are really indispensable for a living, are understandable a priori or with limited instructions that do not imply verbal communication. In my work in Ethiopia, people make me understand the use and even the meaning of things through bodily gestures (Figure 11.1) and this, I believe, creates a sense of common ground between us, a point of convergence between our respective alterities. It is the body and things that tie us together, not words. Language can be a barrier: it creates a sense of isolation and alienation. Things can be a bridge between worlds.

They can be a source of nostalgia as well. My longing for a preindustrial materiality was born through my interaction with the vanishing material culture of peasant Galicia, but it has allowed me to relate to other nonmodern materialities and the people that create and use them. I have a bodily experience of wooden ploughs because I have had them in my hands (I know how much they weigh, how unwieldy they are, and how well they fit one's body). And even when I have no previous experience of certain things (bows and arrows), I can appreciate the woodwork and the ergonomics through my corporeal understanding of similar materials (Figure 11.2).

My experience with the materiality of peasant culture in Galicia was tinged with nostalgia from the beginning. When I was a child, the traditional material assemblage was already collapsing. Yet wooden oxcarts, haystacks and water mills were

FIGURE 11.2 Muturuhũ, an Awá Indian from Brazil, making arrows. Photo: Alfredo González-Ruibal

still something of an ordinary experience in the 1980s. Then, in the 1990s everything disappeared. I have vivid memories of the last water mill grinding corn that I saw, the last decorated yoke fastened to the neck of a cow, and the last iron plough ploughing a potato field, all in the mid-1990s. The memories are vivid because I knew already that it could be the last time I would be glimpsing those things, as in fact it was. Every time I returned to the countryside in the 1990s, it was with the anxiety of finding out that something had disappeared without a trace. One day, for instance, it was *palleiros*, haystacks.

I had a love for those things for many reasons, of which I was not then fully aware. There was their vulnerability, in the sense that they were vanishing before my eyes, but also their often intrinsic fragility, due to the material they were made of (wood, straw, vegetal fibers). There was their immense beauty, too, a raw beauty like no other, that has fascinated writers like John Berger (1992) and Maja Haderlap (2016) and has made me work with traditional material culture ever since. There was the links of those things, their perissological qualities (Lemonnier 2012), the world of artefacts, knowledge, symbols, rules, stories and emotions in which they were immersed. They were an extension of the landscape. They created a continuity between myself, my father and my father's grandfather (skipping by grandparents, who had betrayed their roots).

They also allowed me to appropriate the language from where I had been expelled before I was born: words like *carapucho*, *guincha* or *roucear*, some of them so intrinsic to the experience of the Galician peasant that are impossible to translate. *Roucear* means turning the oxcart slightly to one side on a single wheel, something that you can do with the massive wooden wheels of the traditional Galician cart (Figure 11.3). How do you translate that? These were words like those of Humberto Ak'abal's indigenous tongue, with the flavor of the soil. Rooted words for rooted things. The Arabic and Berber-speaking Algerians, writes Derrida (1998, p. 37), were 'very near and infinitely far away'. This is similar to my experience of the peasant world, with the important difference that this very near does not refer to a spatial relation, but to an emotional one. The smell of ground corn in a water mill is not just almost unbearably near to me, but an inseparable part of myself. Much so than any Castilian word could be.

I have been talking about vanishing things, which seems at odd with the title of this chapter: the thing remains. Indeed it remains. Not everything is lost. Something of the old materiality persists and permeates the landscape. Some things survive behind closed doors – the yoke of my great-great-grandfather, that I keep; others in plain view: the sturdy architecture of the Galician landscape. It is not easy to disassemble a complete material culture. There will always be ruins.

From my late childhood I came to appreciate a masonry wall sustaining an agricultural terrace in front of my home. During the 1990s, most of the village where I spent parts of my childhood underwent drastic changes: vernacular houses were torn down or completely altered with concrete, bricks and synthetic painting. The place where I grew up disappeared before my eyes, but that wall remained unchanged, a wall of schist, perfectly fashioned and covered with moss

FIGURE 11.3 An abandoned wooden cart in Galicia. Photo: Alfredo González-Ruibal

and ruderals. I clung to that wall with anxiety as if it were a tenuous but solid link with the past, with my biography and that of my father and my great-grandfather. The wall has survived so far (Figure 11.4). And that is the other reason for my loving of traditional material culture. It is frail, but also persistent, unbelievably enduring.

It is surely not a coincidence that my research topics for two decades include resistance and non-state communities incorporated into state formations. That is the world of my childhood. This was what I witnessed as a child and a teen-ager: resistance to the storm of progress and the tense juxtaposition of two different worlds: modernity and the premodern, state and statelessness. It is not a coincidence that I am an archaeologist, either. My devotion to archaeology comes from a deep love for material culture and craft and at the same time a feeling of loss. I am an archaeologist that excavates out of nostalgia. I want to retrieve lost worlds because I want to retrieve *my* lost world. But I am an archaeologist also because I believe in the miracle: I think those worlds can actually be retrieved because something of them persists today. Even in the disfigured village of my childhood foundations remain, traces, ruins, walls. And I also believe in that something of those vanishing

FIGURE 11.4 The persistence of things. A terrace wall made of schist in front of my family house in Galicia. Photo: Alfredo González-Ruibal

worlds ought to be recovered and projected into the future – their unfulfilled promise. This is the ethics of archaeology, too.

'Rooting and uprooting, there it is everything nostalgia revolves around,' writes Barbara Cassin (2015, p. 63). To be rooted is to be at home (*chez soi*) and one is *chez soi* when one is welcomed, she argues. I agree with that, but I do not think that the feeling of being welcomed can be limited to human neighbors. Cassin herself notes that in the case of the Odyssey, the tale of return par excellence, Ulysses knows that he is *chez soi* when he sees his nuptial bed. He made it himself out of an olive tree that was not uprooted or cut, but left in place and which determined the location of both bed and bedroom. The olive tree remained rooted and the house was built around it. Here rootedness (*enracinement*) is above all and without any sense of metaphor the rootedness of the bed, made of the wood of a tree literally rooted to the ground on which the house was built (Cassin 2015, pp. 44–5). It is nostalgia for this very material, very unmetaphorical root that I feel. And I would say that this root is the truth itself, at the other side of images and phantasms, that Derrida was looking for in language, beyond language, in vain.

The thing remains: A manifesto for material nostalgia

I have taken you through a nostalgic journey. I have explained from where my nostalgia comes, its material roots. What I would like to do now is to define and reclaim such nostalgia and for that I propose a tentative decalogue.

One. Material nostalgia is based first and foremost on the assumption that the past is vital for the present and the future. 'The future brings us nothing, gives us nothing,' wrote Simone Weil (2001, p. 51),

> it is we who in order to build it have to possess; and we possess no other life, no other living sap, than the treasures stored up from the past and digested, assimilated and created afresh by us. Of all the human soul's need, none is more vital than this one of the past.

But this is not the past as image or discourse, to be consumed or waved as a flag. It is the past as a haunting material presence. A presence that moves between 'promise and terror' (Derrida 1998, p. 73), that is as phantasmatic as it is Real – indeed, it is phantasmatic because it is Real: a hard core resisting symbolization (Žižek 1989, p. 162).

Two. Material nostalgia is a demand for continuity. We need continuity amid endless threats of discontinuity (Davis 1977, p. 420). The experience of historical fragmentation and alienation from history echoes a similar fragmentation and alienation in our identities. Many of us can no longer see ourselves in the time of our grandparents and even in our own childhoods. The sense of loss is not just related to a vanished past, but to the broken links between present and past, which is also a traumatic rupture in our biographies. Continuity means roots: 'To be rooted is perhaps the most important and least recognized need of the human soul,' asserted Simone Weil (2001, p. 43). This essential need has been criticized, as I pointed out at the beginning, by the proponents of mobility and fluid identities. One of the reasons for the critique of rootedness is its frequent translation into nationalistic terms. Yet roots, like languages, are not inevitably nationalistic. Simone Weil was both a strong defender of roots and a staunch anti-nationalist: 'Only human beings have an eternal destiny. Human collectivities have not got one' (Weil 2001, p. 5). The defense of rootedness and continuity can also be subversive and liberating, as in the case of the demands of indigenous peoples, expropriated from their past and evicted from their lands. Continuity does not mean – should not mean – that interruptions between past and present are denied or glossed over. To stress the link between past and present is compatible with emphasizing the rupture, the gap that modernity, capitalism or colonialism opened between past and present (Orser 2012). Archaeology can be a way of stitching the wound. But stitching always leaves a scar. A critical nostalgia respects the scar. It makes it visible. Even more than that: a critical nostalgia is founded on the scar. The pain of nostalgia is not for the longing to return, it is for the gap that prevents any return to be fulfilled – as any emigrant knows.

Three. Material nostalgia reclaims a past that is durable and persistent. We live in a world that is increasingly ephemeral. Materiality itself is engineered to be so. Capitalism transforms everything at an incredible speed. The aspirations to permanence have been criticized in heritage studies, which have rightly emphasized the transient nature of the material legacy of the past, always enmeshed in creative, entropic processes (DeSilvey 2017). Yet the claim to persistence is not only legitimate, but also realistic. It is realistic because it is in the being of things to last, in systemic or archaeological contexts. 'Things are more persistent than thought. They evidently last longer than speech and gestures. Things are concrete and offer stability,' reminds Olsen (2010, p. 158). And they are powerful even as remnants, traces and fragments (Burström 2013). Persistence is a basic need. Byung-Chul Han (2015) has defined contemporary society as the 'burnout society' in which neurological disorders have superseded bacterial ones. Many of these disorders are caused by the lack of stability brought about by modern technologies and artefacts, themselves related to the political economy of capitalism. It is an error to try to find the solution to our malaise in a techno-utopia. It is more reasonable to accept that we need things that last, that do not change or become immediately obsolete. Bjørnar J. Olsen points to the trauma created by losing your belongings – 'house, city, farm, or hunting grounds' – but are we not losing our belongings every single day? My great-great-grandfather's yoke is still in perfect usable condition, but I do not have my cellphone of two years ago. It is not only that this is ecologically unsustainable. It is also psychologically unsustainable: 'Solidity and permanence are thing properties that make a vital difference to human life: not only to society and social bonds, but also to our existencial security' (Olsen 2010, p. 159).

Four. Material nostalgia is about presence (Domanska 2006). Nostalgia, as often presented by critics, is too ethereal: it is more about visual and textual representations than about the past qua past. Yet nostalgia often rejects mediation. From collectors and reenactors to political activists and indigenous people occupying the places of their ancestors, there is a demand for presence. We need the past to be materially here with us and this cohabitation to be acknowledged.

Five. Material nostalgia is a longing for the corporeal. It is not metaphysical or theological. It is experienced – suffered, enjoyed – through the body, as it is through the deployment of the body that things have been traditionally made and used (Leroi-Gourhan 1964, pp. 102–7). Ploughing the land requires every muscle in one's body, typing this text only a very limited set of muscles located in my hands and forearms. Material nostalgia honors the physical effort of being in the world and making the world.

Six. Material nostalgia is about materials and substances – wood, straw, resin, stone. It embraces nonmodern materialities, not for their aesthetic qualities – synthetic materials, such as concrete, provide extraordinary aesthetic affordances – but for ethical reasons: nonmodern materialities are in balance with the world. They are attuned to geology, the weather, the past and ourselves (Figure 11.5). Against the 'flatness, immaterial abstractness and timelessness' of modern materiality (Pallasmaa 2000: 79), nonmodern stuff is concrete, historical, mysterious. The material nostalgic is not afraid of being labeled 'primitivist,' as if anything that precedes or bypasses modernity is regrettable or backward and any praise of the premodern an exercise in obscurantism or naivety – as implied by Miller (2007).

Seven. Material nostalgia is about alternative and heterogeneous temporalities, non-modern experiences of time and regimes of historicity. It is

FIGURE 11.5 A roof made of local schist labs in the mountains of central Galicia. Photo: Alfredo González-Ruibal

anti-presentist and follows the deep temporal roots of everything (Witmore 2013). But above all, it is nostalgia for slower temporalities: the time of the artisan who spent many hours polishing an axe, oblivious of the world. Through archaeological fieldwork, we relate to that temporality and demonstrate its contemporaneity and its value: there is no technique than can speed up the act of digging. We can document faster, but we cannot dig faster. It is the soil and the artefacts that impose their rhythm upon us. Archaeological fieldwork, as a craft (Shanks and McGuire 1996), provides a model for a slow ontology of knowledge production (Ulmer 2017), one that is rooted in activities as old as cultivating the land.

Eight. Material nostalgia does not see past things as historical artefacts or museum exhibits, 'not as the stuff of future memorials, but as something living, breathing' (Tarkovsky 1989, p. 35). As it was experienced, in fact, and is still experienced today by so many nonmodern societies around the world.

Nine. Material nostalgia sees the everyday material world as a miracle and, as such, it is 'governed by the dynamic of revelation' (Tarkovsky 1989, p. 41). This revelation does not mean necessarily that we discover the esoteric meaning of things, but that a chair is actually good for sitting and an axe to cut trees (Olsen 2010). Archaeology is the science of revelation, but also the science of the trivial. Material nostalgia is thus an archaeological nostalgia.

Ten. Material nostalgia is utopian. This utopia, which is Benjaminian at heart (Benjamin 1968), has a material dimension – the impossible but indispensable retention of the past, a temporal one – the time of nostalgia is the time of 'not yet' (Cassin 2015, p. 50) and the 'not yet' is by definition the time of utopia, and a spatial one: we know that it is impossible to return to the same place, in the same way that we cannot see the same river twice (Theseus' Paradox). Julia Kristeva (1991, p. 10) sees the foreigner as the one who lives 'attached to a lost space' and at the same time with 'a passion for another land, always a promised one.' The lost space and the other land can be one and the same place. We know that returning is impossible, but we keep traveling back to where we have never been.

Concluding remarks

Nostalgia is a basic human emotion. It is related to the need for roots and continuity with the past. In this chapter, I have argued that materiality, the longing for things and particularly nonmodern materialities, is a potentially utopian and subversive form of engaging with the past. It is not unproblematic, for sure, nor easy: after all, the idea of pain is at the heart of nostalgia as an affect. That pain, I have argued, is related to the very impossibility of the return. Material nostalgia implies a different ethical relationship to the past: one that refuses to let the past go, because it believes that it has something to offer to the present and the future, but at the same time accepts both the inevitability of loss and the damage already done – the scar, which is itself material. Nostalgia, after all, is the longing for a vanished home. Loss is at the heart of nostalgia. Yet material nostalgia reacts against such loss, not with the attitude of the ironist, but with that of the archaeologist who clings to what is left and takes care of the remains. Material nostalgia, as outlined here, respects – admires – the nonmodern world, but it does not idealize it. It is not about returning to a preindustrial utopia that never was, but about mobilizing traces of the material past for the future.

Acknowledgements

I would like to thank the colleagues of the project *After Discourse: Things, Archaeology, and Heritage in the 21st Century* for inspiring conversations and thought-provoking comments and Caitlin DeSilvey for the insightful suggestions that have helped to improve this paper. I also want to thank Irma Pineda for kindly allowing the reproduction of her poem 'La Nostalgia', which has inspired this text. Any errors remain my own.

References

Arendt, H., 1994. What Remains? The Language Remains: An Interview with Gunther Gauss. In: J. Kohn, ed., *Hannah Arendt, Essays in Understanding, 1930– 1954.* New York: Harcourt and Brace, 1–23.

Beaudry, M. C., and Parno, T. G., eds., 2013. *Archaeologies of Mobility and Movement.* New York: Springer.

Benjamin, W., 1968. *Illuminations. Essays and Reflections.* Edited by Hannah Arendt. (Trans. H. Zohn). New York: Schoken Books.

Berger, J., 1992. *Pig Earth.* New York: Vintage.

Boym, S., 2001. *The Future of Nostalgia.* New York: Basic Books.

Braidotti, R., 2013. *The Posthuman.* Cambridge: Polity.

Buchli, V., 2010. Memory, Melancholy and Materiality. In: D. Borič, ed., *Archaeology and Memory.* Oxford: Oxbow, 204–210.

Burström, M., 2013. Fragments as Something More. In: A. González-Ruibal, ed., *Reclaiming Archaeology: Beyond the Tropes of Modernity.* Abingdon: Routledge, 311–22.

Clifford, J., 1997. *Routes: Travel and Translation in the Late Twentieth Century.* Cambridge, MA: Harvard University Press.

Cassin, B., 2015. *La nostalige. Quand donc est-on chez soi?* Paris: Pluriel.

Castillo, R., 2016. *Sombra roja. Diecisiete poetas mexicanas (1964–1985).* Madrid: Vaso Roto.

Cresswell, T., 2006. *On the Move: Mobility in the Modern Western World.* Abingdon: Routledge.

Davis, F., 1977. Nostalgia, Identity and the Current Nostalgia Wave. *The Journal of Popular Culture*, 11(2): 414–24.

Davis, F., 1979. *Yearning for Yesterday: A Sociology of Nostalgia.* New York: Free Press.

Dawdy, S. L., 2016. *Patina: A Profane Archaeology.* Chicago: University of Chicago Press.

De León, J., 2015. *The Land of Open Graves: Living and Dying on the Migrant Trail.* Berkeley: University of California Press.

Derrida, J., 1998. *Monolingualism of the Other, or, the Prosthesis of Origin.* Palo Alto: Stanford University Press.

DeSilvey, C., 2017. *Curated Decay: Heritage beyond Saving.* Minneapolis: University of Minnesota Press.

Domanska, E., 2006. The Material Presence of the Past. *History and Theory*, 45(3): 337–48.

Friedman, J., 2002. From Roots to Routes: Tropes for Trippers. *Anthropological Theory*, 2(1): 21–36.

Gaffney, J., 2015. Can a Language Go Mad? Arendt, Derrida, and the Political Significance of the Mother Tongue. *Philosophy Today*, 59(3): 523–40.

Giddens, A., 1991. *Modernity and Self-identity: Self and Society in the Late Modern Age.* Stanford: Stanford University Press.

González-Ruibal, A., 2019. *An Archaeology of the Contemporary Era.* Abingdon: Routledge.

Grünewald, R. de A., 2002. Tourism and Cultural Revival. *Annals of Tourism Research*, 29(4): 1004–21.

Haderlap, M., 2016. *Angel of Oblivion* (Trans. T. Lewiss). New York: Archipelago.

Hamilakis, Y., 2017. Archaeologies of Forced and Undocumented Migration. *Journal of Contemporary Archaeology*, 3(2): 121–39.

Han, B. C., 2015. *The Burnout Society.* Palo Alto: Stanford University Press.

Huyssen, A., 2006. Nostalgia for ruins. *Grey Room*, 23: 6–21.

Kristeva, J., 1991. *Strangers to Ourselves.* New York: Columbia University Press.

Leary, J., ed., 2014. *Past Mobilities: Archaeological Approaches to Movement and Mobility.* London: Ashgate.

Lemonnier, P., 2012. *Mundane Objects: Materiality and Non-verbal Communication.* Walnut Creek, CA: LeftCoast.

Leroi-Gourhan, A., 1964. *Le geste et la parole II. La mémoire et les rytmes.* Paris: Albin.

Malkki, L., 1992. National Geographic: The Rooting of Peoples and the Territorialization of National Identity among Scholars and Refugees. *Cultural Anthropology* 7(1), 24–44.

Marcus, G. E., 1995. Ethnography in/of the World System: The Emergence of Multi-sited Ethnography. *Annual Review of Anthropology* 24(1), 95–117.

Millares, S., 2013. *Antología. La poesía del siglo XX en Centroamérica y Puerto Rico*. Madrid: Visor.

Miller, D., 2007. Stone Age or Plastic Age? *Archaeological Dialogues,* 14(1), 23–7.

Olivier, L., 2008. *Le sombre abîme du temps. Mémoire et archéologie*. Paris: Le Seuil.

Olsen, B., 2010. *In Defense of Things: Archaeology and the Ontology of Objects*. Lanham, MD: Altamira.

Orser, C. E., 2012. An Archaeology of Eurocentrism. *American Antiquity,* 77(4), 737–55.

Pallasmaa, J., 2000. Hapticity and Time. *Architectural Review*, 207(1), 78–84.

Pickering, M., and Keightley, E., 2006. The Modalities of Nostalgia. *Current Sociology*, 54(6), 919–41.

Seremetakis, N., 1994. The Memory of the Senses, Part I: Marks of the Transitory. In: N. Seremetakis, ed., *The Senses Still. Perception and Memory as Material Culture in Modernity*. Chicago: The University of Chicago Press, 1–18.

Shanks, M., 2007. Symmetrical Archaeology. *World Archaeology*, 39(4), 589–96.

Shanks, M., 2012. *The Archaeological Imagination*. Walnut Creek, CA: LeftCoast.

Shanks, M. and McGuire, R. H., 1996. The Craft of Archaeology. *American Antiquity*, 61(1), 75–88.

Sheller, M. and Urry, J., 2006. The New Mobilities Paradigm. *Environment and Planning A*, 38(2), 207–26.

Spender, D., 1980. *Man Made Language*. Abingdon: Routledge.

Tannock, S., 1995. Nostalgia Critique. *Cultural Studies,* 9(3), 453–64.

Tarkovsky, A., 1989. *Sculpting in Time: Reflections on the Cinema*. (Trans. K. Hunter-Blair) Austin: University of Texas Press.

Tedder, V., 2019. Crafting a Progressive Nostalgia: Radical Embroidery as a Negotiation of the Past into a Positive Future. In: Burke, C. and Spencer-Wood, S.M. eds., *Crafting in the World*. New York: Springer, 245–54.

Tsing, A. L., 2005. *Friction: An Ethnography of Global Connection*. Princeton: Princeton University Press.

Ulmer, J. B., 2017. Writing Slow Ontology. *Qualitative Inquiry,* 23(3), 201–11.

Weil, S., 2001. *The Need for Roots*. (Trans. A. Wills). Abingdon: Routledge.

Wilson, J. L., 2014. *Nostalgia: Sanctuary of Meaning*. Lewisburg: Bucknell University Press.

Witmore, C., 2013. Which Archaeology? A Question of Chronopolitics. In: A. González-Ruibal, ed., *Reclaiming Archaeology. Beyond the Tropes of Modernity*. Abingdon: Routledge, 130–44.

Žižek, S., 1989. *The Sublime Object of Ideology*. London: Verso.

PART III

Ethics: Caring for things

Caitlin DeSilvey

'To know is to care, to care is to use, to use is to transform the past. Continually refashioned, the remade past continuously remoulds us', wrote David Lowenthal, in his introduction to *The Past is a Foreign Country – Revisited* (2015, 1). Lowenthal's observation reminds us that our interest in the 'things' that have come to us from the past is never innocent or indifferent. The act of knowing – in both an intellectual and affective sense – is an act of extending care, in that it focuses our attention on the specificity of a particular thing and its properties. And while such care may be benevolent or benign, it also, almost inevitably, involves an attempt to enlist things in our own projects and preoccupations (even, paradoxically, when our project is one that seeks to acknowledge the agency and autonomy of things). In this way, as Lowenthal points out, we 'use' the past, and the act of use transforms the object we are attending to – which allows the transformed object to work back on us, in turn.

Questions about how we care for things, and how we use them, are at their core questions of ethics. As noted in the introduction to the volume, however, our focus in this section extends beyond ethics as an exclusively human concern. We seek to understand how an ethical lens may help us reframe our relation to the things we share the world with, and allow those things to touch us (and each other) in unpredictable ways. The chapters in this section share an interest in relations between people and things, and a concern for understanding what 'right' person–thing relations might look like in a world riven with inequality and instability. Themes of encounter, exposure, authority, appropriation, intention and responsibility all emerge in the chapters that follow, though they are treated in in very different ways. This difference is, in part, borne out of the different disciplinary traditions represented: philosophy, cultural geography, archaeology, anthropology, history. But there is also a productive blurring of methodological and epistemological approaches, as the authors take up the invitation presented in this volume to engage with things otherwise, against the grain of inherited academic conventions.

The question of 'touch' is central to Lucas D. Introna's chapter, which opens this section. In his discussion of a handful of discarded and mundane objects – a bolt, a drawer of old spectacles and watches – he explores both the impulse to connect meaningfully with the material world and the ultimate impossibility of this connection. Drawing on the work of Lingis, Nancy, and Derrida, he suggests that 'tactful touch' – which acknowledges its inherent failure – is the condition of possibility for an ethical encounter. In the chapter that follows, I explore similar themes in a radically different context – a section of coastal path vulnerable to erosion and incursion by the sea. Working with the concept of 'foundering,' I ask what the appropriate ethical response might be to transient things, which are crossing the threshold between presence and absence. I explore the potential application of an ethics of attention without intention, which acknowledges the ambiguous energies of things without trying to fit them within anthropocentric systems of meaning and management.

The two chapters that follow both address darker aspects of ethical relation and deliberation. In Doug Bailey's chapter, the discovery of a slide archive – culled from an anthropological collection because of its disturbing content – creates an opportunity for an extended engagement with the troubled politics of academic labour and the limitations of reconciliation and repatriation. Ultimately, Bailey concludes that the release of these images from the archive requires degrees of violence equal to those expended in the original act of capturing images and subjects. In the next chapter, the legacy of historical violence and control is expressed in diseased bodies and landscapes. In the company of Curtis L. Francisco, an indigenous geologist and resident of the Laguna Pueblo, Christopher Witmore explores a partially remediated uranium mine. The chapter registers how radioactivity persists in the landscape and experiments with a mode of expression that cleaves closely to intimate encounter and exposure, witnessing the afterlife of exploitation and contamination.

The final chapter in this section advances a broader argument about the need for reassessment of our relations with non-human others. Tim LeCain argues against human exceptionalism, and explores the ethical relations that may emerge when we ourselves are seen as part of a broader continuum with other organisms and things. Using two empirical case studies of other organisms, he suggests that a more humble understanding of our place in the world may engender increased respect for the dynamic materiality that creates and sustains us.

Reference

Lowenthal, D. (2015), *The Past is a Foreign Country-Revisited*, Cambridge: Cambridge University Press.

12

TOUCHING TACTFULLY

The impossible community

Lucas D. Introna

> *What is touched remains compellingly exterior, so that touch is a contact without possession, without belonging, in difference. It remains an approach, a nearing, a contact without possibility for satisfaction and rest. Nonmediated, pervasive, vulnerable, touch constitutes for mortals the possibility to enter that place of an encounter with things that takes the name of an ethics of things.*
>
> *(Benso 2000, p. 163)*

Allow me to start this chapter by relaying my encounter with a particular bolt. Our lives crossed paths when I stepped on it in the road, walking. It impressed itself on my foot, and thus called for my attention. I picked it up without much attention and deposited it in my pocket. At home, whilst working, I took it out and placed it on my desk, beside my keyboard (Figure 12.1). There it sat, passively, but not quite. Occasionally I would pick it up, to fiddle with it, or to study it intently, feel its contours, the coolness of the steel, and then I'd set it down again. Over time, I became strangely affected by this bolt, in ways that are difficult to express. It was not just its beauty or the fact that it was discarded, as such. It was something more and something less. In some vague sense, it acted as a mirror, revealing me – as one that picks up things in the street.

The bolt afforded me a reflection not only on myself, but also on us humans more generally – as ones that organize things in the world to be available for our purposes (Heidegger 1977) – and much more besides. In being there, it seemed to be posing all sorts of questions, silently and unassumingly: questions such as the sort of being that we humans are when we relate to discarded things like it, and to other-than-human others in the way that we do. In being-with this bolt, I felt in some sense questioned, implicated in something that was difficult to express. I became increasingly aware of our relationships with things – not as tools, or as things that we use for practical purposes. Rather, I became

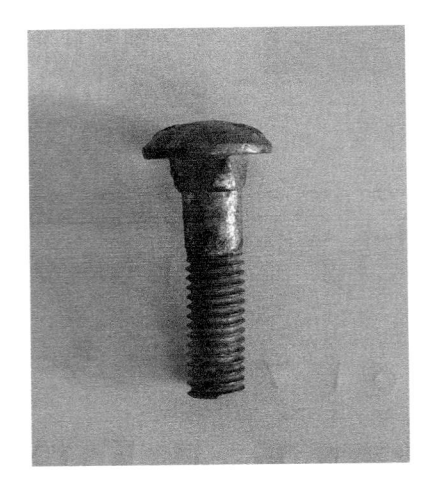

FIGURE 12.1 The bolt. Photo: Lucas D. Introna

aware of our relationships with things, beyond, or despite, their usefulness to us. Our relationship with things, *qua* things, one might say. Importantly, this is not really a question of what ethics becomes (for us humans) if we somehow add the other-than-human to our ethical calculus (Verbeek 2008). It is rather the question of ethics in which such distinctions do not hold or are not taken as valid. It is a question of ethics towards all others that are other-than-me, whatsoever (Introna 2009).

When considering things, we must start by acknowledging that whenever we find ourselves in the flow of everyday life we are already a being-in-the-world, in the very midst of it, already there, surrounded by things that are other than us. Or, perhaps more precisely, we are already entangled with other things – in a world that is more than human. Sometimes things seem, from where we are, passive, friendly, and so forth, and sometimes they seem aggressive, threatening us, pushing against us, and so on. Whatever the case, we never find ourselves alone and self-contained. We seem to be the beings that we are by being always and already in relation with others. In other words, whenever we take note of ourselves, we find ourselves always and already confronted with the other, somehow. That is, we are confronted with a question of how to be with the other: the question, one might say, of ethics (and, of course, politics). Ethics here is understood not in norma-tive terms, of being good or bad, or right or wrong, but rather, in the Levinasian sense as *exposure* (Levinas 1999). What this entails is an ethics that is always and already exposed to, and confronted with, the concrete and weighty reality of all things, in their very thingingness, weighing down on us, somehow (Benso 1996, p. 134). Things, in their being-there, call for our attention, for a response, one way or another. This calling for our attention is not a scream-out-loud call. Rather, it seems to be a very faint, almost indiscernible murmur in the background – almost nothing, easy to miss in the busyness of everyday life. Nevertheless, it is unmistakably present in our peripheral awareness, quietly unsettling us, even if we mostly ignore it.

In being faced with this quiet yet unsettling call, I find myself (not as a self-certain 'I' but rather as an 'I' that is in some sense always and already implicated) in some way needing to respond (Levinas 1989). Not only to the human other, as Levinas would insist, but also for the other-than-human other as Benso (1996) has argued. That is, the otherness of the human and the other-than-human other has already called me into question, quietly disrupting my already assumed right to be. Faced with this faint but incessant questioning, I can do my best to ignore it, to occupy myself with the busyness of daily life, acting as if this voice that calls me into question is not there or does not matter. Of course, we all do it (it is the rational thing to do). Alternatively, I can expose myself to this call. I can respond by saying, here I am. I am always and already implicated – in some way I am already your hostage (Levinas 1989). This responding 'I' is not a pre-existing sovereign 'I.' Rather, this 'I' becomes constituted out of the ether of this encounter with, or exposure to, the other as *the one* that is always and already responsible. In this ethical encounter, my singularity is constituted by the fact that no other can respond on my behalf or take my place in responding. I am not a representative of humanity (or some social category). Rather, I, as the I that emerges from this encounter, am the *one* that is singularly responsible – that is, ethical obligation as the original ground of all being (or, as Levinas would say, ethics is first philosophy). This obsessive experience of responsibility, in a sense, always and continuously 'persecutes me with its sheer weight,' to use Simon Critchley's (2007, p. 61) words.

How do I respond to this weightiness, to the other-than-human facing me, and to the many others that equally surround me? Indeed, especially towards those other-than-human others that seem so utterly other, with whom I seem to have nothing in common – yet, who seem to question me in some way. More specifically, how do I respond without simply turning the other-than-human other into the economy of the same (for example by transforming the other into a category in the traffic of language or reason)? That is, how do I respond, or commune with the other, *ethically*? Not just theoretically (in the intellectual discourse of academia) but also practically, in being with the multitude of others (human and the other-than-human alike)? This is a question that pre-occupies me in the flow of everyday life, when holding the bolt in my hand, when opening my desk drawer, which contains my no-longer-useful eye glasses going back many years, or my old broken watches (Figure 12.2). Why do I keep them? Am I just a hoarder? Perhaps, but it also seems that these things have some sort of a hold on me. In some sense, they are also questioning me. In some way, they are questioning my right to be the 'I' that I already assume I am. How shall I respond, ethically? This is the question that I would like to explore (or at least start to explore) in this chapter.

FIGURE 12.2 Broken watches. Photo: Lucas D. Introna

On the community of those that have nothing in common, or, being-with others outside of identity

It is possible to suggest that I can in some way imagine my ethical obligations to the human other, since they are like me, but what about the other-than-human other? Can there be any sort of ethical communion – understood as exposure – between those who have nothing in common? For Alphonso Lingis (1994), we enter – or become members of – the rational community by expressing ourselves in terms of an institutionally defined 'rational discourse.' One can imagine here the ideas of Foucault (1998), when he talks about discourses as constitutive of regimes of truth (and associated subject positions). For example, when we speak as a scientist, we need to speak in, and through, the discourse of science, and all that that implies. Through our participation in such a discourse, we become enacted as a particular kind of subject (a scientist, in this case). Thus, the rational community affords individuals a way into communication, but this affordance is constituted in a very precise manner. That is, it is a communion that "depersonalizes one's visions and insights, formulates them in terms of the common rational discourse, and speaks as a representative, a spokesperson, equivalent and interchangeable with others, of what has to be said" (Lingis 1994, p. 116). Such participation in the rational discourse gives one a voice, but only a representative voice. The rational community affords us the opportunity to speak, but only on the terms of that particular community – its language, its reasons, its logic. In this form of speaking, it might matter what we say, but it does not really matter who is saying it. In the rational community, all speakers are, in a sense, identical or interchangeable. It is the communality, continuity, and resilience of the rational discourse community that creates the sense of immortality, something that transcends the limits of the individual finitude. In our relations with the other-than-human things, the rational discourse (and communion) is mostly one *of use and utility.* For example, William Morris, a big figure in the Arts and Crafts movement, said "If you want a golden rule that will fit everything, this is it: Have nothing in your houses that you do not know to be useful or believe to be beautiful." This exemplifies the rational community of the more-than-human: it either must be useful (serve our utilitarian purposes) or beautiful (serve our aesthetic purposes) – and even more so if it can be both. In such a rational community of use and utility – in the world of 'fast' and mass production – things are essentially identical, that is, interchangeable. Their singularity is utterly irrelevant; replacement always seems possible. It is what they can do for us that matters (Introna 2009) – be it simple utility, virtue signalling, identity work, and so on. If they are no longer useful (or they break) we 'dump' them, they literally become taken as waste. Is the rational community the only form of communion available to us? Can we speak of a community of *those who have nothing in common,* a community of radically singular others – others that are absolutely other? How do we commune with, or become exposed to, those singular others (human and other-than-human alike) with whom we have absolutely nothing in common?

To explore this question, Lingis (1994) considers a number of limit cases of communion – where the rational community seems to evaporate. The one I will focus on here is the case in which we are with someone who is dying. What can be said in such a situation? It would seem that anything that one might try to say would be ill-conceived. In some sense, one might suggest that to say anything – to somehow suggest that we have something meaningful to say – is itself absurd. Nevertheless, we typically find ourselves fumbling through sentences, desperately trying to speak, to acknowledge the singularity of the event in some way. Lingis suggests that in this situation it does not matter what we say, as such. What matters most is that one speaks. However, in trying to speak one discovers "that language itself does not have the powers" (Lingis 1994, p. 108). It is feeble in the face of death. What do we do? We stretch out our hand, we feel compelled to touch, to hold the dying. The touch of this extended hand,

> communicates no information and brings no relief and knows no hope, is there only to accompany the other in his or her dying, to suffer and to die with him or her. And in this hand there is perhaps an understanding more profound than all apprehension and all comprehension, a force stronger than every efficiency and a compassion beyond and beneath every virtue …
>
> *(Lingis 1996, p. 10)*

In touching the dying other I am not a representative of the rational community. I am instead a finite material being, an earthling, as Lingis (1994) would say, "[o]ne whose flesh is made of earth – dust that shall return to dust …" (p. 117). The community that has nothing in common does not come about by working together, sharing an identity, a common language, a common culture, and so forth. Rather, it is produced by exposing oneself, through touch, to the one who is always and already dying, and with whom one has nothing in common. This exposure reveals our finite being, our mortal existence. The community of those that have nothing in common is a finite community of strangers who are, touchingly, dying together. Of course, Lingis reminds us that we should not see the rational community and the community of those that have nothing in common as two separate communities. These are not two options that we can choose from. Rather, "this [second] communication is other than and prior to, and it doubles up our communication as representatives of the rational community." It "troubles the rational community, as its double or its shadow" (Lingis 1994, p. 10).

When thinking about the communion of community, Jean-Luc Nancy (2000, 2008) starts differently. For him, community is more primordial than personhood (individual subjectivity): "[t]*hat Being is being-with, absolutely, this is what we must think*" (Nancy 2000, p. 61). Our personhood is itself only a derivative form of our original community. Our being is that of always and already being-in-common. Thus, a community is not formed by bringing or adding together independent and self-sufficient beings in order to form some sort of collective. Rather, our original relatedness is already constitutive of who we are prior to becoming an individual. Significantly, however, this community (or relationality) does not have an identity. That is, something *immanent* in it that needs to be brought out and put to work. According to Nancy, such thinking of community – as having something in common, an immanent identity, that must be put to work – is totalitarian (and shared by all totalitarian thought) (Nancy 2000). Such thinking is in effect the closure of the very possibility of an ethical encounter. It assigns to community a common being, an essence, which needs to be brought out by what he calls *subject-work* – or perhaps what one might call *identity work*. We can think of the many violent things being done in the name of identity-work (be it humanity, religion, nation, people, self-affirmation, common good, justice, even ethics). Indeed, identity work has become a major preoccupation for the post-modern subject and late capitalism – mostly in search of transcendence, or as an attempt to cover over the unbearable finitude of our existence.

In opposition to this notion of community, based on identity, Nancy proposes a notion of community based on finitude – "finitude, or the infinite lack of infinite identity, if we can risk such a formulation, is what makes community. That is, community is made or formed by the retreat or subtraction of something …" (Nancy 2000, pp. 18–19). This finitude – or one might say un-working of identity – does not allow us to contain either the world or ourselves – to be a self-sufficient subject, identical to ourselves. Instead, we are lost in a condition of plurality – our always and already being-withness, one might say. The essence of community is this plurality – that we are always and already different from one another. This difference, or heterogeneity, is something we share, something that makes sharing possible as such – it is what we have in common (Nancy 2000; Watkin 2007). This difference, this singularity, is *embodied and ecstatic*. As such, it is exposed and vulnerable to the other. It is always and already affected, touched, and in a sense invaded by the other. This radical openness of the body compels the subject into relations with others, as an already entangled being. This porous, always open horizon – of embodied beings – is where singularities touch, and are touched. It is as singular bodies that community (and ethics) becomes possible. Bodies are 'earthlings' in Lingis' idiom – they have weight and edges. Bodies in-the-world are singular in that no two bodies can occupy the same space (or one might rather say place, in Malpas' (2008) terms). I cannot take the other's place, I cannot speak (or listen) for her. My body is the limit of what can be known. The moment I touch another body I am reminded of this limit. Yet, the touch also allows for exposure, for the possibility of an ethical encounter (Lingis 1994; Benso 2000; Nancy 2000).

I want to suggest, with Lingis, Nancy and Benso, that touch is, in some sense, the condition of possibility of an ethics for those who have nothing in common. Not just the human other, but also all other-than-human others – with whom we have absolutely and utterly nothing in common. As finite singular beings we are all already dying together (that is what we share). The universe as it expands and cools down, the tree as it withers away, the bolt as it corrodes, my body as it slowly shuts down – we are all finite 'earthlings' dying together. What can we do? Not reason it out, not cover it over with desperate identity work (of self and others). We can reach out and touch each other, touchingly. In touch there exists the condition of possibility for ethics to become possible – but it is also fragile, very fragile indeed, and perhaps impossible.

Touching (tactfully) as an ethical encounter with the other, as other

What is touch? How can we understand it? For the traditional Newtonian physicist, touch is nothing other than electromagnetic interactions. What we feel when we touch a tree, a desk, a dog, or another's face is merely the effect of *electromagnetic repulsion*. Indeed, all we really feel is an electromagnetic force pushing us away rather than the stranger whose contact we might seek – in a sense, the other is repulsed by us (as we are by it). However, this is not the case when we consider touch in terms of quantum physics. In quantum wave theory, as Barad (2012) suggests, touching is a very different matter altogether. In some sense, touching is not repulsion but rather hypersensitive-touching:

> All touching entails an infinite alterity, so that touching the Other is touching all Others, including the "self," and touching the "self" entails touching the strangers within. Even the smallest bits of matter are an unfathomable multitude. Each "individual" always already includes all possible intra-actions with "itself" through all the virtual Others, including those that are

noncontemporaneous with "itself." That is, every finite being is always already threaded through with an infinite alterity diffracted through being and time.

(p. 214)

Thus, it seems that, in the language of quantum physics, touch is the state of being entangled (always threaded through with alterity) and of withdrawing at the same time – simultaneous proximity and distance, as the quantum entanglement suggests. This is something that Nancy would certainly agree with. Perhaps this condition of always being entangled with an infinite alterity already touching us is the murmur in the background that Lingis (1994) refers to? How can we think this?

Touch, unlike other senses, involves a proximity and an exposure. For example, sight and hearing are the senses for grasping those objects that are given as coming from elsewhere. I can hear and see at a distance. I cannot touch at a distance. Touch involves the proximity of the body. Touch requires contact, an exposure. The body is given, or made real in some sense, in contact. It has to risk itself in some way. In addition, when I touch, I also feel myself being touched by some other thing or being – there is a certain doubling at work. In touching, we experience the boundary, border, or limit of ourselves. In a sense, touching is what recalls our finitude. It shows up the fact that I am not infinitely extended. I am instead a fragile, finite, and singular being. Thus, touch is always in some sense a limit experience. It can approach the boundary of the other, but it cannot properly go beyond it, even if it is entangled with it. Derrida (2005) expresses this limit of touching as follows:

> It is touching that touches upon the limit, its own "proper-improper" limit, that is to say, on the untouchable on whose border it touches … To touch is to touch a border, however deeply one may penetrate, and it is thus to touch by approaching indefinitely the Inaccessible of whatever remains beyond the border, on the other side.
>
> *(p. 297).*

In touching, the singular reality of the other, 'on the other side', is also given to me, albeit in some ambiguous way. Aristotle (in On Physics and on the Soul) suggested that touching is in itself nothing other than the very experience of heterogeneity. This encounter with heterogeneity is the very experience of being exposed – we feel in touch with something, but also exposed to the edges of an uncertain body, touching us back. In short: I am affected. As a body in touch with the world – affected by it – I become a lived body – touching the world and being touched by it. Or, more precisely, I am a lived body because I am always and already touched or affected by the other, already "threaded through with an infinite alterity." It is perhaps the acknowledgement of this irreducible double sense of touch – of the simultaneity of touching and being touched – that is behind our use of the word 'touching' or 'being touched' to describe the experience of being already affected. However, it is an affectedness where the source of the affection itself is not given, a sort of tactful contact.

In considering the work of Nancy, Derrida (2005) suggests that in touch there is also something else at stake — what he calls the law of tact:

> For there is a law of tact. Perhaps the law is always a law of tact. *And one should understand tact, not in the common sense of the tactile, but in the sense of knowing how to touch without touching, without touching too much, where touching is already too much. Tact touches on the origin of the law. Just barely. At the limit.*
>
> (Derrida 2005, p. 67, emphasis added)

For Derrida, there is always a counter-movement involved in touching. Touching is not just a way of making contact, it is also a mode of distancing contemporaneous with the very touch. Nancy proposes that between bodies there is always a contiguity — we are always and already bodies touching other bodies, indeed, already bodies because of this very touch — but there is not continuity. This extreme proximity to others, of touching, however, simultaneously reveals a profound distance — a distant horizon that never seems to come closer no matter how vigorously we approach it. In spite of this, the other bodies touch us back. Thus, Nancy suggests that "[a]ll of being is in touch with all of being, but the law of touching is separation; moreover, it is the heterogeneity of surfaces that touch each other. Con*tact* is beyond fullness and emptiness, beyond connection and disconnection" (Nancy 2000, p. 5, emphasis added).

Let us explore further these two moments (or one might say movements) of touch — what we might call *touch as contact* and *touch as tact*. It would not be controversial to say that touch as contact is fundamental to the production of knowledge, that is, to epistemology. The only way to know something is to touch it, we know through contact. However, what does this contact do? Touching as contact, in its touching of other bodies, aims to register differences (to make distinctions). The cyberneticist Gregory Bateson (1979), in his book *Mind and Nature*, suggested that in cybernetics *information is a difference that make a difference*. The touch must not just register — or, more properly said, bring to presence — differences (is it hard, soft, cold, wet, positive, negative, or just different, etc.). These differences must also make a difference. That is, they must become, in some sense, relevant differences within a set of propositions, a theory, a cosmology, and so forth. Why? So that they might confirm the self-certainty of the subject (or the rational community, more broadly). To touch, epistemologically, is an attempt to know the stranger by subsuming her into the categories of the same — touch as contact. It is a logic that attempts to place the other in the order of knowledge, precisely. That is, to confer on her a more or less exact identity that would render her body knowable and orderable as either significant or insignificant. In its extreme form, touch as contact will attempt to push forward against every boundary, and invent increasingly complex technologies of touch, in pursuit of bringing to presence these differences that make a difference — think of the Large Hadron Collider, for example. Moreover, in epistemological contact, there should ideally not be any exposure to the other. The scientist must protect herself and actively withdraw herself (anything specific to her, her own singularity) in order to not contaminate, or be contaminated by, the touch of contact. In this contact, we are compelled – if at all possible – to silence the interpellations of the law of tact. Of course, what this notion of contact fails to appreciate is that it is conditioned by something more primordial, the touch of tact.

Touching as tact is different. I would suggest, with Derrida and Nancy, that touch as tact functions by touching without touching, or touching tactfully (or with tenderness, Benso (2000) might say). Such touching does not seek to register differences, but rather withdraws, or steps back, in the very moment of contact. It hesitates and it acknowledges that in touching the other there is always something irreducible which cannot be touched. This stepping back is indeed necessary to touch the other in a truly touching way. This touching touch is acutely aware of the limit inherent in touching (and its potential for violence]. Touch as tact, as Derrida reminds us, is "to break with immediacy, with the immediate given wrongly associated with touch and on which all bets are always placed ..." (Derrida 2005, p. 293). To touch tactfully is *to be utterly indifferent to differences* – a complete passivity. Tactful touching suspends the desire to register differences – it seeks (if it seeks at all) absolutely to not be informed. On the contrary, it resolves to be exposed, to be vulnerable to the possibility of being touched by the other – in some way, beyond the registers of consciousness, of contact, of connection. Indeed, beyond everything that might be brought to present in the touch itself. In the tact of almost touching (but not quite), the other's body offers itself as a weighty matter "without anything to articulate, without anything to discourse about, without anything to add to them" (Nancy 1994, p. 197). Weighty, not in the sense of gravitational force but rather as an ethical force – not to be resisted but purely to be exposed to, silently. Lingis suggests "And in the ethical relationship that makes contact with the other's vulnerability and mortality ... tact is made of silence" (Lingis 2007, p. 5). We should also note, before moving on, that it is indeed possible to touch tactfully with our other senses, as Derrida (2005) suggests. We can see and hear tactfully. In being tactful we become affected, questioned, disturbed, less secure, and as such open to the interpellations of the other, as exactly other.

I would suggest that the radical openness (and ethical weightiness) of tact – as an ethos of dwelling or being-with the other – is further implied in the fact that the least valued in society are often referred to as *untouchables* (think of the Hindu cast system or the waste sites at the edges of our cities). They are believed to be untouchable because touching them would defile or pollute the one that touches. However, perhaps they are deemed to be untouchable because touching them would expose the one touching to the violent injustice (even horror) of their assumed identity (as more or less worthless reality, as waste). Does such untouchability not acknowledge that something is given through touch, something that is irreducible to the immediately given of the contact – and is perhaps too much to endure? In this irreducible exposure, of the tactfulness of any and all touch, there is an ethical murmur in the background, haunting us, even if we desperately try to ignore it – by designating some things as untouchable. To shield us from this disturbing touch of the other we limit our touch – we simply do not touch, except purposefully, that which is knowable, useful, or beautiful (as suggested by William Morris). The rest, it seems, is untouchable – and when we touch them, we touch them tactlessly, preferably with gloves on. Having said that, we need to acknowledge that when we take the gloves off, when we touch touchingly, we are exposed, at risk. For ethics to be a true being-with (an ethos) the 'I' needs to be at risk – always and already at risk, exposed to its own finitude. Indeed, this is what gives ethics its urgency, what makes it more than 'just hanging around' with the other. As Lingis suggests

> community forms when one exposes oneself to the naked one, the destitute one, the outcast, the dying one. One enters into community not by affirming oneself and one's forces but by exposing oneself to expenditure at a loss, to sacrifice.
>
> *(Lingis 1994, p. 11/2)*

Concluding comments

Where does this discussion leave us, practically? Somewhere and nowhere, one might suggest. Can we be ethically with all other others, also the other-than-human others – truly, with all of those with whom we have nothing in common? Can we become attuned to the murmur in the background already touching us tactfully? Indeed, I would suggest that we might. I would suggest that the conditions of possibility for an ethical encounter (or exposure) is given in tactful touching – touching and being touched, tactfully, perhaps. Was that what the bolt already touching me was suggesting, ever so silently, as it lay there passively next to my keyboard? Was it the tactful touching of the old watches and the old eyeglasses in my desk drawers that made me want to hold onto them, to touch them tactfully? Were they, in touching me, exposing me to the community of the dying, recalling in some strange way our shared finitude? But this tactful touching is almost imperceptible, so fragile. We can so easily miss it in the busyness of everyday life. It calls for an attunement outside of reason, knowledge, and so forth. Our ethical challenge is to live tactfully with all others, without the certainty of the rational community, or of contact. It is a radical exposure that is almost too much, and where I am always and already at risk. Having said this, we must also acknowledge that this would be impossible. The sheer weightiness of my being-in-the-world would be unbearable, and my existence would be very precarious – an impossible possibility as Derrida would say. But that is the point. Perhaps the discarded bolt, in touching me tactfully – not as this or that particular thing (it being a bolt is irrelevant) – was exposing me to the faint and indistinct background murmur already there. A faint murmur that recalled the fact that I am always already tactfully entangled with all others – and that this entanglement is finite, fragile and always at risk. A murmur that questions my assumed authority and self-certainty, radically. That allows me to somehow risk myself as one that is always and already dying – not alone, but with all those very many strangers with whom I have nothing in common, already touching me, tactfully. This seems to me to be the ethics of dwelling with all others, human and more-than-human alike, an impossible possibility. But that is all we have.

References

Barad, K., 2012. On Touching – The Inhuman That Therefore I Am. *differences*, 23 (3): 206–23.

Bateson, G., 1979. *Mind and Nature: A Necessary Unity*. 1st ed. New York, NY: Dutton.

Benso, S., 1996. Of Things Face-to-Face with Levinas Face-to-Face with Heidegger: Prolegomena to a Metaphysical Ethics of Things. *Philosophy Today; Charlottesville*, 40(1): 132.

Benso, S., 2000. *The Face of Things: A Different Side of Ethics*. Albany, NY: SUNY Press.

Critchley, S., 2007. *Infinitely Demanding: Ethics of Commitment, Politics of Resistance*. London: Verso.

Derrida, J., 2005. *On Touching, Jean-Luc Nancy*. Stanford, CA: Stanford University Press.

Foucault, M., 1998. *Ethics: Subjectivity and Truth*. 1st edition. New York, NY: New Press.

Heidegger, M., 1977. *The Question Concerning Technology, and Other Essays*. New York, NY: Harper and Row.

Introna, L.D., 2009. Ethics and the Speaking of Things. *Theory, Culture & Society*, 26 (4): 25–46.

Levinas, E., 1989. Ethics as First Philosophy. In: S. Hand, ed. *The Levinas Reader*. London: Wiley-Blackwell, 75–87.

Levinas, E., 1999. *Otherwise Than Being, or, Beyond Essence*. Pittsburgh, PA: Duquesne University Press.

Lingis, A., 1994. *The Community of Those Who Have Nothing in Common*. Bloomington, IN: Indiana University Press.

Lingis, A., 1996. *Sensation: Intelligibility in Sensibility*. Atlantic Highlands, NJ: Prometheus Books.

Lingis, A., 2007. Contact: Tact and Caress. *Journal of Phenomenological Psychology*, 38 (1): 1–6.

Malpas, J., 2008. *Place and Experience: A Philosophical Topography*. 1st edition. New York, NY: Cambridge University Press.

Nancy, J.-L., 1994. *The Birth to Presence*. Stanford, CA: Stanford University Press.

Nancy, J.-L., 2000. *Being Singular Plural*. Stanford, CA: Stanford University Press.

Nancy, J.-L., 2008. *The Inoperative Community*. Repr. Minneapolis, MN: University of Minnesota Press.

Verbeek, P.-P., 2008. Cultivating Humanity: Toward a Non-humanist Ethics of Technology. In: Olsen, J.K.B. Selinger, E. and Riis, S. eds. *New Waves in Philosophy of Technology*. Basingstoke England ; New York: Palgrave Macmillan, 241–63.

Watkin, C., 2007. A Different Alterity: Jean-Luc Nancy's 'Singular Plural'. *Paragraph*, 30 (2), 50–64.

13

FOUNDERED

Other objects and the ethics of indifference

Caitlin DeSilvey

Origins

The English word 'foundered' is an odd one. It usually indicates some form of failure or surrender, but it can apply to a bewildering diversity of different subjects: ships founder when they sink; horses founder due to an infection of the hoof; companies founder when they become insolvent. The use of the term in relation to landscape dates to at least the 17th century. In 1830 Charles Lyell wrote in his *Principles of Geology*, 'We find that the cliffs of Bawdsey and Felixtow are foundering slowly' (1830, p. 274). The word is linked etymologically to the Latin *fundus*, 'bottom', and seems to have arrived in English via the Old French term, *fondrer*. Other inflections have persisted: in Northern Ireland to be foundered is to be chill or numb with cold.[1] In its contemporary use, 'founder' most commonly takes an intransitive form, in that it does not have an object. It was once possible to say 'the river foundered the wall' or 'the sea foundered the path', but this use is now obsolete. The term in its current meaning is notable for the way in which it describes an act that apparently occurs without the intervention of an external agent.

This chapter explores the process of foundering with reference to a stretch of coastal path in Cornwall, in the far south and west of the island shared by England, Wales and Scotland. In the writing, a close engagement with the specificity of language, paradoxically, provides access to material and non-discursive aspects of lived experience. Through dwelling on the state of 'foundering' as I move through the landscape, I open up reflection on themes of care, ethics, and impermanence. My emergent analysis hinges on the recognition that with a 'foundered' object, care is not invited, and the object apparently asks nothing of us. This begs the question, how should we orient ourselves in relation to foundered and foundering things? Is there potential for an ethics of attention without intention? How can we acknowledge energies of transience and impermanence without giving in to the impulse to

FIGURE 13.1 Unstable cliffs, Polurrian Cove, Cornwall. Photo: Caitlin DeSilvey

contain and constrain their meaning? I explore these ideas through my experience of a landscape art commission and my encounters with foundered features along this stretch of coastline.

Wayfinding

The walk from Poldhu Beach to Mullion Cove begins on a on a west-facing beach and rises up along a narrow access road, where it picks up the coastal footpath just past the carpark of a massive white building, once a hotel and now a care home for the elderly. The path edges along high above the sea, and dips down to another beach, posted with warning signs: '*Caution: Unstable Cliffs*' (Figure 13.1). It rises again to cut below another hotel, and then it tracks up to a lane and a string of seaside bungalows. Past the bungalows, the path narrows again briefly, crowded by brambles and heather, and then emerges in front of a third hotel. A sharp drop down a grassy slope reveals a view of a stone harbour sheltering the mouth of a cove. On the elbow of a switchback, the path seems to diverge, the more travelled way cutting back along the contour to pass behind a row of harbour cottages.

The other route cuts downhill to the corner of the harbour, but it appears infrequently used. And then you notice a sign, posted on a sturdy metal post: '*This public footpath has foundered/No further access*'. A triangular black and yellow graphic above the text depicts a stylized human figure falling away from what appears to be a crumbling cliff face, flanked by Cornwall Council logos, with their distinctive silhouette of the cliff-dwelling Cornish chough (Figure 13.2).[2] By using the term 'foundered' to describe the path, the Council is asserting, in a technical and legal sense, that the path no longer exists and the right to public access has been terminated. The term's ontological implacability forecloses any possible intention with regard to the damaged path. It is not awaiting reinforcement or repair; it has passed a threshold into another state, a falling away.

It has becoming increasingly common to encounter such postings of foundered paths along this stretch of coastline. In the ferocious winter storm season of 2013–14, seven sections of coast path collapsed between the town of Porthleven and Lizard Point, a distance of fourteen walking miles. As with many other coastal landscapes in our climate-changed world, erosion that had been background and

FIGURE 13.2 Foundered footpath, Mullion Cove, Cornwall. Photo: Caitlin DeSilvey

incremental is now dramatic and unpredictable. Due to its peculiar geology, in this place the coast erodes in slumps and slides. On the inland edge of the cliffs, soils saturated by increasingly heavy rainfalls become unstable: when cliff bases are battered by intensifying storm swells and subject to the effects of rising sea levels, the result is often a landslip. The most recent Shoreline Management Plan, prepared by the UK Environment Agency, designates the majority of this coastal landscape as NAI – no active intervention. In this landscape, change is inevitable, and there is no current intention to defend vulnerable paths, or properties (of which there are relatively few – the hotels, a handful of homes, a beach café, the harbour).

I've walked along the stretch of coastline from Poldhu to Mullion many times over the last decade, accompanied by family, friends, and students. Depending on why I am walking and who I am walking with, the quality and target of my attention varies, but I rarely slow to focus on the details of specific features. My attention swings and stutters between moments: pulling small boys away from the cliff edge; looking out to ships moving in the Channel; eating a blackberry; navigating uneven terrain. On one walk in the summer of 2016, however, I did stop to look more carefully.

I was with a group of people, led by artist Louise Ann Wilson. Louise had been commissioned to devise a participatory walk for the section of coastline from Poldu to Mullion, as part of a wider programme of events along the Cornish coast. The programme, which was supported by the National Trust and Golden Tree Productions, involved a series of activities to engage people in creative ways with actual and anticipated coastal changes in specific places. Louise's commission, *Mulliontide*, sought to create an experience that 'notices the effects of tide and time, acknowledges deep feelings for place and recognises the challenges of change – personal and topographical' (Wilson 2017, p. 3). Through her engagement with local stories and memories, Louise worked to draw out analogies between lived experience and landscape – surfacing themes of loss and grieving in both contexts. The concept of *care* was central to the framing of the project: participants included elderly residents of the Poldhu Care Home and a palliative care nurse, who was brought into the project to contribute elements of his practice and draw out their resonance with the ideas Louise wanted to explore. The group of us that gathered in July 2016 to walk the route with Louise also included fellow academics, the National Trust ranger responsible for this stretch of coastline and producers from Golden Tree.

As we walked, Louise told us about the memories she was gathering from local residents, and shared her thoughts about how these could be woven into a performative public event due to be held in October. On the stretch of lane lined with bungalows on one side and steep cliffs on the other, Louise had us pause between a picket fence and the cliff edge. She pointed out a section of pebbledash wall, just the other side of a chain link fence. The section formed a rough corner, the wall edges fallen away, the ruined remainder hanging on above a short hanging valley crowded with overgrown rubble, and then dropping to an inaccessible slip of beach (Figure 13.3). I had passed this foundered feature perhaps a dozen times

FIGURE 13.3 Wall remnant. Photo: Caitlin DeSilvey

over the previous decade, but I had no recollection of ever paying it any attention. In her research, Louise had come upon the fragment, and through discussion with local people she identified it as part of a house that had been lost in a cliff collapse decades ago. A photograph surfaced, and the name of the lost house: Pedn-y-ke. One of the local residents that Louise had spoken to recalled the story shared by a friend of hers who used to live in the house: '*One day she came running home from school when suddenly, as she watched, the cliff seemed to rear up. Black mud squelched out, the cliff shrank, the house twisted and groaned then crashed onto the rocks below*' (Wilson 2017, p. 21). In this story, lived memory, passed on down decades and through a third person, takes on a fantastical sheen, as the cliff and the house both seem to become animate – 'rearing up' and 'twisting and groaning'. Louise included the story in her guided walk, and reproduced it in the publication documenting the project.

As we stood looking at the corner ruin on that July day, I felt the story kindling my appetite for more knowledge, and I noticed that suddenly I had an urge to map identity onto other overlooked things in this liminal landscape. A few yards down the road from the wall, we came across a pair of ivy-clad gate posts, opening to a bramble-choked drop (Figure 13.4). Before we knew the story of the house, these posts would have been unremarkable. But the awareness of the story, and their connection to the lost house, infilled these posts with meaning, like a rush of oxygen into a sealed box. Looking back along the coast towards the care home, the

FIGURE 13.4 Ghost gate posts. Photo: Caitlin DeSilvey

posts became elements contained by the narrative that now framed them. When we returned to the ruined wall, my imagination moved closer to the object to find the shape of what could have been an attached shed, or outbuilding. The act of recognition seemed to introduce a need to hold onto these remnants and their story, and to know more. In Haraway's words, '[O]nce we know, we cannot not know. If we know well, searching with fingery eyes, we care. That is how responsibility grows.' (Haraway 2008, p. 287). Although the aim of Louise's commission was to encourage people to understand and prepare for inevitable erosion and loss, according to research by colleague Bryony Onciul, many of the people who experienced the walk reported that it enhanced their appreciation of the vulnerability of coast, and made them want to protect things from further change.

But what if we resist this response, and responsibility? The wall fragment, before the story took hold, did not solicit our concern. Left to its own devices, in various weathers, above the stormy or still sea, it contributed to a background awareness of instability along this coastline, perceived with a mode of attention that involved not concentration but distraction, the feature casually 'absorbed' in the course of daily life (Dawdy 2016, p. 16). The addition of layers of story and image added meaning, and prompted care. Here, care emerges as a self-centred, rather than selfless, impulse, in that it focuses on the process of extending *our* attention and concern. It can be seen as an imposition of the human need to make the world meaningful (for us). Before the story arrived to make sense of it, the foundered wall was 'withdrawn', held in its own relation to the world, and in relation to the ruined fragments in the cove below (Harman 2002).

On indifference

How can we respect this withdrawn state, while still attending to things and their being? One possible way through to an alternative mode of encounter emerges from Hallvard's Lillehammer's writing about the 'ethics of indifference' (Lillehammer 2014, p. 2017). We usually accept that indifference implies 'a lack of interest or attention', but Lillehammer, in a series of papers, goes deeper than this to explore in detail the various orientations of indifference. His discussion includes an analysis of indifference as lack of awareness – not seeing the wall – as distinct from indifference as lack of concern – not caring if the wall falls down. Lillehammer also talks about how it is possible to be in a state of indifferent attention – not committed to a certain outcome or orientation, occupying the same space without paying focused attention to each other. He uses as an example the experience of overhearing a conversation between strangers at a bus stop – or, perhaps a tram stop, like the one at Skarpsno, in Olso, just down the road from the Centre for Advanced Study (Figure 13.5). While beginning to think about the ideas in this paper, I would often stand at this stop waiting for the tram, and sometimes I would be joined by others, who I would politely ignore – partly out of worry that I would invite a

FIGURE 13.5 Skarpsno tram stop, Olso. Photo: Kjetil Ree, 2009. Creative Commons license CC-BY-SA 3.0. https://commons.wikimedia.org/wiki/File:Trikk_Skarpsno_02.jpg

conversation in a language I did not speak. In this context, my apparent indifference to others was an act of courtesy, and also perhaps self-defence. Lillehammer describes this form of indifference as withholding concern out of respect for the autonomy of the other.

> Sometimes people fail to care about something precisely in order to mark their difference or separation from that thing … The virtuous manifestation of a lack of concern that involves this kind of orientation I refer to as *indifference as civility*.
>
> *(Lillehammer 2014, p. 120)*

Perhaps we can find some resources in these ideas for developing alternative ways of approaching foundered things, and allowing them to carry on with their changes with their ambiguous energies intact. Back on the path, between the picket fence and the wall fragment, on that summer day in 2016, I turned to look over the picket fence into a tidy bungalow garden. There, attached to the boundary fence on a small shelf, was what appeared to be a tiny wooden house, about 10 inches high, its gabled roof bearing a slight resemblance to the roofline of the lost Pedn-y-ke (Figure 13.6). I felt an odd leap of delight on seeing it. The model house on its stair-step cliff-shelf seemed to be bound in a sympathetic relation to the foundered

FIGURE 13.6 Model house attached to boundary fence, middle distance, above 'Tamarisk Cottage' sign. Photo: Caitlin DeSilvey

house across the road – a relation that set up a resonance between the two objects, in which we were only observers, caught in the cross-gaze. It was like the moment of recognition between two people at the tram stop, a conversation overheard, but not in a language I recognized. Of course I could have asked whether the tiny house had some significance or symbolism – a talisman against the forces of the eroding cliff edge? A sacrificial object – "if you need to take a house take this one?" Or I could let it be.

What happens when we understand indifference to things as recognition of their difference – and their existence outside our designs and designations – rather than an absence of care? Maria Puig de la Bellacasa, in her recent book on care and relations with more than human worlds, proposes what she calls a 'speculative ethics'. She asks: 'What does it mean to think of agencies of care in more than human terms?' (Puig de la Bellacasa 2017, p. 21). In her reframing, care is not an exclusively human capability, but a capacity, realized in relation. Can we see the tiny model house as caring for the foundered house? What would our role be in this relationship, if any? A reorientation of responsibility requires us to pause, and to examine what motivates our urge to make contact and claim objects with our attention.

On the section of walk between Poldhu and Polurrian beaches, a mile or so north of the collapsed house, there are twin cast iron fence posts separated by a raw gap, where the earth has slipped away (Figure 13.7). The posts are stranded, held

FIGURE 13.7 Ghost fence posts. Photo: Caitlin DeSilvey

apart from each other, and no longer linked by the path that held them. When we passed the posts on that walk in 2016, my impulse was to reach out and place my hand on one of them, to recognize its presence with a gesture. Like touching the top of a mountain, or a lucky statue, the touch was indifferent – in the sense that it did not seek to make any change or invite a response from the object. Puig de la Bellacasa explores the role of touch not as forced connection, but as expressive of the ambivalence of care, a way of keeping close to a thing or a problem without foreclosing on its meaning. Touch, in her terms (as in Benso's writing about touch as 'contact without possession') accentuates 'both the attraction of closeness and the awareness of alterity' (Benso 2000, p. 163; Puig de la Bellacasa 2017, p. 115).

Puig de la Bellacasa goes on to argue that, 'Haptic speculation doesn't guarantee material certainty; touching is not a promise of enhanced contact with "reality" but rather an invitation to participate in its ongoing redoing, and to be redone in the process' (Puig de la Bellacasa 2017, p. 117). How do these ideas about (indifferent) touch relate to Lillehammer's ideas about the ethics of indifference? He argues,

> There is no deep tension between a plausible ethics of indifference and a 'partial' ethics of care … A partial ethics of care should be able to explain why and how some indifferent attitudes or orientations are ethically appropriate and a range of contexts where empathetic caring is either not possible, or is ethically inadvisable or misguided.
>
> *(Lillehammer 2017, p. 34)*

With regard to the coast's foundered features, empathetic caring is, arguably, not an appropriate response. In their foundered state, these things have passed a threshold beyond which such active intervention would require almost complete reconstruction, and an extraordinary commitment of resources. Jem Bendell, in his discussion of 'deep adaptation', presents the concept of 'relinquishment', as the intentional 'letting go of certain assets, behaviours and beliefs where retaining them could make matters worse' (2018). In the context of coastal change, there are places where intervention will be necessary, to protect communities and cultures, and there will be other places where we need to acknowledge that action is not only not possible, but is not desirable. A partial ethics of care acknowledges the impulse to touch (and, as Haraway reminds us, we can touch with our eyes as well as our hands) but does so in a mode of haptic speculation which allows us to engage with other objects in a spirit of 'reciprocal exposure' and shared vulnerability (Puig de la Bellacasa 2017, p. 116). Such engagement does not seek to appropriate or intervene in the lives of other things, but instead leaves open the possibility that we may be 'redone' through our contact with them, whatever form that may take.

Endings

A few months ago I returned to take another look at the sign on the section of path above Mullion Cove: '*This public footpath has foundered*'. A few yards in front of the sign was another more battered sign, which had appeared in summer of 2016, after the partial collapse of the cliff face between the path and the harbour wall. The laminated paper notice read: '*Temporary prohibition of through traffic*', and elaborated, '*The closure will continue from 6th April 2016 to 6th October 2016 or until the works are completed whichever is sooner*'. But the works stalled, the path remained closed, and things moved on. In January 2018 another crack opened in the unstable ground in the cliff above the harbour, below the closed section of path, and chunks of stone and earth started to fall down onto the quay. The harbour itself was closed to public access from January to October. After remedial work to remove hundreds of tons of unstable rock and install a chain link retaining fence to catch stray stones, access to the harbour resumed. The path never reopened, and it never will. When the 'foundered' posting went up it became clear that the path was no longer waiting until the works were completed. The path had taken matters into its own hands.

All along the Cornish coast, unstable sections of cliff threaten to create gaps in the linear connectivity of the coastal path. Occasionally, temporary defensive action is taken by landowners and the local authority before the situation becomes critical, but more often the path is diverted inland and realigned, sometimes by a few yards, sometimes by whole fields. The ranger responsible for the section of path explored in the chapter shared his reflections on the language people use when they talk about this process of coastal erosion – he noted that cliffs are usually said to have 'failed'. But he pointed out that from the cliff's perspective, this is what cliffs do – they collapse, settle into a new form, open up new ecological possibilities, release sediment to the sea. The foundering of the path is also a new beginning, though not in a context we can necessarily relate to. The slumped cliff can be seen to be caring for the sea, depositing necessary sediment, contributing material essential to the functioning of coastal systems. In this sense, the language of failure is a human construct: the cliff fails *for us*, not on its own terms.

In this situation, a partial ethics of care, and a mode of indifferent attention, may work to frame a response that decentres human agencies and acknowledges other energies at work. But it is critically important to recognize that in many other places affected by rapid and extreme climate and coastal change, such as low-lying island nations, indifference is not a form of civility, but potentially a form of violence, complicit in what Ann Laura Stoler calls the 'politics of disregard' (Woodham et al. 2018; Stoler 2010). A decision to withhold care from the people who live in these places – and to continue to act in denial of the 'inverted cruelties of climate change' that inflict the greatest damage on those least responsible for it – is now ethically indefensible (Rich 2019, p. 199). In places of relative stability and privilege like the one explored in this chapter, exercise of a partial ethics of care can perhaps be understood as a strategy to redirect emotional energy and physical resources to places where much more is at stake than the loss of a favourite coastal walking route. Partial care, in this sense, can take many forms, including both the art of active noticing, such as that performed by the *Mulliontide* commission, and experiments with a more detached mode of attentive indifference.

I walked the Poldhu to Mullion path in February this year, with a group of students this time. The wall fragment was still intact and apparently unchanged, but on the other side of the picket fence the tiny house was missing from its perch. I scanned the garden and saw it had toppled into the flower border along the fence. When I saw the little house upturned on the ground in the bare winter soil, I felt I should look away, out of respect, but I could not pull my 'fingery eyes' away. What I experienced in this moment was perhaps the convergence between a plausible ethics of indifference and a partial ethics of care. In Puig de la Bellacasa's terms, I found myself 'redone' in the process of engaging with this landscape and its transience. I was exposed and rearranged by this encounter, but I didn't feel the urge to let myself into the garden to place the house back on its shelf. I just felt a keen awareness of the hazards of living in a foundering world, making connections that will inevitably, invariably, come undone.

Acknowledgements

Natalia Eernstman, Bryony Onciul, Justin Whitehouse, Alastair Cameron, Louise Ann Wilson, Saul Ridley and students on the Heritage and Environmental Change module – thank you for sharing the walking and the talking that shaped the ideas in this chapter. Audiences in Oslo (at the Centre for Advanced Study 'Interdisciplinary Workshop on Ethics and Things') and Aarhus (at the 'Inevitable Ends: Meditations on Impermanence' conference) also made essential critical contributions.

Notes

1 https://blog.oxforddictionaries.com/2016/03/09/northern-irish-verbs/
2 The chough, a relative of the jackdaw, used to be widespread on the cliffs of Cornwall. After years of decline and near extinction, in 2001 a small population established at the tip of the Lizard Peninsula and is now thriving.

References

Bendell, J. 2018, Deep adaptation: a map for navigating climate tragedy, IFLAS Occasional Paper 2, Available from: http://insight.cumbria.ac.uk/id/eprint/4166/ [accessed 9 October 2019].

Benso, S., 2000. *The Face of Things: A Different Side of Ethics*. Binghamton: SUNY University Press.

Dawdy, S., 2016. *Patina: A Profane Archaeology*. Chicago: University of Chicago Press.

Haraway, D., 2008. *When Species Meet*. Minneapolis, University of Minnesota Press.

Harman, G., 2002. *Tool-being: Heidegger and the Metaphysics of Objects*. Peru, IL: Open Court

Lillehammer, H., 2017. The nature and ethics of indifference. *The Journal of Ethics*, 21, 17–35.

Lillehammer, H., 2014. Minding your own business? Understanding indifference as a virtue, *Philosophical Perspectives*, 28, 111–26.

Lyell, C., 1830. *Principles of Geology*. London: John Murray.

Puig de la Bellacasa, M., 2017. *Matters of Care: Speculative Ethics in More than Human Worlds*. Minneapolis: University of Minnesota Press.

Rich, N., 2019. *Losing Earth: The Decade We Could Have Stopped Climate Change*. New York: Farrar, Strauss and Giroux.

Stoler, A. L., 2010. *Along the Archival Grain: Epistemic Anxieties and Colonial Common Sense*. Princeton: Princeton University Press.

Wilson, L. A., 2017. *Mulliontide: A Guide for Walkers*. Lancaster: Louise Ann Wilson Company Ltd.

Woodham, A., Penrhyn Jones, S., Onciul, B., and Gordon-Clark, M., 2018. Enduring connections: Heritage, sustainable development and climate change in Kirbati, *Journal of Museum Ethnography* 31, 199–211.

14

RELEASING THE VISUAL ARCHIVE

On the ethics of destruction

Doug Bailey

Oslo, June 2017: Releasing images

Pouring bleach into the plastic beaker, I look into the face of the women in the image. Posed in front of a gridded background, her eyes wide, she looks sharp right, beyond the frame, as if her attention is drawn to someone shouting or to a door slamming. The wall behind the woman is pink, though an unnatural shade; I wonder if the time that has passed since the photograph was processed has caused the image's colour dyes to deteriorate. The cardboard slide mount and the image it holds are from another era, in terms both of photographic chemistry, of acetate film stock, of emulsion and dye, but also of anthropology, and of anthropometric query into human diversity, race, and sexuality. The gridded background looks hand-made: lines almost parallel but not quite, verticals in a darker colour, perhaps once blue; horizontals lighter, maybe red. The woman's brown hair is short, brushed close over her ears. Eyebrows arch in question or in surprise at what is happening out of our sight: she is in her world, of that place, in front of that camera. Neither now nor here, she is locked inside the fieldwork of a long-retired professor, in a laboratory, in one of the buildings on the campus where I now work, once exposed on a screen for students: since then kept locked out of sight in the drawer of a file cabinet in a museum storeroom. Looking towards the lowest part of the image, I see small beads of a necklace and just a trace of blue fabric across the shoulders of her dress. Her lipstick is bold. Who is this woman? What kind of object is this 35-mm slide? (Figure 14.1).

With plastic tongs pressed tight together with black metal bulldog clips, I have clamped the slide containing the woman. Thus supported and held vertically, the slide stands at the bottom of a straight-sided, wide-based, broad-mouthed, plastic laboratory beaker. I pour in more bleach. The liquid's level rises. Past her chin, then the crown of her head, and then the top edge of the

FIGURE 14.1 Slide 0123: unbleached. Photo: Doug Bailey

slide's cardboard mount. What is this image-thing? Where has it come from? Who created it? When and where was it processed? At what photographic lab? How was it used? Printed across the bottom of the cardboard mount, the words "ROBOT. EASY MOUNT" and in smaller font, two patent numbers. Across the top, "CRAFTSMENS GUILD" in arty typeface, a row of barely discernable human figures printed above the letters; the typographic reference is art deco. Below that, "HOLLYWOOD, CALIF. U. S. A." Running vertically along the right edge of the mount, a strip of white tape, reading "TREG-001_0123," that someone has attached much more recently, long after the photograph was taken, the film was processed, and the square of plastic film inserted and glued between the two faces of its grey cardboard mount.

When the level of liquid has fully covered the slide and its mount, I stop pouring. Closely, I look at the woman. I face her. Immobile, she still looks to her side, in alarm. After four of five seconds, tiny bubbles come away from the slide and drift towards the surface of the bleach. The first bubbles are clear. I look closer as more begin to fizzle out of the slide. I see that they are yellow. They flow in streams, faster, up towards the surface of the liquid. The yellow colour makes me think of smoke swirling from a chemical fire at some neglected toxic waste dump, spontaneously igniting or torched by local trouble makers. Just below the surface of the bleach, a thin hazy cloud of yellow liquid billows to find its shape. With slowly curling wisps reaching outwards, the cloud of pigment moves towards the right under its own power, seeking an escape, exploring new spaces into which suddenly, after long confinement, it has been released (Figure 14.2).

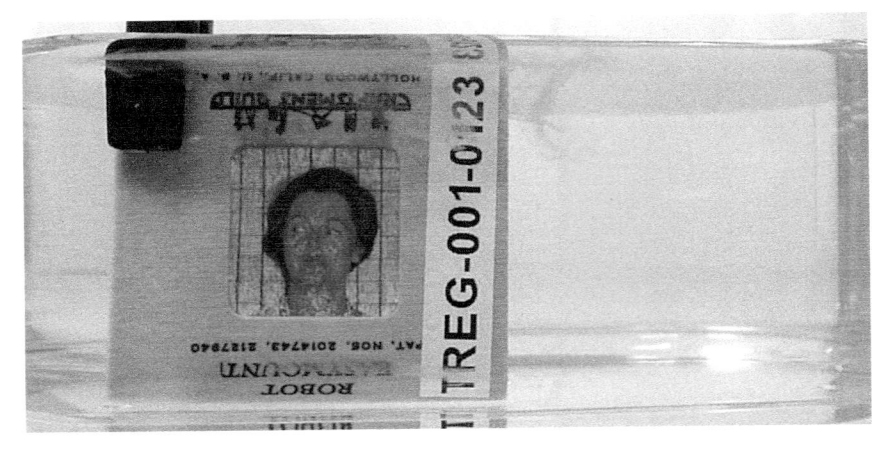

FIGURE 14.2 Slide 0123: bleaching stage 1. Photo: Doug Bailey

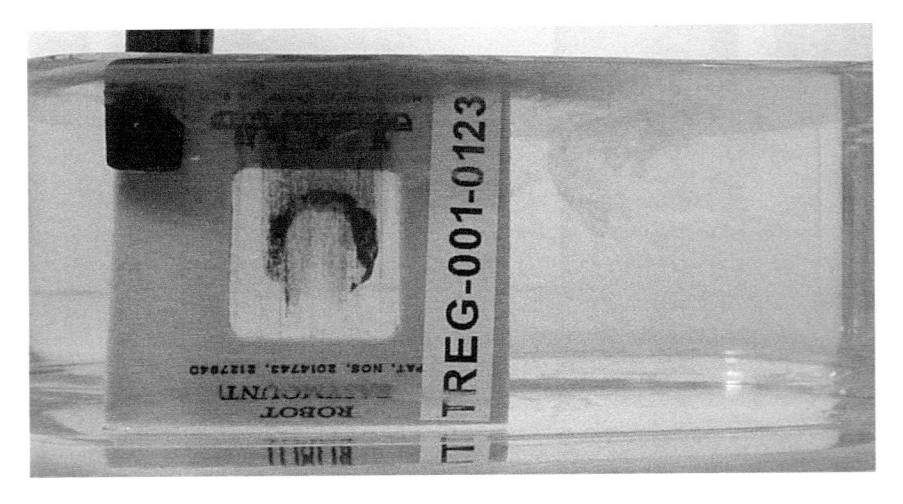

FIGURE 14.3 Slide 0123: bleaching stage 2. Photo: Doug Bailey

From the plastic support of the slide's image, more coloured bubbles (darker) now jet towards the surface. These reds come from every part of the image: the woman's face, her hair, the skin of her neck and ears, the gridded background, from its lines and its pink surface. As if super-heated air-bubbles coming from a deep underwater vent, they hurry upwards. With increasing speed and in greater density, they pour toward the surface of the bleach to form darker sets of clouds mingling with or clashing against the yellows which continue their swirl and spread. More bubbles of red dye release from the image. The woman's face is gone (Figure 14.3). Her hair loses its visible composition, now transformed into

FIGURE 14.4 Slide 0123: released. Photo: Doug Bailey

base molecules: coloured traces freed from emulsion long bonded to the film's plastic. Just below the liquid's surface, the dark, red clouds start a push to the left, the yellow ones move right. The face, the grid, the hair, the woman, gone: their two-dimensional constitution once held rigid in three-colour emulsion dyes, now disarticulated into forms and molecular traces I can no longer identify as visual representation, let alone as a bodied person, never again as a record within an anthropological study. The image no longer exists. The representational thing has dissolved. On the plastic surface where once there had been a woman, previously locked in gelatin layers of cyan, magenta, and yellow, long fixed within an academic study, now all that remains is an empty plastic square held in its cardboard mount (Figure 14.4)

Out of the bleach, I pull the tongs and the slide, now a non-image. In its wake, activated clouds of colour dance through the liquid. They have life. They swim. Dyes swirl and collide under their own strength, graceful in their own energies, on the move, released. One long curving loop, dark purple, arcs from the top of the bleach to the bottom of the beaker, looking for a way out, a final escape. (Figure 14.5).

Dissolving image things

In the early summer of 2017, I dissolved the images from the surfaces of over 1000 colour 35-mm transparencies that had been part of the archive of the anthropological

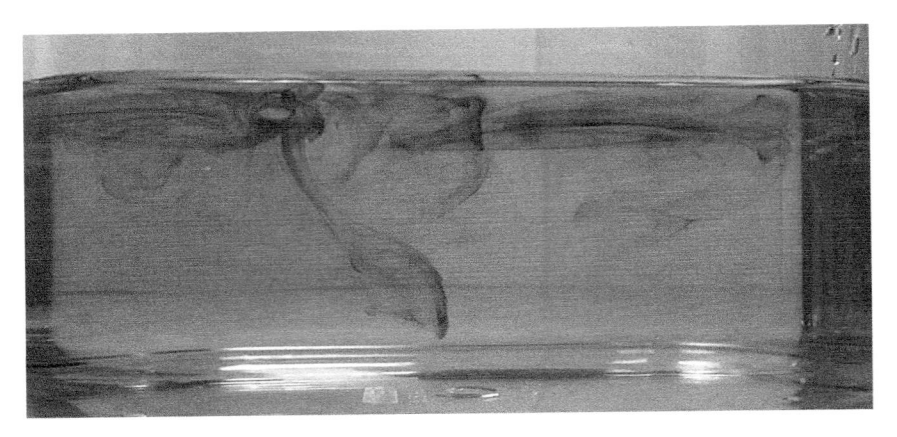

FIGURE 14.5 Slide 0123: clouds of dyes and pigments. Photo: Doug Bailey

museum in the North American university where I work. With some minor variation the description of the process of dissolution of transparency TREG_001–0123 provided above could apply to each of the slides that I immersed in bleach. I applied the same methods, and obtained similar results. The decision to dissolve these images in this way was my imperfect solution to the conundrum that I faced when opening a cardboard box of visual material of dubious ethical foundations: a box of visual things carefully collected and stored in an ethnological archive of a large, federally funded teaching institution. My intentions for handling these transparencies had started within professionally informed standards of image treatment within modern visual anthropology: visual repatriation to descendent communities. As I came to know the images inscribed on the film, however, I realized that normal practices of visual repatriation would not be possible.

In the early stages of work, a series of simple, easily anticipated questions emerged. What were these slides? Who had taken them? Who were those people (and, I realized as I started cataloguing them, what or who were the non-human subjects, the animals and artefacts) captured in these images? Other questions were more complex, though still not unique in discussions of museum collections of visual things. What role should these transparencies play within my institution's research activities and pedagogic practices? How does an anthropological institution resolve its relationship with its cultural archive, especially when so much of it had been obtained through, at best dubious, and, most often, unethical means? What is a curator's moral responsibility either towards images taken without the subject's consent, or towards images originally made under what we now see as outdated and unprincipled practices of examining, recording, categorizing, dehumanizing "exotic" peoples?

Other, increasingly difficult questions surfaced. What rights do I recognize that things like these transparencies hold? What do these things ask of me? What responsibilities do I have to them? Indeed, do I have responsibilities? Do these image-things have their own individual rights? Further, who am I to make decisions about the place, role, or even existence of these things, to adjudicate over what is "best practice," of what I should do to them? Ultimately, what are the ethics of the eventual decision that I took to destroy the slides' images by soaking them in bleach? Did my acts of dissolution violate a broader ethics of care? To the slides? To my institution? To the people captured in those layers of dye, emulsion, and plastic? To my institutional predecessors who loaded the film into the camera, who paid for the processing, who catalogued and stored the slides, and who projected that woman's image on a screen to a lecture hall full of students? My attempts to find answers to those questions led me first to explore these issues and then to find a way to release the emulsified images from the plastic surfaces of those slides.

San Francisco (2010): The box of slides

The slides that are now dissolved came to me in a cardboard box: a selection of images that a museum curator had made from a large archive of similar materials in the months after our university made her job redundant. The university had placed into receivership the collection of artefacts, photographs, audio recordings, field notes, and other ethnographic and archaeological material collected over sixty years of professors' fieldwork and study; with this decision, the curator's job dissolved. For years, she had struggled to care for these things, for the most part without proper or regular financial or administrative support. By the early 2000s, the collection was in poor condition. Textiles from South America were piled in a corner on top of insect infested cardboard boxes of Inuit dolls. Museum inventories and catalogues were chaotic, incomplete, and inaccurate (in fact, two separate catalogues existed, neither cross-tabulated with the other). Some artefacts had disappeared, most probably on their way to eBay or Craigslist or to a faculty member's office bookshelf.

Holding the ultimate legal responsibility (and acting as an agent of the State of California), the university took the critical decision to transfer the collection from the Department of Anthropology to the Department of Museum Studies. The transfer of material and of responsibility came after heated and detailed consultation and collections assessment; not all parties accepted the final solution. Some in the Anthropology Department complained that "their" research and teaching materials had been taken from them; some in the Museum Studies Department complained that their already overstretched budget could not support the work required to properly conserve and store the material. Many consoled the (now ex-) curator, suddenly released into a retirement she had not sought.

Regardless, the decision was made. The museum was closed. The curator lost her job. What many stakeholders did not know until much later, however, was that, even in retirement, the curator had kept a copy of the key to the locked museum stores. As the university eventually discovered, in the month or two before the physical transfer of material from one department to the other could be completed, the retired curator sifted through files and objects, shredding some records and disposing of material which she preferred that the collection's new managers either not receive or not know of its existence. Her motives in doing so will never be known (she passed away not long into retirement), and suggestions founded more on gossip than on fact (as well as on hardened intra-departmental animosities) regularly found voice at end-of-semester, department drinks parties.

What matters, at least for the present chapter, is that one of the final acts that the curator undertook (after she had left the university's employment) was to select over a thousand colour slides which she found particularly offensive, to place them in a cardboard box, to put the box into a large black garbage bag, and to throw the bag into a campus trash dumpster. While her intent was to discard the slides, the result was otherwise. By chance, an adjunct professor walking to the parking lot passed by the trash, wondered what was in the bag, looked inside, recognized the slides' labels and subjects, and carried the box back into the Anthropology Department. As the chairperson of the department at that time, I took a quick look inside the box, glanced at a few of the slides, thought little about them, and stored the box under a table my office.

Excavating a box of slides

When the box was next opened, it had been shipped from San Francisco to Norway, where I had time, now several years later, to examine its contents in detail. One immediate and obvious approach was to take advantage of the collection of slides as an exercise in contemporary archaeology. What could be simpler or more intellectually stimulating than to apply standard methods of excavation and analysis, to treat the box as if it were a site, and to dig down through the layers of slides as if they were artefacts in sedimented strata? With luck, the result would be an engaging contribution to discussions and debates about material culture, the archaeological process, and about both as introductions to archaeologies of the contemporary past. Once excavated and then made the subject of academic study within a contemporary archaeology, the slides could be sent back to rejoin the larger collection of visual materials under the curatorial care and control of the Museum Studies Department and, where possible, to be repatriated to the relevant individuals.

The excavation of the box was straightforward: after removing the initial large features near the site's surface (a boxed carousel tray [Inv. no. Treg-001-0007], and a context sealing cardboard sheet [Inv. no. Treg-001-0017]), excavation continued down through a dense apparently undifferentiated cache of slide-artefacts. Facing a taphonomically undistinguished fill of slide-artefacts, excavation proceeded in 10 cm spits, using a quadrant method to recover as much information as possible about variation among the objects at different levels and in different areas of the site (Figure 14.6). Each slide was numbered with a unique inventory number, and any potential cuts and fills within the cache were noted. Once the sterile layer at the bottom of the box was reached, post-excavation analyses began.

Chronology was straightforward, both through absolute dating, provided by date-stamped months and years on many slide-mounts (Figure 14.7) (ranging from

FIGURE 14.6 Excavation in progress: quadrant method. Photo: Doug Bailey

FIGURE 14.7 Chronology detail. Photo: Doug Bailey

November 1960 to December 1986), and through relative, micro-chronologies that followed slide-to-slide comparison, and through the recognition of handwritten numbered sequences that I identified as orderings of individual slides that had been used in specific lectures. Other sets of sequencing information were recovered; painstaking analyses of the museum's cataloging numbers (hand-written on the slides' plastic, paper, or metal mounts) produced ordered histories of individual slides as they entered the collection's larger storage files. Vital provenience information came from studies of the materials of manufacture of the slide mounts and of the geographic location of processing (e.g., California, Switzerland, Canada). In summary, post-excavation analysis produced robust chronologies and typologies of the material recovered from the site.

Problems emerged, however, when I turned away from the material analyses, typologies, source locations, and chronologies, and started to examine the images inscribed onto the glass or plastic base layers of the slides. Standard methods of archaeological classification were applied, and they produced the following image categories: 1) hominin fossils (and casts of hominin fossils); 2) living animals (exclusively non-human primates in zoos and safari parks); 3) ethnographic field subjects (e.g., ritual dances); 4) subjects for medical anthropology study (primarily of skin pigmentation); 5) human reproduction (ranging from x-rays of pregnant women at full term to line-drawings of reproductive organs); 6) dissection of fetuses of non-identifiable species; 7) human face and head morphology (with notations of ethnic and geographic origin); 8) general human anatomy (including x-rays of individual bone and dental casts). Further sub-categories were delimited. For example, the human reproduction category could be refined to distinguish photographs of live births in delivery rooms, from artist's cut-away drawings of the stages of labor and birth. Other examples of sub-categorization included variation in how the slides had been originally created and obtained. Thus, many of the slides in the human reproduction category had been purchased ready-made as educational aides from medical supply companies (e.g., The Carolina Biological Supply Company, Burlington, North Carolina); others had been made outside of the educational materials industry (e.g., the images of fetal dissections) and had been processed privately away from the costs and oversight of commercial laboratories.

Several preliminary conclusions are of note. First, the assemblage of slides is not a random mixture of images representing a sample of the different subjects present in the many 10,000s of images in the original larger collection of the Anthropology Department. On the contrary, strong connections link particular categories of images that were selected for discard, and these connections cut across other variables that post-excavation analysis recorded and analyzed. Thus, slides of hominin fossils and their casts were present in a wide range of different types of films exposed and of mounts used; they were made at distinct periods of the department's history through the second half of the twentieth century.

What emerged from the study of the images was one theme linking all categories of slides: the visual examination and analysis of, and the experimentation on, living and non-living subjects, all of which are human beings, their relatives, and their ancestors or non-human relatives. One proposal is that the newly retired museum curator selected these particular slides for discard due to their image content, and that she left unselected (and thus retained in the larger museum archive) other images from a much greater range of categories which were present in the slide collection: field excavations, artefacts, and many teaching slides related to the study of linguistic, economic, and cultural anthropology. The selection of slides to be discarded was limited to physical and biological anthropology.

A second conclusion closely follows the first and, I suggest, sheds more light on the curator's decision to select these particular images for disposal. Not only was slide selection focused on the anthropological study of the human, but, in many cases, images selected were of anthropological practices which have come under intense ethical, moral, and professional scrutiny in the last 30–40 years as the discipline of anthropology developed as a self-reflective, politically aware, collaborative, and non-exploitational practice particular as concerns photographs from anthropological study.[1]

Regardless of the curator's actual intentions in her selection of individual slides to remove from the collection before its relocation to a new departmental home, the assemblage of image-artefacts excavated from the cardboard box presents critical questions: what should happen to these slides, or to refer to the questions posed more generally at the start of this chapter, what do these slides demand of me, and what is my ethical responsibility to them? There is no easy or correct set of answers to these questions. One way forward would be to follow the robust, ethical, tradition within visual anthropology and in the practices of a growing number of museums, collections, and archives of visual materials: the physical repatriation of images to members of descendent communities. Within a discussion of visual repatriation rests a second, equally important conversation: what roles do institution and museum collections of images play in their positions as cultural archives? The discussion that follows here places the box of slides within the potentials of the practice of visual repatriation and within the recognition of the power of the archive. This fuller discussion of these two issues helps clarify my deliberations about my ethical responsibility to the 1221 slides.

Visual repatriation and the archive

The disciplinary move towards the repatriation of anthropological photographs developed within a body of scholarship that explored the ethics of visual materials (Gross et al. 1988; Pinney 1989; Binney and Chaplin 1991; Edwards 1994, 2003; Poignant and Poignant 1996; Fienup-Riordan 1998; Peterson 2003; Pinney and Peterson 2003), and is (or should be) the standard practice for archives of images in anthropological and museum collections. Critical to the emergent practice of visual repatriation was a recognition of the exploitative ways that anthropology in the late 19th and early 20th centuries employed technologies of photography and cinematography as efficient and (supposedly) objective means of recording human diversity (Edwards 1992, 2001; Edwards and Hart 2004a, 2004b; Morton and Edwards 2009; Pinney 1992, 2011; Pinney and Peterson 2003; Banks and Vokes 2010). Much of the call to repatriate images developed alongside late 20th century critiques of early anthropology's dehumanization and objectification of indigenous people, first by capturing them on photographic plate or film, and second by collecting and controlling those images within western cultural and educational institutions (Poignant 1992; Edwards 1992, 2009).

The technologies and powers of fixed and moving image recording developed in parallel (both chronologically and conceptually) with the births of ethnography and anthropology in the last half of the 19th century (Pinney 1992, 2011; Grimshaw 2001; Griffiths 2002). Central to the emerging sciences for the study of humankind stood efforts to explain human capabilities and appearances through theories and languages of biological evolution (Spencer 1992) and assumptions of western, Caucasian superiority in matters cultural, social, intellectual, and moral. The images that captured local indigenous (and other non-western) peoples and which were collected in institutions of learning and cultural display were central to the methods of ethnographic study and to the broader intellectual industries of the social sciences (Im Thurn 1893; Portman 1896).

The late 20th century questioning of the assumption that western image producers, archives, and institutions had inalienable rights to obtain, collect, maintain, and control access to (and dissemination of) images of people who were defined at the time as exotic or primitive developed in parallel with similar changes in the status of human remains and cultural material across the social sciences (e.g., The Native American Graves Protection and Repatriation Act in the United States). The result of this shift in understanding the essence and power of the photographed individual was a commitment to return those images and films to local, descendent communities for their own control and use.

Visual repatriation, however, invokes more than just the physical return of photographs and films. Through image repatriation, descendent communities re-engage (or encounter for the first time) long lost recordings of ancestors and disremembered cultural and ritual practices (e.g., Geismar and Herle 2010). In addition, modern communities re-appropriate that original material for new, local, contemporary purposes, often resulting in the creation of novel visual and cultural works (see Morton 2015). Thus, visual repatriation of historic anthropological images instigates, in the present, original creative action and community debate about events and people of the past.

In their discussion of visual repatriation, Marcus Banks and Richard Vokes describe the practice as the "unstitching" of living subjects who had been sutured into older anthropological projects through the technology of photography (Banks and Vokes 2010, pp. 337–8). Visual repatriation unties the imposed connections that had been created in the original anthropological and ethnological appropriations, collections, storages, displays, and publications. In turn, visual repatriation presents the potential for new stitchings as descendent communities re-examine, re-interpret, and use anew images in re-weaving their own histories and political journeys into, though, and out of colonial exploitation and dislocation. In these ways communities exert control over their own histories (Harlan 1995, 1998; Rickard 1995; Tsinhnahjinnie 1998, 2003; Hill 1998; Vizenor 1998; Chaat Smith 1995; Aird 1993, 2003).

These local impacts of visual repatriation are worth noting, particularly in the ways that the children, grandchildren, and great grandchildren of people once photographed now reclaim and re-appropriate the photographs returned. Repatriated images are absorbed, resocialized, and repositioned through modern communities' social structures and repositories of political history and cultural knowledge (Bell 2003; Poignant 1992; Morton and Oteyo 2015). In addition, the moments and conversations that envelope an image's re-entry into a community make visible previously hidden, locally embedded and negotiated sets of restrictions, rights, and responsibilities, for example, that govern who is allowed to see or possess a particular image. Previously unrecognized social topographies of private and public space for the viewing and storing of images become visible in a community's control of photographs, and as the complex rules of quarantine and availability are brought into play, particularly in response to the death of an individual once photographed or filmed (Michaels 1991; Gross et al. 1988, 2003). Usually only visible from a local perspective, variations in image availabilities and rules for viewing them often fluctuate, shifting along dimensions of age, gender, and lineage. Thus, according to local regulation, the rights to view or show an image can alter depending on when and where an image or a person is positioned; rights to view can range in scale from individual to family to initiation group to the community at large, and back again, in ways that may not mesh with (or even be visible to) non-local anthropological observation.

Through the repatriation of images, descendant communities re-appropriate, re-engage, and re-deploy anthropological photographs for their own local, modern purposes, often with an aim to regain control of their own histories or to uncover previously hidden or overwritten events (Harlan 1995, 1998; Rickard et al. 1995; Tsinhnahjinnie 1998; Hill 1998; Vizenor 1998; Chaat Smith 1995; Aird 1993, 2003). In Hulleah Tsinhnahjinnie's terms, the issue is one of the photographic sovereignty that a community (or an individual) recognizes and controls in the act of reclaiming a photograph to tell one's own story (Tsinhnahjinnie 1998; see also Rickard 1995). In some cases, as Binney and Chaplin (1991) show for the Tuhoe Maori at Urewera in New Zealand, the local response to, and use of, repatriated images succeed to confirm and articulate past events, conflicts, and resistances that colonial-authored histories had suppressed or overlooked. The repatriated images bring to life heavily conflicted realities, long forgotten or excluded from the histories or rememberings written or spoken by those who had held power at the time. In many cases, visual repatriation projects (Brown et al.'s [2006] work with the Kainai Nation in Alberta Canada is a robust example) have forced anthropologists to accept not only that they must let go of the photographs (in literal and physical senses) but also that they must relinquish their non-local and industrialized academic, attempts to create, distribute, and adjudicate meanings and values of images, particularly where previous control and determination of meaning had rested with a non-local photographer and the original project's external sponsoring institution.

Also important has been the recognition of variation in the ways that different communities (and indeed different constituents within any single group) understand the status of a person inscribed in a photograph or a film. While any short comment on visual repatriation risks an overgeneralization of local perceptions of the photographed individual, it is reasonable here to note that many non-western communities understand that the physical image of a person (the printed photograph, the photocopy, the slide transparency, the printed reproduction in press or online) contains an essence, soul, shadow, or spirit of that individual depicted. Jocelyn Dudding writes of the Maori concern for the *maui* (or life force) understood to be invested in photographs of ancestors, and of the resulting objections by descendants to the 2001 sale of 19th-century photographs and their concern that the sale, use, and reproduction of those photographs would dissipate and dilute the life forces of the people represented in the images (Dudding 2003; see also Binney and Chaplin 1991). Similarly, Joshua Bell reports how the Purari in Papua New Guinea understand photographs as shadows or reflections of the soul (as *avea*) of the person photographed, and, therefore, that photographs exist as things much more complex and multi-dimensional than a piece of chemically treated paper (Bell 2003, 2008; see also Halvaksz 2008, 2010). In these and other examples, it becomes clear that photographs of people possess materialities both physical (they can be taken away, sent, shipped, kept, sold, traded, stored, locked-up, put on display) and spiritual (they retain, transport, possess essences of the living being contained in the chemical inscription that is the photograph).

Relevance to 35-mm slides

My confrontation with the 35-mm transparencies from my university's museum, that is the subject of this chapter, benefits in several ways from this short discussion of visual repatriation. First, there can be no debate over the ethical responsibility possessed by collections managers, institutional curators, and archivists who maintain control over stores of images of people to repatriate those images to descendent communities, if those communities can be identified and located. Thus, the most straightforward objective for me would be the return each 35-mm slide to the person contained in the image, or to his or her descendant(s). The second benefit of the discussion of repatriation is born of ethnographic collaboration with non-western communities: the recognition of the presence and the strength of non-western definitions of the non-material essences contained in a photograph of a person, whether that essence is understood in terms of spirit, soul, or along some other mobile, fluid, and extra-temporal, extra-physical register. Taken together then, these observations forced me to shift my perception of the 35-mm slides at the center of this chapter: my position is that it is unethical to keep these images in the university's museum collection; I must acknowledge that the images' non-physical statuses and essences most probably extend well beyond the museum's original identifications and uses of them as catalogued artefacts in a collection and in service to academic pedagogy and research.

Taking one step farther, an understanding of the ethical grounds of visual repatriation forced me to confront the moral responsibilities that I have to the subjects contained in the slides' images. I cannot avoid the reality that each person who is photographed in each slide maintains and possesses a life that reaches far beyond traditionally understood limits of chemical dyes, emulsions, and the plastic materials mounted in the cardboard or metal surrounds. Of equal, though less obvious, consequence is the matching reality that the non-human species pictured in the slides (the chimpanzees and bonobos, for example), and the physical objects (the fossilized human bone and the casts of such fossils) have similar spiritual essences. From such a perspective, I realized that I could not avoid the ethical responsibility I had to those slides, perhaps a responsibility that is closer to the one that I have to living beings (human or animal). Before turning back to the slides themselves, to the questions posed at the start of the chapter, and to the practical consequences of this discussion of visual repatriation, it is important to consider these slide-images, in their newly recognized enlivened status, as objects collected and then retained in a museum archive.

Archives

The 1221 slides that the museum curator discarded were one small part of a larger collection of images, artefacts, recordings, and ethnographic materials. Established and then used as a resource for teaching and research, the museum stores were an archive that faculty and students valued and exploited in delivering classroom-based education and in building their individual careers within the political economy of the American academic anthropological tradition: observe, appropriate, classify, interpret, publish. While traditional academic and institutional perceptions have seen archives of images and artefacts as static and neutral repositories of cultural goods and records to be preserved and safe-guarded, it is critical for us to recognize that other, more robust, conceptions of what constitutes an archive have complicated the definition of museum collections and the roles that those collections and their individual contents can or should play. The core text in this more critical approach is Jacques Derrida's *Archive Fever: a Freudian Impression* (1995).[2] Derrida's comments are essential not only for a broader engagement with archives across disciplines (in and outside of academia and cultural institutions) but more directly to the material at the center of this chapter, particularly in the way that Derrida's discussion disrupts the assumption that the correct place for the 1221 slides was the museum stores, that the museum and its curator had a duty to preserve, conserve, and protect them, and most relevant, what responsibilities I had to the slide-images and how I treated them.

At the beginning of his disruption of the status of the archive, Derrida makes the fundamental point that an archive is about authority. Derrida takes us to the Greek origin of the word: *arkheion*, the house of the archons, the place where official documents were kept and consulted (Derrida 1995, p. 2). The documents that were held in the *arkheion* were the documents that spoke, imposed, and recalled the law. As magistrates, the archons held the authority to keep and guard these official documents; they also held the power to interpret them. From this Derrida delivers a second vital point: there is no political control of a community without the control of the archive and, thus, of the documents that speak the law of that community (Derrida 1995, p. 4n1). Democracies, for example, are communities in which people have access to the archive, to what makes up that archive, and to how it should be interpreted. Next, Derrida argues that archives are "institutive and conservative." They keep, they reserve, they save, but they do so in an unnatural fashion. Archives do more than keep the law that the people obey; in the acts and places of keeping the law, the archive itself (and not its contents) creates the law (Derrida 1995, p. 7).

Derrida's next comments make best sense in light of the subtitle to the original lecture and its subsequent publication (*Archive Fever: A Freudian Impression*) as well as to the context of that lecture: a colloquium at the Courtauld Institute in London, but organized by the Société Internationale d'Histoire de la Psychiatrie et de la Psychanalyse and the Freud Museum. Derrida argues that there is something in human nature that both runs against the archive and its existence, but which, in doing so, also brings about the very need for the archive into existence: this is the death drive, which Derrida calls "anarchivic" or "archiviolithic" (Derrida 1995, p. 10). Within human nature, the death drive threatens us with forgetfulness and the destruction of what we know (Derrida 1995, p. 12). Derrida defines this as a "violence of forgetting," an "anarchive," and a potential putting to death of that thing upon which the archive is made: the law (Derrida 1995, p. 79). The archive, thus, comes into being in opposition to the death drive, and an archive fever, therefore, is the internal contradiction aroused in opposition to that natural drive to forget and to destroy (Derrida 1995, p. 19).

Next comes a critical observation: the act of making the archive (for Derrida, the "archivization") produces, more than it records, the events that it stores and preserves (Derrida 1995, p. 17). Thus, the technology of the archive determines the event that is then archived; thus any meaning to be found in an archive will always be determined by the structure of the archive and not by any original event that that archive may contain or reflect (Derrida 1995, p. 18). Another vital point follows. Archives are not about the past as much as they are about the future (in Derrida's terms, an archive is a "pledge" or a "token" of the future) (Derrida 1995, p. 18). An archive does not, therefore, record what happened in the past; it structures the future.

Other observations of importance follow. The archive only exists because it rests on the use and power of titles, of classification, of hierarchization, and of order, all of which are tools that provide the archive with its appearance of legitimization (Derrida 1995, p. 40). Thus, the archive is built with a set of rhetorical instruments: the tools of control and organization. In this sense, we can see that the archive only exists because of itself; it augments itself and in doing so generates its own authority (Derrida 1995, p. 68). And thus we loop back to Derrida's first comment that archives are about authority: they do not respect or follow an authority that comes from outside the archive or from any other body of power; an archive creates its own authority within and for itself.

In sum then, Derrida's work destabilizes the archive as archaeologists, anthropologists, and museographers had come to know, value, respect, use, construct, and maintain it. In the light of his argument, we can now see that what we find in an archive is not an objective and absolute record of past events that thus requires saving, maintaining, curating, preserving, guarding, and protecting. On the contrary what we find in an archive is nothing but the frame of the archive itself, its structure, and its technologies, created in response to a subliminal death drive that is part of human nature. Thus, archives are not repositories of original facts or sets of information, the originality of which requires preservation and protection. In preserving the archive (or the museum stores and collections) we are only ever preserving the structure of a collection and the political structures and imbalances that ordered and funded its creation. The consequences of these observations are both catastrophic and liberating, overturning the standard sacred values that we normally assign to museum collections and other archives, but also opening up rich potentials for what archive contents are free to do, once they are loosened of the limitations imposed on them by regimes of care or by the drive for preservation.

The contents of an archive, therefore, are the victims of archivization: collected, curated, purchased, donated, stolen, registered, catalogued, used (created even) as component parts of larger institutional (and social and political) projects that the museum or institutional collection serves. In many cases, these archiving projects are constructions of particular types of knowledges within specific politicized ways of seeing the world, and for most anthropological museums, this is a vision of the world-out-there, which is thus seen (defined for the first time, even) as other and different, regardless of whether or not that difference is held as derogatory, racist, or culturally devalued. On the other hand, and in a more positive sense, we now recognize the liberating potential that this more robust understanding of an archive presents. We begin to see new and empowered statuses and potentials of the objects and images held within a collection or museum store. We realize that the artefacts, photographs, and other collected materials, which were previously held at the mercy of the politicized structure and technology of the archive, are fully and always eligible for release from the confines of their collections. They are freed from what held them before: the unnatural drive for their preservation and protection, their archivization, their suffering as a side effect of the archive fever that afflicts a large part of the museum community and the heritage conservation industry. Derrida's revelations about the archive thus grant the collections' contents their freedoms. Within the context of visual repatriation, as discussed above, and its call to return images of original communities and descendants, the Derridian undermining and unlocking of the doors of the archive fit comfortably and help me move towards a resolution of the conundra presented by the 35-mm transparencies.

Decay, destruction, and release

These discussions of visual repatriation and of the archive undermined my original perception of the 1221, 35-mm slides that I had cleverly excavated from their cardboard box. Regardless, I still had no clear idea of what were my responsibilities to these image-things and to the people, animals, and other objects held within them.

Visual repatriation requires me to return images to descendent communities, but there were no descendent communities for me to reach out to: no names had been preserved of who had been photographed; no field notes or records of these photographic projects existed.[3] Even more futile would be any attempt to apply a visual repatriation methodology and ethos to the rest of the slides, the subjects of which were non-human primates, of dissected animals, of hominin fossils, and of fossil casts. If I followed my reading of Derrida, then the images were free to depart the archive: but to what destination, and by what means? Releasing the transparencies from their containment in museum file drawers and locked storerooms would take a half-step towards liberation; each person (and each animal and object), however, would remain still trapped within in the dyes and emulsions of each slide.

Part of a solution to the dilemma of how to fully release the subjects held within the slides comes from a reading of anthropologist Liam Buckley's work on collections of colonial era photographs in the National Archives of The Gambia (Buckley 2005). Buckley writes of the social lives of colonial images and of the role that the National Archive played (and continues to play) in colonial and post-colonial states, particularly in Africa. More importantly, however, Buckley makes us think about the realities of the unexpected and positive potentials that live within the processes of decay and of loss, potentials that he could not avoid as he carried out his fieldwork.

> One afternoon, while doing research in the National Archives, I was told by the Keeper of the Records. "Liam, you have something stuck to your forehead." It was a piece of a page about the size of a postage stamp from one of Bahoum's [a Gambian civil servant who photographed state events from 1947–56] albums. The power had gone down that day, the ceiling fan had stopped, and I was sweating – a piece of the brittle page must have broken off and stuck to my hand and had been transferred to my forehead as I wiped off the sweat. My hands and face were filthy and covered in brown dust. Around me, piles of newspapers stacked haphazardly filled the tables. I would open up manila folders to find small ants crawling within, files would fall apart, rusty paper clips would break, and pages would easily tear.
>
> *(Buckley 2005, pp. 249–50)*

Working in an archive that was in active decay, Buckley encountered difficult decisions that needed to be made about the archive he studied in The Gambia. Buckley makes a strong case against the need to preserve that archive, suggesting that the best course of action may be to allow the archives to decay. Buckley argues eloquently for letting decay happen, indeed for decay to have a right to be allowed to happen (Buckley 2005, p. 250). He wrestles with questions of why we work so hard to prevent loss and decay, asking who has the right to look after "material culture as they inevitably expire" (Buckley 2005, p. 250). In this, I am reminded of the ethics that drive visual repatriation, and the question of who has the right to retain, collect, use, or publish historic anthropological photographs.

Echoing Derrida, Buckley notes that the source of institutional order, regulation, command, and control is grounded in modernity and its political desires and economic contexts (Buckley 2005, p. 250). Taking the argument farther, however, Buckley shows us that archived colonial photographs are valued and monitored according to a set of local moral expectations, and that while those expectations include the rights to care for materials, they also include the rights to destroy. In this reasoning, decay becomes a central practice of archiving (Buckley 2005, pp. 250–1). In the local Gambian context, Buckley elevates the value of decay, as opposed both to the currencies of preservation and (for the community where he lived while carrying out his research) to assumptions (and desires by museographers) that members of the public should donate historically valuable photographs and documents to government archives. On the contrary, Buckley notes that local families felt no pressure to give their recently deceased relatives' possessions and records to state institutions of cultural archiving and remembering; in fact, a more likely practice was for descendants to destroy the deceaseds' objects and images. Buckley's article is a detailed account of decay as a process that invokes feelings for an intimacy with objects, as well as with the political and social contexts in which images, in particular, were made. In the context of colonial photographic archives, the discussion, Buckley suggests, "asks us to imagine ways of letting go" (Buckley 2005, p. 250).

Releasing the slide archive

In reading Buckley, not only did I come to see that decay was an appropriate, ethical, and professional response to questions of how best to handle archives, but further, I was drawn powerfully to the potentials that could result not only from decay, but from accelerating the processes of decay, particularly though the intentional destruction of materials held in archives and museum collections. If the normal voyage of visual repatriation (back to descendant communities) was not available to the 35-mm slides from the my university's archive, and if I no longer believed that my approach to an archive must adhere to sacred codes of preservation, containment, and the protection of its contents, then I could start to see an ethical route coming into focus: I could release the people, animals, and objects held in the slides that had been trapped in the museum collection. If, as noted from the ethnography of repatriated photographs, those images existed as spiritual essences, then the methods that should be employed in that release would require a capacity and a strength satisfactory enough to allow those essences to escape into spiritual realms of existence, most probably in media and through forms that irreversibly de-constituted them as the visual representations in which they had been held since the moment that each image had been locked down onto the glass and plastic supports in the dyes and emulsions.[4]

As described at the beginning of this chapter, the agent of release that I found to have this capacity and strength was sodium hypochlorite as present in the form of domestic cleanser *Clor*.[5] While there is nothing particularly special about *Clor*, its application to the transparencies had both the intended chemical effects as well as unanticipated, less tangible, references: bleach is used in domestic contexts in the Western industrialized world to clean, to remove stains, to kill germs, to "make things right." Though I had not thought about the use of sodium hypochlorite in these ways when I was pouring the bleach into the plastic beakers, I started to make these connections as I sat and watched the static materials of dyes and emulsions transform from recognizable shapes (of faces, bodies, fossils, and bones) into amorphous clouds, bubbles, streams of colour, and soaring, semi-transparent, liquid vapors: movement from static and material to mobile and essential. Once I saw the material images release into liquid form, I faced new questions that came unexpectedly with the spontaneity of the success of the bleach releases. Where should I put the liquefied de-constituted essences of people, animals, and objects? What was their final destination? My answer was to send the fluid back into the natural world, down through the plumbing of the Academy of Sciences and out into the Oslo fjord.[6]

Some might see this action of bleaching, the dissolving, the dissolution (and indeed of the introduction of toxins into the Norwegian waterways) as violent, unnecessarily (and permanently) destructive acts. Others might ask what right did I have to enact these image releases, particularly when I am a white, male academic, employed by the very institution that captured and imprisoned these image that held these people, animals, and objects. Others, still, might object that in using a toxic chemical, I was doing damage in a fully industrial way, and they might ask if it was not possible for me to achieve the same results with less violent, more environmentally harmful agent of release.[7] These questions and objections worried me as well, until I came to see that the levels of violence that I sought were necessary (required even), and that the agent (i.e., me) of dissolution, of destruction, and of release needed to be a member of that same academic community that had captured the people, animals, objects on film and held them in its archive. In defining the process of release in terms of an essential, almost ritual, act that transformed a fixed, trapped image into a liberated and mobile spread of essences, I recognized that the success of this transformation between media and between states of being would rely on an equivalence of violence.[8] Violence defined the original acts of capturing each person, animal, and object's image with a camera, of processing that transparency film, of cataloging and labeling each mounted slide, of suspending each in slide files, of exposing to the public each slide with white projector light in a lecture hall, and of returning each to its place of containment in the museum files and stores. The release of individuals from within each image required an act of equal violence carried out by a similarly positioned institutional academic.

Acknowledgements

Grateful appreciation to the many people who commented on the process and concepts included in this text. Special thanks to the After Discourse: Things,

Archaeology and Heritage in the 21st Century team at the Centre for Advanced Study at the Norwegian Academy of Sciences in Oslo (Hein B. Bjerck, Mats Burström, Caitlin DeSilvey, Alfredo González-Ruibal, Tim LeCain, Saphinaz-Amal Naguib, Þóra Pétursdóttir, Chris Witmore) with special thanks to Bjørnar J. Olsen who led that team and who invited me to join them. In addition, I gained immensely from the comments and critique from colleagues at the following institutions who participated in workshops about the box of slides and the ethics of release: Department of Anthropology (UC Berkeley); Institute for the Study of the Ancient World (New York University); Saxo Institute (University of Copenhagen); Museum of Antiquities (University of Gothenburg); Department of Archaeology (Arctic University of Norway, Tromsø); Department of Archaeology and Classical Study (Stockholm University); Archaeology Center (Stanford University); Cotsen Institute of Archaeology (UCLA); Historical Museum (Oslo); Society for Visual Anthropology (American Anthropological Association); Material and Visual Worlds Program (SUNY Binghamton); Department of Art History (Rutgers University).

Notes

1 Excellent and important discussions of these developments include the following: Green 1984; Binney and Chaplin 1991; Edwards 1992, 2001; Turner 1995, 2002; Faris 1996; Banks and Morphy 1997; Ginsburg 1998, 1999, 2011; Ginsburg et al. 2002; Lydon 2005, 2010, 2014; Morphy and Edwards 2009; Grimshaw 2001; Pink 2003; Ruby 2005; Banks and Ruby 2011; Conor and Lydon 2011; and Pinney 2011.
2 A large literature and debate have formed over the status of the archive: Sekula 1983; Schwartz 2000; Hamilton 2002; Morton 2005; Stoler 2009; Rand 2010; Derrida 2010; Banks and Vokes 2010; Lydon 2010; Conor and Lydon 2011.
3 There remains the possibility that a person represented in the slides reproduced in this chapter or in an audience with which I discuss this material will recognize herself or himself. The potential consequent shift in agency and "ownership" will add a further, open-ended, dimension of responsibility to this project and its things.
4 There are other ethical concerns that emerge, and though it is not the task of this chapter to address these fully, it is worth raising them here. First, is a recognition that although I dissolved the images from the slides (with the result that the slide no longer exists as it once was – I have altered it, literally, beyond recognition and, as such, that original slide cannot be stored, projected, studied, or viewed as it once was) now, however, there exist electronic facsimiles of those original images. These copies live on in an unexpectedly large number and range of forms and places: here in the illustrations in this chapter; in the electronic files (as jpegs and tiffs) that I retain of the scans that I made of the slides before I treated them with bleach; and in the electronic files of PowerPoint presentations that I have created and presented at conferences, in classes, and at workshops. Furthermore, all of those electronic ghosts of the images currently drift in and out of being, rematerializing among a large, and seemingly always expanding range of electronic repositories (themselves perhaps also to be understood as archives): the hard-drive of the laptop I am using to type these words; the external hard drive where I hold a copy of the files for the original Oslo dissolving project; the two cloud-based backup systems that I use as second and third copies of all of my work; and, in an unintended turn of events, on the hard-drive of a laptop that was stolen from my car while writing this text.

Second, is the revelation that there also exist paper copies of many of the slides, most clearly in the five photo-books that I created during the Oslo project (Bailey 2017a–e), and that these books are openly available via Amazon (search for *The Book of Miko*). In further, perhaps unending, expansions of the distances that electronic representation can reach, there also exist downloadable pdfs of those photobooks (again from Amazon), as well as the sample images available on the relevant Amazon webpages offered as tasters to potential purchasers. One can add to this list the electronic versions of the image files held on the servers of the photo-books' publisher. In addition, Vimeo.com hosts a copy of the video of one of the slides as its image is detached and dissolved by the bleach.

In all of this, I have come to realize that in undertaking my assault on the archive of images and in my efforts to release the images by dissolving them, I may have done the opposite of what I had originally intended; I have reproduced and distributed them, and I have done so in a way that is almost without control or recall. How do I respond to members of a lecture's audience or from this book's editors and peer-reviewers when they tell me that in claiming to have dissolved and destroyed, I have actually done the opposite?

A first reply is that one of (unexpected) and powerful consequences of recording the dissolutions of the slide imagery and then, more powerfully, of showing those videos in public was the affect that the videos had on the people watching. Some were appalled. One was moved to tears. Others reported that in the clouds of pigment and chemicals they found characteristics and qualities similar to what they would expect in an art gallery, of a performance work, or from video art. Regardless of the content or the mood of these reactions, I remain convinced that the only (or perhaps, the most effective) way to draw in, stimulate, and provoke the viewers (to push them to commit to the work) was to show videos of the dissolutions in action; to do that required that I have imagery (both video clips of slides as they dissolved, and photographs revealing the before, during, and after stages for individual slides). In this sense, the work (the images, the videos, the photobooks, the PowerPoints, this chapter) is performative. A second reply is that the dissolving project, the lectures that are based on it, the PowerPoint presentations, the photo-books for sale on Amazon, and again, this book chapter itself (with its illustrations) have a primary goal of sparking conversation, argument, debate, support, and (inevitably, as it turned out) consternation about taking radical action within the realm of archive thought and action, be that photographic, archaeological, or otherwise. The act of dissolution as rhetorical stimulant.

The alternative step to take, or perhaps better, another direction in which to head would be to destroy all of these facsimiles. All of the electronic files. All of the printed copies. This chapter included. I see no reason to object to taking that path. My decision to record, reproduce, distribute, and disseminate, however, is a decision based on my belief that it is more important (or at lease of equal importance) to use these images and my contested, performed, rhetorical destructions of them, as "things" themselves that provoke debate within the politics of archives and images, especially within anthropological and archaeological institutions and among museum curators, archivists, and educators.

5   Dissolutions of the images took place in Oslo, at the Center for Advanced Study in the Norwegian Academy of Sciences; the local commercially available bleach is sold under the trade name, *Klor*.

6   For the record, soaking the transparencies was one the last of a series of attempts I had made to explore how to accelerate the decay of the images. Earlier attempts included punching holes with a stationery hole maker, cutting with scissors, and burning over an open flame. The open flame treatment helped me recognize the need to transform the material from solid slide to non-solid smoke or vapor. The experiments with scissors and hole-punch had given me the feeling that I was physically abusing both the slides and the

essential people and objects contained. Indeed, the hole punching reminded me of the 1930s Farm Security Administration's Roy Stryker's treatment of negatives that he judged did not follow the shooting scripts that agency photographers were meant to follow (Jones 2010).

7 Indeed, these where the most frequent questions and reactions from audiences to whom I presented this work in Binghamton, Copenhagen, Gothenburg, New Brunswick, New York, Stockholm, and Tromsø.

8 I am indebted to Geneviève Godin and her cohort in the Department of Archaeology at Arctic University of Norway at Tromsø for helping me recognize the importance of violence and its balance.

References

Aird, M. 1993. *Portraits of Our Ancestors*. Brisbane: Queensland Museum.

Aird, M. 2003. Growing up with aborigines. In C. Pinney and N. Peterson (eds.) *Photographies Other Histories*, pp. 23–39. Durham, NC.: Duke University Press.

Bailey, D.W. 2017a. *The Book of Miko*. Volume 4, number 4 (Reproduction and Fossil). San Francisco, CA.: Blurb.

Bailey, D.W. 2017b. *The Book of Miko*. Volume 8, number 3 (Subjects and Dissection). San Francisco, CA.: Blurb.

Bailey, D.W. 2017c. *The Book of Miko*. Volume 17, number 1 (Ethnicity and Sexuality). San Francisco, CA.: Blurb.

Bailey, D.W. 2017d. *The Book of Miko*. Volume 23, number 6 (Grid and Classification). San Francisco, CA.: Blurb.

Bailey, D.W. 2017e. *The Book of Miko*. Volume 43, number 6 (Release and Destroy). San Francisco, CA.: Blurb.

Banks, H. and Morphy, H. (eds.) 1997. *Rethinking Visual Anthropology*. New Haven, Conn.: Yale University Press.

Banks, M. and Ruby, J. (eds.) 2011. *Made to be Seen: Perspectives on the History of Visual Anthropology* . Chicago, IL.: University of Chicago Press.

Banks, M. and Vokes, R. 2010. Introduction: anthropology, photography and the archive. *History and Anthropology* 21(4): 337–49.

Bell, J.A. 2003. Looking to see: Reflections on visual repatriation in the Purari Delta, Gulf Province, Papua New Guinea. In L. Peers and A. Brown (eds.) *Museums and Source Communities: A Routledge Reader*, pp. 111–22. London: Routledge.

Bell, J.A. 2008. Promiscuous things: Perspectives on cultural property through photographs in the Purari Delta of Papua New Guinea. *International Journal of Cultural Property* 15(2): 123–39.

Binney, J. and Chaplin, G. 1991. Taking photographs home: The recovery of a Maori history. *Visual Anthropology* 4: 431–42.

Brown, A.K., Peers, L.L. and members of the Kainai Nation. 2006. *Pictures Bring Us Messages: Sinaakssiiksi Aohtsimaahpihkookiyaawa: Photographs and Histories from the Kainai Nation*. Ontario: University of Toronto Press.

Buckley, L. 2005. Objects of love and decay: Colonial photographs in a post-colonial archive. *Cultural Anthropology* 20(2): 249–70.

Chaat Smith, P. 1995. The ghost in the machine. *Aperture* 139 (*Strong Hearts: Native American Visions and Voices*): 6–11.

Conor, L. and Lydon, J. 2011. Double take: Reappraising the colonial archive. *Journal of Australian Studies* 35(2): 137–43.

Derrida, J. 1995. *Archive Fever: A Freudian Impression.* (trans. Eric Prenowitz). Chicago, IL.: University of Chicago Press.

Derrida, J. 2010. *Copy, Archive, Signature: A Conversation on Photography.* Stanford, CA.: Stanford University Press.

Dudding, J. 2003. Photographs of Maori as cultural artefacts and their positioning within the museum. *Journal of Museum Ethnography* 15: 8–18.

Edwards, E. (ed.) 1992. *Anthropology and Photography, 1860–1920.* New Haven, CT: Yale University Press.

Edwards, E. 1994. Visualizing history: Diamond Jenness's photographs of D'Entrecasteaux Islands, Massim, 1911–1912: a case study in re-engagement. *Canberra Anthropology* 17(2): 1–25.

Edwards, E. 2001. *Raw Histories: Photographs, Anthropology, Museums.* Oxford: Berg.

Edwards, E. 2003. Introduction: "locked" in the archive. In L. Peers and A.K. Brown (eds.) *Museums and Source Communities*, pp. 83–99. London: Routledge.

Edwards, E. 2009. Evolving images: Photography, race and popular Darwinism. In D. Donald and J. Munro (eds.) *Endless Forms, Darwin, Natural Sciences and the Visual Arts*, pp. 167–93. New Haven, CT.: Yale University Press.

Edwards, E. and Hart, J. (eds.) 2004a. *Photographs Objects Histories: On the Materiality of Images.* London: Routledge.

Edwards, E. and Hart, J. 2004b. Mixed box: The cultural biography of a box of 'ethnographic' photographs. In E. Edwards and J. Hart (eds.) *Photographs, Objects, Histories: On the Materiality of Images*, pp. 48–64. Routledge, New York.

Faris, J.C. 1996. *Navajo and Photography: a Critical History and the Representation of an American People.* Albuquerque, NM: University of New Mexico.

Fienup-Riordan, A. 1998. Yup'ik elders in museums: Fieldwork turned on its head. *Arctic Anthropology* 35 (2): 49–58.

Geismar, H. and Herle, A. (eds.) 2010. *Moving Images: John Layard, Fieldwork and Photography on Malakula Since 1914.* Honolulu, HI: University of Hawai'i Press.

Ginsburg, F. 1998. Institutionalizing the unruly: Charting a future for visual anthropology. *Ethnos* 63(2): 173–201.

Ginsburg, F. 1999. Shooting back: From ethnographic film to the ethnography of media. In T. Miller and R. Stam (eds.) *A Companion to Film Theory*, pp. 295–322. London: Blackwell.

Ginsburg, F. 2011. Native intelligence: A short history of debates on indigenous media and ethnographic film. In M. Banks and J. Ruby (eds.) *Made to Be Seen: Perspectives on the History of Visual Anthropology*, pp. 234–55. Chicago: University of Chicago Press.

Ginsburg, F., Abu-Lughod, L., and Larkin, B. (eds.) 2002. *Media Worlds: Anthropology on New Terrain.* Berkeley, CA.: University of California Press.

Green, D. 1984. Veins of resemblance: Photography and eugenics. *Oxford Art Journal* 7(2): 3–16.

Griffiths, A. 2002. *Wondrous Difference: Cinema, Anthropology and the Turn of the Century Visual Culture.* New York: Columbia University Press.

Grimshaw, A. 2001. *The Ethnographer's Eye: Ways of Seeing in Modern Anthropology.* Cambridge: Cambridge University Press.

Gross, L., Katz, L. and Ruby, H. (eds.) 1988. *Image Ethics: the Moral Rights of Subjects in Photography.* New York: Oxford University Press.

Gross, L., Katz, L. and Ruby, H. (eds.) 2003. *Image Ethics in the Digital Age.* Minneapolis, MN: University of Minnesota Press.

Halvaksz, J. 2008. Photographing spirits: Indigenous photography, ancestors and the environment in Papua New Guinea. *Visual Anthropology* 21(4) (special issue *Haunting Images: The Affective Power of Photography*, edited by B. Smith and R. Vokes): 310–26.

Halvaksz, J. 2010. The photographic assemblage duration, history and photography in Papua New Guinea. *History and Anthropology* 21(4): 411–29.

Hamilton, C. (ed.) 2002. *Refiguring the Archive*. New York: Springer.

Harlan, T. 1995. Creating a visual history: A question of ownership. *Aperture* 139 (*Strong Hearts: Native American Visions and Voices*): 20–32.

Harlan, T. 1998. Indigenous photographies: A space for indigenous realities. In J. Allison (ed.) *Native Nations: Journeys in American Photography*, pp. 233–45. London: Barbican Center.

Hill, R.W. 1998. Developed identities: seeing the stereotypes and beyond. In T. Johnson (ed.) *Spirit Capture*, pp. 139–60. Washington, DC.: Smithsonian Institution.

Jones, W.E. 2010. *Killed: Rejected Images of the Farm Security Administration*. New York: PPE.

Lydon, J. 2005. *Eye Contact: Photographing Indigenous Australians.* Durham, NC: Duke University Press.

Lydon, J. 2010. Return: The photographic archive and technologies of indigenous memory. *Photographies* 3(2): 173–87.

Lydon, J. (ed.) 2014. *Calling the Shots: Aboriginal Photographies*. Canberra: Aboriginal Studies Press

Michaels, E. 1991. A primer of restrictions on picture-taking in traditional areas of Aboriginal Australia. *Visual Anthropology* 4: 259–75.

Morton, C. 2005. The anthropologist as photographer: Reading the monograph and reading the archive. *Visual Anthropology* 18(4): 389–405.

Morton, C. 2015. The ancestral image in the present tense. *Photographies* 8(3): 1–18.

Morton, C. and Edwards, E. (eds.) 2009. *Photography, Anthropology and History: Expanding the Frame*. Farnham: Ashgate.

Morton, C. and Oteyo, G. 2015. The Paro Manene Project: exhibiting and researching photographic histories in Western Kenya. In A.E. Coombes and R.B. Phillips (eds.) *Museum Transformations: Art, Culture, History*, pp. 311–35. Chichester: Wiley Blackwell.

Peterson, N. 2003. The changing photographic contract: Aborigines and image ethics. In C. Pinney and N. Peterson (eds.) *Photography's Other Histories*, pp. 119–45. Durham, NC.: Duke University Press.

Pink, S. 2003. Interdisciplinary agendas in visual research: Re-situating visual anthropology. *Visual Studies* 18(2): 179–92.

Pinney, C. 1989. Other people's bodies, lives, histories? Ethical issues in the use of a photographic archive. *Journal of Museum Ethnography* 1: 57–69.

Pinney, C. 1992. The parallel histories of anthropology and photography. In E. Edwards (ed.) *Anthropology and Photography, 1860–1920*, pp. 74–95. New Haven, CT: Yale University Press.

Pinney, C. 2011. *Photography and Anthropology*. London: Reaktion Books.

Pinney, C. and Peterson, N. (eds.) 2003. *Photography's Other Histories*. Durham, NC: Duke University Press.

Poignant, R. 1992. Surveying the field of view: The making of the RAI photographic collection. In E. Edwards (ed.) *Anthropology and Photography*, pp. 42–73. New Haven, CT: Yale University Press.

Poignant, R. and Poignant A. 1996. *Encounter at Nagalarramba*. Canberra: National Library of Australia.

Portman, M.V. 1896. Photography for anthropologists. *Journal of the Anthropological Institute of Great Britain and Ireland* 25: 75–87.

Rand, R. 2010. Thoughts on "Archive Fever." *Communication and Critical/Cultural Studies* 7(2): 207–11.

Rickard, J. 1995. Sovereignty: A line in the sand. *Aperture* 139 (*Strong Hearts: Native American Visions and Voices*): 51–54.

Rickard, J., Longfish, G., Jackson, Z., Carroll, P.S., Carraher, R. and Tsinhnahjinnie, H.J. 1995. Sovereignty: A line in the sand. *Aperture* 139 (*Strong Hearts: Native American Visions and Voices*): 50–9.

Ruby, J. 2005. The last 20 years of visual anthropology: A critical review. *Visual Studies* 20(2): 159–70.

Schwartz, J. 2000. Records of simple truth and precision: Photography, archives, and the illusion of control. *Archivaria* 50: 1–40.

Sekula, A. 1983. Reading an archive: Photography between labour and capital. In B.H.D. Buchloch and R. Wilkes (eds.) *Mining Photographs and Other Pictures: a Selection from the Archives of Shedden Studio, Glace Bay 1948–1968*, pp. 193–202. Halifax: Nova Scotia College of Art and Design, University of Breton Press.

Spencer, F. 1992. Some notes on the attempt to apply photography to anthropometry during the second half of the nineteenth century. In E. Edwards (ed.) *Anthropology and Photography*, pp. 99–107. New Haven, CT: Yale University Press.

Stoler, A.L. 2009. *Along the Archival Grain: Epistemic Anxieties and Colonial Common Sense.* Princeton, NJ: Princeton University Press.

Im Thurn E.F. 1893. Anthropological uses of the camera. *Journal of the Anthropological Institute of Great Britain and Ireland* 22: 184–203.

Tsinhnahjinnie, H.J. 1998. When is a photograph worth a thousand words? In J. Alison (ed.) *Native Nations: Journeys in American Photography*, pp. 41–55. London: Barbican Art Gallery.

Tsinhnahjinnie, H.J. 2003. When is a photograph worth a thousand words? In C. Pinney and N. Peterson (eds.) *Photography's Other Histories*, pp. 40–52. Durham, NC: Duke University Press.

Turner, T. 1995. Representation, collaboration, and mediation in contemporary ethnographic and indigenous media. *Visual Anthropology Review* 11(2): 102–6.

Turner, T. 2002. Representation, politics, and cultural imagination in indigenous video: General points and Kayapo examples. In F. Ginsburg, L. Abu-Lughod, and B. Larkin (eds.) *Media Worlds: Anthropology on New Terrain*, pp. 75–90. Berkeley, CA.: University of California Press.

Vizenor, G. 1998. Fugitive poses. In M. Katakis (ed.) *Excavating Voices: Listening to Photographs of Native Americans*, pp. 7–15. Philadelphia, PA.: University Museum of Archaeology and Anthropology.

15

THROUGH THE JACKPILE-PAGUATE URANIUM MINE

Christopher Witmore with Curtis L. Francisco

Note to reader

Moving in the company of Curtis L. Francisco, this chapter documents the partially remediated Jackpile-Paguate uranium mine, registering how features such as radioactive reservoirs, eroding slopes, and radon-emitting walls both weigh upon pueblo communities, plants, and animal others, and shape engagement, mood, conversation. To encompass an erstwhile uranium mine from a comfortable distance with maps or satellite photography (as if that were even possible) seems to me to ignore or dismiss the debt that all who live in zones of nuclear-energized comfort owe to those humans and nonhumans who struggle with the radioactive consequences of our lifestyles. Therefore, the mode of writing embraced here is chosen for how it confronts this dark object, opening an intimate path through that which dwarves us, allowing it to suggest something of itself over the course of the encounter, while witnessing how others live with it. What is here presented as a single journey was recorded and compiled over three separate outings at the invitation of Francisco, an indigenous geologist and resident of the Laguna Pueblo, for the purpose of bringing this story to people's attention.[1]

The journey up

Curtis Francisco is waiting at the bottom of the ramp by the entrance to his home. Under a glaring sun he had been sitting on a walker thumbing through a stack of papers. Upon seeing the car he rises, places the documents into a seat compartment, and sets out into the driveway before I come to a full stop. With a passing greeting he asks me to pop the trunk.

'The journey into the mine and on to Paguate should take about an hour.'

Curtis is short, stocky, and in his mid-fifties. His hair is long, which he wears in a way not atypical of Pueblo Indians. A member of the Laguna Pueblo, and a geologist, he lived with his grandparents in Paguate during the summers. His grandfather was a Yuke driver, then a gate guard, who worked at the Jackpile-Paguate mine, once the world's largest open-pit for uranium extraction. As a child, Curtis spent as much time as any of the miners among the waste dumps, protore stockpiles, access roads, and pits.

After wrestling the walker into the trunk, we both climb into the car. We're headed for what has become of the uranium mine. Curtis seeks to share the story of this more-than-massive object, and convey some sense of the crushing weight it has exerted upon his people and the land to which they belong. I, for my part, have come to learn from him and gain an awareness grounded in what lies here by grappling with the staggering heft of the mine and its afterlife in the wake of industrial uranium-ore extraction.

'Take Old Route 66 west.'

We drive down a long, gravel way framed by chain-linked fencing, passing under the water tower for the Pueblo of Laguna. We turn onto Old Route 66, then west on 66/NM 124. Ahead, Old Laguna rises as a collection of brown adobe houses crowned by the white Mission of San José and the Catholic church. While the Pueblo predates all listed inception dates, the mission and church were built in 1699, in the wake of the Pueblo Revolt. They persist as testaments to the Catholic presence under the Spanish, which is contentious (Flint 2015).

'Lagunas,' I inquire, 'were required to attend church services under the Spanish?'

'Yes.'

'The church dominates the pueblo.'

> It was placed at the top so that the priests can see everything that was going on. When we held religious activities, we did so outside of the village. Under the watchful eyes of the priests, the plazas were not used as they were in the past.

We pass over the Rio San Jose, through a cut in the south flank of Two Feathers Hill, then across the Santa Fe railroad. We turn onto NM 279.

'The Grants Mineral Belt holds forty percent of the US uranium,' Curtis says. 'Ninety percent of the uranium in the Grants is locked up in the lacustrine deposit that is in the Jackpile mine.'

'Lacustrine? So, it was a lake?'

> Yes. Uranium wants to go into solution. It typically forms in streambeds as roll-fronts, small and concentrated deposits in the shape of crescents. Common in the western portion of the mineral belt, these oxbow lakes were left to evaporation. Calcium salts, manganese salts, gypsum, and uranium remained. Still, the Jackpile is unlike any other deposit.

Before us a view opens north towards the flanks of flat mesa, a southeastern extension of Wheat Mountain and Mount Taylor. To the northeast broad flats cut by the Rio San Jose encompass Flint Peak. Curtis points directly ahead. 'In the edge of the mesa you can see all four units of the Dakota Sandstone. The light-colored, white material is the Jackpile Sandstone. It contains the high-grade uranium ore.'

'Those are the lacustrine-formed deposits?'

> It was an estuarian marsh in the Jurassic. Tidal flats, not unlike that of the Carolina coast, received river-deposited material. There was a great deal of bioaccumulation by plants, which uptake uranium water. Uranium likes to stick to calcium and over deep time the deposit formed.

The tarmac surface curves right with the Santa Fe Railroad. Curtis directs my attention north towards a linear, finger-shaped mesa that comes into view between two peaks. 'There are a series of ruins up there called *Dyu-pe Tsa-ah-shche-tra*,[2] which translates as the Badger Village.[3] It was built for defensive purposes – outsiders could not get to them easily.'

'That mesa bleeds white with Jackpile Sandstone.'

'They built directly upon it. However, they raised their walls with sandstone hauled down from the Morrison formation above. Radiation would have been a very real problem for them.'

Curtis motions for me to turn onto a dirt road at the convergence of Old 279 and New 279. We cross a cattle grate and continue southeast.

The mine was opened at the beginning of the Cold War. From 1953 until 1982 it was operated by the Anaconda Minerals Company, a division of Atlantic Richfield (ARCO). 'How,' I ask, 'was Uranium revealed here?'

> A Navajo sheepherder named Paddy Martinez found uranium in a railroad cut at the foot of Haystack Butte, just west of Grants. He thought the yellow rock was gold. A flight survey of the wider area with Geiger Counter in 1950 was followed by ground truthing, and that is how Jackpile was found.

We turn east onto the service road. Uranium occurs predominately as two isotopes, 235 and 238. 'Here,' Curtis adds, 'we also have 234.'

'While the number of protons are consistent, 92, the number of neutrons differ.'

'Yes, and 235 is the main fissable isotope. A low percentage can be used in most nuclear reactors, but highly concentrated amounts are necessary for a warhead.'[4]

We cross an old rail spur without tracks or ties. 'It was the line from the mine,' Curtis continues, 'It is very contaminated.'

The progeny of exploding supernovae, uranium originated as early as 6.6 billion years ago. Primordial ingredients out of which the earth was formed, some scientists argue that uranium decay contributes to the vital heat that stirs beneath the earth's lithosphere. Out of the lacustrine deposit at Jackpile the ore was mined, then transported in open hopper cars along the spur to the Santa Fe Railroad and on to

Anconda's Bluewater Mill, 40 miles west of here. There the ore was crushed and milled, then sent on as yellow cake to enrichment facilities.

At the reservoir

The spur road follows along the top of the earthen dam. Constructed in the 1930s to supply the village of Mesita with irrigation water from the Paguate creek, the former reservoir is now completely silted in. 'There is,' Curtis says, 'about 30 feet of accumulation at the center of the dam. All of the silt is screaming radioactive.'

Among cattails behind the dam cattle graze on the yellowing grasses that emerge from the unstable sludge. Noting my reaction, Curtis remarks: 'They now pasture cows out here, but they shouldn't.'

'Because they ingest radionuclides.'

'Correct. People have been told not to graze animals here, but they claim to have nowhere else.'

Curtis directs me to look off to the right.

> Beyond the base of the embankment, there are three different ponds. The Bureau of Indian Affairs (BIA) put those in to contain water that seeps out of the reservoir and mine. Cattle drink from them because they have no other water source. The bottom pond is very radioactive.

Russian olives grow less green from the top pool to the bottommost pool. Those clustered around the lowest pond appear to be under stress. According to Curtis,

> when the Environmental Protection Agency (EPA) undertook the pre-CERCLIS[5] assessments they collected numerous samples of soil, water and

FIGURE 15.1 Road over reservoir. Photo: Christopher Witmore

sediment. During the proposed listing to the National Priority List (NPL), an ASPECT[6] flyover identified this area as being just as hot as the open pits in the mine.

The reservoir is among the most radioactive areas due to the accumulation of silt resulting from erosion within the mine (see USDOI 1985, 2-32-35).

Curtis assisted in an effort to have the mine listed as a Superfund site, which funds the cleanup of the most toxic locales in the United States. 'The mine was listed in December 2013.'

'I understand three of the sixteen listed Superfund sites in New Mexico are in this county.'

'Yes, Cibola County has more than its fair share.'

We pass over the old water-control gate. Though the gate is completely silted in, it still conveys some water.

'Surely, this is not used for irrigation?' I ask.

It is no longer usable for agriculture. The bioaccumulation factors are too high. We have sampled the plants below the reservoir, and also taken samples of native food – corn, chili, beans, and squash – and they were very high.[7] Mesita, which gets little water from the Rio San Jose, during the growing season, now has no irrigation water and has not been able to grow anything.

'We,' he continues, 'are primarily an agrarian culture and ninety percent of what we grow is used for our own consumption. The same with livestock.'

'Your people were known for raising sheep.'[8]

'My family maintained one of the largest herds. During the Second World War, Laguna Pueblo was one of the major producers of wool for military clothing and blankets. We also produced lanolin.'

'For skin cream?'

'For bullets.'[9]

We come to a stop at the end of the earthen dam and get out to inspect the diversion box and spillway. 'The BIA,' Curtis points out,

added the concrete wall extension in the 1980s in hopes of retaining water above the silted-in portions. Uranium salts have degraded the seam between the old spillway and the new addition to the point that it cannot hold any more water.

Water seeps over, under, and through the spillway which the BIA tried to improve. 'So, while the reservoir forms a sink for the heavy metals, salts, and radio-active materials that move down the watershed, the uranium passes through?' I ask.

'And on down. The Jackpile-Paguate mine is one of the three major contributors of radionuclides to the Rio Grande. The others are Los Alamos and the Sandia National Laboratories.'

'A legacy which exceeds that of the Manhattan Project.'[10]

'Yes.'

Here, radioactivity is dependent on the source of water.

> After rains the water is diluted by surface runoff and life enters. I have seen catfish and brine shrimp, though I have wondered whether skin blotching on the catfish is related to radioactivity. If the water is supplied predominately by the Paguate and the Moquino rivers, it can still sustain life. However, when the water derives solely from the local water table, it turns blue, life struggles and dies.

'Up in the mine,' Curtis recalls,

> there used to be a lake; a beautiful, turquoise-blue lake. There was no life in it at all, no algae, no fish, no plants around it, no mosquitos, no insects, no birds. You wouldn't see waterfowl around it. Rabbits would not go near it. Deer would not go near it. Even the sheep would stay away. But as a child you always wanted to get into it or drink there, because it looked so very inviting. But then there was the smell.

'What did it smell like?'

'Even now the odor is familiar, though I can't quite describe it. I guess the best that I can say is that it smelled like an oxidized metal.'

'Oxidized metal?'

> Like ozone. I don't know how to adequately describe that smell. If you have been next to a lightning strike, it is akin to the scent of burnt metal that follows. But then you have to oxidize it. The odor is distinctive.

'It smells salty here.'

'Yes, you could smell the salts, which adds the scent of the ocean.'

We return to the car and retrace our path over the earthen dam. As we near the retaining ponds, ten mustangs come to drink. Before I can comment, Curtis interjects:

> Grandpa spoke of the turquoise lake in terms of death. It was called *Shu-mu Gu-ywie-tro*. The precise translation of this Keresan toponym is 'this is where death lives.' 'This is death's home.' It looked beautiful, but it was deadly. Death is not someone you want to affiliate with.

We both watch as the mustangs enter the middle pool. 'If you destroy Death's house where is he going to go?'

FIGURE 15.2 Mustangs drink from containment pond below reservoir. Photo: Christopher Witmore

Into the mine

We reach the far side of the dam and continue along the dirt road. We note more cattle grazing in the area. 'I understand that the economic base of the Pueblo shifted from agriculture to mining in the wake of opening the first pit in 1953. I have read that its closure left an unemployment rate of over fifty percent.'[11]

'Even so, the Laguna people did not want the mine,' says Curtis. 'The old timers fought against it. It was considered raping our Mother. And we said no, we don't want this.'

'Then how did it come about?'

> In those days, other than a little Spanish, and Navajo, which we used for the sheep herders, Keres was the only language. Only a few people could speak English; people who had been sent off to Carlisle Indian Industrial School. Their translation skills were less than adequate.

'So, it was a matter of miscommunication?'

> Essentially. As far as we understood it, the government only gave us two options. 'Either you let us mine and you will get something out of this to benefit your people' – and we couldn't figure out how it was going to benefit

our people. Or, the government will condemn the area and take the land. 'You will get nothing.' Those were the options that we were given.

'Or the interpretation your people were compelled to bear?'

Indeed. For people who don't speak English, translating that over, what was presented as a demand, was not something that was easy to do. We didn't know that they could not actually condemn the area. We didn't know that they couldn't take our land. One has to recall that the parents and grandparents of those Lagunas presented with this choice remember the transition from Mexico to the United States. We didn't trust the US government.

'And so it was also a matter of exploitation.'
'Yes.'

Upon returning to the intersection with State Highway 279, Curtis gestures ahead to the old roadway for 279 to Paguate, which descends from the top of Oak Mesa by cutting a line across the slopes of what is known locally as Questa. 'The new road was rerouted in tandem with the remediation project.' He follows this observation with a few choice words concerning the folly of routing a state highway through a uranium mine. We turn right.

The remediation project was designed to encircle the mine with a sphere of protection. Though it reduced the radiological hazards associated with the exposed ore deposits, it fell short of walling off humans, other animals, and plants against the full onslaught of gamma radiation, radionuclides in their food, or uranium in their water.

'When,' I ask, "did the remediation take place?'
'The process was initiated in 1987, but the actual work did not begin until after 1989.'
'Remediation was not without its struggles …'[12]

There were many. Our governor at the time was embroiled in a battle with ARCO.[13] They offered 40 million for remediation, which was a drop in the bucket. So, he fought and got 7.9 million more.

'And, unsurprisingly, ARCO didn't want to take on responsibility for the remediation.'

No. It fell to the Pueblo. That 47.9 million was used to build Laguna Construction Company in 1989, which is now all but defunct. Of course, 47.9 million was nowhere near enough to undertake all of the necessary remediation. It didn't even pay for a third of it. That is why the South Paguate pit was never touched. There was not enough money.

'And any accountability for the shortfall falls back on the Pueblo?'

'It does. Regrettably, our own ignorance is our defense. ARCO took advantage of Pueblo innocence.'

The road meets with the rail spur and soon skirts the east base of South Oak Canyon Mesa. To the left, Curtis points out the shop up Oak Canyon. 'That is where they use to work on vehicles for the mine.' He points out a small shack built of stone on the left. 'That was an old sheep camp. The shepherd was known as the "Chinese Colonel." '

Curtis motions for me to slow down and pull off the road by a metal gate. 'We will only be a second. This is the official point of entry to the mine.'

I look ahead into a valley cut by the Rio Paguate. To the east, even slopes, devoid of vegetation and lacerated with parallel rills, fall from the broken crests of what was the flat-topped Gavilan Mesa. 'The mine took seven eights of the mesa,' according to Curtis. Beyond the crests, the Jackpile Pit opened a 300-acre crater 625 feet deep. Farther north, below the village of Paguate, the North Paguate Pit was blasted to a depth of 200 feet, while to the west the South Paguate Pit was cut deep enough to accommodate a thirty-two story building. In addition to three open pits, nine underground mines were also exploited (USDOI 1-1, 2-1).

'To those who pass here this river valley appears to look like the natural landscape of buttes and ridges,' says Curtis.

'They attempted to make what had been waste dumps, protore stockpiles, open pits, and highwalls blend into the surrounding topography.'

'They put benches and terraces in, but they could not recreate the rock structures like you see on the Mesas on the other side of the road. If you are aware of this, the difference is blaring.'

'Very little vegetation grows on the remediated slopes.'

'The dirt they used has no nutrient content whatsoever. It is sterile. There is no organic matter in what they retrieved from two-hundred feet below.'

'I have read the Department of Interior (DOI) environmental impact statement. The most conservative proposal included a stipulation for a foot of topsoil.'

'There was an inch, at best!'

Curtis waves his arm to the right. Beyond the green gate, a concrete road fords the river. On the opposite side, where several salt cedars (tamarisks) now grow, a guard shack once stood.

> In his later years, my grandfather worked there as a guard; this was the main entrance to the mine. The contoured slopes beyond mark where they kept stockpiles of ore. I have measured the uranium content of the stream here.[14] The highest measurements that I obtained were about 496 picocuries per liter when the water was flowing nice and blue.

'What is the limit for drinking water?'

'Twenty picocuries per liter.'

We drive on. As we round the turn, remnants of a rock wall call my attention. 'It was,' according to Curtis, 'built by the old timers and it denotes the jurisdiction of the village of Paguate.'

The company housing area

Curtis motions for me to pull over. We stop off the far side of the road near a cattle grate. I hurry to grab Curtis's walker and offer it as he rises out of the car. We cross the road to the grate and stand by a cable cordon.

'This is what remains of the company housing area.'

A concrete slab marks the footprint of the geology lab. In the distance a line of foundations mark where eighteen houses once stood (see inventory in USDOI 2–10).

'All the Anaconda executives and managers lived here,' Curtis continues.

A breeze-block barbeque pit stands as a memory to anonymous gatherings. Nearby an abandoned tennis and basketball court is encircled by a high, chain-link fence. A swing set, chin-up bars, and climbing frame are what remain of a playground. A hanging trapeze bar dangles in the wind.

'They lived here with their families. Children were born here. Conceived here. They grew up and went to school here.'

'The entire town was separated from the pueblo?'

> It was considered too good for our people to live here. Even in the trailers that were here. They had a guard shack nearby that would stop us if we came over here. We had to be on a specific task with a specified purpose. We were not allowed to stay. We had to leave at dark.

FIGURE 15.3 Barbecue pit and playground persist mid-distance at company housing area. Photo: Christopher Witmore

'Such company towns tend towards isolation and separation,' I add. 'They "reproduce the logic of colonial outposts." '[15]

'Yes, not unlike the Spanish with their missions.'

Curtis turns to point east towards the slopes across NM 279. Contoured terraces bereft of vegetation mark what has become of the loading station.

> Ore chutes once stood there. Twenty-four, seven, they were constantly loading ore and all the uranium-laden dust blew across the valley to cover everything here. Radioactive dust was also thrown up during the blasts and that too covered this area.

'How often did they blast?'

'Three times a day: six am, twelve noon, and six pm.'

'Were there sirens?'

'They were loud enough to be heard for miles,' Curtis affirms.

> I remember as a kid my grandmother timed her routines around the blasts. After the dust settled from the morning explosions, she would pack all the clothes in the car. My grandpa, who worked the graveyard shift, would come home from work to drive us all to the laundry mat in Grants. She would wash all the white clothes there and, when we returned home, she would hang them out on the line by 11 am.

'That didn't leave much time to dry before the next explosion.'

> I remember that the sirens caught us by surprise one day. My grandparents had been arguing incessantly over something. Then came the sirens; followed by a huge blast. It was very close to the village. The sky turned black. The street lights came on. We had to dive under the table. Cracks formed in the walls. Chunks of plaster fell from the ceiling. Dishes tumbled from the cabinets. Cabinets ripped off the wall. And then, my grandmother remembered the laundry. What had been gleaming white was now brown.

FIGURE 15.4 Afterlife of ore-loading station area. Photo: Christopher Witmore

'Those who lived here must have had similar experiences, and problems, with radioactive dust. Inhalation of airborne radionuclides is one of the principle pathways to contamination and the corruption of one's DNA.'

'Yes. And people living in the company housing area started having health problems. Then the mine was shut down.'

'Do you know what became of those who lived here?'

Not really. The foreman lived over there. He had a swimming pool at his house. He died from cancer. But, they did not attribute it to the mine. He was a heavy smoker, so they attributed his death to smoking.

'All of the houses were torn down … I presume because of the radioactivity?'

Yes. Radioactive dust was absorbed into the paint, into the wood. They bulldozed all of the buildings and dumped them into the South Paguate Pit. I don't recall whether they covered the area with soil. It doesn't appear that they did.

'Everything,' I note, 'has been reclaimed by vegetation.'

'What there is of it. All the elm trees have died.'

'Uranium doesn't discriminate.'

We turn to look east to the slopes where the train cars were loaded. In his twenty-ton dump truck, Curtis's grandfather hauled radioactive ore to the chutes. 'The primary ore was a pitch blend, it was black. It was so hot that they had to mix it with aggregate to get it into the ore cars.'

'But the rail line was not here in the beginning?' I ask.

'No. In the 1950s there were no regulations for radioactivity on the highway. They hauled uranium in open ore trucks.'

'That paints a less than nostalgic image of Route 66.'

Yes. Of course, later the ore was found to be so radioactive that it could only be hauled by train. They also used open ore cars on the railroad. A lot of uranium ore jostled loose. A number of cars even tipped over and spilled their contents. Along the spur line, the rails and the wooden ties were taken up, but the roadbed is still highly radioactive.

Over the course of a generation, approximately 400 million tons of overburden (topsoil and alluvium, shale and sandstone) was shifted to remove 25 million tons of uranium ore. Locked in deeply buried sandstone beddings, workers with drills and dynamite blasted through 250 million years of accumulated insulation. With steam shovels, large front-end loaders, and Yukes hauling twenty cubic yards of earth over twenty-five miles of road, they resurfaced the land over the course of a generation. Shifting ore, protore (low grade ore, which was stockpiled), and waste

FIGURE 15.5 Remediated slopes by NM 279. Photo: Christopher Witmore

dumps they blocked drainages, altered stream courses, increased sediment loads, and transformed waters through uranium uptake, whether here or downstream. Blasting and dumping unleashed a radioactive blitzkrieg on the company housing area and Paguate, all flora and fauna in the area. When the winds came, radioactive dust was blown over Albuquerque, 45 miles to the east.

Whereas uranium-235 has a half-life of 700 million years; that of 238 is 4.46 billion. Uranium lies here in wait, extending well before and far beyond anything human or otherwise. It precedes life on earth, outlasting Jurassic flora and its primordial lands only to return to the surface and remix with everything here and elsewhere, in the past, now, and beyond. 'How,' I ask, 'can a few years of remediation balance out the labors of a generation, much less those of deep time?'

'It can't.'

There is no way to repay the debt that comes with undoing what was formed over geologic eons. Such a legacy will press on into the deep future, far beyond Anaconda, the EPA, the state of New Mexico, the people of Laguna, or the more-than-monstrous aftermath of one of the world's largest open-pit mines.

Into Paguate

We return to the car. We place the wheeler in the back, close the trunk, then pause to look above the erstwhile housing area. An outcrop of sandstone cuts a broad swath across the east face of the mesa. At the northern end stone lines break the monotony of the rock-laden slope.

> That is an old sheep corral. On the opposite side of the arroyo, at the base of the other cliff face you can see another rock wall. That is also a sheep corral. Those were here well before they built this housing area.

A herding map was published in 1957; it shows the locations of lambing camps and corrals and lists the names of those associated with them. 'Rafael Lente and Jose Gaco were associated with this area,' I add.[16]

'This was also agricultural land. Paguate,' Curtis recalls,

> was the bread basket for Laguna and the mine gobbled up half to two-thirds of our fields. We grew everything down here – primarily wheat, but also corn, chili, melons, squash, and alfalfa. Because we had a very good supply of water, there were also orchards – apricot and peach.

Archaeological studies were undertaken throughout the lease area (Anschuetz, et al. 1979; Beal 1976; Carroll and Hooten 1977; Carroll et al. 1977; Grigg et al. 1977). Of the 217 archaeological sites that were documented in the 1970s, seven were excavated, five were deemed too insignificant for investigation. All twelve were destroyed. 205 were left. Of course, these numbers do not account for what was obliterated over the decades of extraction prior to the survey. And no inventory of individual sites can evince the full scope of Laguna heritage; here, ten square miles were saturated with meaning and association. No metrology can do justice to the valleys, mesas, or rivers it purports to measure; here, the land is understood as mother, as nurturer, as womb for the people, for plant and animal others. Of course, some places are more saturated than others.

'We had the mine carve out sites which had more religious significance for us. Basket Mountain was one of them.' Curtis points west. 'They began mining up the saddle, and our most significant site is up there. *Ah-tra-ne Ku-tu*, Wheat Mountain, is a small shield volcano on top of that large basalt plateau that is just below Mount Taylor.'

'Mount Taylor is now a Traditional Cultural Property (TCP).'[17]

> Yes, everything 8000 feet and above off the reservation is in the TCP. At Acama they bring it down to 6300 ft. In the Laguna reservation the elevation comes down to 7000 feet, I think. The area protected is over 400,000 acres; the entire top of Mesa Cevato and Mount Taylor.

The total Anaconda lease covered nearly 8000 acres (7868 acres). Yet, what remains of ARCO's monstrous intervention now marks all Pueblo heritage in the shadows of Mount Taylor. 'What has become of the mine,' I add, 'will continue to crush other objects of Pueblo heritage under its tremendous weight, outlasting them into the future deep of geological time.'

Curtis says nothing. We return to the car, then take to the road. The exploitation of uranium not only radically changed the Laguna peoples' routines of interaction, it redefined what it was to live with this land. Only gradually did those who lived in the pueblos, those who worked the mines, come to understand how their principal milieu had turned out to be perilous in the wake of massive human-technological intervention. Within their midst, the removal of overburden to extract uranium, opened a wide valley of discordancy.

'How,' I ask, 'did the Pueblo people live with uranium prior to its discovery?'

'We have always known that something was there that wasn't good.'

'As with the turquoise lake?'

'Yes. It killed things. It was there, it was something to be respected, but we shouldn't have anything to do with it.'

We pass the confluence of the Rio Paguate and the Rio Moquino. 'The salt cedars,' Curtis says, 'are dying. I guess the radioactivity is finally killing them.'

A valley opens before us and the village of Paguate can be seen on the bluffs. Below a cliff stripped back by the mine is bracketed by remediated slopes. Chain-link fencing enclose ponds too radioactive to drain into the watershed. Four horses graze what was the North Paguate Pit. 'They shouldn't be here.'

I focus on a chestnut mare for a moment before returning to topic. 'Prior to its disclosure through science, the efficacy of uranium was hardly something that was naively given. Your worldview,' I continue, 'accounted for the dangers of what is later revealed as uranium. Of course, none of this was understood in terms of radioactivity and radiation, which was made explicit from the angle of science ...'

'... which is an Anglo-American mode of understanding, used by the corporation behind the mine, by state and federal agencies. In any case, we have no way of expressing radiation or radioactivity in our language.'

'All language falls short of radioactivity.'

'Nonetheless, we have tried. We had to. The closest we could come for our old people to understand is the energy that comes from the wood stove.'

'Which hardly carries negative connotations.'

'For our old people, heat is a good thing. It keeps us warm. Some equate it to a wood fire; others, the touch of the sun.'

'Radiation was recognized as solar radiation?'

'Yes.'

'So, coming to understanding was not only an issue of language, but of experience.'

'Absolutely. Except if you can feel heat coming from that radioactivity, you are dead.'

The road before us is bracketed by barren objects – the highwall of the North Paguate Pit on the left, a rill-ridden remediated slope on the right.

'Our senses cannot cope with radiation,' I continue.

'You can't see isotopes or gamma rays. You can't smell them. You can't taste them. For many, it is out of sight, out of mind. I suppose it makes it easier for them to sleep at night.'

I briefly contemplate how the phenomenological emphasis on *being there* provides so little ground for understanding uranium. 'What did your people make of the dark clouds generated by the explosions or the dust that covered the laundry?'

'It was dirty. My grandmother never understood radioactivity. My grandfather did not understand radon until about six months before he passed.'

'How did you bring your grandfather to understanding?'

My dad and I worked on a translation. We reworked and reworked it. I broke down the science to about a tenth-grade level. Even though my father has a master's degree in Elementary School education, it didn't help with translating the scientific concept into something understandable within our language.

'So, where there is an experiential blindness, science remains.'
'Or religion.'
We turn left on Postal Road. With the uranium that comes from deep beneath Pueblo land, there is dissonance of language, which forms a boundary object to mutual understanding. There is the disjuncture of experience, which gives no ground to find purchase with unstable particles or gamma rays. Here we leave aside any questions of ontologies, in how the world is understood to actually exist, and stay with matters of epistemology. 'So,' I query, 'the incongruity comes down to ways of knowing?'

> 'For a people that lived by the natural world and lived in harmony with nature there are no words, there is no knowledge to explain things that could not be experienced by the physical senses of taste, sight, smell, touch, or hearing'.

'Indeed, the only way for invisible harm to step forward into view is through the technologies of science. In living without dosimeters or Geiger-counters one comes to recognize radiation over the course of a generation through the formation of cancer, abscesses, and transformations of the body that are alien and foreign. Providing one had acquired an awareness of radiation and its consequences. In any case, the body is a slow indicator and by time any suggestion of harm appears, it is too late'.
'Of course, there were many ways of explaining those indications.'
'Such as?'
'Someone was practicing witchcraft, someone did something wrong. Things that could not be explained outright were explained by superstition or supernatural events.'
'Or, that someone was a smoker.'
'Many were.'
We come to a stop at a crossroads. Clusters of adobe dwellings rise out of the earth from which they are made. Two stone structures endure in ruin. The Catholic church stands at the center of the village. The nearby Post Office forms a gleaming contrast to its surroundings. No one is on the streets. A late summer storm is brewing off Mount Taylor to the northwest. We drive through the village center, past huddles of houses associated with the Bear Clan, past the kiva, past the central plaza towards the edge of the bluff. We park beside a stonewall.

Paguate village

Well-shaped blocks, of hues red and orange, rest upon deeply weathered stone of beige color. Portions of walls which formed part of a ruined compound have

FIGURE 15.6 Radioactive wall in Paguate. Photo: Christopher Witmore

collapsed through instability. The layered wall inverts the bedding of the land, stone from more recent strata below, deeper, older masonry above. The base layer of fretted flagstone was collected here. Older pueblo houses are built of it; that is, what could be gathered from the surface around the village. The upper, well-formed, and more recent blocks comes from the mine. They are radioactive.

'The wall emits radon,' says Curtis.

A small shop is set in the corner of the radioactive ruin. Before its whitewashed façade, surmounted by an espadaña, a patio umbrella unfurls over a small courtyard. 'The shop belongs to Greg and he has cancer.'

'How old is Greg?' I ask.

> Greg is probably just in his sixties, not much older than me. He smokes a lot. He drinks a lot. His house, built of the same material as the wall, was one of the most radioactive in the village, like that of my grandparents.

'Your grandparents' house was built of stone from the mine?'

> Yes. It is a traditional pueblo house fashioned from rock and mud. My grandpa built it in the 1950s with stone that he hauled from the mine. Their house has the highest radon levels of any in the village. It stays at about 20 pCi/L (picocuries per liter) year round. It is not livable.

'Of course, more injurious stones were collected from the mine.'

'Such as?'

> Petrified wood was often encountered in the course of mining. With its laminar coloring it was really pretty, but it is highly radioactive. My neighbor in Laguna collected a piece from the mine and had it in his yard. He used to sit on it. It had a count so high that it could only be guessed – upwards of 3000 counts per minute on the Geiger counter. That is beyond screaming hot. My grandfather did the same thing – he had big chunks of petrified wood in the front yard.

'They lived in a radon-emitting house with radioactive objects in the yard, as you did. How did living within such a house affect the health of your grandparents?'

'Dementia and Alzheimer's robbed my grandmother of her memory. A lot of people in the village of Paguate have dementia and Alzheimer's, perhaps one in five.'

'That is quite high.'

'Much higher than the rates across the country.'

'My father,' Curtis continues,

> has *retinitis pigmentosa*, as does his sister. The degenerative eye decease affects the normal population at a rate of 1 in 10 million, yet within the village of Paguate we have more than thirty cases of it out of a population of 1750.

I recall other cases from Paguate about which Valerie Kuletz had written in her book, *The Tainted Desert* (1998, 19–20). Interviewing a Paguate resident and anti-nuclear activist, Dorothy Purley, she learned of the terrible toll cancer had taken here just after the completion of remediation in 1995. Dorothy had lost her mother and her brother, aunts and uncles to cancer. She spoke of a nineteen-year old who died from prostate cancer. A fifteen-year old who died from leukemia. Struggling with an enlarged thyroid she too was battling cancer. Dorothy died from lymphoma in 1999. 'How well did you know Dorothy Purley?'

> Dorothy was a direct family relative of mine. She worked in the mine for eight years as a Yuke driver, like my grandfather. However, it was after 1972, so she was not eligible for RECA, the Radiation Exposure Compensation Act.

'Which would have provided restitutions for those who developed certain cancers or illnesses.'

'Provided that they worked in the mine for over a year.'

'And, ascertaining causation was not a requirement of RECA.'

'No.'

Establishing a causal link between reported illnesses and the presence of a radio-active mine is not easy. Epidemiological studies, as Kuletz pointed out twenty years ago, are still costly. A decease such as *retinitis pigmentosa*, can be written off as inherited, even though uranium corrupts DNA. 'Indian Health Services diverts blame away from the mine,' Curtis declares.

'Despite the fact that low-dose exposure to radiation contributes to carcinogenesis and has nonetheless been linked to a throng of nonmalignant diseases?'[18]

'Yes.'

Dorothy's house sits upon bluff at the edge of the village not far from here. Below, less than a 1000 feet from her kitchen window, lays the threshold of the North Paguate Pit.

'RECA,' I say, 'compensates "uranium miners, millers, and ore transporters." There are no provisions for communities perched so precariously on the edge of mines.'

> Nor are there protections for those who must now struggle with the aftermath of mining. We lived with the dust-enveloped mine. We lived with a wasteland of radioactive devastation. We now live with a partially remediated ruin, which continues to affect our groundwater, our surface water, our soil, our soul.

I consider pressing the discussion on, but I now detect a certain reticence on Curtis's part to take the topic any further. It is clear that this is a dissonant land, tragic, heartbreaking, dark in its radiance. It is also clear, through Curtis's example, that this community cannot succumb to anger and despair over its own carcinogenic stigmata. Anyone who subscribes to those contemporary modes of living encircled behind the shared walls of nuclear protection and underwritten by the new energy regime of nuclear power is implicated in what was, and what now transpires, here. Though accountability is distributed, the weight of uranium is disproportionate. For the uneven distribution of a nuclear legacy falls squarely upon this community who now struggle with the afterlife of what was one of the world's largest open-pit mines.

I turn to inspect the nearby stonewalls. My archaeological curiosity is swiftly dulled by the knowledge of what lies here. It is somewhat unnerving to stand so close to radon-emitting walls. It is unsettling to stand above a radioactive pit, remediation or not. Yet, I quickly push away such thoughts. For what does it matter if I share in the dangers of this place but for a few moments when compared to what Curtis and his people have endured? *Being here* is part of a necessary witnessing that those in zones of comfort owe to those who live here, to the land for which they care so deeply, and to that which exceeds that care.

The return journey

Raindrops splatter on radioactive stones. Lightning clouds threaten. We return to the car and set out for Laguna. 'We will take the old road by the mine shop.'

At the center of Paguate, numerous rock and adobe structures are in ruin. Many houses were abandoned because damages wrought by the daily triptych of explosions emanating from the mine rendered them hazardous. Others were abandoned due to radon levels too high for habitation. Tattered walls, broken windows and collapsed roofs offer testaments to devastation beyond the confines of the mine (also see Lorenzo 2016, pp. 98–9). They also attest to detonations within this native community; an indigenous culture, like so many others, struggling against its own oblivion.

We follow a road named for a revered school teacher, Elizabeth Bender. 'She was an inspiration to a generation of Pueblo children, including my father,' Curtis interjects. We pass fallow fields north of the Rio Paguate. 'All of this area was farmland, now only a few plots are maintained.'

The road soon crosses the Rio Paguate and doubles back below a reservoir, which supplies water to the village. Some fields south of the river are under cultivation. Plots of corn, sunflower, beans, and squash are encircled by runs of barbedwire. These lines are held fast and high on railroad ties turned fence posts. 'A lot of people still plant crops out here. Our biggest problem now is elk. No matter how high the fence, they will find a way in to eat the corn.'

We drive along an unpaved road around a mesa. In the rain, the upper half-inch of dirt has turned to mud. Curtis points out a few houses on the flat-topped hill. 'That is where the Parrot people came from. My grandpa was born there. My great grandmother used to live in this house up here.'

Soon we return to the edge of the mine, and pause at Old 279. From here one gains a clear sense of the area's verticality. Clean water, good agricultural lands, above. Radioactive water, devastated lands, below. But this image is too simple. It doesn't account for wall-cracking detonations or hellish clouds of uranium dust. It shatters against the emanant efficacy of uranium or the scale of what was taken from here, which is hard to fathom. 400 million tons of overburden. 25 million tons of ore. More-than-mammoth pits and mounds suggest little concerning the relationship between locality and the world objects of nuclear energy and warheads.

We turn right. How many of the radionuclides dispersed around the planet through thousands of US nuclear detonations were once locked in the Jurassic strata formerly buried here? No doubt they are legion. A potential marker of the so-called Anthropocene (Hancock et al. 2014), what was taken from the jurisdiction of Paguate to be milled and enriched, detonated or expended will endure across enormous swaths of time and space. We should contemplate uranium and its spawn of radiogenic nuclides as "hyperobjects" that are molten and sticky, massively distributed and nonlocal, independent of those objects that give rise to them, thereby exceeding their local manifestations (Morton 2013). We need such concepts to elicit "an appropriate level of shock and anxiety" concerning our collective lot as global humanity and the devastation wrought upon other beings that share our planet (ibid., 8; also see Macfarlane 2016). And yet, driving along the edge of a partially remediated mine, having borne witness to this ravaged land alongside my escort, such concepts seem somewhat out of place. We also need to draw our focus to what is here, out of respect for these disenfranchised people, out of a fidelity to this greater-than-gargantuan object of a mine (Witmore 2019), out of empathy and a shared sense of outrage, in order to accept some level of culpability, and to learn how we all might return to our *shared* ground (Latour 2018).

Ahead the road cuts through waste material for the mine. 'As the mine grew they moved the road here.'

Curtis indicates a wooden headframe on the right.

> It marks the outlet for an air vent that supplied mine shafts below. Just east of here the open pit stopped and the underground galleries began. They went down 2000 feet beneath this road using open-stope mining, or what is known as room and pillar. They even had a grill down there.

'A grill?'

'Yes. A burger bar. My grandpa remembered eating hamburgers 2000 feet below the ground. Radon was a killer.'

There is no way for me to reconcile this image of a burger grill with that of the dark uranium underworld. The combination of pragmatism, ignorance, and indifference becomes too ghastly to contemplate.

To the east, exposed grey terraces rise above the South Paguate Pit where winds continue to whip up radioactive dust. Ahead we can now see the whole of the shop area. A half-dozen buildings stand on flat ground above Oak Canyon. Two large-machine shops with huge bay doors tower above various one-storey, prefab warehouses. In places, sheet-metal siding has pulled away to reveal skeletons of steel raised upon concrete slabs. On the adjacent dirt-covered parking lot a stockpile of machinery worth millions of dollars stands at ready, rusting – bulldozers,

FIGURE 15.7 South Paguate Pit with the Jackpile Pit in the distance. Photo: Christopher Witmore

FIGURE 15.8 The shop. Photo: Christopher Witmore

road graders, backhoes, utility vehicles. 'Even though the site is heavily radioactive,' Curtis says, 'in the wake of the mine, it housed Laguna Construction Company.'

'What are your hopes for the Superfund listing?' I ask. 'What is to be done?'

'That with the help of the EPA we will return the area of the mine to background normal.'

'Yet, it can never be as it was, can it?'

'No, the grievous harm which has been done to our land, our Mother, is irreparable.'

For the last couple of miles we have been passing along a hill riddled with access roads. 'It is perforated with drill holes,' Curtis explains. 'They were planning to mine the entire slope out, but they never did. The holes went down hundreds, and in some cases thousands of feet. They were looking for the extent of the ore body.'

'By measuring the top and bottom of the ore-containing strata.'

'Yes. With that measure one can generate an estimation for tonnage.'

'And, therefore, profitability.'

'Indeed. With so little thought to the true costs of what would remain in its wake.'

'Perhaps, remediation is entirely the wrong word for what must be done here. What remedy can there be given the scale of the mining and the unruly potency of uranium?' I ask.

'Over ten square miles of open pit and the reservoir can never be used by our community again. Our people don't understand that. The water will always be unusable for drinking and growing crops. The land will always be unsuitable for pasturing sheep or cattle. It will never again sustain wheat and peach or apricot trees. We can never hunt the deer or elk that graze there. We can never eat the rabbits or the waterfowl that dwell there. We can no longer fish. We can no longer harvest the wild herbs due to bioaccumulation. For the same reason we can never gather fuel wood there to burn. Fire catalyzes uranium. Cedar and juniper in a wood stove or pinion in an open fire would release strontium, thorium, and radon into the house. We can't use the rocks to construct new dwellings. We can't use the caliche to make plaster or dry grasses to bind it all together.'

We come to a stop at the junction of New 279. We both look ahead. In its afterlife, a mine will continue to weigh upon this community, it will crush our animal and plant others. In its afterlife a reservoir will press ahead as a poisonous pasture for livestock. Ponds will continue to provide toxic waters for mustangs, coyotes, and Russian olives. I begin to wonder whether living with the afterlives of super-monstrous things is a portent of what elsewhere is to come. Perhaps, no; if only because to different degrees their effects are already there.

We turn for Laguna. 'We long,' Curtis says, 'to walk across our land without fear of harm. Though it falls far short of what we had, that would be a gift.'

Notes

1 The first visit occurred in September 2017 in the company of Chris Taylor and students with the Land Arts program. The second outing followed two months later with Bjørnar J. Olsen and Þóra Pétursdóttir. The third journey was in August 2019.
2 There is no definitive lexicon for Keresan. We are grateful to Eldon Francisco for his help with the phonetic spelling of words presented in this article.
3 Ellis (1974, p. 58) seems to record this as LM 8, a defensive site called *Kawakaisha*, where women and children took refuge in times of danger (also see Akins 1993, p. 81).
4 See Wilson 2001.
5 Comprehensive Environmental Response, Compensation and Liability Information System.
6 EPA's Airborne Spectral Photometric Environmental Collection Technology (ASPECT). www.epa.gov/emergency-response/aspect
7 Also see Gorospe 2013, pp. 71–92.
8 See Hopkins, Colwell, and Ferguson 2016.
9 Lanolin is used as a lubricant for bullet casings among other things.
10 Both Los Alamos and SNL played significant roles in the Manhattan Project. Though the project drew to a close in 1946, its nuclear aftermath presses on into the future.
11 USDOI 2–79.
12 See Kuletz 1998, pp. 29–30.
13 ARCO was later bought out by British Petroleum (BP) in 2000.
14 Curtis gathered data on behalf of the Pueblo. Testing upstream and downstream of the mine, he observed the release of uranium into surface waters. This data helped to drive the listing of the mine for Superfund.
15 González-Ruibal 2019, p. 153.
16 See Ellis 1974, p. 210; on sheepherding in the area of the mine, see Cattle 1979.

17 Benedict and Hudson 2008; also see Colwell, C. and T.J. Ferguson 2014.
18 Chernobyl provides comparative examples, see: Iablokov et al. 2009.

References

Akins, N.J. 1993. *Traditional Use Areas in New Mexico.* Archaeology Notes 141. Santa Fe: Museum of New Mexico, Office of Archaeological Studies.

Anschuetz, K.F., S.C. Lent, M.E Harlan, and P. Whitely. 1979. *An Archeological Survey of Approximately 3,800 Acres within the Anaconda Company Jackpile Uranium Mine near Paguate, New Mexico.* Manuscript. Office of Contract Archaeology, Albuquerque, NM: University of New Mexico..

Beal, J.D. 1976. *An Archaeological Clearance Survey of Eight Parcels of Land at the Anaconda Company's Jackpile Mine, Paguate, New Mexico.* Manuscript. Office of Contract Archaeology, Albuquerque, NM: University of New Mexico.

Benedict, C.B. and E. Hudson. 2008. *Mt. Taylor Traditional Cultural Property Determination of Eligibility for the National Register of Historic Places.* Heritage Resources Report #2008-03-021. Mt. Taylor Ranger District, Cibola National Forest, Albuquerque, NM.

Carroll, C.H. and L.J. Hooten. 1977. *An Archaeological Survey of Eight Parcels of Land within the Anaconda Company's Jackpile Mine, Paguate, New Mexico.* Manuscript. Office of Contract Archaeology, Albuquerque, NM: University of New Mexico.

Carroll, C.H., L.J. Hooten, and D.E. Stuart. 1977. *An Archaeological Survey of the Anaconda Company's Proposed P-15/P-17 Jackpile Mine, New Mexico.* Manuscript. Office of Contract Archaeology, Albuquerque, NM: University of New Mexico.

Colwell, C. and T.J. Ferguson. 2014. The Snow-Capped Mountain and the Uranium Mine Zuni Heritage and the Landscape Scale in Cultural Resource Management. *Advances in Archaeological Practice.* 2(4), 234–51.

Ellis, F.H. 1974. *Pueblo Indians II. Archaeologic and Ethnologic Data: Acoma-Laguna Land Claims.* New York: Garland Publishing.

Flint, R. 2015. Laguna Pueblo History Revisited. *New Mexico Historical Review* 90, 7–30.

González-Ruibal, A. 2019. *An Archaeology of the Contemporary Era.* London: Routledge.

Gorospe, M.J. 2013. *Uranium mobility in vegetation, soils and water below the Jackpile Uranium Mine, New Mexico.* Master's Thesis. Socorro, NM: New Mexico Institute of Mining and Technology.

Grigg, P.S., S.P. Fosberg, and R.P. Gauthier. 1977. *An Archaeological Survey of the Anaconda Company's Oak Canyon Tract in the Jackpile Mine, Paguate, New Mexico.* Manuscript. Office of Contract Archaeology, University of New Mexico. Albuquerque, NM.

Hancock, G.J., S.G. Tims, L.K. Fifield, and I.T. Webster. 2014. The release and persistence of radioactive anthropogenic nuclides, in *A Stratigraphical Basis for the Anthropocene*, 265–81. London: Geological Society of London.

Hopkins, M.P., C. Colwell, and T.J. Ferguson. 2016. Laguna Sheepherding. *Kiva*, 82(3), 278–322.

Iablokov, A.V., A.V. Nesterenko, V.B. Nesterenko, and J.D. Sherman-Nevinger. 2009. *Chernobyl: Consequences of the Catastrophe for People and the Environment.* New York: The New York Academy of Sciences.

Kuletz, V.L. 1998. *Tainted Desert. Environmental Ruin in the American West.* London: Routledge.

Latour, B. 2018. *Down to Earth: Politics in the New Climate Regime.* Cambridge: Polity Press.

Lorenzo, J.L. 2016. Paguate Village Attitudes and Beliefs on Preservation and Renovation of Traditional Structures: Remembering Our Connection to Our Mother. *Journal of American Indian Education.* 55(3), 91–110.

Macfarlane, R. 2016. Generation Anthropocene: How humans have altered the planet forever. *The Guardian.* www.theguardian.com/books/2016/apr/01/generation-anthropocene-altered-planet-for-ever

Morton, T. 2013. *Hyperobjects. Philosophy and Ecology after the End of the World.* Minneapolis, MN: University of Minnesota Press.

US Department of the Interior. 1985. *Jackpile-Paguate. Uranium Mine Reclamation Project. Environmental Impact Statement.* Albuquerque, NM.

Wilson, P.D. 2001. *The Nuclear Fuel Cycle: From Ore to Wastes.* Oxford: Oxford University Press.

Witmore, C. 2019. Hypanthropos: On Apprehending and Approaching That Which Is in Excess of Monstrosity, with Special Consideration Given to the Photography of Edward Burtynsky. *Journal of Contemporary Archaeology.* 6(1), 136–53.

16
TOWARDS A POST-ANTHROPOCENTRIC ETHIC

Timothy James LeCain

The evidence these days against human exceptionalism has never been stronger. Pick almost any trait once proudly counted as uniquely human – intelligence, creativity, tool making, altruism, language, emotion – and some scientist somewhere has discovered some other animal that has some trait like it. Indeed, a full reckoning with the steady human slide in status is arguably well over due. It has been half a millennium since Copernicus and Galileo kicked us out of the center of the universe, while Darwin's mid-nineteenth century theory that humans are really just an odd species of mammal has long been established fact. Even the truism that our species is a bit odd at the present moment in the planet's history increasingly looks to be more or less a quirk. Just 100,000 years ago there were at least six species of fairly intelligent creatures of the genus *Homo* on the planet, and scientists fully expect to find more species in the years to come. At least some of these now extinct species of human now look to have behaved much like the current modern models, making tools and art, living in complex social groups, and communicating abstract ideas. True, *Homo sapiens* are the only species of humans that managed to survive into the present, which by definition does make us unique. Yet that should not keep us from recognizing the bigger point that the material world seems to churn out human-like creatures and traits rather freely.

Being human is clearly not all it was once cracked up to be. Yet despite all these insults to our *amour propre*, the faith in human greatness has in some ways scarcely wavered. In recent years there has been a spate of books and articles seeking to explain why, despite all the humbling news to the contrary, we humans are still special. The Australian psychologist Thomas Suddendorf (2013), for example, went straight to the heart of the matter in the title of his book, *The Gap: The Science of What Separates Us from Other Animals*. In 2018, the editors of *Scientific American* (2018) devoted a special issue to explaining: "Why we're unlike any other species on the planet." Most recently, the science writer Adam Rutherford (2019) stakes out a somewhat similar position in his book, *Humanimal: How Homo sapiens Became Nature's Most Paradoxical Creature*, concluding that while we may share many continuities with tool-using crows and fashion-loving chimpanzees, "humanimals" are still extraordinary in the pronounced degree to which these and many other traits have developed.

Surely it is no coincidence that this defense of human exceptionalism is reaching a crescendo at the very moment when other scientific evidence is driving home the point that we might do better to abandon our longstanding sense of self-importance. All these efforts to hang on to some semblance of human pride increasingly appear to be a bit desperate and defensive. Even when we consider a name for the disastrous modern era of global climate change and mass species extinction, we cannot seem to help but give ourselves a backhanded compliment and name it after ourselves: the Anthropocene, or the Age of Humans. But to be fair, these rear guard champions of human exceptionalism do obviously have a point. No other animal on the planet has ever achieved anything close to what *Homo sapiens* have accomplished, at least by our own standards of what counts as achievement. Crows may make and use simple tools, but they don't build nuclear reactors. Great apes may be capable of fairly complex communication when given the necessary training and tools, but they don't write books and organize discussion groups. Likewise, there are legitimate scientific questions about the precise nature of this quantitative (if perhaps not qualitative) human-animal divergence and how and why it occurred. What has permitted humans to outpace all the other smart animals on the planet, including those six (or more) other species of human who went extinct over the last 100,000 years? Current thought suggests it was the result of some combination of our unusually big brains, hyper-developed abilities to communicate and use language, and sophisticated social skills, but there is a lively debate over which of these, or other factors yet, should be given causal priority. Still, many scientists and science journalists more or less agree on the key point: while it is true that many traits we once thought were solely human have now been found in other animals, these are so much more developed in contemporary human beings that we are still justified in seeing ourselves as unique – and thus, in a narrower but still formidable sense, still special.

The scientific focus on the role of communication, language, and culture in making humans special also finds a surprising parallel in the humanistic disciplines. Having gone to the rhetorical extreme of naming their discipline after themselves (a forerunner to the Anthropocene), humanists have long been happily and unapologetically anthropocentric. This self-obsession reached something of an extreme in recent decades when the post-modern cultural turn and focus on language and discourse at times seemed to suggest that humans were entirely unmoored from the material world, free to create and recreate themselves in whatever manner their abstract thoughts and ideas suggested. While relatively few humanists embraced the extremes of post-modernist solipsism, many did see their subjects of study as largely self-created and, to the degree they gave it much thought, distinctly separated from the other creatures and things of the merely material world (LeCain 2017). This should not surprise us. Even well before the post-modern turn, most humanists embraced a human exceptionalism based on two erroneous beliefs that persist today. First, many still assume that while we humans are animals at a biological level, in terms of intelligence, creativity, and culture, humans alone occupy a uniquely *immaterial* realm of abstract thought. We may *look* like animals, but in our minds we are as gods, liberated from and thus free to remake the stolid materiality of the world in our own image. Which points to the second mistaken belief – that the material world of mere things, raw materials, and non-human organisms is indeed stolid, passive, and fixed – the very antithesis of the quicksilver brilliance that is "us," the raw material that bends to our will.

There are good reasons – from the recent insights into the microbiome to new understandings of cognition and intelligence – to question both of these assumptions, and I have done so at length elsewhere (LeCain 2017). In this chapter, I want instead to challenge these foundational humanist ideas from a somewhat different angle using two empirically driven case studies. These two examples, I argue, suggest a very different view of humans and the humanities, one in which we become human not in *distinction or contrast* to a passive material world, but rather through our intimate engagement with a dynamic material world that generates the opportunity for the expression of all of the traits we once considered to be uniquely human. The aesthetic taste of a seemingly modest little bird and the social intelligence of a common domestic animal will help make my points. I conclude by considering what ethical and political approaches might logically emerge from embracing the truly post-anthropocentric worldview and ethic these examples point us towards.

Clever birds and the evolution of beauty

In 1872, the respected Italian botanist Odoardo Beccari was searching for novel biological specimens in the jungles of New Guinea, which were rich in species never before seen or identified, at least by western scientists. While out hunting specimens one day, Beccari stumbled across a strange hut on the jungle floor. As he later wrote,

> I found myself in front of a piece of workmanship more lovely than the ingenuity of any animal had ever been know to construct. It was a cabin in miniature, in the midst of a miniature meadow, studded with flowers.
>
> *(Strycker 2015)*

Beccari assumed that the small "cabin," which was about four feet high and wide, must have been made by local tribespeople. Yet to what end? Was it some sort of ceremonial altar, or perhaps just a small child's forest hideaway? Its purpose remained baffling – until, as Beccari stood contemplating the mysterious structure, the builder himself returned: a small olive brown bird who is today known as the Vogelkopf Bowerbird (Figure 16.1).

Beccari's astonishment notwithstanding, none of this would have surprised the native peoples of the area who were well aware of the little bird and its strange habits – though the New Guineans arguably had a better name, calling it the *burung pintar*, or "clever bird." Yet it was Beccari who brought the news to a wider world, and ever since, biologists have debated why and how such elaborate and seemingly human-like behaviors should have evolved. The tiny 150 gram male Bowerbird expends a tremendous amount of time and energy painstakingly building his bower from twigs, constantly rearranging and perfecting the often highly colorful decorations. However, this elaborate bower serves not as a shelter or food trap that might increase the ability of the bird to survive in the competitive jungle environment. To the contrary, in terms of the traditional "survival of the fittest" concept of natural selection, the Bowerbird's efforts appear to be deeply mal-adaptive: every moment spent building a bower on the jungle floor was a moment the bowerbird could otherwise have been feeding himself – or worse yet, becomes some predator's lunch. So why do it?

Darwin had already grappled with this general problem when thinking about the evolution of other seemingly useless and costly traits in other birds and animals. As a possible answer he developed a second and much less well-known evolutionary mechanism – not natural selection, but sexual selection. To explain such risky and costly traits as the male peacock's immense tail, which if anything made the bird *more* vulnerable to predators, Darwin theorized that female peahens must be choosing sexual partners based on the male peacocks' showy plumage. In the case of the rather plain looking male bowerbird, the nest would stands in for the plumage. Indeed, ornithologists have confirmed that the female bowerbird selects

FIGURE 16.1 A male Satin Bowerbird with his bower. Photo: Courtesy of Pixabay Photos

her mate based at least in part on her exceedingly critical evaluation of the male's bower. The male with the most pleasing bower-building skills would thus be the one most likely to mate and pass on the genes for his abilities.

Importantly for my purposes here, though, most evolutionary biologists, both then and now, still did not stray very far from what they considered to be Darwin's more central idea of fitness and (largely) male competition. It surely could not be, as one nineteenth-century biologist put it, that the mercurial whims of mere female *aesthetic* taste were the prime evolutionary driver. (Gorman 2017) Rather, they argued that the peacock's tail or the Bowerbird's bower were *really* just indicators of the health and fitness of the male – what evolutionary biologists term "honest signaling." Only the fittest male specimens could afford to build an impressive bower or sport a truly impressive tale, so the female's choice was really nothing more than a preference for the strongest and thus most competitive bird. Sexual selection, in this view, was just natural selection in a slightly different form.

The story of this "clever bird" offers a good example of the potential utility of a post-anthropocentric approach as it points so clearly to the modernist tendency to dismiss the creativity of non-human things and organisms in preference for a reflexive, and as in this case, sexist, anthropocentrism. Yet there is another and less obvious anthropocentric subtext at work, because just as ornithologists dismissed the role of the female they also dismissed an even more radically destabilizing possibility: that the female Bowerbird chose the most impressive bower not because it was an "honest signal" of male reproductive fitness, but rather simply because she found it to be the most *beautiful*. She was attracted to her mate not solely, or perhaps even primarily, because he was physically fit, but rather because he was capable of creating a more beautiful work than his competitors. In an intriguing parallel with the humanist colleagues they are often mistakenly seen as largely distinct from, most biologists have long assumed that beauty was not something the harsh material world of nature generated, but was solely the product of big-brained humans with a capacity for symbolic thought and discourse. The female Bowerbird surely could not be picking a bower simply because she found it to be the most pleasingly beautiful. Or could she? In a recent controversial book, *The Evolution of Beauty,* the Yale ornithologist and evolutionary biologist Richard Prum (2017) dares to argue that the female's judgment of the bowers is in fact something far more subjective. The bowerbird and many other animals, he suggests, have the capacity to make what we would consider to be aesthetic judgments – they have preferences that Prum argues can only logically be understood as a taste for beauty, that may even encompass subtle differences or preferences among individuals. Even more importantly for my purposes here, Prum thus suggests that the material world in and of itself simply generates both the capacity to create and to appreciate beauty. There is nothing *categorically* different between the female bowerbird's preference for a certain bower over another and the much-vaunted human aesthetic sense, however much more the latter is elaborated. Likewise, the human artistic impulse is as rooted in material evolutionary processes as the bowerbird's, suggesting that the functional and the aesthetic are one and the same thing. "Birds are beautiful," Prum writes, "because they are beautiful to themselves" (Gorman 2017). In this sense, the natural material world generates a capacity to appreciate and create beauty simply because it is pleasing to the organisms in question, regardless of what other signals it might convey.

Prum's argument is controversial and few other evolutionary biologists agree with him entirely – the standard argument remains that bowers and peacock tails can largely be explained as honest signals of an organism's fitness. In this view, the bowerbirds have no sense of beauty that might be akin to that of that of humans – whose sense of beauty instead remains safely in the conventional realm of abstract culture and discourse – and the actual appearance of the bowers is largely arbitrary and trivial. Yet if we return to Beccari's initial discovery of the Bowerbird's elaborately decorated little hut – or if we simply look for ourselves at their creations – one can't help but recognize that there are some intriguing parallels between what humans and bowerbirds find beautiful. Indeed, Beccari himself first assumed that the nests must have been made by humans. Obviously, humans do not always find their own diverse tastes in accord with that of other organisms – if a dung beetle were to evolve a sense of beauty, it would probably be very different than ours. And yet in the case of the bowerbird there seems to be a surprising convergence towards a broad concept of beauty that many humans also share, suggesting perhaps a larger biological continuum between humans and other organisms even in this most abstract realm of what we typically view as solely a cultural matter. As noted earlier, the evidence continues to accumulate that all sorts of traits that humans once considered uniquely their own – tool use, language, altruism, culture, art – are in fact found among at least some other organisms, albeit often at a considerably diminished level. Why should a sense of beauty be any different?

Yet if the material world has a pronounced tendency to generate traits like intelligence, creativity, and an appreciation for beauty, it seems apparent that we should escape our persistent allegiance to anthropocentric exceptionalism and see ourselves – both biologically and culturally – as products of what the political ecologist Jane Bennett identifies as a vibrant materiality (Bennett 2010). Not only did the material world generate many (perhaps all) of our most human attributes, it also seems to have generated them in many other organisms. Yet if this is true then the earlier post-modern turn increasingly looks to have been the product of a hyper-anthropocentrism that mistakenly claimed the realm of culture as both strictly human and strictly rooted in the human capacity for abstract thought and discourse. At the heart of such an anthropocentric approach lies the modernist refusal to accept the possibility that things, organisms, and environments might have creative powers in and of themselves, and thus that there could be a material basis for human creativity at both a biological and cultural level. This does not, of course, require that we dismiss the importance of abstract human thought and discourse which obviously may generate all manner of fantastical elaborations of these traits. Yet too often the post-modernist view neglected or even deliberately rejected the role of the material in favor of placing all of the agency in human hands. How much might be gained at an analytical level if we humanists learned instead to recognize creativity not so much as a human trait or ability, but rather as a phenomenon or process that emerges from the diverse human interactions with a vast, dynamic, and generative world of sometimes beautiful material organism and things?

For the purposes of humanists and social scientists, however, perhaps the more useful aspect of a post-anthropocentric view and ethic is not so much that evolutionary processes freely generate intelligence, creativity, beauty, and culture, but rather how the creativity of the material world sparks and enables human creativity and power. To better understand this type of material creativity, we will need the assistance of cows rather than birds.

Smart cows and American imperialism

Historians have long understood that the American West was taken from the indigenous peoples through a combination of violent armed conquest and aggressive settler colonialism. Yet what is often overlooked is that at a sizeable part of "the West" was conquered not by human colonists alone, but rather by Euro-Americans working in partnership with an intelligent, creative, and powerful animal: *Bos taurus*, the domesticated cows and bulls that we raise, slaughter, and eat. Historians of the American open range ranching industry of the late nineteenth- century western high plains point out how cattle first bioconcentrated the dispersed plant energy of the western range, and then carried the stored caloric energy to cattle towns and slaughter houses where it could be efficiently processed for human consumption.

However, in recognizing the way cattle physically stored and moved energy, historians reinforce an understanding of cows and the humans who worked with

Conrad Kohrs

DEER LODGE CITY.

FIGURE 16.2 The pioneering Montana rancher, Conrad Kohrs. Public Domain, original in M. A. Leeson, History of Montana, 1739–1885 (Chicago: Warner, Beers and Co., 1885: 557)

them as merely economic units, thus ironically giving support to the abstracted separation of humans and materiality that modernist neo-liberal market theories depend upon. What is lost with such economic abstractions is that the western open-range industry was entirely dependent upon the social and cognitive abilities of the millions of individual cows and steers who made these flows of energy and capital possible.

Take for example, the capital and power accrued by one of the West's pre-eminent cattle barons, the German immigrant Conrad Kohrs (Figure 16.2). Many of the cows and bulls that Kohrs initially raised on his isolated Montana ranch in the second half of the nineteenth century were Texas Longhorns, smart, self-sufficient animals who could defend themselves with great sharp horns as much as six feet from tip to tip in some steers (Figure 16.3).

During the brief but pivotal decades of the open range, ranchers relied upon a delicate social and cognitive balance between the Longhorns' hardy independence and their grudging willingness to tolerate humans (LeCain 2017, pp. 153–61). Profitability depended on the intelligent ability of the animals to largely take care of themselves, seeking out food and water, raising and defending their young, and using their sophisticated social intelligence to maintain a cohesive herd that protected the majority from deadly predators – in part by relegating their weaker compatriots to the edge of herd where they were vulnerable to attack.

FIGURE 16.3 The dangerous horns, powerful long-legged body, and sharp social intelligence of the Texas Longhorns equipped them to fend off predators and survive without human assistance. University of North Texas Library, George Ranch Historical Park (c. 1940)

A simple thought experiment suggests just how important the self-reliance and social intelligence of the Longhorns was. Imagine if Kohrs' Longhorns had been less social mammals, preferring to spread out over the wide open plains in small groups rather than cooperating by more or less sticking together. Imagine that the human cowboys who went out twice a year to "round them up" for branding or shipment for slaughter had to track down these small widely dispersed groups and then try to force them, entirely against their will, to congregate in some central place (Ward 2013). Immediately you will recognize that such a system would demand the expenditure of vastly more human time and energy in order to function, if it could even function at all. Yet humans had obviously not *created* the desire of Longhorns and other cows to form herds or (reluctantly) cooperate with humans. To the contrary, the early ancestors of modern cows developed this type of social herding behavior as social and defensive measures entirely for their own purposes.

Likewise, consider the much storied case of moving cows in the aptly named "cattle drive." While closely managed cows will sometimes learn to follow a human leader (usually because they have learned that the human is leading them to food, water, or shelter), range cattle with relatively little contact with their keepers typically do the opposite: if a cowboy moves directly in front of a line of cows as if to *lead* them, the cows at the front will typically turn to the right or left or stop altogether. To get the cows to move in a desired direction, cowboys must instead ride *behind* the lead animals at roughly a 45 degree angle, and they must take care neither to get too close nor stray too far away. The contemporary expert on cattle behavior, Temple Grandin, explains that this dynamic is entirely logical from the perspective of a cow responding to a potential predator or other threat (Grandin and Deesing 2013). With large eyes positioned on the sides of their heads, cattle can see almost all the way around them, except for a small blind spot immediately behind. If a potential threat – the cowboy in this case – approaches from behind at about 45 degrees yet does not move too close, a cow will typically elect to move straight ahead, a route that keeps the cowboy at a comfortable distance but still in full view. But if the cowboy moves too near or into her blind spot, the cow will often choose to turn and face him, preparing either to defend herself or run to either side.

In sum, the ranchers and cowboys were entirely dependent on the sophisticated social intelligence and defensive behaviors of their animals, even though these humans had no real understanding of the complex origins and dynamics of these behaviors at the time. Given this, it seems obvious that however much "intelligence" or cultural sophistication we might wish to assign to successful open-range cattle ranching, it was a *distributed* animal intelligence and culture – never solely or even primarily human. Likewise, the much-storied "culture" of the western open range resided not as an abstract idea or narrative in the minds of the cowboys and ranchers, but rather was inseparable from the intelligent animals who helped to create and maintain it.

Most importantly from a post-anthropocentric political and ethical point of view, if we fail to recognize the essential cognitive and cultural materiality behind the open range cattle industry, we provide unwitting support to the view that there was something superior about the Euro-American culture that explains its rise to power. That is, that the ideas, creativity, and technologies of one group of humans were somehow superior to those of another. From a post-anthropocentric perspective, however, this puts the causalities exactly backwards. It was not an abstract immaterial Euro-American "culture" that proved decisive in the successful settler colonialist conquest of the western high plains, but rather a materially rooted deep culture – one that was inextricable from the non-human cognitive abilities of the Longhorns that had helped to create this culture in the first place. Of course, open-range ranching was not the only or even primary means by which Euro-Americans came to remove the indigenous peoples and dominate the North American continent – violent invasion, oppression, and even genocide played equal roles. (Though all of these were also embedded in other material things and organisms.) But to the degree that ranching furthered the course of settler colonialism and imperial conquest, it was not so much because Euro-Americans possessed a powerful *culture*, but rather because they possessed a powerful *creature* that allowed them to think and act in wholly novel ways.

Towards a post-anthropocentric ethics of things

As these two empirical historical examples suggest, it no longer makes sense to think of humans and their cultures as clearly separated from the material world around them, or to argue that whatever culture resides in "material culture" has been put there solely by humans. An ability to create and appreciate beauty or art has long been held up as a uniquely human attribute, a quasi-divine gift that sharply distinguished our species from all others on the planet. Yet if, as Prum convincingly argues, the male and female Bower Birds also have an "eye for beauty," we begin to suspect that the material world at least occasionally (and perhaps frequently) simply generates the capacity to apprehend and create beauty through the process of evolution, perhaps most frequently through the mechanism of sexual selection. As I discussed at the start of the essay, the more recent defenders of human exceptionalism rightly point out that this sense of beauty, and certainly the related culture of art and aesthetics, is much more highly developed and elaborated in humans. Obviously no one is suggesting that an affinity for Picasso's abstract cubism is entirely reducible to an evolutionarily useful sense of beauty. (I will resist the too-obvious temptation to parallel the bowerbird's bower with the clichéd idea of male artists inviting potential partners to "come up to their flat and see some etchings.") Yet the realization that even a phenomenon as seemingly ephemeral and abstract as beauty is rooted in the quotidian functioning of biological systems, does suggest we should see its much-elaborated human expressions as occupying one pole of a broad continuum with other animals. It seems increasingly likely that the same might well be said about intelligence, empathy, communication, emotion, and many other traits that were once assumed to be uniquely human.

The case of the American Longhorn offers a related but distinct insight: that regardless of whether other animals truly share in human traits, some significant part of what we previously considered to be solely human attributes are better understood as emerging from our interactions with a dynamic living material world. Whatever intelligence there was behind the success of American open range cattle ranching was clearly generated in the *interactions* between two social animals, and thus it cannot logically be said to reside in either one of those animals alone. To be sure, the unusually large and supple human brain permitted ranchers and cowboys to adapt much more easily and rapidly than the Longhorns they worked with. Yet rather than seeing this solely as evidence of superior human intelligence, we might also see it as an indication that humans are particularly well prepared to think with and through other species and things. We have long assumed that what makes humans special is their separation and difference from the natural or material world. Yet the story of Longhorn suggests instead that we become most fully human through our interactions with other organisms – which, as we have seen with the case of the Bowerbird, should not surprise us because their own abilities evolved from the same materiality that created us. In this sense, humans are creative and intelligent because their material world generates the capacity for creativity and intelligence, both through a historical evolutionary process and as they interact with other organisms and things at any particular moment in time. We might thus say that humans, more than any other extant species, have evolved to generate intelligence, creativity, and other aspects of culture through an unusually pronounced ability to interact with a wide array of others things and organisms.

If we accept these broader points, what then might a less anthropocentric and more materially rich worldview and ethical approach be? I am a historian, not an ethicist, and I am certain there are many possibilities and consequences here that I have not considered. Nonetheless, the following four points strike me as offering a good starting place for a post-anthropocentric ethics of "things," by which I mean all the various organisms and materials that constitute our diverse environments, the biotic and abiotic and the anthropogenic and non-anthropogenic alike:

1. *A respect for things:* If Longhorn cows and countless other organism and things are indeed how we become most fully human, then they clearly deserve a much greater measure of appreciation and respect than we have heretofore accorded them. (Without engaging the issue at depth, which would take an essay in its own right, this seems especially important when we propose to slaughter and eat the organism in question.) A post-anthropocentric ethic would ask that we better recognize how a diverse array of other things in our environments are critical not only to our biological and ecological health – a point already well recognized in contemporary environmental ethics – but also to our cultural and social health, both for the good and the bad. To care for our things is to care for ourselves. During the age of western imperial expansion, Europeans dismissed the not-infrequently animistic beliefs of their newly colonized subjects as superstitious and backwards. Yet modern scientific

insights increasingly suggest that such indigenous ways were in a certain broad sense more accurately descriptive of the material world as we understand it today than the crudely reductionist western views of the time. As the anthropologist Philippe Descola argues, there is much we might learn from such "pre-modern" societies, to create what I think of as a sort of scientific animism. To truly embrace the idea of a creative materiality would also demand a level of respect even for those things that we may not be interacting with in the present moment. We can never predict what seemingly useless mineral or bacteria or animal might yet spark some new aspect of human existence. Thus while every organism inevitably alters its environment (or niche), an ethic of things suggests we should whenever possible avoid unnecessary or careless damage. The contemporary environmental ethic recognizes the centrality of other things to our survival as a biological organism – a post-anthropocentric ethic would also include their centrality to our survival as a cultural organism.

2. *Embracing caution:* One of the most dangerous aspects of the modernist anthropocentric worldview is the belief that humans can manipulate and control the non-human world without *necessarily* making any significant changes to themselves and their cultures. Yet in shifting our focus from humans to things, we can better recognize the many ways in which we become entangled with things, which not only push us down certain historical paths, but may also change our very nature as human beings. Post-modern social constructivist theory tended to criticize such ideas as deterministic, preferring to emphasize the ability of humans to shape material evolution and determine their own destinies. There is much of value in this perspective, yet it also tends to underestimate the power of things and provide a (likely unintended) measure of support for neo-liberal politics that permit supposedly free markets to determine what new technologies and environments are adopted. A post-anthropocentric ethic, however, can better recognize and respect both the potential dangers and benefits of things, suggesting that we should be much more cautious and conservative (using the older meaning of the word, not its entirely contradictory modern usage) in adopting new technologies and materialities. Although it is inherently difficult to predict the future consequences of any new thing or environment, a post-anthropocentric ethic suggests a pressing need to develop effective democratic means of studying the potential risks and benefits of novel things *before* they are permitted to alter the nature of human society.

3. *A humble global politics:* As noted in my discussion of the Longhorn's central role in creating American power and imperial expansion, a post-anthropocentric understanding of things might also help us to create a more humble and just system of global politics and economics. The modern worldview often suggested that national power and success were the product of superior *human* ideas, inventions, and cultures, thus justifying global inequities as the natural outcome of a competition between stronger and weaker human societies. From a post-anthropocentric perspective, however, the power and success of any nation is understood as resulting primarily from the alliances it has

struck with countless powerful non-human things, the availability of which are unevenly distributed around the globe. As we have seen, the Longhorn fueled the successful conquest of the American West every bit as much as the ideas or culture of the American rancher and cowboy. Yet if national (or individual) power and wealth are not human achievements so much as the gifts of a dynamic material world, then it seems logical that their benefits should be to all people, not just the one group that happened through geography or luck to stumble on these powerful organisms and things first.

4. *The humble human*: Finally, perhaps the most difficult challenge presented by a post-anthropocentric ethic would be the need to abandon – or at least sharply reduce – our pervasive admiration and worship of ourselves. The modern worldview often celebrates the achievements of individuals, particularly the inventors and entrepreneurs who introduce new technologies, consumer items, and other material things into our societies. A post-anthropocentric ethic, however, deemphasizes the individual creator in favor of placing much of the creative potential in the peculiar material environment of things that exist at any moment in time. It is the material environment of existing technologies, organisms, and other things that sparks new inventions, not just the presence of one key heroic inventor. The world would still have steam engines even if James Watt had never lived, and there were dozens of inventors and entrepreneurs who would have developed a practical electric light bulb had Thomas Edison not gotten there first. A post-anthropocentric ethic warns us we should give up the still popular fairy tales of individual human genius, as they dangerously obscure the immense power of our material environment to shape our lives, our minds, and our histories. As the French *Annales* school historian Fernand Braudel observed decades ago, many of the stories we humans find most interesting are epiphenomena, "the crests of foam that the tides of history carry on their strong backs." (Trevor-Roper 1972, p. 475) To be fair, our fascination with ourselves is perhaps one of the traits we share most broadly with other creatures. Every organism is uniquely well positioned to appreciate and admire itself – humans have just once again taken this self-obsession to an extreme. But now, when the realities of global climate change demand that we recognize the immense power of the non-human world to shape our destiny, a post-anthropocentric ethic could help us move beyond the Promethean dreams of control and instead foster a more humble and cautious vision of our place on the planet.

Some may no doubt criticize such a post-anthropocentric ethic as anti-humanist and demonstrating a problematic lack of appreciation for the brilliance of our species. Others will argue that to put so much weight on the power of the non-human is to lose sight of the many ways in which a minority of privileged humans, corporations, and nations rig the system to their own benefit. As I noted previously, social constructivists will surely object to my embrace of a certain manner of material determinism as both overly fatalistic and politically disempowering.

Yet while these criticisms raise important issues, they also reflect the very same anthropocentrism that I argue has caused many of our problems in the first place. Being humble, as an individual or as a species, is never easy. Yet at this late point in the modernist global experiment, when just a few centuries of human arrogance and over confidence have created an unprecedented existential crisis, it is surely time to consider what might be gained from shifting our focus away from ourselves and towards the material world that created us. Ironically, the most exceptional thing we humans might do at this moment is to fully embrace how unexceptional we are.

References

Bennett, J. 2010. *Vibrant Matter: A Political Ecology of Things.* Durham: Duke University Press.

Editors. 2018. "Special Issue: Humans: Why We're Unlike Any Other Species on the Planet." *Scientific American.* 319 (3), cover.

Gorman, J. 2017. "Challenging Mainstream Thought about Beauty's Big Hand in Evolution." *New York Times* 29 May 2017.

Grandin, T and Deesing, MJ., eds. 2013. *Genetics and the Behavior of Domestic Animals.* New York: Academic Press.

LeCain, T. 2017. *The Matter of History: How Things Create the Past.* Cambridge (UK): Cambridge University Press.

Prum, R. O. 2017. *The Evolution of Beauty: How Darwin's Theory of Mate Choice Shapes the Animal World – and Us.* New York: Doubleday.

Rutherford, A. 2019. *Humanimal: How Homo sapiens Became Nature's Most Paradoxical Creature – A New Evolutionary History.* New York: Workman.

Strycker, N. 2015. *The Things With Feathers: The Surprising Lives of Birds and What They Reveal About Being Human.* New York: Riverhead Books.

Suddendorf, T. 2013. *The Gap: The Science of What Separates Us from Other Animals.* New York: Basic.

Trevor-Roper, H. R. 1972. "Fernand Braudel, the *Annales*, and the Mediterranean." *The Journal of Modern History* 44: 468–79.

Ward, F. E. 2013. *The Cowboy at Work: All About His Job and How He Does It.* New York: Skyhorse Publishing.

INDEX

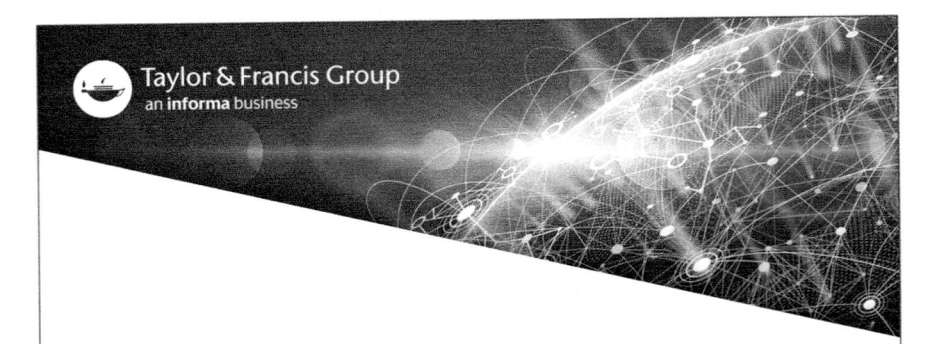